URBAN ECONOMIC ISSUES
READINGS

URBAN ECONOMIC ISSUES
READINGS AND ANALYSIS

STEPHEN L. MEHAY
San Jose State University

GEOFFREY E. NUNN
San Jose State University

Scott, Foresman and Company   Glenview, Illinois

Dallas, Texas   Oakland, New Jersey   Palo Alto, California   Tucker, Georgia   London, England

Library of Congress Cataloging in Publication Data
Main entry under title:

Urban economic issues.

    Includes bibliographical references and index.
    1. Urban economics—Addresses, essays, lectures.
2. United States—Economic conditions—Addresses, essays,
lectures. I. Mehay, Stephen L. II. Nunn, Geoffrey E.,
1942-
HT321.U2915 1984   330.973'0927'091732   83-23525
ISBN 0-673-16624-4

PREFACE

Despite a relatively short history, the field of urban economics has generated an extensive and still growing body of literature. This collection of readings presents a small sample of that body of literature, appropriate for undergraduate students with a limited background in economics. These readings show how the standard tools of microeconomic analysis can elucidate important but troublesome urban problems.

According to some of the writers included in this collection, many urban problems—such as highway congestion or fiscal crisis—result from government policies that either ignore or deliberately distort market forces. Other writers trace the source of urban problems—including housing and transportation problems—to the inherent weaknesses of the public sector and the political process in allocating resources efficiently.

In a form accessible to undergraduate students, this book attempts to discuss current issues in urban economics, including land-use restrictions and zoning, local-growth restrictions, fiscal impact analysis, income redistribution, and the flight of urban residents to the suburbs. Many of the readings also address traditional issues, such as urban transportation, urban growth and structure, and housing. Some of these readings—including those by Tiebout, Stigler, Alonso, and Thompson—have become classics in the field. The 33 readings in this collection are grouped into eight parts: an introduction to urban economic analysis, city growth and structure, zoning and growth control, housing, transportation, public finance, local government services, and policy issues.

The readings selected naturally reflect the personal biases of the editors. We believe, however, that these readings accurately reflect economists' general approaches to urban problems. In a field where city planners and political scientists often hold sway, there is probably more agreement among economists on methodological approaches and policy prescriptions than in some other fields of economics.

We would like to acknowledge the valuable comments and suggestions of several reviewers—Randall Eberts (University of Oregon), John Vahaly, Jr. (University of Louisville), and Larry Singell (University of Colorado)—and the assistance of our colleague David Shapiro.

S. L. M.
G. E. N.

v

CONTENTS

PART 1

INTRODUCTION TO
URBAN ECONOMIC ANALYSIS

*The field of urban economics emerged only about two or three decades ago.
Originally, urban and regional economics were combined as a single field of
study. Some overlap between the two fields still remains, particularly concerning
interurban spatial questions such as long-run patterns of urbanization,
development of systems of cities, and city growth and decline. The theoretical
topic that distinguishes urban from regional economics is the modeling of
economic activities within metropolitan areas. Urban economic theories explain
patterns of land uses and land rents, city form, and the spatial allocation of
resources in metropolitan areas.*

*The rapid growth of the field of urban economics has not been motivated
so much by interest in the traditional questions of spatial-allocation patterns as
by concern for the social problems spawned by the rapid postwar growth of
metropolitan areas. Urban economics has become issues-oriented and
encompasses such topics as crime, poverty, blighted housing, highway
congestion, sprawl, and pollution. Efficiency of resource allocation in the urban
public sector has also become an important area of inquiry. Other notable
topics of inquiry in the urban public economy include fiscal disparities between
central cities and suburbs, local government tax structures, and efficiency in the
provision of local public goods.*

*Each discipline provides its own unique perspective and methodological
approach to urban problems. The economic approach to an urban problem is
to first identify the features of the relevant market (for example, transportation,
housing, or land) and then determine whether resources are allocated efficiently
in that local market. If resources are misallocated, an attempt is made to
identify the type of market failure that might be frustrating economic efficiency.
One pervasive type of market failure in urban areas is the external effect of
individual actions in market situations. Because of high population densities,
externalities affect almost every urban market. Whenever externalities are
significant, economists attempt to identify the nature of the inefficiency and to
recommend appropriate corrective action.*

1

The reading by Geoffrey Nunn sketches an overview of the process of resource allocation in competitive markets. While he emphasizes the inherent efficiency of that process, he also points out various sources of market failure, instances in which the normal workings of the market cannot be relied upon to yield efficient results.

The selection by Wilbur Thompson refines and elaborates on this theme by analyzing the adverse consequences of public policies that ignore market forces and market prices. Thompson assigns the cause of numerous urban problems—such as traffic congestion, sprawl, and crowded public facilities—to the failure of municipal governments to use market prices or to use them correctly. In the short term, market-clearing prices can ration scarce public facilities more efficiently, especially during peak demand periods. In the long term, prices can signal the strength of users' demand for additional capacity and, therefore, determine whether additional investment in public facilities is warranted. The absence or misuse of prices leaves the problems of rationing and long-run investment entirely to the vagaries of the political process.

The selection by Geoffrey Nunn and Stephen Mehay focuses on how the political mechanism allocates resources, especially at the local-government level. The political mechanism is contrasted with the market mechanism. This reading elucidates features of the political process that tend to produce government failure, a situation whereby public bodies fail to select efficient policies or to operate programs efficiently. Special-interest groups, rational voter ignorance, and political shortsightedness all interfere on the demand side with accurate transmission of voter preferences to political decision makers. On the supply side, government bureaucracies—operating in a nonprofit, monopoly environment—tend to either produce an excessive amount of output or to require an excessive budget to produce a given output.

The economic approach to urban problems reminds public officials that formulating effective urban policy requires an appreciation of the constraints imposed by scarcity. If alternative ways of achieving desired ends are identified and the opportunity cost of each alternative is explicitly recognized, decision makers can make choices with better information about the economic background and consequences. But just as the political decision maker must be aware of the strengths and weaknesses of the market mechanism, so too must he or she be mindful of the advantages and disadvantages of the political mechanism. Government is not a deus ex machina that can be expected automatically to intervene prudently, wisely, or efficiently in the market.

GEOFFREY E. NUNN

1 The Price System, Markets, and Urban Problems

This selection describes the social functions of prices and markets. It provides the background for understanding many of the subsequent readings in the book. Urban problems are introduced as examples of market failure. In addition, the planning approach to solving urban problems is contrasted with the market approach.

Millions of consumers in the United States make decisions about what goods to buy, and millions of businesses decide what goods to produce. Although the two sets of decisions do not synchronize perfectly, they mesh together rather well. When urban residents go shopping they find a vast array of goods for sale and do not normally encounter either gluts or shortages. When gluts or shortages do appear, forces will appear that begin whittling them away. Yet, there is no central authority, no single board of directors, no manager, whose job it is to coordinate the vast number of decisions and to see that order is preserved. In fact, this task would be so enormously complex that it would swamp the capabilities of the most ingenious planning board or the largest computer. Since there is no oversight board to organize and coordinate the millions of activities, it is remarkable that we do not observe complete chaos.

THE PRICE SYSTEM

In the U.S. economy the regulating mechanism that coordinates individual decisions is the *price system*. The essence of the system is that goods are produced for exchange, that exchange is voluntary, and that exchange is regulated by prices. Trade is facilitated by markets, which bring buyers and sellers together. All inputs and outputs have prices. Competition among buyers as well as among sellers, each pursuing individual self-interest, normally determines the price at which trade takes place.

Prices perform several functions that are essential to an efficiently operating economy. One of the most important roles is to capsulize and transmit information. Suppose, for example, that consumers suddenly want more health-food products. When the demand for these products increases, prices rise. The higher prices transmit a signal to health-food firms to expand production. Because higher prices fatten producers' profits, firms will seek to expand. Meanwhile, a slackening demand for nonhealth foods leads to lower prices and profits, signaling firms in these industries to produce less. Prices transmit information concerning consumer preferences to producers. Health-food firms need not know why the sudden shift in tastes occurred. Nor is it necessary to know that demand has gone up (or down). All they must know is that someone is willing to pay more for their product and that the higher price makes it worthwhile to satisfy that demand.

Prices transmit signals not only from buyers to sellers but also from sellers to buyers. Suppose that silver miners in Mexico suddenly strike. This production halt would likely bump up the world (and U.S.) price of silver. The boost in price transmits a signal to silver-using firms, such as manufacturers of photographic paper, jewelry, dentistry materials, and tableware, to retrench on silver. But no central authority is needed to assure that retrenchment takes place. Each firm is prodded by the profit motive to retrench. Much of the retrenchment would probably take place among firms that are able to substitute for silver or that are unable to pass on the price increase. The higher price spurs consumers as well as producers into action. Stiffer prices for photographic paper, silver jewelry, and so on, are a signal to consumers that these products have become more scarce. Once again it is not necessary that any individual know why the price is higher or why the good is less plentiful in order for economizing behavior to occur.

Scarcity and Costs

Scarcity is a central fact of economic life. Economic resources are limited and are dwarfed by society's wants and needs. In societies where living conditions are poor, scarcity is obvious. Yet, even comparatively rich societies, such as the United States, must also constantly struggle against scarcity. Scarcity is an inescapable bugaboo that makes it impossible for individuals or societies to fulfill all their wants.

Most of us would gladly accept additional goods and services if they could be obtained costlessly (that is, without giving something up). When resources are limited, however, choices must be made. To have more of one thing means to forgo something else. Production of a particular good has costs, in the form of other goods that could have been produced by the same resources. The forgone benefit—the forgone best alternative—connected with a good is called its *opportunity cost*. If a family chooses to spend more of its budget on shoes or recreation, the cost is its reduced consumption of furniture, private education, or savings. The same principle applies to government. If we insist upon having more public parks, better streets, or cleaner air, something must be given up, such as additional police protection. The familiar expression that "there is no such thing as a free lunch" means that even if a good appears to be free it is not, because someone had to give something up in order for it to become available.

In a *competitive economy* (many buyers and sellers in each market) the equilibrium price of any good will match its cost of production, which is the total opportunity cost of the resources embodied in the good. Production costs, expressed in dollars, are payments to resource suppliers (laborers, suppliers of materials and capital, etc.) that induce them to spurn opportunities that exist elsewhere. Under competitive conditions, these payments just match what the resource owners could have earned elsewhere. The payments that would have been earned in the alternate use depend upon how highly consumers value that use. In sum, in a competitive economy the price of each good reflects the value of the resources needed to produce it, as valued by consumers. In other words, *relative prices reflect the relative opportunity costs of scarce resources*—a crucial condition for economic efficiency.

Efficiency

A community pursues numerous economic goals. One of the most important undoubtedly is *efficiency*—getting the most from available resources. Resources are efficiently allocated when the total benefit (utility) to members of society is maximized. Of course, society will also be concerned with *equity*—how fairly the benefits are distributed among individual members of society. But note that no society, least of all a poor one, can afford to disregard efficiency. If efficiency is shrugged off, a smaller pie of benefits will be delivered. Unfortunately, many public policies are often geared strictly to equity considerations, while efficiency is either not understood or simply disregarded.

To examine a simple example of inefficiency, suppose that to help the poor the government hands out wood-frame sewing machines free. The poor would benefit, of course, but it doesn't require much imagination to realize that consumers may use sewing machines for nonsewing purposes—perhaps firewood, for example. While it is tempting to think that no government would do anything so ill conceived, one did—in the Soviet Union not long ago. While sewing machines were not free, the price was low enough to assure that most families could afford one. In fact, the price was so attractive that many consumers purchased several sewing machines. But Soviet authorities finally discovered, much to their dismay, that many consumers were removing and simply discarding the sewing machine, in order to use the remaining

wooden frame as a lamp table. Sewing machines were priced below lamp tables! When *relative price*—the relation of one price to another—does not reflect relative opportunity cost, resources will become inefficiently allocated.

Allocative efficiency occurs when resources are funneled into their most highly valued uses. A correct understanding of this concept uses *marginal analysis*, which compares the incremental benefit and incremental cost to society from producing a little bit more or less of some good. It is simply a question of comparing the value of resources employed in one use with their value employed elsewhere. In the sewing-machine fiasco, resources were inefficiently allocated. The value to consumers of a sewing machine, at the margin, was no greater than that of a lamp table, although the sewing machine cost more to produce. Too many sewing machines were produced and too few lamp tables. When resources are efficiently allocated, the output mix—the ratio of one quantity to another—maximizes total benefits to society. Allocative efficiency is not to be confused with *technical efficiency*—producing a particular good at minimum cost. It is possible to imagine technical efficiency existing throughout an allocatively *inefficient* economy.

Efficiency and the Market System

A well-known theorem in economics states that an individual's marginal benefit *(MB)* is equivalent to his or her demand for a commodity. If we aggregate the benefits accruing to all individuals for a particular commodity, we can obtain a market demand curve (see Figure 1). As an individual's rate of consumption rises, marginal benefits will tend to fall. Therefore, for the

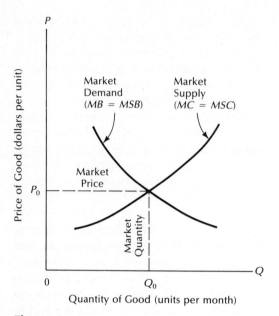

Figure 1.

market as a whole the demand curve is downward-sloping. Further, if the entire benefits from this good are captured by paying customers, then the marginal *private* benefits *(MB)* are identical to the marginal social benefits *(MSB)*.

What an individual will pay for the good is determined by the value (marginal benefit) he or she places on it. Consider the case of an everyday item such as men's shirts. A man will not purchase another shirt if the price exceeds his marginal benefit. For him to do so would be to forgo greater benefits elsewhere. Conversely, he will always pay the price if it is less than his marginal benefit, which means he will buy additional shirts as long as marginal benefit exceeds price. The consumer acquires shirts up to the point where price equals marginal benefit $(P = MB)$. At this point there is no opportunity for further gain. In short, the market price of shirts

will match the marginal private (and social) benefit for each consumer when the market is in equilibrium.

In a competitive economy prices are controlled by the interaction of supply and demand (see Figure 1). The reader may recall from an economics principles course that in purely competitive markets the supply curve of a commodity duplicates the marginal cost curve. That is, the height of the supply curve at each quantity indicates the marginal cost *(MC)* of producing one more unit. If the private firm bears all of the relevant opportunity costs of producing a good, then the supply curve also will reflect the full marginal social costs.

A *competitive market economy generally will deliver an efficient allocation of resources.* Efficiency requires that marginal social benefits equal marginal social costs in every market. In Figure 1, the market-determined quantity, Q_0, is precisely the quantity where $MSB = MSC$, and efficiency is realized. If a little bit less than Q_0 is produced, the marginal benefit resulting from one more unit of output exceeds marginal cost, implying underproduction. The value of additional resources absorbed here exceeds their value elsewhere, which is wasteful. Resources are also misallocated if production exceeds Q_0. Now, too much is produced because the marginal benefit of the last unit is less than its marginal cost. Since the value of the marginal unit elsewhere exceeds the value here, society will gain if production is cut back, allowing the unleashed resources to gravitate to more highly valued uses.

Allocative efficiency is not the only way in which the price system promotes efficiency. Working in tandem with the profit motive, free prices also promote technical efficiency. Whenever a firm discovers it can manufacture its product with fewer—or less costly—resources, it can profit by taking appropriate action. In a competitive economy, the price of a given resource will be bid up to reflect the highest valued use of that resource. That is, resource prices reflect opportunity costs. Hence, a firm's efforts to minimize production costs will free up scarce resources, which may then be employed elsewhere in society. Prices create the necessary incentive for firms to seek technical efficiency. Even if the profit motive within a firm is not all-powerful, competitive pressures will eventually force a laggard firm to shape up. High-cost firms that fail to adopt efficient methods of production will be unable to compete and over the long run will not survive.

When all markets attain long-run, competitive equilibrium, the resulting allocation of resources is characterized by *pareto optimality* because no reallocation of resources can make someone better off without making someone else worse off. Both technical and allocative efficiency are embraced within this concept. For example, if a good is not being produced efficiently, then resources could be employed elsewhere to increase production, benefiting those who value that particular good while harming no one. Similarly, if the overall mix of goods fails to agree with consumer preferences, a reallocation of resources is potentially beneficial because the gains from exchange have not been exhausted. Pareto optimality is a widely agreed upon criterion for evaluating government policies.

PRICE CONTROLS AND EFFICIENCY LOSS

Governments often impose price controls on some commodities to achieve equity. While the usual purpose is to make the good cheaper to individuals who cannot otherwise afford it, price controls usually impair efficiency (that is, they create waste). When controls distort the relationship between price and opportunity cost, relative prices no longer reflect relative scarcities. We earlier examined the damaging effects of pricing sewing machines in Russia below the value of the resources needed to manufacture them.

Local government controls on apartment rental rates is another example of the distortive effects of price controls. As inflation and other factors drive up apartment rents, controls become increasingly popular. The alluring appeal of rent controls has spread despite predictably adverse experiences with them in many European and U.S. cities, especially New York City. The simple model of competitive market allocation predicts fairly accurately what one can observe in these cities. As rental rates are held below market levels, shortages appear. Over time, owners allow apartments to decay more rapidly because of the low rents. As dramatic evidence of this, New York City during a recent period was the only major U.S. city in which the proportion of substandard housing actually rose. In the long run, resources may be diverted from rental housing altogether because the low rents do not make rental housing profitable. When newcomers seek housing in the city, the shortage worsens. A housing shortage in Stockholm grew so bad before rent controls were rescinded in 1975 that 40 percent of the city's population was on official waiting lists for rationed housing.[1] In New York, rent control is partly to blame for abandoned apartment buildings. Another blow to the rental market is condominium conversion, which is more prev-

1 F. A. Hayek et al., *Rent Controls: A Popular Paradox* (Vancouver, B.C.: The Frazier Institute, 1975).

alent in New York than in similar cities without rent control.

Of course, one might be willing to accept these distortions if rent control met its objective of assisting the poor. However, there is only meager evidence that rent control has had any leveling effect on income distribution. About the best that can be said is that the benefits of below-market rents are not distributed across income classes in any consistent fashion. Middle- and higher-income tenants may benefit perhaps as much as the poor.

THE PRICE SYSTEM AND EQUITY

While the price mechanism promotes efficiency, it does not necessarily deliver a "fair" distribution of income. The income each person receives by means of the market is determined by the factors of production that he or she owns and makes available. Factors of production are rewarded according to their marginal productivity—that is, according to the additional satisfaction to society that their output makes possible. In the United States the single major productive resource many of us possess is our human capital: skills, knowledge, experience, and willingness to work. About three fourths of all income in the United States is paid in wages and salaries (plus supplements). Of course, some individuals also cash in on property holdings, such as stock dividends, savings, and income-producing real estate. The monetary values that the market assigns to the services of these resources also depends upon their productivity. In general, the highest rewards go to the resources that are the most useful in satisfying wants expressed in the marketplace.

Some economists grudgingly praise the price system as a coordinating mechanism and a system that promotes efficiency but nevertheless ultimately reject it on the grounds that it produces unacceptable inequalities. Ideally, they would prefer to split off income distribution from its other functions. Yet, the distributive function of the price system is interwoven with its other functions. The information that prices convey is wasted unless individuals have an incentive to act. To illustrate, a higher demand for semiconductors will boost the wages of assemblers, signaling that assemblers now are in greater demand. Some individuals who previously felt indifferent about becoming assemblers may now change their minds. Young people entering the labor market may now choose to become assemblers. If they do, the economy becomes more productive. If, however, what a person received did not depend upon the type and amount of work chosen, that individual would have no incentive to act on the signals provided by the market. When prices are prevented from distributing income, they probably will also be impeded in performing their other functions.

MARKET FAILURE: PROBLEM AREAS FOR THE MARKET

Although the general outcome of the market system is efficient resource allocation, important exceptions exist. The reader may recall that allocative efficiency is concerned with the *relative* quantity (the ratio of one quantity to another) of each good. The test for allocative efficiency is that the marginal social benefit equal the marginal social cost for every commodity. But for efficiency to emerge, *all* costs and benefits must be reflected in the decisions made by producers and consumers. There are important instances where individuals will not necessarily consider all the costs or benefits associated with their actions.

Market Power

Any claim that unregulated markets allocate resources efficiently assumes that competition is flourishing in each market. Strictly speaking, this means that each market must fulfill the textbook conditions of pure competition. In a purely competitive market, there is a large number of buyers and sellers, and no single buyer or seller is large enough to influence the price. That is, all buyers and sellers are *price takers*. When a firm is powerless to influence the price,. it adjusts output so that marginal cost equals price. When price and marginal cost are unequal, then the essential condition for efficiency, $MSB = MSC$, no longer holds. Although the model of pure competition is rare in practice, there are numerous markets in which it seems roughly to hold—agricultural markets, for instance.

In imperfectly competitive markets, the $P = MC$ relationship may be violated. One such market is a pure *monopoly*, in which a single seller sets the price. A general rule that shall not be proven here is that market power prompts firms to restrict output below what it would be under competition, driving the price above marginal cost. In Figure 1, monopoly output would fall short of the amount Q_0, violating the condition for allocative efficiency. Resource misallocation (waste) occurs because resources are not channeled to their most highly valued uses.

Some urban problems are often attributed, rightly or wrongly, to monopoly power. For example, it is often argued that the housing market is in the clutches of monopoly landlords, whose market power should be checked with government controls. Similarly, it is often argued that monopoly land speculators are to blame for excessive urban growth, sprawl, congestion, pollution, and high housing prices. In these cases government land-use controls are necessary, it is argued. Yet, available evidence seldom supports the contention that major urban problems are traceable to excess market power. However, other types of market failure—particularly externalities—do underly many urban problems.

External Costs and Benefits

External costs, or *negative externalities,* occur when costs are imposed, perhaps by a producer, on someone who is not compensated for the harm done. For example, when a steel mill blankets the surrounding atmosphere with dirt or dumps effluents into local waterways, costs are imposed on residents in the form of health risks, property damage, or psychic losses of utility. Social costs associated with steel production are *external* to the firm because it does not take them into account when making decisions to produce steel.

Negative externalities lie at the heart of numerous urban problems. Pollution and highway traffic congestion are two obvious examples where the private costs that influence individual decisions diverge from the social costs. The commuter's decision to drive to work during the rush hour depends upon that commuter's average time costs. A commuter completely disregards the additional time cost he or she inflicts on thousands of other drivers. Similarly, some land uses (such as a noisy, smelly factory) impose costs on other property owners. As another example, the deterioration of urban housing is often attributed, at least in part, to externalities. The distortion of housing prices by externalities has been cited to justify government urban renewal programs.

Some production activities generate *external benefits,* which are also bestowed upon third parties. If a dilapidated house is sold to someone who restores and beautifies it, adjacent property owners will benefit. If an individual obtains a smallpox immunization, people who come into contact with that person are also better protected. External benefits bypass the interplay of the market since a recipient cannot be compelled to pay for them.

When market activities produce external effects, prices no longer allocate resources efficiently. *Private* costs and benefits no longer coincide with *social* costs and benefits. When a producer firm imposes spillover costs on others, its private cost falls below the full social cost. The producer ignores the external cost and thus is able to sell more of its product at a lower price than it otherwise could. External costs result in overproduction of the firm's product, whereas external benefits imply underproduction.

In principle, the market inefficiencies that result from spillover effects may be remediable by government. There are two general types of intervention. One approach is simply to regulate spillovers directly. For example, government may force producers to accept standards that limit the amount of pollution they cause.

Alternatively, inefficiencies can be remedied through taxes and subsidies. A tax on polluters raises the cost of production and this cost is passed on to consumers, thereby dampening consumption and eliminating overproduction. Conversely, a subsidy can be granted to those who immu-

nize themselves against smallpox. This subsidy will lower the effective price of immunization, thereby boosting consumption and eliminating underproduction. A large body of literature has focused on the question of the respective merits of the two approaches: regulation versus taxes and subsidies. This issue will not be discussed here except to mention that the tax and subsidy approach is more efficient in most cases. The general problem with mandatory controls is that they fail to recognize demand and cost differences among industries and fail to achieve their goals with minimum cost.

Public Goods

Private firms may not find it profitable to produce some desired goods. These goods, once produced, benefit all members of the community. Because no one can be excluded from sharing the benefits, these goods are called *public goods.* An example of a public good is police service. Once police services are provided, everyone benefits and one person's benefit does not subtract from the benefits obtained by others. If a firm is unable to exclude *free riders,* it will encounter difficulty in financing the good. Even though the good may be highly desired, it may not be produced. In principle, government provision of public goods may bring about a more efficient allocation of resources. For this reason government provides national defense, public-health services, mosquito-abatement programs, law enforcement, and flood control.

PLANNING VERSUS THE MARKET

Under some conditions, a system of markets and prices promotes efficient resource allocation. The necessary conditions are that goods be private in nature, that markets be competitive, and that external effects be absent. Whenever these conditions are violated, direct government intervention may be justified.

Disagreement about the efficiency and equity of market outcomes often underlies conflicts between a *planning approach* to urban problems and a *market approach*. The planning approach often favors direct government controls to suppress or supplement market forces. For example, if *urban sprawl* results from inefficient land uses, the planning remedy invokes controls on private landowners that would prevent the conversion of land from one use to another. Zoning regulations that stipulate a minimum lot size are one example of such a control. On the other hand, supporters of the market approach have suggested that, given the actual nature of the urban land market, sprawl may not necessarily imply inefficient land use. If it does, the best remedy may be simply to adjust the pricing system by charging fringe residents more for utilities and for public services. One advantage of using the price structure to correct inefficiencies is that it requires little, if any, additional government action.

One commonplace planning approach to the problem of urban congestion is to subsidize the construction of new mass-transit systems. Advocates of the market approach, on the other hand, have suggested that subsidies to private automobile travel first should be eliminated—especially by charging higher prices to rush-hour highway users. This charge would have the effect of smoothing out traffic flows at various times of day, of utilizing existing highway capacity more efficiently, and even possibly of avoiding the enormous costs of new transit systems. These examples should serve to indicate how fundamental and deep is the gulf between the planning and market approaches.

The choice between market and government approaches to urban problems depends not only on benefits but also on costs. For example, while intervention may be needed to deal with monopolization of private markets, government itself sometimes stifles competition and creates and protects monopolies. For example, in many cities monopoly franchises are awarded to taxi companies. By not permitting open competition among cab companies, this policy leads to limited service and higher fares.

Finally, government programs inevitably affect individual liberties. One characteristic of government institutions is the ability to use the police power of the state, which, in irresponsible hands, can be all too often used to reduce individual freedoms in the name of improved public welfare. When the costs and benefits of government policies are appraised, the harm to individual economic and personal freedom should be counted as one of the costs. In contrast, market solutions are voluntary and, therefore, allow freedom of choice.

By stressing the issues of efficiency, equity, and freedom, the urban economist strives to inform policy makers of the special trade-offs underlying urban problems. By highlighting what the market does well and what it often does poorly, the economist provides tools with which urban problems can be approached and analyzed. Only then can the costs and benefits of proposed government actions be fully and reasonably assessed.

KEY CONCEPTS

allocative efficiency	*opportunity cost*
competitive economy	*Pareto optimality*
efficiency	*planning approach*
external benefits	*price system*
external costs	*public goods*
market approach	*relative prices*
marginal social benefit (MSB)	*scarcity*
monopoly	*technical efficiency*

WILBUR THOMPSON

2 The City as a Distorted Price System

Professor Wilbur Thompson of Wayne State University, a pioneer in the field of urban economics, observes that the price system is either neglected entirely or badly misused in the public sector of the urban economy. Numerous serious urban problems can be traced to the misuse or lack of a basic set of prices for scarce public services. Correcting the price system will improve the short-run and long-run allocation of resources in both the private and public sectors of the urban economy. In addition, a wider use of prices would improve the distribution of income.

We treat the scarcest thing in our cities—street space at the rush hour—as if it were free goods. We offer "free" such public facilities as museums, marinas, golf courses. We insist on equal pay for teachers everywhere throughout the urban area. All of these are instances of bad economics, the result of public failure to understand the city as a price system. And small wonder, since the complex prices that shape the city are largely subtle, hidden prices, a subterranean maze of rewards and penalties. It is doubtful that the local public managers of any city in the country can even roughly describe, much less defend, the network of "prices" that push and pull at the fabric of the city and so hamper them at every turn.

The failure to use price—as an *explicit* system—in the public sector of the metropolis is at the root of many, if not most, of our urban problems. Price, serving its historic functions, might be used to ration the use of existing facilities, to signal the desired directions of new public invest-

Reprinted from *Psychology Today* Magazine, August 1968. Copyright © 1968 Ziff-Davis Publishing Company.

ment, to guide the distribution of income, to enlarge the range of public choice and to change tastes and behavior. Price performs such functions in the private marketplace, but it has been virtually eliminated from the public sector. We say "virtually eliminated" because it does exist but in an implicit, subtle, distorted sense that is rarely seen or acknowledged by even close students of the city, much less by public managers. Not surprisingly, this implicit price system results in bad economics.

We think of the property tax as a source of public revenue, but it can be re-interpreted as a price. Most often, the property tax is rationalized on "ability-to-pay" grounds with real property serving as a proxy for income. When the correlation between income and real property is challenged, the apologist for the property tax shifts ground and rationalizes it as a "benefit" tax. The tax then becomes a "price" which the property owner pays for benefits received—fire protection, for example. But this implicit "price" for fire services is hardly a model of either efficiency or equity. Put in a new furnace and fireproof your building (reduce the likelihood of having a fire) and your property tax (fire service premium) goes up; let your property deteriorate and become a firetrap and your fire protection premium goes down! One bright note is New York City's one-year tax abatement on new pollution-control equipment; a timid step but in the right direction.

Often "urban sprawl" is little more than a color word which reflects (betrays?) the speaker's bias in favor of high population density and heavy interpersonal interaction—his "urbanity." Still, typically, the price of using urban fringe space has been set too low—well below the full costs of running pipes, wires, police cars and fire engines farther than would be necessary if building lots were smaller. Residential developers are, moreover, seldom discouraged (penalized by price) from "leap frogging" over the contiguous, expensive vacant land to build on the remote, cheaper parcels. Ordinarily, a flat price is charged for extending water or sewers to a new household regardless of whether the house is placed near to or far from existing pumping stations.

Again, the motorist is subject to the same license fees and tolls, if any, for the extremely expensive system of streets, bridges, tunnels and traffic controls he enjoys, regardless of whether he chooses to drive downtown at the rush hour and thereby pushes against peak capacity or at off-peak times when it costs little or nothing to serve him. To compound this distortion of prices, we usually set the toll at zero. And when we do charge tolls, we quite perversely cut the commuter (rush-hour) rate below the off-peak rate.

It is not enough to point out that the motorist supports road-building through the gasoline tax. The social costs of noise, air pollution, traffic control and general loss of urban amenities are borne by the general taxpayer. In addition, drivers during off-peak hours overpay and subsidize rush-hour drivers. Four lanes of expressway or bridge capacity are needed in the morning and evening rush hours where two lanes would have served if movements had been random in time and direction; that is, near constant in average volume. The peak-hour motorists probably should share the cost of the first two lanes and bear the full cost of the other two that they alone require. It is best to begin by carefully distinguishing where market tests are possible and where they are not. Otherwise, the case for applying the principles of price is misunderstood; either the too-ardent advocate overstates his case or the potential convert projects too much. In either case, a "disenchantment" sets in that is hard to reverse.

Much of the economics of the city is "public economics," and the pricing of urban public services poses some very difficult and even insurmountable problems. Economists have, in fact, erected a very elegant rationalization of the public economy almost wholly on the *non*-marketability of public goods and services. While economists have perhaps oversold the inapplicability of price in the public sector, let us begin with what we are *not* talking about.

The public economy supplies "collectively consumed" goods, those produced and consumed in one big indivisible lump. Everyone has to be counted in the system, there is no choice of *in* or *out*. We cannot identify individual benefits, therefore we cannot exact a *quid pro quo*. We can not exclude those who would not pay voluntarily; therefore we must turn to compulsory payments: taxes. Justice and air-pollution control are good examples of collectively consumed public services.

A second function of the public economy is to supply "merit goods." Sometimes the majority of us become a little paternalistic and decide that we know what is best for all of us. We believe some goods are especially meritorious, like education, and we fear that others might not fully appreciate this truth. Therefore, we produce these merit goods, at considerable cost, but offer them at a zero price. Unlike the first case of collectively consumed goods, we could sell these merit goods. A schoolroom's doors can be closed to those who do not pay, *quite unlike justice*. But we choose to open the doors wide to ensure that no one will turn away from the service because of its cost, and then we finance the service with compulsory payments. Merit goods are a case of the majority playing God, and "coercing" the minority by the use of bribes to change their behavior.

A third classic function of government is the redistribution of income. Here we wish to perform a service for one group and charge another group the cost of that service. Welfare payments are a clear case. Again, any kind of a private market or pricing mechanism is totally inappropriate: we obviously do not expect welfare recipients to return their payments. Again, we turn to compulsory payments: taxes. In sum, the private market may not be able to process certain goods and services (pure "public goods"), or it may give the "wrong" prices ("merit goods"), or we simply do not want the consumer to pay (income-redistributive services).

But the virtual elimination of price from the public sector is an extreme and highly simplistic response to the special requirements of the public sector. Merit goods may be subsidized without going all of the way to zero prices. Few would argue for full-cost admission prices to museums, but a good case can be made for moderate prices that cover, say, their daily operating costs (e.g., salaries of guards and janitors, heat and light).

Unfortunately, as we have given local government more to do, we have almost unthinkingly extended the tradition of "free" public services to every new undertaking, despite the clear trend in local government toward the assumption of more and more functions that do not fit the neat schema above. The provision of free public facilities for automobile movement in the crowded cores of our urban areas can hardly be defended on the grounds that: (a) motorists could not be excluded from the expressways if they refused to pay the toll, or (b) the privately operated motor vehicle is an especially meritorious way to move through densely populated areas, or (c) the motorists cannot afford to pay their own way and that the general (property) taxpayers should subsidize them. And all this applies with a vengeance to municipal marinas and golf courses.

PRICES TO RATION THE USE OF EXISTING FACILITIES

We need to understand better the rationing function of price as it manifests itself in the urban public sector: how the demand for a temporarily (or permanently) fixed stock of a public good or service can be adjusted to the supply. At any given time the supply of street, bridge and parking space is fixed; "congestion" on the streets and a "shortage" of parking space express demand greater than supply at a zero price, a not too surprising phenomenon. Applying the market solution, the shortage of street space at peak hours ("congestion") could have been temporarily relieved (rationalized) by introducing a short-run rationing price to divert some motorists to other hours of movement, some to other modes of transportation, and some to other activities.

Public goods last a long time and therefore current additions to the stock are too small to relieve shortages quickly and easily. *The rationing function of price is probably more important in the public sector where it is customarily ignored than in the private sector where it is faithfully expressed.*

Rationing need not always be achieved with money, as when a motorist circles the block over and over looking for a place to park. The motorist who is not willing to "spend time" waiting and drives away forfeits the scarce space to one who will spend time (luck averaging out). The parking "problem" may be re-interpreted as an implicit decision to keep the money price artificially low (zero or a nickel an hour in a meter) and supplement it with a waiting cost or time price. The problem is that we did not clearly understand and explicitly agree to do just that.

The central role of price is to allocate—across the board—scarce resources among competing ends to the point where the value of another unit of any good or service is equal to the incremental cost of producing that unit. Expressed loosely, in the long run we turn from using prices to dampen demand to fit a fixed supply to adjusting the supply to fit the quantity demanded, at a price which reflects the production costs.

Prices which ration also serve to signal desired new directions in which to reallocate resources. If the rationing price exceeds those costs of production which

the user is expected to bear directly, more resources should ordinarily be allocated to that activity. And symmetrically a rationing price below the relevant costs indicates an *uneconomic* provision of that service in the current amounts. Rationing prices reveal the intensity of the users' demands. How much is it really worth to drive into the heart of town at rush hour or launch a boat? In the long run, motorists and boaters should be free to choose, in rough measure, the amount of street and dock space they want and for which they are willing to pay. But, as in the private sector of our economy, free choice would carry with it full (financial) responsibility for that choice.

We need also to extend our price strategy to "factor prices"; we need a sophisticated wage policy for local public employees. Perhaps the key decision in urban development pertains to the recruiting and assignment of elementary- and secondary-school teachers. The more able and experienced teachers have the greater range of choice in post and quite naturally they choose the newer schools in the better neighborhoods, after serving the required apprenticeship in the older schools in the poorer neighborhoods. Such a pattern of migration certainly cannot implement a policy of equality of opportunity.

This author argued six years ago that

Egalitarianism in the public school system has been overdone; even the army recognizes the role of price when it awards extra "jump pay" to paratroopers, only a slightly more hazardous occupation than teaching behind the lines. Besides, it is male teachers whom we need to attract to slum schools, both to serve as father figures where there are few males at home and to serve quite literally as disciplinarians. It is bad economics to insist on equal pay for teachers every-

where throughout the urban area when males have a higher productivity in some areas and when males have better employment opportunities outside teaching—higher "opportunity costs" that raise their supply price. It is downright silly to argue that "equal pay for equal work" is achieved by paying the same money wage in the slums as in the suburbs.

About a year ago, on being offered premium salaries for service in ghetto schools, the teachers rejected, by name and with obvious distaste, any form of "jump pay." One facile argument offered was that they must protect the slum child from the stigma of being harder to teach, a nicely surely lost on the parents and outside observers. One suspects that the real reason for avoiding salary differentials between the "slums and suburbs" is that the teachers seek to escape the hard choice between the higher pay and the better working conditions. *But that is precisely what the price system is supposed to do: equalize sacrifice.*

PRICES TO GUIDE
THE DISTRIBUTION OF INCOME

A much wider application of tolls, fees, fines and other "prices" would also confer greater control over the distribution of income for two distinct reasons. First, the taxes currently used to finance a given public service create *implicit* and *unplanned* redistribution of income. Second, this drain on our limited supply of tax money prevents local government from undertaking other programs with more *explicit* and *planned* redistributional effects.

More specifically, if upper-middle- and upper-income motorists, golfers and boaters use subsidized public streets, golf links

and marinas more than in proportion to their share of local tax payments from which the subsidy is paid, then these public activities redistribute income toward greater inequality. Even if these "semiproprietary" public activities were found to be neutral with respect to the distribution of income, public provision of these discretionary services comes at the expense of a roughly equivalent expenditure on the more classic public services: protection, education, public health and welfare.

Self-supporting public golf courses are so common and marinas are such an easy extension of the same principle that it is much more instructive to test the faith by considering the much harder case of the public museum: "Culture." Again, we must recall that it is the middle- and upper-income classes who typically visit museums, so that free admission becomes, in effect, redistribution toward greater inequality, to the extent that the lower-income nonusers pay local taxes (e.g., property taxes directly or indirectly through rent, local sales taxes). The low prices contemplated are not, moreover, likely to discourage attendance significantly and the resolution of special cases (e.g., student passes) seems well within our competence.

Unfortunately, it is not obvious that "free" public marinas and tennis courts pose forgone alternatives—"opportunity costs." If we had to discharge a teacher or policeman every time we built another boat dock or tennis court, we would see the real cost of these public services. But in a growing economy, we need only not hire another teacher or policeman and that is not so obvious. In general, then, given a binding local budget constraint—scarce tax money—to undertake a local public service that is unequalizing or even neutral in income redistribution is to deny funds to programs that have the desired distributional effect, and is to lose control over equity.

Typically, in oral presentations at question time, it is necessary to reinforce this point by rejoining: "No, I would not put turnstiles in the playgrounds in poor neighborhoods, rather it is only because we do put turnstiles at the entrance to the playgrounds for the middle- and upper-income groups that we will be able to 'afford' playgrounds for the poor."

PRICES TO ENLARGE
THE RANGE OF CHOICE

But there is more at stake in the contemporary chaos of hidden and unplanned prices than "merely" efficiency and equity. *There is no urban goal on which consensus is more easily gained than the pursuit of great variety and choice—"pluralism."* The great rural to urban migration was prompted as much by the search for variety as by the decline of agriculture and rise of manufacturing. Wide choice is seen as the saving grace of bigness by even the sharpest critics of the metropolis. Why, then, do we tolerate far less variety in our big cities than we could have? We have lapsed into a state of tyranny by the majority, in matters of both taste and choice.

In urban transportation the issue is not, in the final analysis, whether users of core-area street space at peak hours should or should not be required to pay their own way in full. The problem is, rather, that by not forcing a direct *quid pro quo* in money, we implicitly substitute a new means of payment—time—in the transportation services "market." The peak-hour motorist does pay in full, through congestion and time delay. But *implicit choices* blur issues and confuse decision-making.

Say we were carefully to establish how many more dollars would have to be paid in for the additional capacity needed to save a given number of hours spent commuting. The *majority* of urban motorists perhaps would still choose the present combination of "under-investment" in highway, bridge and parking facilities, with a compensatory heavy investment of time in slow movement over these crowded facilities. Even so, a substantial minority of motorists do prefer a different combination of money and time cost. A more affluent, long-distance commuter could well see the current level of traffic congestion as a real problem and much prefer to spend more money to save time. If economies of scale are so substantial that only one motorway to town can be supported, or if some naturally scarce factor (e.g., bridge or tunnel sites) prevents parallel transportation facilities of different quality and price, then the preferences of the minority must be sacrificed to the majority interest and we do have a real "problem." But, ordinarily, in large urban areas there are a number of near parallel routes to town, and an unsatisfied minority group large enough to justify significant differentiation of one or more of these streets and its diversion to their use. Greater choice through greater scale is, in fact, what bigness is all about.

The simple act of imposing a toll, at peak hours, on one of these routes would reduce its use, assuming that nearby routes are still available without user charges, thereby speeding movement of the motorists who remain and pay. The toll could be raised only to the point where some combination of moderately rapid movement and high physical output were jointly optimized. Otherwise the outcry might be raised that the public transportation authority was so elitist as to gratify the desire of a few very wealthy motorists for very rapid movement, heavily overloading the "free" routes. It is, moreover, quite possible, even probable, that the newly converted, rapid-flow, toll route would handle as many vehicles as it did previously as a congested street and not therefore spin off any extra load on the free routes.

Our cities cater, at best, to the taste patterns of the middle-income class, as well they should, *but not so exclusively.* This group has chosen, indirectly through clumsy and insensitive tax-and-expenditure decisions and ambiguous political processes, to move about town flexibly and cheaply, but slowly, in private vehicles. Often, and almost invariably in the larger urban areas, we would not have to encroach much on this choice to accommodate also those who would prefer to spend more money and less time, in urban movement. In general, we should permit urban residents to pay in their most readily available "currency"—time or money.

Majority rule by the middle class in urban transportation has not only disenfranchised the affluent commuter, but more seriously it has debilitated the low-fare, mass transit system on which the poor depend. The effect of widespread automobile ownership and use on the mass transportation system is an oft-told tale: falling bus and rail patronage leads to less frequent service and higher overhead costs per trip and often higher fares which further reduce demand and service schedules. Perhaps two-thirds or more of the urban residents will tolerate and may even prefer slow, cheap automobile movement. But the poor are left without access to many places of work—the suburbanizing factories in particular—and they face much reduced opportunities for comparative shopping, and highly constrained participation in the community life in general. A truly wide range of choice in urban transportation would allow the rich to pay for fast movement with money, the middle-income class to pay for the privacy and convenience of the automobile with time, and the poor to economize by giving up (paying with) privacy.

A more sophisticated price policy would expand choice in other directions. Opinions differ as to the gravity of the water-pollution problem near large urban areas. The minimum level of dissolved oxygen in the water that is needed to meet the standards of different users differs greatly, as does the incremental cost that must be incurred to bring the dissolved oxygen levels up to successively higher standards. The boater accepts a relatively low level of "cleanliness" acquired at relatively little cost. Swimmers have higher standards attained only at much higher cost. Fish and fisherman can thrive only with very high levels of dissolved oxygen acquired only at the highest cost. Finally, one can imagine an elderly convalescent or an impoverished slum dweller or a confirmed landlubber who is not at all interested in the nearby river. What, then, constitutes "clean"?

A majority rule decision, whether borne by the citizen directly in higher taxes or levied on the industrial polluters and then shifted on to the consumer in higher product prices, is sure to create a "problem." If the pollution program is a compromise—a halfway measure—the fisherman will be disappointed because the river is still not clean enough for his purposes and the landlubbers will be disgruntled because the program is for "special interests" and he can think of better uses for his limited income. Surely, we can assemble the managerial skills in the local public sector needed to devise and administer a structure of user charges that would extend choice in outdoor recreation, consistent with financial responsibility, with lower charges for boat licenses and higher charges for fishing licenses.

Perhaps the most fundamental error we have committed in the development of our large cities is that we have too often subjected the more affluent residents to petty irritations which serve no great social purpose, then turned right around and permitted this same group to avoid responsibilities which have the most critical and pervasive social ramifications. It is a travesty and a social tragedy that we have prevented the rich from buying their way out of annoying traffic congestion—or at least not helped those who are long on money and short on time arrange such an accommodation. Rather, we have permitted them, through political fragmentation and flight to tax havens, to evade their financial and leadership responsibilities for the poor of the central cities. That easily struck goal, "pluralism and choice," will require much more managerial sophistication in the local public sector than we have shown to date.

PRICING TO CHANGE TASTES AND BEHAVIOR

Urban managerial economics will probably also come to deal especially with "developmental pricing" analogous to "promotional pricing" in business. Prices below cost may be used for a limited period to create a market for a presumed "merit good." The hope would be that the artifi-cially low price would stimulate consumption and that an altered *expenditure pattern* (practice) would lead in time to an altered *taste pattern* (preference), as experience with the new service led to a fuller appreciation of it. Ultimately, the subsidy would be withdrawn, whether or not tastes changed sufficiently to make the new service self-supporting—provided, of course, that no permanent redistribution of income was intended.

For example, our national parks had to be subsidized in the beginning and this subsidy could be continued indefinitely on the grounds that these are "merit goods" that serve a broad social interest. But long experience with outdoor recreation has so shifted tastes that a large part of the costs of these parks could now be paid for by a much higher set of park fees.

It is difficult, moreover, to argue that poor people show up at the gates of Yellowstone Park, or even the much nearer metropolitan area regional parks, in significant number, so that a subsidy is needed to continue provision of this service for the poor. A careful study of the users and the incidence of the taxes raised to finance our parks may even show a slight redistribution of income toward greater inequality.

Clearly, this is not the place for an economist to pontificate on the psychology of prices but a number of very interesting phenomena that seem to fall under this general heading deserve brief mention. A few simple examples of how charging a price changes behavior are offered, but left for others to classify.

In a recent study of depressed areas, the case was cited of a community-industrial-development commission that extended its fund-raising efforts from large business contributors to the general public in a supplementary "nickel and dime" campaign.

They hoped to enlist the active support of the community at large, more for reasons of public policy than for finance. But even a trivial financial stake was seen as a means to create broad and strong public identification with the local industrial development programs and to gain their political support.

Again, social-work agencies have found that even a nominal charge for what was previously a free service enhances both the self-respect of the recipient and his respect for the usefulness of the service. Paradoxically, we might experiment with higher public assistance payments coupled to *nominal* prices for selected public health and family services, personal counseling and surplus foods.

To bring a lot of this together now in a programmatic way, we can imagine a very sophisticated urban public management beginning with below-cost prices on, say, the new rapid mass transit facility during the promotional period of luring motorists from their automobiles and of "educating" them on the advantages of a carefree journey to work. Later, if and when the new facility becomes crowded during rush hours and after a taste for this new transportation mode has become well established, the "city economist" might devise a three-price structure of fares: the lowest fare for regular off-peak use, the middle fare for regular peak use (tickets for commuters) and the highest fare for the occasional peak-time user. Such a schedule would reflect each class's contribution to the cost of having to carry standby capacity.

If the venture more than covered its costs of operation, the construction of additional facilities would begin. Added social benefits in the form of a cleaner, quieter city or reduced social costs of traffic control and accidents could be included in the cost accounting ("cost-benefit analysis") underlying the fare structure. But below-cost fares, taking care to count social as well as private costs, would not be continued indefinitely except for merit goods or when a clear income-redistribution end is in mind. And, even then, not without careful comparison of the relative efficiency of using the subsidy money in alternative redistributive programs. We need, it would seem, not only a knowledge of the economy of the city, but some very knowledgeable city economists as well.

KEY CONCEPTS

merit goods

pluralism

price system

public goods

GEOFFREY E. NUNN   STEPHEN L. MEHAY

3   A Public-Choice Perspective on Urban Problems

The political process is an alternative to the market mechanism for allocating scarce resources. This selection analyzes how the political mechanism reaches basic allocative decisions. Two major questions are posed: (1) Is the political process likely to generate efficient policies? (2) Are government agencies likely to provide services at minimum cost? Government failure occurs when the political process fails to produce efficient outcomes.

While the strength of the free market economy lies in its ability to allocate resources efficiently, several factors can disrupt the market mechanism. Externalities, monopoly, and pure public goods are notable cases where the market may fail in the task of allocating resources efficiently. Numerous urban problems, such as highway congestion, pollution, and blighted housing, may be created in part by market failure. In all of these cases government intervention may be necessary to correct market signals and improve allocative efficiency.

While the need for government intervention is often undeniable, recent research has shown that the political process is itself an imperfect mechanism, one that may also generate serious inefficiencies. The study of how the political process allocates resources is called *public-choice theory*. This theory utilizes traditional tools of economics to analyze various aspects of the formation of government policy, the means adopted to carry it out, and the results. How well government works in practice is contrasted with how it is intended to work.

Studies in public choice have concluded that the inefficiencies born of government failure may rival or even surpass those of the private market. No guarantee exists that the government policies formed to correct market failure will resemble either an efficient ideal or what voters actually desire.

The public-choice approach treats urban governments as entities that produce numerous services, such as police and fire protection, education, hospitals, and recreation. The public enterprises that offer these services are comparable in some respects to private firms. Taxpayers are viewed as consumers of urban government services who register their preferences through the ballot box rather than through dollar voting. The analysis of government, at least at the local level, is framed in terms of the demand and supply aspects of public services.

An important test of economic efficiency is how well consumer/voter demands are met by government. *Allocative efficiency* requires that the mix as well as the level of government services reflect the desires of general voters. Instead, the mix of services often reflects the desires of special-interest groups or bureau managers instead of voters.

Productive efficiency is a second goal in allocating scarce resources to their best uses. Studies have found that the cost of providing a particular service—such as fire protection, solid waste disposal, electricity, or education—is usually higher when provided by government than it is when produced by profit-seeking firms.[1] Public-choice analysis points out that the elements that prod private firms to be efficient—competition, markets, and prices—are often missing in government.

THEORETICAL APPROACHES TO THE PUBLIC SECTOR

Public-choice economists have proposed simple theories to explain and predict the actions of participants in the political process, such as voters, elected representatives, government employees, and bureau managers. The public-choice approach assumes that government decision makers, like the rest of us, are interested in maximizing their own utility. This assumption does not imply that those who work in the public sector are selfish or act totally in disregard of others. It simply means that they are concerned about such things as their salaries, job security, expense accounts, peer recognition, and the size of the organization they may control. The assumption that political participants are motivated by *utility maximization* is an important feature of public-choice theory. Once we accept the view that public deci-

sion makers are motivated by personal gain and self-interest—although they may also be influenced by altruism—it is easier to understand how public policies are formed and carried out.

DEMAND

The political mechanism in which individuals reveal their preferences for public services differs markedly from the market system. In the private sector individuals enter into voluntary exchanges. The price paid for a good or service reveals its value to the buyer. In contrast, in the public sector individuals' preferences are registered through a variety of indirect, often clumsy, vehicles. Foremost among these vehicles are voting, lobbying, participation at public hearings, and the writing of letters to representatives. Voting, which is the primary means of signaling preferences, contains several serious weaknesses in comparison to the price system.

First of all, voters normally choose a single representative to an elective body who then votes directly on each issue. A representative may share a given voter's viewpoint on some issues but probably will not on others. The voter must either support or reject a candidate who has endorsed an entire bundle of separate policies. Because the individual is unable to vote separately on each issue, he or she is unable to spend his or her taxes in an optimal (efficient) manner. The voter's dilemma is not unlike that of a mythical grocery shopper who is somehow forced to choose (and pay for) one of several, predetermined market baskets. Even when individuals can vote directly on a single issue, such as in school bond elections, they must make an all-or-nothing choice. They are unable to adjust the amount upward or downward to meet

[1] For a survey of research on this question, see Robert Spann, "Public versus Private Provision of Governmental Services," in Thomas Borcherding, ed., *Budgets and Bureaucrats* (Charlotte, N.C.: Duke University, 1977).

their own preferences, as they can in private market purchases.

The Principle of
Rational Ignorance

A recent public opinion poll revealed that only about 46 percent of all voters could correctly identify their U.S. Congressional representative. Voters are not particularly knowledgeable about public issues. Most voters, for example, greatly underestimate the cost of government programs. One study showed that the typical voter may be aware of only about 17 percent of the actual cost of the social security system.[2]

Why are voters so uninformed about issues and candidates? The explanation, surprisingly, lies in the fact that individuals are rational, making decisions on the basis of costs and benefits. To become well-informed, a voter must spend hours studying the issues, poring over newspapers and journals at the library, and perhaps attending public hearings. The costs of becoming politically well-informed, therefore, can be substantial. On the other hand, voters may perceive little, if any, tangible benefit from voting. When the size of the electorate is large, the probability that a single vote will decide the outcome is virtually nil. The expected benefit from becoming well informed is, therefore, likely to be small. The *rational ignorance effect* does not mean that voters are apathetic. To the contrary, voters may feel strongly about some issues, but they may find that the time and other costs of casting an *informed* vote simply exceed the expected benefits.

One can compare voters acting in the political process with consumers acting in the market. Consumers of private goods often go to considerable trouble to acquire information. For example, many individuals would not purchase an automobile without first driving it, reading consumer reports, or perhaps even hiring a mechanic to examine it. Of course, the cost of becoming *perfectly* informed would be too high for most consumers. The actual amount of information individual consumers will acquire will depend upon the complexity of the item, its cost, and other factors. Rational ignorance applies more to voting decisions, however, than to market decisions. The cost of registering an uninformed vote is small because a single vote probably will not decide an election. Even it if does, much of the cost will be imposed upon others. In contrast, the costs of making an uninformed market decision may be substantial since the individual bears the entire costs.

Rational voter ignorance may reinforce a tendency of vote-maximizing politicians to support policies that offer visible short-term benefits and hidden long-term costs. For example, rent control may be favored by politicians because it offers immediate and obvious benefits to renters, with only vaguely perceived long-term costs. Another example of an issue elected officials frequently support is generous pension and retirement programs for public employees. The fiscal effects of these programs are often unknown and may not be felt for many years, but by then they have become someone else's problem. That politicians tend to favor policies combining immediate payoffs with long-term costs is sometimes called the *shortsightedness effect*.

The Problem of
Special-Interest Groups

Special-interest groups exert an important—and often distorting—influence on govern-

[2]Edgar Browning, "Why the Social Insurance Budget Is Too Large in a Democracy," *Economic Inquiry* 13 (September 1975).

ment. A *special-interest group* is defined as a relatively small number of constituents who tap the government for direct and often sizable benefits, the costs of which are spread over all taxpayers. Because of rational voter ignorance, politicians may be much more easily swayed by special-interest groups than by the interests of unorganized individual voters, particularly when the cost *per capita* of special-interest legislation is small.

Consider a mayor's or a city council's decision to grant a generous pay raise to transit workers. However likely the pay increase, taxpayers are unlikely to feel very concerned. The additional tax burden will be spread over many taxpayers and is, therefore, small for each individual. The transit workers, of course, stand to gain a great deal from the outcome. Their union can be expected to support politicians who uphold their cause and oppose politicians who do not. Edward Gramlich describes the potential voting power of public employees in New York City:

> If each (city government employee) was married, lived in the city, and had one close friend or relative who would vote alike on city issues, conceivably 1,350,000 votes, 30 percent of the entire voting age population and roughly half the probable number of voters, could be marshalled in favor of making some concessions to, or dealing leniently with, unions.[3]

This effect helps explain why unionized public employees often earn more than comparable workers in the private sector.

Because the gains available to politicians (votes, contributions, etc.) who yield to a special-interest group frequently will exceed the cost, which is the disillusion-

ment of general voters, state and local (and federal) governments often make decisions that clash with the interests of general voters. This special-interest effect prompts state and local governments to set price floors on milk (favored by the dairy industry), to set artificially high minimum prices on liquor (championed by small liquor retailers), to license taxicabs and to prohibit jitneys (favored by existing cab companies), or to require iron pipe instead of equally durable but cheaper plastic pipe in building codes (favored by plumbing suppliers and the pipe fitters union), to cite only a few examples.

Special-interest legislation may thrive not only because of rational ignorance but also because of the costs of organizing opposition. The information costs of fighting an issue or a candidate may be substantial. Why bother to become informed if it is exceedingly costly to do anything about the problem discovered?

SUPPLY

Voting is an imperfect mechanism for expressing consumer/voter preferences and represents one source of government inefficiency. Other inefficiencies arise when government agencies attempt to implement the programs and policies legislated by elected politicians. Three important characteristics influence the efficiency of government firms: (1) the difficulty of defining and measuring output and performance; (2) the lack of sufficient incentives to produce services at minimum cost; and (3) the weakness of the constraints imposed on government.

Measuring output and evaluating performance are major problems for most public services. For example, measuring the output of public schools, the police, the

---

[3]Edward Gramlich, "The New York City Fiscal Crisis," *American Economic Review* 66 (May 1976): 415–29.

parks and recreation department, and the court system have proven difficult for analysts. A consequence of this difficulty in measuring output is that the productivity of labor—the major input in local government services—is also difficult to measure. Labor productivity is the criterion normally used by employers to determine wage increases and other employment policies, such as promotions, personnel assignments, and layoffs. In addition, difficulties arise in setting unambiguous goals for public agencies and, therefore, in assessing whether an agency's goals have been met. If an agency provides a service that has a private counterpart—such as garbage collection or water supply—then external yardsticks can be used to evaluate the agency's performance. However, in most cases only internal guideposts are available to determine whether the agency has met its goals. How can one determine, for example, what would be a reasonable yardstick by which to measure the performance of a municipal zoning and planning department?

These problems are not unique to the public sector. They also appear in the private market. Dentists, lawyers, and retail stores also encounter the problem of measuring productivity. In stark contrast to the public sector, however, the private sector employs an unambiguous measuring rod—profit. Profit is a clear-cut indicator of performance because it allows independent comparisons to be made. General Motors, for example, can be judged not only by its own profits, but by Ford's and Chrysler's profits. When competition is present, profits usually indicate how effectively private firms are serving their customers' interests. Profits also indicate how efficiently the firm operates. Lower profits can be a signal that the firm is lapsing into inefficient practices.

The performance of public and private firms is also affected by differences in the structure of ownership rights. When the performance (profit) of a private firm suffers, its owners can sell their ownership rights (stocks). The new owners may take steps, such as replacing the current management, to improve the firm's performance. In contrast, ownership rights for government agencies are neither well-defined nor transferable. When a government agency operates inefficiently, its "owners" may be unable to induce the agency to improve its performance. Through voting it may be possible "to throw the rascals out," but this mechanism is imperfect as we have seen; other mechanisms for influencing agency behavior do exist—such as organized opposition, taxpayer revolts, or writing one's congressional representative—but they are costly.

The constraints faced by a public or private enterprise are crucial to its performance. If an enterprise is fully constrained to a particular goal, it has little choice but to pursue that goal. If such constraints are weak, it becomes more likely that the enterprise will pursue the private interests of the managers and employees. A government bureau that is not closely monitored is likely to devote a higher portion of its budget to excessive salaries, larger staffs, lax work standards, and other nonmonetary perquisites of the job. The task of monitoring public bureaus falls on the shoulders of legislative committees that seldom can devote full-time attention to the job or have full information about the bureau's activities.

Overall, the constraints on public enterprises are comparatively weak. Private firms must compete with other firms for consumer acceptance and also generate a profit. They are subject to the discipline imposed by the competitive marketplace, which at times can be fierce. Public enterprises, on the other hand, almost always possess some monopoly power and seldom are forced out of business. The power to tax ensures government bureaus of a source of revenue regardless of their performance. All these factors—the absence of a profit motive, the power to tax, and monopoly power—combine to make it unlikely that government agencies will produce at minimum cost.

Competition is not entirely absent in the public sector of the economy, however. As every important election makes clear, competition between the two major political parties is often intense. Political parties and candidates must formulate a set of policies to attract a majority of votes to win an election. Public-choice theory shows that, under certain restrictive conditions, voters will be decisive in determining public policies and that the voter (or group of voters) with the median preferences will determine electoral outcomes.[4] Unfortunately, the conditions necessary for this result are seldom met in real-world voting situations. The practical importance of political competition is that elected officials cannot entirely ignore voters' preferences, which may serve as a significant constraint on the behavior of these officials.

A second important constraint may exist in metropolitan areas where there are often large numbers of local jurisdictions providing the same public services. While some political analysts decry the chaotic pattern of local government in metropolitan areas, this very diversity may offer options to local residents to vote with their feet. Insofar as consumers/voters are mobile, they can select among local governments to find that district which best satisfies their preferences for public-service levels and tax rates. Voter mobility may force local governments to compete by offering service levels and tax prices to attract a sufficient population size to exhaust economies of scale. A city that allows taxes to balloon or services to deteriorate, or that produces the wrong mix of services, risks losing residents and taxpayers. In this way, interjurisdictional competition may limit public-sector inefficiency.[5]

CHARACTERISTICS OF GOVERNMENT BUREAUS

The public-choice literature offers some illuminating models of government bureaus. These models assume that individual decision makers in both public and private institutions maximize their utility. Unlike private firms, public bureaus have the following set of unique characteristics:[6]

1. The bureau receives its budget from periodic appropriations by a granting agency, called a *sponsor* (e.g., a city council) rather than from direct payments for its services. Thus, the bureau is accountable to elected officials and not directly to the public.

2. The bureau enjoys an advantage over the sponsor in information concerning its internal production and cost functions. The bureau can use this advantage in order to obtain larger budget appropriations.

---

[4]David Hyman, *Public Finance: A Contemporary Application of Theory to Policy* (Hinsdale, Ill.: Dryden Press, 1983), chapters 5 and 6.

[5]For a complete exposition of this theory, see Charles M. Tiebout, "A Pure Theory of Local Expenditure," *Journal of Political Economy*, 64 (October 1956). This article is reprinted later in this volume.

[6]For an elaboration of the economic theory of bureaucracy, see William Niskanen, *Bureaucracy and Representative Government* (Chicago: Aldine-Atherton, 1971).

BOX 1

EFFICIENCY LOSS WITH A NET-REVENUE MAXIMIZING BUREAU

A typical bureau is depicted in Figure 1. For simplicity, we assume that the bureau's service can be produced at constant marginal cost. An efficient bureau would produce quantity Q_0, and the marginal cost would be MC_1. But MC_1 represents the minimum necessary cost of producing this service. The sponsor (city council) will be unlikely to know what this minimum cost is, and the bureau will not have an incentive to reveal full information about its operation and costs. On the other hand, the bureau will tend to have fairly good information about the community's demand curve, D, for the bureau's services. This information advantage will allow the bureau to operate at a higher cost, MC_2, instead of producing at the minimum cost MC_1. If this bureau faced competition from other firms, it would find itself losing money. In the long run, it would either reduce its costs or go out of business. However, a government agency faces no such constraint and can operate indefinitely at the higher cost, MC_2.

(The net benefit that the community derives from output Q_0 (called *consumer surplus*) is represented by the area below the demand curve and above the marginal cost curve. If marginal cost is MC_1, then the community's benefit would equal the area of the triangle ACD. As marginal cost rises from MC_1 to MC_2 consumer surplus becomes fully expropriated by the bureau because the area of triangle ABF—representing the consumer surplus obtained by the bureau—equals the area of triangle EFD. At this point, the bureau has fully exploited its monopoly and information advantages.)

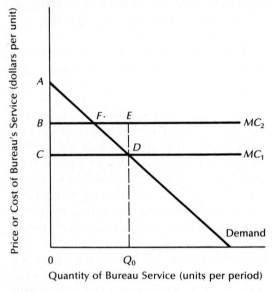

Figure 1.

3. Neither the sponsor nor the bureau can benefit directly (increase their wealth) by operating the organization more efficiently. This absence of financial incentives is a serious shortcoming of government bureaus, which can even be penalized for improved performance. If a bureau fails to spend its entire appropriation it will risk a cut in its budget in the next fiscal period. Consequently, many agencies go on a spending spree at the end of each fiscal period.

4. The bureau's position relative to the sponsor is like that of any other special-interest group. The bureau will routinely lobby for more funds, using its voting power and political contributions as weapons.

5. Bureaus normally enjoy monopoly power and need not fear that competitors will force them out of business. Thus, the bureau is not immediately penalized for operating inefficiently or providing poor service.

What goal can a bureau be expected to follow in order to maximize the managers' utility? One widely accepted hypothesis is that bureaus seek to maximize their net revenues. When a bureau's budget grows, both managers and employees generally benefit. Both share in the increased opportunities for promotion and higher salaries. A bureau manager will enjoy added prestige and power as well as more job perquisites when the size of the budget and staff he or she controls is larger. In general, net-revenue maximizing bureaus are inefficient, as shown in Box 1.

IMPROVING GOVERNMENT EFFICIENCY

How can bureaucracies be reformed to become more efficient and more responsive to the community? It should be obvious that the answer does not lie in such simplistic answers as "electing better people to public office" or "assigning public-spirited officials to manage public agencies." These solutions will not work because they do not alter the reward structure or constraints that guide bureaucrats' behavior.

One possible solution is to introduce competitive market forces when possible. One such approach is to contract out government services. For example, the government could solicit competitive bids from private firms to provide the service. The contract probably would specify a price ceiling on the service as well as terms relating to quality. If past experience is any guide, private contracting leads to lower costs and improved quality.

For example, cities that use private contracting to obtain garbage collection incur costs that are less than two thirds the costs of government-operated garbage collectors, according to a study of 260 U.S. cities by

E. S. Savas. Savas explains why the municipal agencies were less efficient:

> Compared to private firms performing contract collection, city agencies: (a) use larger crews, (b) experience more absences due to vacation, illness, and all other causes, (c) serve fewer households per hour, (d) are less likely to use incentive systems, (e) use less productive vehicles, and (f) are less likely to use vehicles that the driver can help load.[7]

Fire protection may also prove considerably cheaper when contracted out, as Scottsdale, Arizona has discovered. Scottsdale is served by a private, profit-seeking fire company, the Rural Metropolitan Fire Protection Company. The evidence again suggests that private firms, which have an incentive to produce at lower cost, will do so. In 1972-73, the per capita cost of fire protection in Scottsdale was $5.70 compared to a national average for cities of similar size of $24.39. In other years Scottsdale's costs stood higher but were still only about 50 percent of the national average. These savings do not appear to have been achieved by sacrificing the quality of service. On the contrary, the average annual fire loss in Scottsdale is estimated at $4.44 per capita, compared to $12 nationwide.

How does the Scottsdale fire department do it? The company is innovative, both in using labor more efficiently to bring costs down and also in developing new equipment. One labor-saving innovation is the use of supplementary fire fighters, most of whom are city employees who are on call one week per month. The company recognized that the large, traditional, full-time work force is seldom necessary. When serious fires do arise—perhaps once or twice a

[7]E. S. Savas, "Do More With Less," *Taxing and Spending,* February 1979, p. 11. Also see E. S. Savas, *The Organization and Efficiency of Solid Waste Collection* (Lexington, Mass.: D. C. Heath, 1977).

year—trained reservists are called upon. The company also has been innovative in developing small "attack trucks" and robot fire fighters, both of which have attracted national attention. Although private fire companies are rare in the United States, they are common elsewhere, particularly in Europe. In Sweden, 65 percent of the fire departments are privately owned.

Contracting out services is one way to introduce competition into the supply of public services. Another way to build competition is to allow government agencies to compete with one another. In large urban areas containing many separate jurisdictions, government enterprises are unable to avoid some competition. The school system run by one jurisdiction, for example, is forced to compete with other school systems or risk losing patronage as parents vote with their feet. The idea that many small governments, not one big one, are desirable flies in the face of the conventional wisdom that the way to improve efficiency in government is to merge agencies to eliminate duplication. In the private sector, duplication essentially means competition. General Motors, Ford, Chrysler, and Toyota, just to name a few, duplicate each other's product. But the competition that flourishes reduces the cost and prices of automobiles and provides consumers with products they prefer. Requiring government agencies to compete with one another when possible could improve their efficiency.

CONCLUDING REMARKS

Efforts to improve efficiency in government historically have involved either hiring efficiency experts or instituting management techniques, such as program budgeting, systems analysis, and cost/benefit analysis. The problem with these techniques is that they seldom, if ever, by themselves alter the basic reward structure confronting government officials. Cost/benefit analysis, for example, merely provides information to government decision makers. It does not alter the incentives for officials to act on that information. Because of the way property rights are structured in nonmarket environments, if these management devices generate some efficiency gains, no single person has a well-defined claim to these gains—neither bureaucrats, legislators, nor voters. Since no one can appropriate the rewards from achieving these gains, installing management reforms is unlikely to alter bureaucrats' behavior.[8] The use of market-like competition, where possible, remains the most promising way of generating better cost information to sponsors and of improving governmental efficiency.

KEY CONCEPTS

production efficiency

public-choice theory

rational ignorance effect

shortsightedness effect

special-interest groups

tax prices

utility maximization

voting with one's feet

[8]For a discussion of this point see Roland McKean, "Property Rights Within Government, and Devices to Increase Governmental Efficiency," *Southern Economic Journal* 39 (October 1972).

PART 2

GROWTH AND STRUCTURE OF CITIES

Analysis of the growth of U.S. cities normally focuses on the Standard Metropolitan Statistical Area (SMSA) as defined by the U.S. Census Bureau. To qualify as an SMSA an area must contain a central city with a population of at least 50,000. The SMSA includes the entire county in which the central city is located and any adjoining counties that are economically tied to the central city. In the 1980 Census there were 318 SMSAs, and they contained roughly 75 percent of the U.S. population.

One consistent migration pattern in the United States has been the exodus of population from rural areas and small towns to urban centers. This pattern of increased urbanization persisted from the earliest days of the census until the 1970s when the pattern of migration appears to have changed. For the first time ever, the population of nonmetropolitan counties grew faster (growing 15 percent from 1970 to 1980) than the population of metropolitan areas (which grew only 10 percent). While metropolitan areas have not stopped growing, their growth rates have fallen behind those of nonurban areas. It appears that the economic attraction of big cities, which have provided increased real incomes for generations of Americans and foreign immigrants, may have become diluted.

Within metropolitan areas, the growth of suburban areas continued unabated in the 1970s. Between 1970 and 1980 the 429 central cities in the United States grew at a rate of only 0.1 percent, while their suburbs grew by a robust 18 percent. Many major central cities, especially those in the northeast and north central regions, lost population. As examples, New York City lost 11 percent of its population between 1970 and 1980, Cleveland lost 24 percent, St. Louis 28 percent, and Chicago 11 percent. Even some central cities located in the sunbelt lost population, including Atlanta, Denver, and San Francisco.

These recent trends pose some intriguing questions. Why have metropolitan areas begun to lose their allure? What has caused the flight of population from central city to suburb? What are the effects of the flight to the suburbs on the location of economic activities, housing, and employment? How bright is the future of metropolitan areas? Will central cities make a comeback, or will they

31

continue to decline? These questions are complex and somewhat speculative, yet they can be illuminated with traditional economic tools, as the readings in this section demonstrate.

The now classic reading by Charles M. Tiebout outlines the features of the urban economic (or export) base model of urban growth. An economic base study is a simple, yet practical, technique for analyzing the external factors that may stimulate the growth of income and employment in a city. The major assumption of the model is that the exports (or base activities) of a community are the main force generating employment and income. The ratio of service (or non-basic) employment to base employment is assumed to be fixed. This ratio serves as a rough measure of the multiplier effect on total employment of any change in export employment. Although the fixed-ratio assumption is somewhat unrealistic and has been a major source of criticism by economists, the simplicity and low cost of the technique make it popular among city planners and practicing urban analysts.

More sophisticated analytical techniques are growing in popularity among both academic and practicing urban economists. Econometric forecasting models, which were originally developed to interpret economic forces for the entire U.S. economy, have been applied successfully to regions, states, and metropolitan areas. These models consist of systems of equations that mirror the cause-and-effect relationships in the local economy. A set of equations may represent entire sectors of the local economy, such as housing, employment, population, and local government. Small-scale models may consist of as few as 35 equations, but some regional models consist of several hundred equations. Once these models have been estimated and calibrated with actual historical data, they can be used to forecast key variables for the local economy, such as employment, income, retail sales, housing starts, tax revenues, or government expenditures. Econometric models can also be used to simulate the impact on the local economy of a specific change (such as a plant closing).

The urban land market in econometric studies is usually modeled after a well-known theory by William Alonso. Drawing on the classical theory of agricultural rent, Alonso suggests that urban residents balance accessibility against site costs when choosing a housing location. He assumes that the central business district (CBD) is where all employment is located. Abstracting from topographical and other features of the metropolitan area, a household will bid less for a site located farther from the CBD because transportation costs will be higher than for a site located closer to the CBD. Thus, we should expect to observe land values declining with distance from the CBD. Various land uses (commercial, industrial, etc.) will bid more or less for each site depending on how much value they place on accessibility to the CBD, but in general one would expect bid-rent curves to be negatively sloped. This simple prediction of the model has been confirmed for most cities, even for sprawled cities such as Los Angeles.

While Alonso offers a static equilibrium model of the urban land market, the allocation of land among alternative uses is in fact a dynamic process of some complexity, particularly on the urban fringe where some land is developed while neighboring parcels are withheld from development. This pattern of "leapfrog" development is sometimes termed urban sprawl. In an attempt to understand the causes of sprawl, Marion Clawson discusses the characteristics of the market for undeveloped suburban land. Clawson stresses the uncertainties inherent in assessing the present value (that is, the price) of undeveloped land located on the urban fringe. Among these uncertainties are the date when the land will be developed and its value when developed. Because investors may hold different expectations concerning these variables, and also because the land market is not characterized by perfect information, Clawson argues that speculation in suburban land is a normal process. That some parcels are developed before others is shown to be the natural result of an efficiently operating land market. Clawson's results are consistent with other studies that have found that the rates of return on holding vacant urban land do not exceed those on comparable investments elsewhere and that speculation on the urban fringe appears to perform a useful function.

The shift of population from the central city to the suburbs has generated a host of employment problems for central-city residents as well as fiscal problems for central-city governments. Benjamin Chinitz analyzes the assets and liabilities of central cities as locations for private firms. The liabilities of higher rents and congestion are weighed against the assets of agglomeration economies and of greater proximity of activities to one another. Chinitz also analyzes various types of external economic changes that have altered the net attractiveness of central cities. The growth of the service sector of the economy and the decline of manufacturing has improved office employment in central cities. However, improvements in transportation and communications technology have harmed central cities as desirable locations for private firms. Chinitz concludes that the future will likely bring continued suburbanization and the further decline of the central city. (An alternative perspective on central-city growth is provided in the reading by Kenneth A. Small in Part 8 of this volume).

CHARLES M. TIEBOUT

4 A Method of Determining Incomes and Their Variation in Small Regions

In this reading Charles M. Tiebout touches on the major features of a technique that has been widely used to analyze the factors underlying urban economic growth—the economic (or export) base study. The major advantage of this technique is its simplicity. Its major disadvantage is that it is not a comprehensive model of the urban economy. Other techniques—notably, input-output analysis and econometric models—are more comprehensive but considerably more costly and difficult to implement.

INTRODUCTION

This paper is concerned with the determinants of income of a small region (community).[1] The approach will be through modified national (regional) income accounts, especially the international sector. The analysis is cast largely in terms of aggregative national income analysis, but in some cases differs by more than a matter of degree. What is sought is the classification and theoretical analysis of the major exogenous and endogenous variables of a community. Finally, the results of some empirical research in the area will be noted.

ALTERNATIVE APPROACHES

This framework is presented in contrast to two other approaches to community economic research: the more general approach and input-output studies.[2]

Until recent years many studies in community economics tended to be of a descriptive character. Research undertaken by city planners and chambers of commerce tended to be of this nature. Some interesting work of this broader type may be familiar. Often these studies did not deal with any specific question, but merely tried to shed some light on the structure of the region.

In recent years input-output matrices have become a popular tool of regional research.[3] The limitations of input-output

From *Papers and Proceedings of the Regional Science Association,* 1 (1955): 93–103. Reprinted by permission of the Regional Science Association.

[1]The author is indebted to W.F. Stolper and F.G. Adams of the University of Michigan for their help and suggestions.

[2]An example of the former: Homer Hoyt. "Homer Hoyt on the Economic Base," *Land Economics.* Vol. XXX, No. 2 (May 1954), pp. 183–91. (Note especially the bibliography.) For an example of input-output see: W. Isard, R. Kavesh, and R. Kuenne. "The Economic Base and Structure of the Urban-Metropolitan Region," *American Sociological Review.* Vol. XVIII, No. 3 (June 1953), pp. 117–21.

[3]One of the classics of this type is: Robert Haig. *Major Economic Factors in Metropolitan Growth and Arrangement.* Vol. I of *Regional Survey of New York and Its Environs.* N.Y.C., 1928.

have been noted by Dorfman and Isard[4] and, perhaps, a more serious limitation by Vail.[5] Nevertheless, the input-output technique is still a fascinating tool for regional research. There is no desire to quibble over whether or not the approach presented below is a supplement to or alternative for input-output analysis.

REGIONAL SIZE

This paper deals with the incomes of small regions; for the sake of a number say under 200,000 population. As used here "size" is taken as a composite of population and space. A region is considered small if, and only if, it has neither a large population nor is geographically large. Of course, if regions are too small the usefulness of aggregation is nil. The income determinants of a one tank town are not very interesting even to an alcoholic.

It is necessary to note this size feature since the determinants of income are themselves a function of regional size. Illustrative of this point is the case of exports. For example, if the region under consideration is the whole world, then by definition exports could not be a determinant of income levels. On the other hand, in an exchange setting, a region defined as one person in space has its whole income determined by exports. Obviously, for the regions between these extremes, the importance of exports tends to be inversely correlated to the size of the region considered.

Here it is assumed that the region for study is small enough in relation to the overall space of which it is a part that there is no foreign trade multiplier feedback. This means shocks are a one way affair. For example, a decrease in demand for Argus Cameras would lower the income of Ann Arbor, Michigan and, consequently, the Ann Arbor demand for imports. As usually formulated the foreign trade multiplier tells us the reaction would proceed by lowering the income of the rest of the nation due to the fall in Ann Arbor demand. This is explicitly ruled out by assumption. In international trade this is the small nation case quite analogous to the situation of the competitive wheat farmer.

ANALYTICAL FRAMEWORK

The problem now becomes to construct a framework in which the exogenous elements of the community income can be isolated. Since, by definition, these activities are assumed to generate the community's income, let us go along with the term "basic activities." Those variables of the community income which are considered as endogenous are termed "non-basic activities." Hence, the income of the community has two sectors: the basic corresponding to the exogenous sector and the non-basic or endogenous sector. No doubt this may be familiar to some of the readers, since the concept of the "economic base" has recently come up in the literature.[6] Since this analysis draws on this sort of approach, it is worth a moment's look.

[4]Robert Dorfman. "The Nature and Significance of Input-Output," *The Review of Economics and Statistics.* Vol. XXXVI, No. 2 (May 1954), pp. 121–33, and Walter Isard. "Regional Commodity Balances and Interregional Commodity Flows," *American Economic Review.* Vol. XLIII, No. 2 (May 1953), pp. 167–80.

[5]Stefan Valavanis-Vail. "Leontief's Scarce Factor Paradox," *Journal of Political Economy.* Vol. XII, No. 6 (Dec. 1954), pp. 523–28.

[6]See among others: John Alexander. "The Basic-Nonbasic Concept of Urban Economic Functions," *Economic Geography.* Vol. XXX, No. 3 (July 1954), pp. 246–61. R.B. Andrews, "Mechanics of the Urban Economic Base," *Land Economics.* Vols XXIX-XXXI, (May 1953 and continuing). Isard, Kavesh, and Kuenne, *op. cit.* Homer Hoyt, *op. cit.*

Quoting from a summary article on this subject:

> ...*The economic base of a city is by definition made up of export activities of the community. These activities involve the export of goods, services, and capital to purchasers who are outside the community or come from the outside.*[7]

Those industries which serve only local needs are called non-basic.[8] Retail trade is, for the most part, considered non-basic. Here the discussion generally stops except for the details of measurement, definition, and the like.

BASIC ACTIVITIES OF THE COMMUNITY

Let's leave this basic activity approach for a moment and consider the community in an interregional setting. Traditional analysis of the foreign trade multiplier, somewhat simplified, tells us that the level of exports and domestic investment are the exogenous variables in setting the nation's income. With these known and the propensities to consume and import given, the system is solved for the income.[9]

In like manner for the community, those activities whose level is set either by non-economic forces or by forces beyond the control of the community are the ones classed as basic or exogenous. These need not be the same as those termed basic in the literature. The reason they are called basic here is that *given their level, the system is determinate.* Before contrasting these with the non-basic activities it would be well to see what sectors fall under this basic classification.

Gross exports, for the most part, constitute the main element in determining regional income.[10] One would expect the "value added by export" sector to be the major item in the "community income arising out of basic activity" account. Also included in this account would be the income arising in "export linked" activities. Using the example of Argus Camera in Ann Arbor, a local firm supplying them with buffing wheels would be considered as exporting even though its sales are to a local firm, i.e. Argus. Conceptually, the way to find the linked firms is to drop the exports to zero while holding other demands (consumer, housing, etc.) constant. Those firms which fall out are export linked.

But merely to list export activities as basic as is done in the literature misses the point. Exports are important as a determinant of income. In this connection one important case should not be overlooked. This is the case of exports to the contiguous area. Even though it is over 200,000 population New York City will illustrate this point. New York exports to the suburban area in the form of retail sales. These are exports as much as any manufacturing sales as most base studies point out. But the point here is that the level of retail

---

[7]Richard B. Andrews. "Mechanics of the Urban Economic Base: Problems of Base Area Delimitation," *Land Economics.* Vol. XXX, No. 4, (Nov. 1954), p. 309.

[8]It appears that the term "economic base" as used by Isard, Kavesh, and Kuenne, *op. cit.* differs from the above. In their case to the total exports of a new steel mill is added the exports of agglomerating industries as well. Along with this is added the local expansion of activities including households who "also behave like industries." (p. 118). If this interpretation is correct, it would appear that in a town that arose because a steel mill was erected in a desert, *all* economic activity is basic.

[9]See the classic article: Lloyd Metzler. "Underemployment Equilibrium in International Trade," *Econometrica.* Vol. X, No. 2, (April 1942), pp. 97–113.

[10]See: W.F. Stolper. "The Volume of Foreign Trade and the Level of Income," *Quarterly Journal of Economics.* Vol. LXI, No. 2 (Feb. 1947), pp. 285–310; J.J. Polak. "The Foreign Trade Multiplier," *American Economic Review.* Vol XXXVII, No. 5 (Dec. 1947), pp. 889–97.

sales to the suburbs is itself tied to the level of New York income via the commuters. A drop in New York income will drop suburban income and in turn will cut retail exports to the suburbs. Hence, the level of retail exports is not necessarily an exogenous variable. On the other hand, retail sales may be exogenous if the demand is not determined by the city itself. A different example will illustrate this point. It may be that the export demand for retail sales in the city of Peoria, Illinois is largely derived from sales to farmers. Unlike the commuters the income of the farmer does not depend on the income of Peoria itself, but on the demand for farm products. In this case the account "value added by retail sales to non-residents" is exogenous. In the New York example it is not. The point is that one needs to know something about the market in the contiguous area before activities can be classed as basic or non-basic. It involves a question of the overlap of the labor market area with the shopping area.[11]

NON-BASIC ACTIVITIES: ENDOGENOUS VARIABLES

The usefulness of this analysis depends on the validity of the assumption that one group of the communities' activities are in fact endogenous. This implies that given the level of income generated by basic activities, i.e., "income arising out of basic activities," one is theoretically able to predict total community income. Its usefulness would be enhanced if it could be further demonstrated that the proportion of the

non-basic activities, measured in dollars, is the same for similar communities. Put another way, two communities with the same "value added by basic activities" accounts would be expected to have the same "value added by non-basic activities" account.[12] Two conditions are necessary for this conclusion about the similarity of non-basis activities: (1) that consumption habits do not vary among communities and (2) the production actually undertaken is similar. It is worth considering each of these conditions in a bit more detail.

The chief activities in the "income arising from non-basic activities" sector are retail and service trades. By making some assumptions about the nature of two communities the position of these non-basic activities will become clear. Suppose two communities have the following in common: (1) per capita income in basic activities is the same, (2) both cities are located in approximately the same position in a Lösch spatial system, and (3) as (2) implies both communities are of approximately equal size. *In these communities one would expect the level and distribution of the spendings on non-basic activities to be the same.* In communities where the above conditions are not fulfilled, but the differences are known, the level and distribution of non-basic activities spendings can still be predicted. Looked at another way it merely states that how much, on what, and where people spend their incomes does not vary from community to community.[13] Empirical evidence on this point will be noted later.

The second assumption that the produc-

---

[11]Let: W = wages paid foreigners; R_f = retail purchases abroad by residents; and R_e = retail export to foreigners. Then a shopping center might be defined as satisfying the following conditions: $W_f + aR_f = aR_e$ where a = 1/propensity to consume retail goods.

[12]The above remark should be qualified by noting that a community located in the proximity of a large city would be expected to have a smaller part of its income created by non-basic activities, since shopping would be done in the city.

[13]Obviously less is spent on heat in California than in Minnesota, but this can be accounted for.

tion actually undertaken is similar is more critical. In effect what is said is that if the level of exogenous variables is set and the "income arising in basic activities" is given, the level and structure of non-basic activities will follow. Alternatively, for every dollar of basic activity income there will be created two cents worth of barbering. The fact that this is largely the case is due to the low entry costs of these activities. The cost of entering the trades and services is low both in terms of capital requirements and managerial know-how. Experience in communities points up this feature. The number of automobile dealers, barbers, shoe stores and the like varies with the size of the community. One community will not experience a shortage of shoe stores while another has too many. If there is a shortage, in all probability, it will be a temporary affair. This need not be the case in basic activities. The closing of a manufacturing plant and the consequent drop in community income does not necessarily produce a reaction to fill the void. No young entrepreneur or branch plant comes in to offset the drop. In many cases the solution is a migration of population and a reduction of the community size to fit its new and lower "income arising from basic activity" account.[14] In some cases the community, although more likely the economic system, induces new firms into the area. The point is that this may not happen.

In summary, the argument has been that for any community there exists a fairly sharp division of the community's national income. Part of this income, "income arising out of basic activities," is exogenous in that its size is determined either by non-economic forces or by forces outside the community. It was pointed out the export demand need not be exogenous with respect to exports to the contiguous area even though one assumes no foreign trade multiplier feedback for distant spaces. Finally, it was shown that as opposed to basic activities one may define a sector, "income arising from non-basic activity." Non-basic activities are characterized by high mobility and with common consumption habits known, appear in a predictable array given the basic activities.

EMPIRICAL EVIDENCE

Although statistical work in this area is limited, some support of this thesis is noted. That exports do act as a determinant of income is shown by a variety of international trade studies. Simpson's interesting study of the Pacific Northwest points up the role of exports in regional analysis.[15]

Studies concerning the basic/non-basic premise have had varied results. Hildebrand and Mace, in a study of Los Angeles, found a high correlation over time between the basic/non-basic ratio.[16] In a study of the Wichita multiplier the Federal Reserve Bank of Kansas City was less successful in relating the basic to non-basic ratio in Wichita.[17] In part, this failure

[14]This is the sort of problem that comes up in communities whose solution to a recession is to try and open more barber shops. If successful through a shop at home campaign, it raises the ratio of non-basic to basic activities. This raises the communities' multiplier by reducing the propensity to import and makes it all the more sensitive to a future given dollar drop in basic activity levels.

[15]Paul B. Simpson. Regional Aspects of Business Cycles and a Special Study of the Pacific Northwest. Study prepared for the Bonneville Administration, and supported by the University of Oregon, and the Social Science Research Council, 1953.

[16]G. H. Hildebrand and Arthur Mace. "The Employment Multiplier in an Expanding Industrial Market: Los Angeles County, 1940–47," Review of Economics and Statistics. Vol. XXXII, No. 3 (Aug. 1950), pp. 241–49.

[17]. . ."The Employment Multiplier in Wichita." Monthly Review. Federal Reserve Bank of Kansas City. Vol. XXXVII, No. 9 (Sept. 1952), pp. 1–7.

reflects the big production changes in the bomber plant. One interesting series of studies of this sort has been carried on by John Alexander.[18] Here, unlike the above studies, the non-basic and basic activities were determined by survey methods. The similarity in structures of the non-basic activities in the two communities studied is striking. . . .

[18]Alexander, *op. cit.*

KEY CONCEPTS

basic activities

economic base

endogenous variables

exogenous variables

export demand

non-basic activities

5 A Theory of the Urban Land Market

William Alonso of Harvard University argues that the demand for land in metropolitan areas depends in large measure on its accessibility to the central business district. Because transportation costs are greater for sites located more distant from the core, land values (or site rents) should decline with distance from the core. Empirical studies have verified the existence of negative bid rent curves for various land uses.

The early theory of rent and location concerned itself primarily with agricultural land. This was quite natural, for Ricardo and Malthus lived in an agricultural society. The foundations of the formal spatial analysis of agricultural rent and location are found in the work of J. von Thunen, who said, without going into detail, that the urban land market operated under the same principles.[1] As cities grew in importance, relatively little attention was paid to the theory of urban rents. Even the great Marshall provided interesting but only random insights, and no explicit theory of the urban land market and urban locations was developed.

Since the beginning of the twentieth century there has been considerable interest in the urban land market in America.

R. M. Hurd[2] in 1903 and R. Haig[3] in the 1920s tried to create a theory of urban land by following von Thunen. However, their approach copied the form rather than the logic of agricultural theory, and the resulting theory can be shown to be insufficient on its own premises. In particular, the theory failed to consider residences, which constitute the preponderant land use in urban areas.

Yet there are interesting problems that a theory of urban land must consider. There is, for instance, a paradox in American cities: the poor live near the center, on expensive land, and the rich on the periphery, on cheap land. On the logical side, there are also aspects of great interest, but which increase the difficulty of the analysis. When a purchaser acquires land, he acquires two goods (land and location) in only one transaction, and only one pay-

From William Alonso, "A Theory of the Urban Land Market," *Papers and Proceedings of the Regional Science Association* 6 (1960): 149–59. Reprinted by permission of the Regional Science Association and the author. Copyright 1960.

[1]Johan von Thunen, *Der Isolierte Staat in Beziehung auf Landwirtschaft und Nationalekonomie,* 1st. vol., 1826, 3d. vol. and new edition, 1863.

[2]Richard M. Hurd, *Principles of City Land Values,* N.Y.: The Record and Guide, 1903.

[3]Robert M. Haig. "Toward an Understanding of the Metropolis," *Quarterly Journal of Economics,* XL: 3, May 1926; and *Regional Survey of New York and its Environs,* N.Y.: New York City Plan Commission, 1927.

ment is made for the combination. He could buy the same quantity of land at another location, or he could buy more, or less land at the same location. In the analysis, one encounters, as well, a negative good (distance) with positive costs (commuting costs); or, conversely, a positive good (accessibility) with negative costs (savings in commuting). In comparison with agriculture, the urban case presents another difficulty. In agriculture, the location is extensive: many square miles may be devoted to one crop. In the urban case the site tends to be much smaller, and the location may be regarded as a dimensionless point rather than an area. Yet the thousands or millions of dimensionless points which constitute the city, when taken together, cover extensive areas. How can these dimensionless points be aggregated into two-dimensional space?

Here I will present a non-mathematical overview, without trying to give it full precision, of the long and rather complex mathematical analysis which constitutes a formal theory of the urban land market.[4] It is a static model in which change is introduced by comparative statics. And it is an economic model: it speaks of economic men, and it goes without saying that real men and social groups have needs, emotions, and desires which are not considered here. This analysis uses concepts which fit with agricultural rent theory in such a way that urban and rural land uses may be considered at the same time, in terms of a single theory. Therefore, we must examine first a very simplified model of the agricultural land market.

[4]A full development of the theory is presented in my doctoral dissertation, *A Model of the Urban Land Market: Locations and Densities of Dwellings and Businesses*, University of Pennsylvania, 1960.

AGRICULTURAL MODEL

In this model, the farmers are grouped around a single market, where they sell their products. If the product is wheat, and the produce of one acre of wheat sells for $100 at the market while the costs of production are $50 per acre, a farmer growing wheat at the market would make a profit of $50 per acre. But if he is producing at some distance—say, 5 miles—and it costs him $5 per mile to ship an acre's product, his transport costs will be $25 per acre. His profits will be equal to value minus production costs minus shipping charges: $100 - 50 - 25 = 25. This relation may be shown diagrammatically (see Figure 1). At the market, the farmer's profits are $50, and 5 miles out, $25; at intermediate distance, he will receive intermediate profits. Finally, at a distance of 10 miles from the market,

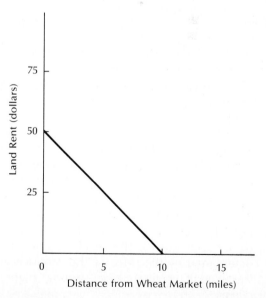

Figure 1.

his production costs plus shipping charges will just equal the value of his produce at the market. At distances greater than 10 miles, the farmer would operate at a loss.

In this model, the profits derived by the farmers are tied directly to their location. If the functions of farmer and landowner are viewed as separate, farmers will bid rents for land according to the profitability of the location. The profits of the farmer will therefore be shared with the landowner through rent payments. As farmers bid against each other for the more profitable locations, until farmers' profits are everywhere the same ("normal" profits), what we have called profits becomes rent. Thus, the curve in Figure 1, which we derived as a farmers' profit curve, once we distinguish between the roles of the farmer and the landowner, becomes a bid rent function, representing the price or rent per acre that farmers will be willing to pay for land at the different locations.

We have shown that the slope of the rent curve will be fixed by the transport costs on the produce. The level of the curve will be set by the price of the produce at the market. Examine Figure 2. The lower curve is that of Figure 1, where the price of wheat is $100 at the market, and production costs are $50. If demand increases, and the price of wheat at the market rises to $125 (while production and transport costs remain constant), profits or bid rent at the market will be $75; at 5 miles, $50; $25 at 10 miles, and zero at 15 miles. Thus, each bid rent curve is a function of rent vs. distance, but there is a family of such curves, the level of any one determined by the price of the produce at the market, higher prices setting higher curves.

Consider now the production of peas. Assume that the price at the market of one

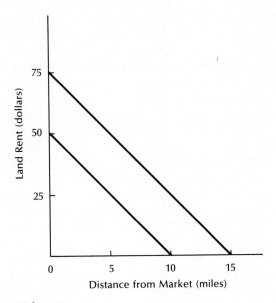

Figure 2.

acre's production of peas is $150, the costs of production are $75, and the transport costs per mile are $10. These conditions will yield curve MN in Figure 3, where bid rent by pea farmers at the market is $75 per acre, 5 miles from the market $25, and 0 at 7.5 miles. Curve RS represents bid rents by wheat farmers, at a price of $100 for wheat. It will be seen that pea farmers can bid higher rents in the range of 0 to 5 miles from the market; farther out, wheat farmers can bid higher rents. Therefore, pea farming will take place in the ring from 0 to 5 miles from the market, and wheat farming in the ring from 5 to 10 miles. Segments MT of the bid rent curve of pea farming and TS of wheat farming will be the effective rents, while segments RT and TN represent unsuccessful bids.

The price of the product is determined by the supply-demand relations at the market. If the region between 0 and 5 miles produces too many peas, the price of the

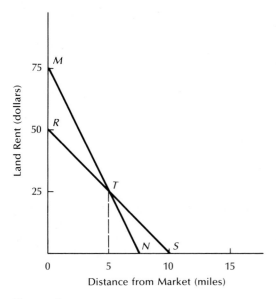

Figure 3.

product will drop, and a lower bid rent curve for pea farming will come into effect, so that pea farming will be practiced to some distance less than 5 miles.

Abstracting this view of the agricultural land market, we have that:

1. land uses determine land values, through competitive bidding among farmers;
2. land values distribute land uses, according to their ability to pay;
3. the steeper curves capture the central locations. (This point is a simplified one for simple, well-behaved curves.)

Abstracting the process now *from* agriculture, we have:

1. for each user of land (e.g., wheat farmer) a family of bid rent functions is derived, such that the user is indifferent as to his location along any *one* of these functions (because the

farmer, who is the decision-maker in this case, finds that profits are everywhere the same, i.e., normal, as long as he remains on one curve);
2. the equilibrium rent at any location is found by comparing the bids of the various potential users and choosing the highest;
3. equilibrium quantities of land are found by selecting the proper bid rent curve for each user (in the agricultural case, the curve which equates supply and demand for the produce).

BUSINESS

We shall now consider the urban businessman, who, we shall assume, makes his decisions so as to maximize profits. A bid rent curve for the businessman, then, will be one along which profits are everywhere the same: the decision-maker will be indifferent as to his location along such a curve.

Profit may be defined as the remainder from the volume of business after operating costs and land costs have been deducted. Since in most cases the volume of business of a firm as well as its operating costs will vary with its location, the rate of change of the bid rent curve will bear no simple relation to transport costs (as it did in agriculture). The rate of change of the total bid rent for a firm, where profits are constant by definition, will be equal to the rate of change in the volume of business minus the rate of change in operating costs. Therefore the slope of the bid rent curve, the values of which are in terms of dollars per unit of land, will be equal to the rate of change in the volume of business minus the rate of change in operating costs, divided by the area occupied by the establishment.

A different level of profits would yield a different bid rent curve. The higher the bid rent curve, the lower the profits, since land is more expensive. There will be a highest curve, where profits will be zero. At higher land rents the firm could only operate at a loss.

Thus we have, as in the case of the farmer, a family of bid rent curves, along the path of any one of which the decision-maker—in this case, the businessman—is indifferent. Whereas in the case of the farmer the level of the curve is determined by the price of the produce, while profits are in all cases "normal," i.e., the same, in the case of the urban firm, the level of the curve is determined by the level of the profits, and the price of its products may be regarded for our purposes as constant.

RESIDENTIAL

The household differs from the farmer and the urban firm in that satisfaction rather than profits is the relevant criterion of optional location. A consumer, given his income and his pattern of tastes, will seek to balance the costs and bother of commuting against the advantages of cheaper land with increasing distance from the center of the city and the satisfaction of more space for living. When the individual consumer faces a given pattern of land costs, his equilibrium location and the size of his site will be in terms of the marginal changes of these variables.

The bid rent curves of the individual will be such that, for any given curve, the individual will be equally satisfied at every location at the price set by the curve. Along any bid rent curve, the price the individual will bid for land will decrease with distance from the center at a rate just sufficient to produce an income effect which will balance to his satisfaction the increased costs of commuting and the bother of a long trip. This slope may be expressed quite precisely in mathematical terms, but it is a complex expression, the exact interpretation of which is beyond the scope of this paper.

Just as different prices of the produce set different levels for the bid rent curves of the farmer, and different levels of profit for the urban firm, different levels of satisfaction correspond to the various levels of the family of bid rent curves of the individual household. The higher curves obviously yield less satisfaction because a higher price is implied, so that, at any given location, the individual will be able to afford less land and other goods.

INDIVIDUAL EQUILIBRIUM

It is obvious that families of bid rent curves are in many respects similar to indifference curve mappings. However, they differ in some important ways. Indifference curves map a path of indifference (equal satisfaction) between combinations of quantities of two goods. Bid rent functions map an indifference path between the price of one good (land) and quantities of another and strange type of good, distance from the center of the city. Whereas indifference curves refer only to tastes and not to budget, in the case of households, bid rent functions are derived both from budget and taste considerations. In the case of the urban firm, they might be termed isoprofit curves. A more superficial difference is that, whereas the higher indifference curves are the preferred ones, it is the lower bid rent curves that yield greater profits or satisfaction. However, bid rent curves may be used in a manner analogous to that of indifference curves to find the equilibrium location and land price for the resident or the urban firm.

Assume you have been given a bid rent mapping of a land use, whether business or residential (curves $brc_{1,2,3}$ etc. in Figure 4). Superimpose on the same diagram the actual structure of land prices in the city (curve SS). The decision-maker will wish to reach the lowest possible bid rent curve. Therefore, he will choose that point at which the curve of actual prices (SS) will be tangent to the lowest of the bid rent curves with which it comes in contact (brc_2). At this point will be the equilibrium location (L) and the equilibrium land rent (R) for this user of land. If he is a businessman, he will have maximized profits; if he is a resident, he will have maximized satisfaction.

Note that to the left of this point of equilibrium (toward the center of the city) the curve of actual prices is steeper than the bid rent curve; to the right of this point (away from the center) it is less steep. This is another aspect of the rule we noted in the agricultural model: the land uses with steeper bid rent curves capture the central locations.

MARKET EQUILIBRIUM

We now have, conceptually, families of bid rent curves for all three types of land uses. We also know that the steeper curves will occupy the more central locations. Therefore, if the curves of the various users are ranked by steepness, they will also be ranked in terms of their accessibility from the center of the city in the final solution.

Thus, if the curves of the business firm are steeper than those of residences, and the residential curves steeper than the agricultural, there will be business at the center of the city, surrounded by residences, and these will be surrounded by agriculture.

This reasoning applies as well within land use groupings. For instance, it can be shown that, given two individuals of similar tastes, both of whom prefer living at low densities, if their incomes differ, the bid rent curves of the wealthier will be flatter than those of the man of lower income. Therefore, the poor will tend to central locations on expensive land and the rich to cheaper land on the periphery. The reason for this is not that the poor have greater purchasing power, but rather that they have steeper bid rent curves. This stems from the fact that, at any given location, the poor can buy less land than the rich, and since only a small quantity of land is involved, changes in its price are not as important for the poor as the costs and inconvenience of commuting. The rich, on the other hand, buy greater quantities

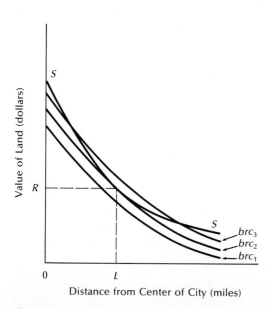

Figure 4.

of land, and are consequently affected by changes in its price to a greater degree. In other words, because of variations in density among different levels of income, accessibility behaves as an inferior good.

Thus far, through ranking the bid rent curves by steepness, we have found the relative rankings of prices and locations, but not the actual prices, locations, or densities. It will be remembered that in the agricultural case equilibrium levels were brought about by changes in the price of the products, until the amount of land devoted to each crop was in agreement with the demand for that crop.

For urban land this process is more complex. The determination of densities (or their inverse, lot size) and locations must be found simultaneously with the resulting price structure. Very briefly, the method consists of assuming a price of land at the center of the city, and determining the prices at all other locations by the competitive bidding of the potential users of land in relation to this price. The highest bid captures each location, and each bid is related to a most preferred alternative through the use of bid rent curves. This most preferred alternative is the marginal combination of price and location for that particular land use. The quantities of land occupied by the land users are determined by these prices. The locations are determined by assigning to each successive user of land the location available nearest the center of the city after the assignment of land quantities to the higher and more central bidders.

Since initially the price at the center of the city was assumed, the resulting set of prices, locations, and densities may be in error. A series of iterations will yield the correct solution. In some cases, the solution may be found by a set of simultaneous equations rather than by the chain of steps which has just been outlined.

The model presented in this paper corresponds to the simplest case: a single-center city, on a featureless plain, with transportation in all directions. However, the reasoning can be extended to cities with several centers (shopping, office, manufacturing, etc.), with structured road patterns, and other realistic complications. The theory can also be made to shed light on the effects of economic development, changes in income structure, zoning regulations, taxation policies, and other. At this stage, the model is purely theoretical; however, it is hoped that it may provide a logical structure for econometric models which may be useful for prediction.

KEY CONCEPTS

bid-rent curves

equilibrium land rent

equilibrium location

indifference curves

MARION CLAWSON

6 Urban Sprawl and Speculation in Suburban Land[1]

Urban sprawl is often viewed as one of the greatest evils of urban development, second only to air pollution. Moreover, it is often attributed to a failure of the market process to work efficiently. In this selection Marion Clawson argues that the timing of development of urban land cannot be regular because it is a dynamic process characterized by uncertainty. Sprawl is seen as a natural outgrowth of an efficient market allocation of urban land to various uses over time.

"Sprawl" has been widely criticized as leading to unnecessarily high costs of social services and of private transportation, as well as for the frequent lack of publicly available open areas. It is also responsible for, or associated with, much wastage of land, since the intervening unused areas are mostly not used at all. Others have tended to minimize these deficiencies, arguing that they are but part of a growth process, not too serious in nature. . . .

The purpose of this article is to explore the economic process in suburbanization—why some areas are developed, why intermingled ones are not, why land speculation invariably accompanies the process, and the like. The economic forces wil be described, as far as possible, and some judgment offered as to which are manipulatable and which are not, and how. A basic premise is that no significant progress

From *Land Economics*, May 1962, p. 100–108. Reprinted by permission of the University of Wisconsin Press, copyright 1962.
[1]In preparation of this article the author has benefited greatly from discussions with colleagues at Resources for the Future, notably Harvey S. Perloff and T. Lowdon Wingo. The views expressed are those of the author.

can be made in developing better suburbanization until the present processes are better understood. . . .

CHARACTERISTICS OF THE MARKET FOR RAW SUBURBAN LAND

The market for raw, undeveloped suburban land has several peculiar characteristics. First of all, land for suburban development is not a homogenous commodity, any more than is land for any other possible use. While differences in soil texture and fertility may be less important, as compared to these same qualities for agriculture, they are not negligible. Slope of land may be highly important, as affecting building costs. The risks of flood damage differ greatly from area to area. In these and in other ways, the native or natural qualities of potential suburban land may differ greatly.

The history of land ownership usually results in a present ownership pattern of variable size tracts of land owned by different owners. Some pieces are large, others small. Some owners have one objective, others another. A potential new owner must deal with what he finds, buying as he can. He will find it impossible to buy exactly as he wishes but must deal with discrete tracts in different ownerships. Subdivision of large tracts often creates a "plottage" value, which is at its peak when the size of tract coincides with the tract best suited to the use for which the land is intended. Tracts either larger or smaller than the optimum have lower value. The passage of time may change the use of land and hence the optimum size of tract. It is significant, we think, that since the war the major railroads of the country have purchased potential industrial sites along or near their tracks when they could, largely to prevent subdivision which would spoil the larger tracts for industrial development.

The owner of a discrete tract often must sell it all, or a major part, if he wishes to sell any. Suburban land, equally with or perhaps more than other land is not, perhaps cannot be, sold in incremental pieces, but rather in relatively large chunks—chunks not necessarily adjusted to the needs of the buyer or seller.

Society, acting through government at some level, has given suburban land further special characteristics. Location with respect to transportation, to water supply, to sewerage, and to other services vitally affects potentiality of land for suburban development. These qualities were given the land without action by the landowner, except as far as he was able to influence the public action which resulted in these services. Individuals may buy and sell land to take advantage of the services provided by group action but they are not responsible for the services.

Society has affected the value of suburban land in other ways—by taxes, by zoning and building codes, and the like. If master plans, zoning, and building codes were explicit, firm, enforceable, and enforced, and if there were confidence they would remain so, they would greatly limit if not completely determine land values in many areas. In fact, zoning in particular and other policies to some degree can be changed under political and other pressures. Even the courts do not always accept values consistent with zoning regulations, when private land is condemned for public use. Public action through zoning and other related measures affects land values; but the major effect may be through the uncertainty created. While some of these services or action by society affect land over rather large areas more or less equally, yet some have a highly local effect.

Suburban land also differs greatly in accessibility, especially to major highways and sometimes to rail lines. The quality of accessibility may affect its price and its saleability greatly. Accessibility is generally not provided by the individual landowner but rather through the public, as in the case of highways, or by large private undertakings, as in the case of rail lines.

The market for suburban land is a derived one, dependent upon the market for the dwellings, shopping centers, or industrial plants erected on it. As such, it is subject to the uncertainties of market for the final product, compounded by the uncertainties of the conversion process. The market for suburban housing is a fragmented and not wholly consistent one, often variable in short distances or over brief times. Differences in price for houses are often reflected back into differences in price for undeveloped land, but in varying degree.

Lastly, the market for suburban land is usually very thin. There are very few buyers and very few sellers at any one time. Annual turnover in relation to total area is small. For almost any commodity there is a liquidation value at forced sale; a normal value between willing seller and willing buyer; and a forced purchase price when for some reason the buyer must buy almost regardless of price. For suburban land these prices might well stand in the ratio of 50 or less, to 100, to 200 or more, respectively. The time required to make a sale of land may be considerable, and directly related to the price obtainable. Part of these variations may be due to lack of information on the part of buyers and sellers but much is probably due to the character of the commodity itself. One need only contrast these characteristics of the market for suburban land with the market for wheat or even for autos. For these latter and for many other commodities there are many buyers and sellers; and forced sale, normal sale, and forced purchase prices stand in much closer relationship to one another. Some of these characteristics we have described for urban land do apply to all kinds of land for any purpose. Although empirical studies are lacking we hazard the judgment that these factors are more serious for urban than for other land.

VALUE-MAKING PROCESS FOR UNDEVELOPED SUBURBAN LAND

Undeveloped suburban land, not yet in use for urban purposes but already taken out of other land uses, obviously must derive its value from the expectation of its later development as urban land. . . . The conversion value of the raw potential suburban land into actual developed suburban land is somewhat uncertain at any date, depending in part upon the action of the community as a whole, and in part upon the skill of the subdivider and developer himself.

The date at which there will be an active demand for the raw suburban land for actual development is to a large extent uncertain. In some instances a piece of land may lie close to areas developed within the past few years and toward which the tide of development is flowing. Under such circumstances its present value is moderately forecastable on the basis of estimated probable future conversion date and value. In other cases, land may lie at greater distance or in directions where future development is less certain; then both its conversion date and its conversion value are more uncertain. The timing of development of a particular piece of suburban land is partly outside of his control. He may obviously withhold it for later development, if he thinks a greater net income can be obtained thereby—he is less able to speed up its development. The large, well-financed, skillful developer can bring about the development of a particular tract more nearly on his terms than can a smaller developer; but each operates within the general market structure.

An expected future income or value can be discounted back to a present worth or value. An interest or discount rate is required to do so. The discount rate may be thought of as having two parts; a more or less normal interest rate based upon alternative sources of investment or alternative sources of funds in competitive money markets; plus an uncertainty factor. The latter relates not only to the date of future conversion from raw to developed status for the land—and even as to "whether" as well as "when"—and the value at that date, but probably should include a large allowance for illiquidity as well. As we have noted, suburban land can be sold quickly or at forced sale only at prices substantially below its normal value when ample time is available to negotiate a sale. In practice a single discounting figure will be used, large enough to include all these and perhaps other factors as well. . . .

In addition to delays and uncertainties as to time and value of suburban land for conversion to development, there are some holding costs to be taken into account. Taxes over a period of years may be considerable even at low assessments and low rates. Occasionally charges other than taxes must be met annually. One cost of holding is interest on the value of the land if sold, but of course the discounting formula includes this factor.

One could easily construct or adopt formulae to show these relationships, or give illustrative tables of different time periods, different final conversion values, different discount rates, and different holding charges. The best guess as to land values 10 years from now will justify present values well under half of that level; and the best guess as to values 20 years from now will justify present values much less than a fourth as high. It is altogether possible that normal or free market values may be higher than this because of widespread optimism over ultimate values, time of conversion, costs of holding, uncertainties, and the like.

The ownership of any suburban land for a rise in value is a speculative undertaking. Profits, when all factors are taken into account, are by no means assured nor large on the average. Everyone knows, or at least has heard, of others who have made substantial gains from holding suburban land for a rise in price. This type of common knowledge nearly always is ignorant of or ignores the cases, perhaps more numerous, when increases in value were much less or even negative. The chance for profit in holding suburban land for development arises entirely out of error in consensus or out of individual judgments more astute than the consensus. If there was complete knowledge as to the time of future conversion, as to value at that time, as to holding costs and as to discount rate, then obviously everyone would be in complete accord as to present worth. There would be no opportunity for speculative gain, because all future value would have been fully and accurately discounted into present value. It is altogether possible that at times the consensus on these matters is in error—everyone is sure of something which later history proves not to be true. Under such circumstances, a sounder judge with a minority view may reap a profit. At other times a consensus may be lacking but one view may prove in time to have been closer to the fact than any other; if the person who held it acted upon his convictions, he may have profited.

As long as the price of land ripe for conversion from undeveloped to developed status is relatively high, then the price of land less ripe for development will be somewhat lower until at the margin the prospects for conversion into developed status are so uncertain or so remote that even the most optimistic will not bid up the value of this land. As long as we have free markets in suburban land and as long as the total effect of the various factors in the formula promise some present value above alternative use value, and given imperfections of knowledge and incomplete consensus, then we can reasonably expect speculative bidding up of suburban land values. Viewed in this way, land speculation in and beyond the suburbs is not only normal but inevitable. . . .

FORCES LEADING TO DEVELOPMENT OF PARTICULAR SUBURBAN TRACTS

Given the nature of the market for raw suburban land and given the value-making process for such land, what are the forces leading to the development of particular tracts of such land? How can we account for the fact that a relatively few of the many possible suburban tracts are developed in a particular year and how can we predict which ones will be developed and which left for a later future?

One basic factor is the overall market demand for urban land for the whole urban area concerned. Some cities or metropolitan areas are growing rapidly, others at a more modest pace, and some are essentially stagnant. The amount of new land needed for urban purposes annually will obviously vary greatly among cities, depending upon this factor. At some times the real estate and building market is much more active than at others, depending in large part upon credit availability as well as upon general economic demand. When the demand for new urban land is high, not only is more land needed but the profitability of conversion is probably greater. This means not only greater profits to landowners, on the average, but also that some tracts or types of development which would be marginal in other circumstances will now be promoted—it is the time for the long chance, for the unusual deal.

The extension of essential public services to particular areas or districts will bring land within such areas or districts closer to the point of actual development or building. Provision of new roads, schools, water supply, sewerage, and other services, or marked improvement in them, add greatly to the impetus for development. The possi-bility of alternative devices, such as septic tanks instead of trunk sewer lines, may have the same effect. Viewing the subdivision developments which actually take place, one can hardly say that these public services, which he is tempted to call essential, are in fact either essential or necessary to building development on specific sites—one sees too many areas that get built up, at least to a degree, without them, or at least without satisfactory services. Yet the provision of new services undoubtedly gives a fillip toward development. On the other hand, it is unlikely, of itself alone, to be sufficient. That is, mere extension of one public service, or even of a group, to an area previously lacking them, may not lead to much actual building. Other factors—above all, overall demand—must be present.

Though empirical data are lacking, at least to this author, yet one cannot but suspect that the personal desires, projections, and preferences of present landowners must be a major factor responsible for some tracts developing while other intermingled ones do not. Institutional factors, such as estate holdings, trusts, defective titles, covenants, and others, may affect marketability of particular tracts, especially in the short run. Some present landholders may be optimistic about future increases in value of their land, others more cautious; some may have ample capital for which they seek investment outlets; others may have pressing need of any capital they can raise by sale of their land; and in other ways landowners may differ considerably. It seems wholly probable that owners of identical land (if one can imagine such a thing) might react quite differently to exactly the same offers for their land. Moreover, the differences between individual landowners may well be so great that a small increase in offered price, such as another year or two might bring, will be insufficient to move the man who wants to hold for later profit. Anyone familiar with urban real estate knows of many tracts remaining vacant for many years while all around them development proceeds apace. Surely one major factor must be the characteristics of the landowner himself.

As we have noted above, raw suburban land differs greatly in physical suitability for development and also in size of parcel which each owner possesses. A residential builder may wish a moderate size tract; some will appear too small for his needs, others larger than he needs, but not available in part. An industrial development is likely to need a relatively large tract, as well as one of specific locational and other qualities and thus many smaller tracts are practically unavailable or nonexistent to him.

When all of these factors are combined one should expect a rather hit-or-miss type of suburban development as normal; it will not normally be incremental, even regular. Instead, some tracts will be developed, other nearby ones remain vacant for long periods, relatively more distant ones developed sooner than some nearby ones, and so on. One should, in fact, anticipate exactly what we have experienced: sprawl! The frontier of urban land use or building will not move slowly and regularly, taking in all land as it goes; instead, development will leap ahead to more distant tracts, passing over nearby ones, taking in some large and some small tracts, and leaving others of assorted sizes. While there has been much criticism of sprawl, and even a little wonder at why it looks as it does, in fact, given the institutional and economic forces we have described, one should have expected exactly the same kind of sprawl we have experienced in such a large way since World War II. . . .

KEY CONCEPTS

conversion value of land

discounted present value

discount rate

thin market

holding costs

BENJAMIN CHINITZ

7 The Economy of the Central City: An Appraisal

Benjamin Chinitz of the State University of New York, Binghamton, adds up the economic advantages (assets) and disadvantages (liabilities) of central-city locations. He also discusses dynamic changes in external forces that alter the attractiveness of the central city over time. These include improvements in transport technology and communication technology as well as the shift toward the production of services. Finally, the author attempts to predict the future of the central city as an advantageous location for employment.

INTRODUCTION

It is virtually impossible to be original in describing the status of the central cities of our major metropolitan areas. The problems abound: congestion, pollution, slums, poverty, racial strife, crime, drug addiction, dirt, noise. People still argue about whether conditions are better or worse than they used to be and whether the people who now live in these cities are or are not better off than they used to be. This much is certain: not many are happy with conditions as they are.

What also seems to be beyond debate is that the fiscal condition of the local governments of these cities is as bad as or worse than it has ever been. The diagnosis is quite simple. The problems put pressure on the demand side: more money for wel-

fare payments; more money for education; more money for police and fire protection, sanitation, and almost everything else on the list of locally provided goods and services.

Then there is the pressure for higher wages for city employees. That pressure stems, in part, from the general rise in earnings in the private sector of the economy, which makes it increasingly difficult to recruit people to the public sector at lower wages. But it also reflects the impact of the unionization of public employees and explicit pressure, via strikes and other devices, to increase wages and improve working conditions even for those who may not have the option of moving over to the private sector.

Finally, and this is my main concern here, there is the faltering private sector of the central city that provides a weak base for local taxation. The big city mayors—Republican and Democrat and Independent—are all pleading for greater financial aid from their respective states but mainly from the federal government. Federal money and state money, one might suppose, are to be preferred over local money in all circumstances. But whether or not that is true, there can be no doubt that the urgency in the current plea for outside support reflects greater reluctance than ever to impose higher taxes on local business and households.

Such reluctance, in turn, can be attributed in part to the political consequences of proposing higher local taxes. Voters persist in an illusion which can be fatal to the incumbent, namely, that while the "old" man wants new taxes, the "new" man is likely to get by with the old taxes. But even a daring mayor has to contend with the competitive aspects of local taxation. Households and businesses can move to nearby suburbs where taxes are more favorable. Some people and some enterprises might even be induced to move to more distant areas.

This constraint, which was always there to some extent, is now deemed to be much more binding because it is assumed that the central city, taxes aside, is increasingly vulnerable to competition for the location of people and jobs. Nobody really knows with any precision how that competition is affected by increased local tax burdens. But when the city's hold on industry and people is assumed to be weakening, increased taxes are not likely to help matters.

I will focus here on the central city as a location for private sector activities. I want first to examine the assets and liabilities of the city as a location, much as we viewed them in the early days of urban economics, before the current sense of crisis set in. I then want to show how these assets and liabilities interact with exogenous forces to shape the changing competitive position and the growth of the city's economy. Third, I want to suggest that municipal policies can affect the local economy's competitive posture and that taxation is only one of many issues in this regard. Finally, I want to speculate about the future of the city as a place of employment.

THE CENTRAL CITY: A BALANCE SHEET

There is a vast literature on the subject of the city as a location for industry [(3)Hoover, 1959; (4) Hoover, 1963; (10) Vernon, 1959]. But in the heat of the current preoccupation with the urban crisis, many of the simple points have been submerged if not forgotten.

By *assets*, I mean those characteristics of a city location that increase productivity and reduce costs. By *liabilities* I mean the converse: those characteristics of a city location that reduce productivity and increase costs. The latter are more readily identified and articulated; the former are more subtle and require greater elucidation. Let me take the easy side first.

The city's liabilities should perhaps more appropriately be termed "constraints" rather than liabilities. These are *rents* and *congestion*. The competition for space increases rents and acts as a deterrent to the location of some activities which might otherwise prefer to be located in the city. Outside the city, we assume the supply of land to be much more elastic.

The density of activity creates congestion. In simple terms, it takes more driver time and more gasoline to traverse a given distance. The same density that gives you congestion may also yield a lower cost per unit of business transacted, despite the higher operating costs but that's on the other side of the equation. Congestion gets translated into higher rents for space by increasing construction costs. Lately, particularly in New York, congestion has assumed other dimensions: deterioration in telephone service and power cutbacks on very hot days. Some of these manifestations of congestion are also experienced in the suburbs.

Rents and congestion are inherent in the logic of central city growth. Their precise levels are of course not inherently determined. Elevators make a difference; size of cars makes a difference; relative use of private and public transport makes a difference; street layout and building design make a difference. We shall deal with some of these as "exogenous" influences in the next section. But planning and clever design can only temper the inelasticity of supply of space for activity and mobility; they cannot render supply completely elastic.

Do we capture all of the liabilities under the twin concepts of rent and congestion? How about higher wages and higher taxes? How about crime and insurance rates? On wages the evidence is mixed [(9) Segal, 1959]. On taxes, congestion is again the root problem to the extent that public services are in greater demand and harder to provide in conditions of high density. But the welfare burden and such problems as crime insofar as they affect the cost of doing business directly or indirectly via taxation, would be hard to subsume under the heading of congestion. These are more appropriately dealt with in the next section as "exogenous" developments.

The asset side is more complex. Face-to-face contact with a wide variety of related individuals and activities is often defined as the root or fundamental advantage of a city location. This is the other side of the congestion coin. You can't walk too fast, traffic is bumper-to-bumper, telephone service is unstable, restaurants are crowded; but you can achieve a great variety of contacts in a day because of the sheer number and diversity of people and activities concentrated in such a small area. What it boils down to is that the unit cost of information is cheaper.

But the facilitation of face-to-face contact is only one of the assets of high density, and high density does not exhaust the asset side of the balance sheet. More basically, the city derives its strength from Adam Smith's famous dictum about specialization and the extent of the market. Density permits a much higher order of specialization because proximity of specialists, one to the other, keeps down the costs of trade for a given scale of operation. Thus each unit can concentrate on doing one thing very efficiently and on drawing its auxiliary needs at low cost from neighboring units. In short: the city is a mechanism for enlarging the market by containing transportation and communication costs, thus permitting a greater degree of specialization and hence higher productivity. Face-to-face communication and short-haul goods movements are the visual by-products of the process.

Another way to view the favorable impact of high density is in terms of capital saving. An enterprise in isolation must substitute capital for what might be current expenses for an enterprise in the city. It might take the form of higher inventories, more workers on the payroll, a computer, cars and trucks—all of which are designed to shield the firm against its isolation. In the city, the firm can augment its supplies on short notice and can purchase transport services, computing services, and the like from other firms which—to get us back where we were before—can afford to specialize in these services because there is a large market at close call.

All these considerations relate to concentration *per se*. They would be relevant if the city were lifted up bodily and put down in the middle of a desert. They might even apply with equal force if part of the city were lifted up and relocated. This is why the thought of relocating the whole garment center out of New York City, for example, is so tempting to some city planners. To the extent that the most vital inter-firm linkages are contained within a given industrial complex, the dream has a certain appeal.

But there are at least two other forces making for concentration in the center that do not derive their fundamental logic from the economies of concentration *per se*. One has to do with the natural attributes of the areas where most cities are located, principally, their access to water. The other has to do with the "centrality" of the city in relation to the metropolitan area. These advantages motivate firms to seek city locations to minimize transport costs on freight and to maximize access, on average, to the region's labor supply. Each firm independently seeks a central location, and concentration is the *result*. By contrast, the gains which accrue from specialization, easy face-to-face contact, saving of capital, result *from* concentration. When you put the two sets of forces together in some kind of historical dynamic model, you have the essentials of the well-known concept of agglomeration.

Before we move on to consider those exogenous forces which erode the city's

assets or aggravate its liabilities (and vice-versa), a few further comments on the balance sheet may be helpful. First, the relevance of and the weights attached to each asset and liability will vary according to the needs and the objectives of the prospective locator. That's why we observe at any point in history that the city is relatively more attractive to some activities than to others.

Second, the flavor of my comments suggests a preoccupation with the Central Business District (CBD) of the central city rather than the whole central city. This is a correct inference, but it should not be overdrawn. Obviously, the asset-liability balance will come out differently for the same firm at a given point in time, for different locations in the city. But we want to keep the whole city in view, at least through the next section.

Finally, we should distinguish between *micro* dynamics and *macro* dynamics. The same firm over its own lifetime, even when the parameters of the larger system are constant, will strike a different balance for the city as a location because of its *own* changing needs and requirements. Hoover and Vernon have told that story well in *Anatomy of a Metropolis* [(3) Hoover and Vernon, 1959]. Furthermore, the city itself, as it grows and ages, even if the exogenous forces are unchanging—technology, tastes, etc.—will go through a revision of its balance sheet from the perspective of a given firm with fixed requirements. The latter tale is unfolded in Hoover's essay, "The Evolving Form and Organization of the Metropolis" [(5) Hoover, 1968].

In other words, there is a lot of dynamics—internal to the firm and internal to the city—that would prevent the city from taking on a very static image even if nothing were happening "outside" to shake things up. But in the sections that follow, we want to focus on the external dynamics.

Dynamics I:
The Changing Industrial Mix

It is an elementary proposition in regional analysis that the relative growth of different areas will inevitably be affected by the changing industrial composition of the national economy. It is equally well established that the industrial composition of a nation's economy is roughly related to the state of development. At first, agriculture and other resource-oriented activities predominate. As productivity in these activities increases, labor is released for industrialization, and the manufacturing sector grows very rapidly as a share of the total. Finally, at very high levels of income, the service sectors—government, trade, finance and the like—move into first place. Currently in the United States, these service sectors account for 64 percent of total employment, manufacturing[1] 31 percent and extractive industries 5 percent.

This transformation of the national economy, it is generally agreed, is responsible for, or at least is highly correlated with the relative decline of rural areas and the rapid growth of cities and metropolitan areas. Progress and urbanization go hand in hand. What is not so obvious is how these industrial trends have affected *intra*-metropolitan patterns and the competition between city and suburb. The fact is that the city has been favored by these trends because precisely those sectors for which the city has a stronger attraction have grown most rapidly in the national economy. While the city continues to yield ground to the suburbs in

almost all sectors, the overall performance of the city is sustained by the favorable industrial composition of national economic growth.

The impact of these trends is manifested in the very dramatic growth of "office" employment in the nation as a whole, and particularly in cities. By office employment, we mean employment that occurs in detached buildings that are entirely devoted to paper work. Office employment cuts across all sectors as traditionally defined, but as one might expect, it is far more important in the service sector than in the manufacturing sector. Corporate headquarters in the manufacturing sector do give the "office" component considerable status even in that sector. According to the only study of the office sector done so far, "jobs in detached office buildings account for about one-quarter of all white-collar jobs in the nation (or 12 percent of total employment) and 40 percent in the New York Region. These proportions have been rising in recent years, both here and abroad" [(1) Armstrong, 1970, p. 3].

In the simplest terms therefore the central city, which always boasts a larger share of the metropolitan area's offices than of its factories, while losing ground in each, is benefiting from the fact that the national trend favors offices over factories.

If nothing else had happened, central cities would have been expected to grow even faster in response to *Dynamics I* than they had before. So now, we must turn to the factors that have adversely affected the city in its competition with the suburbs.

Dynamics II:
Transport Technology and
Transport Policy

Economic theory suggests that reductions in transport costs extend market areas and

---

[1] Manufacturing in this context includes Construction which, in a more detailed classification, is treated as a separate category.

expand the opportunities for specialization and trade. From this point of view, the city would be expected to gain from the transport revolution of the twentieth century. In some respects it has, but one would be hard put to argue that the city has not lost out, on balance.

The gain occurs if, and only if, the city retains its advantages as a production site; all that happens is that it can now serve a wider market. For example, if the Metropolitan Opera remains in New York City, as it apparently must, then New York City stands to gain from the fact that more people can now reach the opera for a given amount of travel time and cost than before automobiles and highways were available. Similarly, if the Port of New York retains its hold on international traffic, then the fact that a trailer-truck can bring freight in from 200 miles a lot faster and cheaper expands the market area served by the Port.

Unfortunately for the city, however, the automobile and the truck and even the airplane do more than simply reduce the cost of transport relative to other things, which would favor greater concentration. As alternatives to traditional modes—rail and water—they alter the balance of advantages and disadvantages at different locations and therefore undermine the very motive for concentration at particular points, e.g. the central city, for particular activities. The central city cannot accommodate highway and air facilities too well. The substitution of these new modes for the old modes, therefore, favors other locations in the metropolis as logical points at which to concentrate activities that make heavy use of these new modes.

The substitution of automobiles for public transit further undermines the special advantage of the center for labor supply. True, the automobile makes it possible for the worker to commute longer distances. The employer who sticks to the center for other reasons will benefit from the extension of the radius of the labor market. But now a large labor force can be conveniently assembled at almost any point served by the highway network; and the center is hardly the best place to assemble an auto-oriented work force.

The auto and the truck also modify the basic spatial character of specialization and concentration. Assume an employer who calculates that he must retain a presence in the center despite its liabilities—old and new. Under the old technology, that decision would entail a much greater commitment to the center than it does now because with improved mobility, there is greater opportunity to "fine-tune" one's commitment to the center. The front office, the showroom, and those related activities that call for face-to-face contact can be located in the center while production and distribution activities can be located further out where space is cheaper, access to transport service is better, and access to labor as good or better. This spatial separation is facilitated by the new transport technology. In the extreme case, the production can go to Japan, to be linked to the home base by air freight.

Thus, every asset of the city is challenged by new transport technology, and some of its liabilities are aggravated. The substitution of automobile travel for mass transit to and from the center and within the center increases the desired space per capita, and in a very real sense, diminishes the overall capacity of the center to accommodate people and jobs. More space is taken up for parking. The greater speed and maneuverability of the truck compared to the horse-and-wagon by itself represents an improvement. But the potential gain from that source is frustrated by the high cost of rearranging the already developed center to accommodate the new vehicle. A city that is built with the new technology in mind can better compete with its suburbs.

On the whole, public policy has supported the thrust of the new technology. Nobody can tell us with certainty what would have happened if transport investments were entirely managed by the private sector and if the prices of all transport services reflected marginal social costs. The fact is that the public sector was relatively quick to supply the complementary capital investments in roads and terminals for the new modes and relatively slow in responding to the agonies of decline in the old modes. Since the center city had more to gain from the preservation of the old, it certainly was not favored by the dominant thrust of public policy.

Nevertheless, there is one aspect of *Dynamics II*, as suggested earlier, that has worked in the city's favor. *Dynamics I* has enlarged the national basket of activities, as symbolized by the growth of the office sector, in which the city retains a strong comparative advantage. The potential for the continued concentration of such activities in the center is enlarged by the revolution in air transport, which makes it easier for an activity of this type to serve an ever-wider market. In this respect, the classic theorem about the impact of transport costs on specialization and trade applies.

When you add it all up, you have to conclude that the center has been adversely affected competitively by technological progress in transport and the public policies which have embodied that progress in physical investments. The impact, however, is not only to hold back the city's growth but also to refine the character of

the city's economy forcing it to specialize increasingly in those activities that gain most from the city's assets and suffer least from its liabilities.

Dynamics III:
Technological Progress in
Other Sectors

There are at least three other kinds of technological progress that have important implications for the competition between city and suburb. We will refer to them as *Dynamics III (A)*, *III (B)*, and *III (C)*.

Dynamics III (A) is technological change in goods handling in plants and warehouses other than those occasioned by *Dynamics II*. The key here is the use of electric power, in combination with engineering design, to favor horizontal as against vertical layouts in such facilities. As a result, the twin pressures of high rents and congestion in the city act even more forcefully to favor outlying areas for the location of production and distribution facilities.

Dynamics III (B) is technological progress in communication and data processing, as symbolized by TV and the computer, which are well established but continuously evolving new forms and remote access. At first, these new gimmicks favor the center because their limited availability and high unit costs compel sharing of a kind that is more readily achieved in a dense market. But as unit costs go down and remote access is achieved, they tend on balance to reduce the disabilities of remote locations and alleviate the pressure to be in the center. They also contribute to the potential, as with *Dynamics II*, of achieving a finer spatial specialization by permitting the top decision-makers in the center to be in close contact with the information and other paper processing activities that can then be located at lower cost in outlying areas.

Many have speculated that further progress in communication will ultimately undermine entirely the "face-to-face" aspect of concentration which favors the center of the city. Even if that were true, it would not necessarily lead to the demise of the center, in terms of our balance sheet above. "Face-to-face" is the reflection of a complex pattern of specialization, the logic of which rests essentially on a large dense market. Easy communication removes one motive for employers to want to be located in close proximity to each other. But they can substitute close-circuit TV for lunch at the club and retain their location in the center if there are other good reasons for doing so.

Dynamics III (C) takes us farther away from our subject but its relevance is soon obvious. I have in mind the technological revolution in agriculture which was alluded to above under *Dynamics I.* There we stressed the shifting industrial mix of the economy and the implications of such shifts for the city center, from the perspective of growth in employment. Here I want to stress the population migration effects.

Historically, the city, especially in the Northeast, was favored in its growth by a very elastic supply of labor. Hordes of immigrants came to these cities from abroad and from America's rural areas because they, like their contemporary counterparts, found the center city a more congenial atmosphere for launching their assimilation into the modern American economy. The happy coincidence of demand and supply worked in everybody's favor.

In recent decades, two factors have operated to create a very serious divergence of interests. On the demand side, the city's economy generates fewer opportunities for the uneducated, untrained, immigrant worker. On the supply side, these workers continue to favor the city voluntarily for the traditional reasons, or involuntarily because of suburban discrimination against racial minorities and poor whites. The city would prefer to make more living space available for workers who are in demand at the center. The immigrants frustrate this objective, in part by competing for scarce space, in part by adding to the tax burden because of their public service requirements, and in part by making the center generally less attractive to the middle- and upper-income groups. Obviously the movement of these groups to the suburbs has been motivated by "pull" factors as well, but the "push" factors cannot be denied.

In summary, *Dynamics III (C)* cuts into the labor supply advantages of the center. *Dynamics III (B)* reduces the need for proximity insofar as it rests on easy communication. *Dynamics III (A)* feeds the demand for space per worker and aggravates a long-standing liability.

Dynamics IV: Capital Accumulation and Higher Incomes

The city, as we said, is a capital-saving device. It is a device for sharing the costs of indivisible units of capital, thus reducing the unit cost per capita or per unit of output. In part, this saving is achieved at the expense of higher operating costs arising from congestion.

Dynamics I, II, and *III* all relate to various facets of progress. But if you can imagine achieving economic progress through capital accumulation alone, a process certainly theoretically possible, you would already have identified a reason for the relative decline of central cities. As wages rise relative to interest rates, there is increasingly less incentive to economize on capital. You go outward, where you can reduce operating costs, even if you have to incur higher capital costs in the process.

The same logic applies to the resident as to the employer. Living in relative isolation calls for greater commitment of capital. You have to own your own home, provide for your own mobility and for a host of other services, available on a current account basis, albeit at higher prices, in the congested center. As your assets and borrowing power improve, you have less incentive to conserve capital and can give vent to your desire for easy, spacious living.

Thus, even with the state-of-the-art held constant, capital accumulation and rising incomes render the savings arising from density less relevant and the advantages of sparsely settled territory more relevant for both producers and consumers.

THE ROLE OF MUNICIPAL POLICY

In the previous section, we view the changing location of jobs and people as reflecting inexorable forces in the economy and society at large. Rural to urban migration is mainly attributed to the decline of job opportunities in agriculture and other resource-oriented industries and the concomitant growth of employment in service industries, which are city-oriented in their location. Technological change in transport—people and goods—accompanied by higher incomes are held to be responsible for the far more rapid rate of growth of the suburbs as compared to the central cities.

Typically, when we think of public policy as an influence on geographic patterns of development, we are more likely to consider aspects of federal government policy than local policy. We credit the Federal Interstate Highway Program and the Federal Housing Program with having accelerated the impact of the automobile on metropolitan growth patterns. We think of the geographic distribution of federal contracts as having significant effects on the distribution of economic activity and population. By contrast, we generally think of local policy as being restricted to a passive role. "How do we adjust to what is happening to us?" is the perspective we have on local policy.

In recent years, there has been a growing presumption that local policy can assume an active role in determining what happens, at least as far as employment is concerned. Local governments have increasingly adopted the view that they can influence the demand for labor in their jurisdictions by adopting and implementing policies that improve their competitive position. Some communities have offered subsidies in one form or another to prospective employers; others have attempted to ease local tax burdens. These measures directly affect the operating costs of the firm. Other measures operate indirectly by enhancing potential productivity. These include improved public services, better transport, and friendlier bankers.

Communities have, of course, also used local policy to discourage the location of certain industries inside their boundaries. The main instrument is zoning, which establishes the legal basis for saying "NO" to a prospective employer. Such communities also have the power to influence the composition of population within their borders. They do so not by inducing changes in the demand for labor but by defining the terms under which people can locate their residences within their borders.

Whether or not localities pursue explicit policies to influence employment and population inside their borders, programs and policies designed to serve other objectives are bound to have such side effects. Taxes are the prime example. The aggregate tax burden and the way that burden is distributed within the community both affect job and residential location even if they are largely decided on other grounds. But other policies are also relevant in this regard.

New York City, for example, is undergoing considerable change in the pattern of job and population growth. In the main, these changes reflect the workings of forces far beyond the control of city government. On the demand for labor side, the impact of these changes has been to retard the overall growth of jobs in the city but mainly to reduce absolutely the number of low-skill jobs. On the supply side, the reverse has occurred. On balance, the city as a place to live is increasingly less attractive to high-skill, high-income employees while low-skill, low-income populations are increasingly attracted there.

Insofar as city policy has been at all addressed explicitly to this problem, the focus has been on the supply side. Very simply, the city has attempted to arrest the decline of blue-collar low-wage employment by assisting employers who might otherwise leave the city to find suitable space for their operations. Although one cannot estimate with certainty the importance of space as a factor in relocation of production facilities, it is reasonable to assume that, in many instances, the proximate if not the ultimate factor motivating relocation is the lack of an adequate site at an acceptable price. Sometimes, the difficulty arises from plant expansion; at other times, from displacement caused by renewal or private preemption for higher-value uses. In any case, it is felt that intervention by the city can augment the supply of space to those producers who would otherwise find it in their own best interests to locate outside the city.

The merits of this particular policy instrument will not be appraised here. Suffice it to say that it appears to have been of limited impact in dealing with the fundamental supply-demand imbalance. Moreover, there are other city policies motivated by noneconomic objectives of the city that have tended to exacerbate, not resolve the basic labor market imbalance. I will focus on two such policies which have received detailed treatment in research: housing and welfare.[2]

The essential dilemma of the government has been clear for some years. To finance a very large and growing welfare burden along with conventional city services whose costs keep rising rapidly, it has had to extract revenue from a productive sector that is growing very slowly and is increasingly sensitive to comparative cost pressures. The dilemma seems difficult enough to resolve by itself; yet it is further aggravated by city policy. In other words, the city is actually making worse an already bad situation.

Let me suggest two criteria for judging such policies. The first is short-run and static: it says that you should pursue those policies that do the least damage to your productive capacity while yielding the maximum effectiveness in combating poverty. The second criterion is longer-run and dynamic: it says that you should prefer those policies which contribute to the automatic or natural resolution of the problem over policies which perpetuate or

---

[2]The research referred to here is in progress at the New York City Rand Institute which the author serves as consultant. So far, the only published work is that of Lowry [(7) 1970].

even exacerbate the problem. Generally, although not always, the two criteria reinforce each other to create a strong preference for one set of policies over another.

As applied to the case in hand, these criteria would argue for bringing relief to the needy in ways that do least damage to the local economy and provide maximum incentive to escape from poverty through gainful employment. A federally financed family-assistance plan which does not tax earnings at 100 percent is readily seen as passing these criteria with the highest possible scores. In the absence of such an ideal resolution of the city's dilemma, it is unfortunately hard to argue that the second-best alternative is being pursued.

The sad fact is that the city is transferring *assets* to the poor, rather than just *income*. It is doing so by creating artificial incentives for the poor to occupy space that is either directly or indirectly in great demand for productive use. The full force of city policy can be made clear by imagining that the Pan-American Building were to be condemned by the city so it could be made available as housing for the poor. Nothing like this has happened to my knowledge; yet this is the logical limit of current city policy.

Which aspects of city policy give rise to this interpretation? First, there is the welfare practice of treating housing costs as an extra. Within reason, a household on welfare can compete for housing with no budget constraint; the city will simply pay whatever bill is incurred. Thus, space, which in its current condition or more likely through clearance or renovation would be attractive to firms or their employees wishing to locate in the city, is likely to be retained in the "poverty" market. Instead of deriving maximum value from the property and taxing that value to subsidize poor people to live elsewhere where the alternative uses are not so productive, the city, in effect, transfers assets to the poor, which they are not able to use anywhere nearly as productively. The net social loss is large and unambiguous.

The policy not only fails on the first criterion but its failure on the second is equally apparent. Paradoxically, the space which is most valuable to the potential producer, e.g., in Manhattan, is least relevant to the welfare recipient in terms of ultimately providing him with job opportunity and wages to displace welfare benefits. If the welfare recipient could be induced to seek cheaper space elsewhere, thus preserving a vital productive asset, he could, at the same time, increase the probability of locating closer to the relevant potential employer who is compelled by the nature of his business also to seek out cheaper space.

Again, to bring the point home, let us imagine the (politically) impossible: the city of New York derives revenue from its own industry to subsidize the co-location of low-skill jobs and workers in open tracts in the suburbs. But failing this, can we justify the indiscriminate use of space within the city for anti-poverty purposes?

The illogic of this policy is reinforced by the city's housing policy, specifically, rent control. To begin with, rent control is a very inefficient anti-poverty policy for the simple reason that 45 percent of the occupants of rent-controlled housing are not poor [(7) Lowry, 1970]. Viewed as a tax on the rich landlord, rent control is deficient in the sense that landlords can escape the tax through disinvestment. But what is most relevant to the issue at hand is the effect that rent control has on relative prices. Rent control confers a far greater bargain on the occupant in Manhattan than it does in other boroughs of the city. Median rents for controlled housing hardly vary from borough to borough ($21.80–$26.90 per room per month) whereas median rents for uncontrolled housing vary substantially ($30.00–over $50.00 per room per month), suggesting that rent control conceals the relative opportunity cost of space within the city.

The very high figure for Manhattan attests to the ongoing validity of a Manhattan location in the private sector despite all the heralded pressures to suburbanize. There is every reason to suspect that the city could enjoy greater private output and greater public welfare if its scarce resources—mainly space—were more strategically employed. At the same time, the resolution of the labor market imbalance might better be served in the long run by such policies.

NET IMPACT AND FUTURE PROSPECTS

Despite the widespread interest in the economic welfare of the central city, there are no standard data sources that permit easy calculation of comparative rates of growth of employment except for manufacturing, wholesale, retail, and a category called "Selected Services" in the U.S. Census. These four categories account for only slightly more than half of total employment. More comprehensive measures have been developed for a limited number of areas for selected time periods by painstaking research [(2) Birch, 1970; (6) Lewis, 1969; (8) Noll, 1970].[3]

[3]In the New York Metropolitan Region Study, for example, estimates were developed for New York City, covering all categories of employment. Similar estimates have been developed for other areas in connection with special studies of these areas. The most comprehensive attempt to go beyond the readily available sources is that of Wilfred Lewis, Jr., in an unpublished paper entitled "Urban Growth and Suburbanization of Employment—Some New Data."

Both the standard sources and the special studies show a very mixed picture as between areas and as between time periods if we look only at the absolute growth of employment in the central city. When, however, we compare the central city to the rest of the metropolitan area and control for industrial mix,[4] the trend to the suburbs is rather persistent and pervasive. There are also some interesting surprises. For example, in a study of 12 metro areas over the period 1953–1965 [(6) Lewis, 1969] the author found that New York City, which grew very slowly, experienced less suburban competition than places like Atlanta, Denver, and Washington, D.C., which grew much more rapidly in absolute terms.

The pattern of national growth was found to be favorable to the growth of central city employment in every case but one, as suggested above in *Dynamics I*. Also, while the suburbs grew faster than the central cities in all industrial categories, the suburban drift was more pronounced in manufacturing and retail trade than in the service sectors, as suggested in *Dynamics II*. When the national economy is growing rapidly, the favorable effect of national growth tends to outweigh the unfavorable impact of competition from the suburbs.

What will happen to employment in the central city in future decades? *Dynamics I* should continue to operate with considerable force in favor of the central city. The triple trend to white collar, service, and office employment shows no signs of abatement. *Dynamics II* offers considerable ground for speculation. Although the automobile is still chipping away at mass transit patronage and finances in many cities,

[4]That is, we take into account the industrial structure of the city's economy and control for the influence of overall national rates of growth by industry.

there are significant counter-developments. New transit systems are being built, and there is some hope that rail-commuter travel will be put on a more solid basis by federal action. The revolution in differential access wrought by the automobile is irreversible, but we don't see in the cards another revolution with similar effects and small incremental measures in favor of the city are definitely possible.

Dynamics III (A) is the great imponderable. We need more research on the extent to which sophisticated communication devices do, in fact, substitute for face-to-face contact before we can make any assessment of the locational implications of *Dynamics III (A)*. The relevance of *Dynamics III (B)* will wane as goods-handling activities continue to shrink as a share of the total economy. The rural-to-urban shift that underlies *Dynamics III (C)*, the 1970 Census already tells us, is less of a factor in shaping the demographic characteristic of metropolitan areas. As for *Dynamics IV*, I see no reason why it should not continue to work in favor of lower densities.

What all this adds up to is that the city will most likely continue to lose competitively to the suburbs, but the aggregate demand for labor in the city will be sustained by overall national growth and the favorable "mix" aspects of that growth. To the extent that we continue to rely on local revenues to finance city needs, extreme caution is called for to protect the goose that lays the golden egg.

REFERENCES

(1) Armstrong, R. B. *The Office Industry.* New York: Regional Plan Association, 1970, Final Pre-Publication draft.

(2) Birch, D. L. *The Economic Future of City and Suburb.* New York: Committee for Economic Development, 1970.

(3) Hoover, E. M. and Vernon, R. *Anatomy of a Metropolis.* Cambridge: Harvard Univ. Press, 1959.

(4) _____. *The Location of Economic Activity.* New York: McGraw-Hill, 1963.

(5) _____. "The Evolving Form and Organization of the Metropolis," in Perloff, H. S. and Wing, L., Jr., eds. *Issues in Urban Economics.* Baltimore, Md.: Johns Hopkins Press, 1968.

(6) Lewis, W., Jr. *Urban Growth and Suburbanization of Employment.* Some New Data, Unpublished, Revised Draft, 1969, available through Mr. Lewis at *National Planning Association.*

(7) Lowry, I.S. *Rental Housing in New York City.* Volume 1. *Confronting the Crisis.* New York: New York City Rand Institute, 1970.

(8) Noll, R. *Metropolitan Employment and Population: Distribution and the Conditions of Urban Poor.* Washington, D.C.: The Brookings Institution, 1970 (Reprint).

(9) Segal, M. *Wages in the Metropolis.* Cambridge: Harvard Univ. Press, 1959.

(10) Vernon, R. *The Changing Economic Function of the Central City.* New York: Committee For Economic Development, 1959.

KEY CONCEPTS

capital accumulation

capital saving

communication technology

economies of agglomeration

economies of concentration

industrial mix

specialization

transport technology

PART *3*

ZONING, GROWTH CONTROLS, AND CITY SIZE

One of the most important issues confronting urban policymakers is land-use regulation and control. One common device to control land-use decisions is municipal zoning, which has been employed in varying degrees in U.S. cities since colonial times. Originally, the purpose of zoning was to control or prohibit negative spillover effects, such as noise, blight, or offensive odors. Massachusetts passed a law in 1692 that authorized towns "to assign places in each town, where least offensive, for slaughter houses, still houses, and houses for drying tallow and currying leather." Except for Houston, Texas, zoning is practiced today in all major U.S. cities.

In principle, municipal zoning may prevent irrational land-use patterns and, therefore, may improve allocative efficiency. In practice, however, zoning itself often results in serious inefficiencies. The rationale underlying zoning is that a city can be segregated into zones of homogeneous land uses to prevent "lower" land uses—such as commercial establishments—from harming "higher" uses—such as single-family homes. But this approach may prohibit commercial uses that benefit, as well as those that harm, residential areas. The principle that all "lower" land uses impose negative externalities on single-family homes has not been supported by empirical research.

Another inefficiency may also occur because of fiscal zoning, a zero-sum game often played by separate jurisdictions within a metropolitan area. Each jurisdiction attempts to maximize its own revenue, even at the expense of neighboring jurisdictions. Therefore, each jurisdiction tends to restrict land uses to activities that produce high property-tax revenue, low demands on public services, or both. Because businesses ordinarily make few demands on public services (schools, roads, police, etc.) compared to residences, fiscal zoning leads to overzoning for commercial and industrial uses. Moreover, since expensive homes pay more property taxes, fiscal zoning encourages them while discouraging lower-income housing and mobile homes. Fiscal zoning overallocates resources into land-intensive commercial and industrial developments and expensive residential housing at the expense of moderate- and lower-priced housing.

The selection by Walter Block attempts to show that zoning is not necessary to guide land into the best uses. Block argues that in the absence of zoning, natural market forces would bring about fairly orderly land-use patterns, partly because private legal covenants would supplant much public zoning. The free-market system would operate more efficiently if many of the wasteful encumbrances associated with public zoning were removed. Block cites substantial evidence for his arguments, including the case of Houston, Texas, the only major U.S. city without zoning. Block does not argue that private zoning is a panacea, capable of resolving all externality conflicts. The real issue is not which approach to zoning—public or private—is ideal, but rather which one creates the least amount of chaos and waste and which one is more equitable.

While public zoning originally was introduced as a device to resolve externality conflicts, it has been employed increasingly during recent years as a tool to suppress growth. Urban areas have stopped identifying growth with prosperity. Concerns about spillover effects, especially environmental concerns, have led an increasingly large number of cities to perceive growth as more detrimental than beneficial. The case for intervention recognizes the fact that growth may have adverse, communitywide effects on population densities, traffic congestion, real-estate prices, land-use patterns, and local tax burdens.

The danger of suppressing economic growth, thereby restricting the mobility of resources, is that the economy may become increasingly inefficient over time and that living standards may decline. Daniel Orr analyzes the causes and effects of rapid growth using Orange County, California as a case study. Orr applies traditional tools of microeconomics, which are well suited to illuminating the dramatic changes and economic conflicts that swept Orange County. Although Orange County has become one of the most productive regions anywhere in the world, the adverse environmental changes that have occurred there have helped to inspire opposition to further growth both locally and elsewhere.

Robert H. Nelson analyzes the methods and effects of local-government land-use regulations. As Nelson shows, one of the principal effects of growth control is to harm less well-off people by raising their housing costs. Opportunistic suburban communities have discovered the laws of supply and demand, according to Nelson, and these communities have found environmental protection to be a convenient way to hide their real intention: exclusionary zoning. By imposing minimum lot sizes or maximum densities or by requiring some land to be left as "open space," zoning drives up the price of houses, land, and apartment rents. The end result, whether intentional or not, is to reduce the number of apartment dwellers and the poor who can afford to live in the area.

Fiscal-impact analysis is an analytical tool that allows city officials to estimate the likely effects of proposed developments—residential, commercial, or industrial—on local-government revenues and expenditures. Thomas Muller and Grace Dawson provide an overview of this technique. The effect of growth on expected city costs and revenues is an important aspect of new projects. However, the narrow perspective of fiscal-impact analysis ignores the overall benefits (such as new employment) to the community as well as the total costs (such as traffic congestion).

An implicit assumption in many public-policy discussions is that an ideal city size exists. Local restrictions on growth, for example, must have in mind some ideal city size beyond which the quality of life begins to decline. Using the tools of microeconomics, William Alonso examines the issue of whether an optimum city size exists. He compares public-service costs as well as other social costs of alternative city sizes with the economic benefits of higher productivity and income. He concludes that there are several different sizes that can be considered "optimum" depending upon whether a national or local viewpoint is taken. Other analysts have concluded that there is clearly a minimum, or threshold, size of city necessary for economic self-sufficiency, and that there may well be a maximum size of city beyond which urban diseconomies are excessive, but that no single optimum city size can be identified theoretically or empirically.

DANIEL ORR

8 Who Took the Orange Trees Out of Orange County?

Few American cities have experienced economic growth and change on the dramatic scale of those in California. Daniel Orr, of Virginia Polytechnic Institute and State University, analyzes the causes of rapid development in Orange County, California, but the analysis is applicable to any rapidly growing metropolitan area. Orr also outlines the effects of development on land and housing markets. One of the unique aspects of his analysis is the attempt to identify the various groups that are either benefited or harmed by development.

THE "EVIL" OF ECONOMIC DEVELOPMENT

Because of improved transportation, increased job opportunity, and the attractions of climate and environment, immigrants have, since the Depression and World War II, wrought truly fantastic changes upon the sunny slopes and fertile valleys of California. Nowhere are the changes more visible or more dramatic than in Orange County.

In 1930, a single two-lane highway wound down the coast of Southern California, connecting the region's metropolis with Mexico. Los Angeles was certainly a major city—a few years earlier, it had passed Detroit to become the fourth largest city in the nation, with a population of just over 1.2 million. However, to the south, the only semblance of a city was at

Condensed from Daniel Orr, *Property, Markets, and Government Intervention* (Glenview, Ill.: Scott, Foresman, 1976). Reprinted with permission.

San Diego, where some 150,000 residents basked in the sun beside a spectacular harbor, and devoted themselves mainly to the business of the United States Navy and to the entertainment of visitors from Los Angeles.

The drive between the two cities was an experience: miles of untouched seacoast, thousand-foot hills hugging the shore, and an electric blue sky. On a side trip across the coastal hills that stretch from Newport Beach to Capistrano, one could visit a pristine valley bordered on the east by the mile-high rise of the Santa Ana range. Scattered through the north end of the valley were trees—the orange groves that gave the county its name. The coastal communities of the county were idyllic—Newport Beach, Laguna Beach, San Juan Capistrano, San Clemente—all picturesque, isolated retreats for the vacationer, the artist, the retired. Since then, what has happened?

Freeways, tract after tract of monotonously similar new homes, shopping centers, dragstrips, a major league ballpark, Disneyland, California State University. Fullerton and the University of California, Irvine have all happened. The beauty and seclusion and charm and clear air have been transformed into a mess that is increasingly hard to distinguish from any of the smog-blanketed suburban jungles surrounding Chicago, or Houston, or Washington, or you name the city.

Some numerical evidence may help you to grasp the profound nature of change west of the Santa Ana Mountains... In 1930, Orange County was home to 118,674 people. A total of 63,803 acres were planted in citrus trees, which yielded a crop valued at $41,636 million. By 1970, population had surged to 1.420 million (more than a tenfold increase); citrus cultivation declined to 15,360 acres, and the crop value was $12,551 million. If the dollar value of the citrus crop is corrected to reflect general price-level changes, the drop in crop value is far more dramatic—in constant dollars of 1970 purchasing power, the 1930 crop would have been valued at $101,255 million.

There are numerous other counties in the United States that show substantially the same pattern of explosive growth: Fulton (Georgia), Nassau (New York), Arlington (Virginia), Du Page (Illinois), Maricopa (Arizona) are a few that have developed along similar lines since World War II. All are part of a pattern that is of increasing concern to civic and conservation groups. In the view of such groups, more and more open land is destroyed forever to no good purpose, and in nearly every instance, at the core of the expansion is a great central city, becoming progressively more decayed and dispirited and dangerous.

SCARCITY AND CHANGE IN ORANGE COUNTY

The rhetoric of the concerned reflects the depth of their concern. In Orange County, would it not be better to go on raising oranges? Think of the ravaged beauty, the steadily increasing problem of smog, the annoyance of congestion and crowding! Think of the unemployment and hardship wrought upon the most disadvantaged of socioeconomic groups, the agricultural laborers! Must we continue to rob future generations of their heritage by sacrificing our scenic treasure on the altar of profit? We only do so to benefit the big tract builders and big highway builders, and the cement and lumber monopolists who supply them.

Fortunately, economics is useful in understanding, explaining, and evaluating processes of change and accompanying conflicts of economic interest like the ones that are unfolding in Orange County. Economics teaches us that a central problem in society is *scarcity*—not enough clean air, or open space, or high-salaried jobs, or beautiful and comfortable homes to make everyone happy. Noneconomists (and indeed, even some who call themselves economists) are continually offering us simple explanations of the observed events in Orange County, explanations which usually run in terms of too many people, or the greed of a powerful and ruthless few. Experience reveals that the attempt to provide comprehensive explanations of complex social events in such simple terms is almost sure to be unsuccessful. Only when situations of conflict and change are approached with some coherent and proven perspective can understanding be expected to develop, and understanding is

necessary. Without it, the actions of a concerned citizenry can do harm instead of
good. . . .

How do individuals respond to scarcity?
We will assume that everyone who has a
stake or a role in the changes that are taking place in Orange County seeks to make
himself better off, to enhance his own subjective sense of well-being to the greatest
possible extent. Society denies an individual the use of naked force or power in the
pursuit of his own interest. It is the
essence of a civilized social order that an
individual cannot coerce others in order to
obtain what he wants. Two important
processes—economic and political—are
accepted by society as instruments by
which individuals can try to move events
in directions that they deem best for themselves. Both processes are concerned in
important ways with the resolution of the
conflicting and competing claims of different individuals for scarce resources.

The most important economic process is
one whereby claims are settled through a
system of voluntary and impersonal interaction called the *market exchange* process.
We will understand better what is going
on in Orange County after seeing how the
market exchange process affects events
there. Our first analytic undertaking, then,
will be informally to define and describe
the mechanism of market action, with reference to the provision of housing in
Orange County. . . .

FACTORS AFFECTING
DEMAND AND SUPPLY

A number of important considerations will
determine the demand for housing in
Orange County. For example, the price of
housing elsewhere in Southern California
will affect the number of people who
search for a place to live in Orange
County. If for some reason housing
becomes relatively cheap in the San Fernando Valley, in the north of Los Angeles,
then many Los Angeles commuters will
choose to settle there instead of in Orange
County. This leaves a smaller group of
potential purchasers or renters to bid for
housing in Orange County; and the
demand curve for housing will shift as
shown in Figure 1, from D to D'. A lower
price of housing elsewhere means a
reduced demand for housing in Orange
County. It is not necessary that *all* potential
buyers or renters of Orange County housing have the choice of settling in the San
Fernando Valley; if *some* potential Orange
County buyers have that choice, then the
price of San Fernando Valley housing will
affect the demand for Orange County
housing.

A second factor that affects the Orange

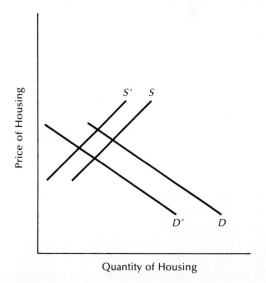

Figure 1.

County housing demand is the income of the population of potential residents. The higher that income, the greater the amount available to spend on housing, and the higher the housing demand. A drop in income will lead to a demand shift like the movement from D to D' in Figure 1.

Finally, the weather, atmosphere, and climate of Orange County will affect the demand for housing there. As the county becomes more smoggy relative to other nearby areas, the more likely it is that at any given housing price, a potential resident will choose to settle elsewhere, or that a current resident will move elsewhere. An increase in smog in Orange County can also cause a demand shift like the D to D' shift shown in Figure 1. In general, the *alternatives* confronting residents and potential residents will be decisive in determining how strongly they value the prospect of life in Orange County.

A similar story may be told about the potential suppliers of housing—the owners of homes already built, and the developers and builders. If development work in San Diego to the south or the San Fernando Valley to the north is expected to pay off better than new housing for Orange County, then the resources necessary to provide new housing are more likely to be used in those other areas. If the price level for housing in Orange County is low relative to housing prices elsewhere, then owners are not as likely to be induced to sell out in favor of moving elsewhere. Thus, housing prices elsewhere will affect the supply of housing in Orange County, as well as the demand. An increase in prices elsewhere will reduce supply, shown as the movement from S to S' in Figure 1.

The cost of resources used in providing housing also will affect the housing supply.

Higher resource prices lead to a supply reduction, like S to S'. ...

THE EFFECTS OF DEVELOPMENT: THE BENEFITED AND THE INJURED

When you want to know *why*, ask: *who gains*?

That Sicilian proverb, freely translated, leads us into a consideration of why Orange County is developing, and how the forces that produce development work through the market process. Obviously, to repeat a contention of the conservationists who deplore events in Orange County, highway contractors and tract builders do reap significant financial benefits from the great stimulus that development affords to their lines of activity. They in fact stand among the groups most obviously benefited. However, on the basis of the supply and demand analysis that we just completed, we may conclude that the largest group to realize financial benefits from development, in terms of the number of persons involved, is composed of Southern California renters and home buyers. A part of this group benefits in a direct and obvious way—they rent or purchase in Orange County, and their decision to live there reveals that they regard it as superior to any alternative living site they can afford. But people moving into the San Fernando Valley, 40 miles to the north, also benefit from the availability of housing in Orange County. This is a result of the fact that some people who settle in Orange County would otherwise have bid up housing prices in the San Fernando Valley.

We see, then, that home buyers in Southern California as a group are made financially better off by development. Does it follow in a symmetric way that home *owners* and especially home *sellers* are made financially *worse* off? There are two effects of development to consider in answering this question.

1. First, anyone selling an old house finds himself in competition with the sellers of new houses. The price received for the old house is lower than it would be if no new houses were available. If somehow all other aspects of development could continue, but the supply of new houses could be cut off, then sellers of old houses would be able to get much higher prices.

2. But second, there are other aspects of development that we cannot ignore: new roads transform once-inaccessible outlying areas into places from which people may easily commute; and better schools, hospitals, and shopping facilities develop. These aspects of development increase the value of old houses in the developing area.

Thus, we cannot judge *a priori* whether development leads to higher or lower values of existing housing, because the depressing effect of competition from new housing works against the enhancing effect of the better services that are made available in the area in the course of development. In the case of Orange County, the prices of older houses have risen dramatically over time. The question of interest is: would they have risen even *more* in the absence of development? If the answer to that question is yes, then owners of old houses would have been better off financially if development had been avoided.

Another large group that benefits from Orange County's development consists of businessmen who serve the residents of the new housing in the County, and

employers who operate establishments within commuting distance. The incomes of businessmen are significantly increased; and the employers find that their task of attracting new employees (and hanging onto old ones) is made easier by the availability of more (and consequently cheaper) housing in the vicinity of their operations.

Fairly large groups, then, are benefited (but only in a small way, in some cases) by the development of Orange County. Who is made clearly worse off?

As a first instance, it is tempting to point to the agricultural laborers who had previously derived a substantial part of their livelihood from picking in the citrus groves. Their array of employment alternatives is reduced; they are forced farther afield and to compete more vigorously to find jobs. It follows that their incomes are reduced and they are made worse off, *if they all continue to work as agricultural laborers.* What other occupation could they turn to? For one, the new houses will predictably have gardens, and where there are gardens there are jobs for nurserymen and gardeners. These lines of work require different and more diverse skills than do fruit picking; and they require some *physical capital* (equipment used to produce a good or service: tools, spray equipment, mowers, and a truck are capital to a gardener). However, by apprenticeship to men already in these trades, and by frugality (or perhaps a lucky borrowing opportunity) the requisite skills and equipment can be acquired by some of the more fortunate among the former pickers.

What signals light up to indicate that new workers will be rewarded in these new lines of activity? Do the builders and developers, with great foresight, anticipate the future "needs" of their customers for gardening services, and seek to provide an adequate supply of gardeners in advance? By what mechanism are gardening and nursery services made available? The answer is "the market provides": in this case, markets for ornamental plantings and garden care. When new homeowners begin to install and tend their landscaping, their demands are felt as higher prices for plantings and gardening services. New nurseries are opened in the area, and gardeners take on helpers who are enabled to learn the trade. This all happens because it has become profitable.

Thus, it is not clear a priori whether development will benefit or injure the agricultural laborers of Orange County. If the effect of suburbanization is to increase the demand for "unskilled" or "semi-skilled" workers, the farm workers may be made better off as a group. If, instead, job opportunities are reduced by the change from citrus ranch to suburb, the agricultural workers are injured (displaced geographically, and subjected to lower income).

What about long-term, old-time residents of Orange County? Development subjects them to smog, congestion, and reduced natural beauty. Are they clearly injured? We have already seen that any property they hold within the county may rise in value owing to development activity, and to the extent that this happens, the wounds of urbanization are in part compensated by financial benefits. But for many, no solace is to be had from market processes. In the face of an increasingly less pleasant environment and higher rents, they may feel compelled to move on.

That brings us to a very interesting concerned group, the orange growers. Interesting, because they are faced with strong pressures to relocate or find a different livelihood; but at the same time the value of their land is growing rapidly. Economic

pressures on the fruit growers stem from two sources. One is the market (higher prices can be obtained if they wish to sell their property), and the other is political in nature. With suburbanization, land values rise, a reflection of the fact that land is now quite desirable for use in housing, as well as for its current use, agriculture. As the value of a grower's land rises, in a very real sense it becomes more costly for him to continue producing fruit on it. For by persisting as a fruit grower, he passes up an opportunity to sell out and thereby obtain a sum of money sufficient to increase his economic well-being greatly. As an alternative to continued fruit farming in Orange County, he could sell his valuable grove, use a part of the proceeds to buy a similar grove in northern San Diego County, and have considerable money left over.

But consider the case of a sentimental grower, who is so devoted to his own home, land, and way of life that no reasonable price can induce him to move, even just down the road to San Diego County. The high price he could get for his land will not induce him to move; but he almost certainly will feel that second type of pressure accompanying development, the one that comes from collective (or political) action. As land values rise, county and municipal real estate taxes will rise also, in order to pay for all those public services—such as schools, streets, and sewers—that are made necessary by population growth. One consequence of the higher taxes is to force the sentimental grower to stop growing fruit on land that is highly prized for housing development. And so he finds that the value of his property has increased as a result of adjacent suburban development. The array of alternatives open to him has also increased; but the alternative that may be most precious to him—that of remaining where he is—becomes less and less feasible with time, owing to higher and higher taxes.

Finally, we should ask about the effects of development on the most interesting group of all—ourselves, the ordinary citizens—the people who have no economic stake in Orange County, but drive through from time to time perhaps; or who used to enjoy the abalone diving near Dana Point, having spent numerous weekends there in quieter times. Nearly all of us prefer orange groves to smog and billboards, and so the process and result of development seems a horror story. What recourse do we—the casual, or mildly interested, or totally engaged bystanders—have whereby we can make our preferences felt? Without property rights in the county, our only recourse is political. We can advocate laws and statutes to be directed at such problems as pollution of air and water, and the size and placement of billboards along public highways. Additionally, we bystanders can hope that the county and its municipalities will enact ordinances to stipulate building standards; design streets and highways to prevent avoidable traffic chaos; and provide for public parks and beaches. We can further hope that all these state and local laws, statutes, ordinances, and provisions will do some good in terms of the purposes for which they are conceived. But to keep the land as we may remember it, we can do virtually nothing.

INDIRECT EFFECTS OF DEVELOPMENT: AN EXAMPLE

To illustrate how pervasive and widespread the effects of market action are, suppose (as is true) that the newer areas of Orange County are virtually all white in terms of the racial composition of residents. Does the development of Orange County then have any positive impact on the welfare of excluded ethnic groups such as blacks? We must recognize that if blacks are excluded arbitrarily on grounds of race, then they will feel less well off; injured by being excluded, and being told that their freedom of choice is restricted. But even if some minorities are totally excluded from the newer areas, the development of Orange County will convey some *economic* benefit to members of the excluded group. The benefits will be the result of an indirect process, in which *all* housing in Southern California becomes somewhat cheaper, as people respond to the available new housing in Orange County. Fewer whites will be *competing* with blacks (bidding against them) for housing in Los Angeles, because some whites will elect to buy or rent in Orange County. The reduction in the number of whites bidding against blacks means that blacks will pay less for housing in Los Angeles than they would have to pay if Orange County were not being developed. The benefits of Orange County development would be more significant for blacks if exclusion were not practiced; but even if blacks are excluded or feel excluded from direct participation, the market process conveys to them some measure of indirect benefit from Orange County development. The market process conveys a benefit, in the form of lower housing prices in other nearby locations, even to groups of people who suffer the injury of exclusion. Stated more abstractly: one need not be a potential trader in a particular market in order to benefit from the action of that market. This is true because markets affect each other: a change in the price observed in one market can affect the price that will prevail in another market. This is the same point that was made earlier when it was asserted that buyers of housing in the San Fernando Valley derive some small benefit from Orange County development. . . .

THE SPIRIT OF INTERVENTION

We must be careful to avoid dismissing as sentimentalists all those individuals who express dismay over Orange County's development. The foregoing remarks came close to suggesting that all critics are people who long only for "what was" when they view "what is." Nostalgic or sentimental observers are numerous and vocal, but they aren't the most important critics of the development process. Another group (let us call them interventionists) look at "what is," and instead of marking down unpleasant events as inevitable consequences of "progress," they speculate on ways of achieving progress with less destruction of such valuable goods as clean air and natural landscape. The criticisms that interventionists offer take several forms: (1) there are aesthetic as well as economic and technical dimensions to efficient operation. Thus, highways shouldn't slash through hills, even if routing them around entails longer travel times for highway users. (2) Individuals should be compelled to consider common aspects of their own private property—aspects that affect the well-being of many people in subtle ways. Thus, a Main Street men's clothing salesman should not locate a thatched-roof replica of Shakespeare's birthplace next door to a starkly modern glass-and-steel bank office, even though such a choice would be extremely appropriate as a setting for the sale of men's tweeds. (3) Individuals who control the use of resources are greedy and myopic. The result is that too much is spent in advertising the new

houses built by a handful of developers in Orange County. The houses that get built aren't actually needed, and the consequence of the whole process is that we use up the precious resource of open land without due concern for the needs of future generations.

. . . Is there any hope that our customary methods of resource allocation can accommodate the criticisms? Will that accommodation be made spontaneously through the actions of individuals if a sufficiently large part of the population can be educated to understand the critics? Or will it be necessary to change the allocation process, as, for example, by more direct government control, in order to effect the recommended reforms? Many people who would like to see a better outcome from the processes of allocation suggest that direct government participation in the allocation process is necessary if a better outcome is indeed to be obtained. Their view should not be accepted without careful consideration of alternative possibilities: it often turns out that government involvement in the processes of allocation is neither necessary nor beneficial.

It must be recognized that intervention is a process that can lead to general and widespread harm unless it is intelligently justified, designed, and carried out. . . . To perceive a problem, and to be willing to undertake its remedy, is not enough. It is further necessary to know what we are doing if intervention is to result in benefit. In forecasting the benefits that may be realized from government involvement in allocation, it is interesting to trace the effects of existing government policies. When we do this, we often find that effects differ significantly from what is intended. Programs and policies intended for social betterment may work in the opposite direction. To consider only one example: the highway construction program, conceived as a device that contributes to the convenience of the population at large, is in fact an important contributor to the problem of smog. In recent years we have witnessed the passage of government anti-smog programs, in response to a problem that is as severe as it is only because of earlier government programs. It may be worthwhile to wonder in advance what unanticipated secondary effects will arise out of the anti-smog programs. . . .

Despite persistently incorrect predictions of environmental disaster, and unfulfilled objectives of greater equality, people today more than ever appear to be convinced that land use controls are necessary for noble purposes of conservation and equalization. Why?

One answer contains two major components or dimensions. First, people are mistrustful of unadministered mechanisms. It is the miracle of social order that occasionally unplanned and unadministered institutions evolve spontaneously, with great net benefit to nearly everyone. The most important of these institutions is the market; but it is hard to convince any typical or average bystander that good things emerge from unimpeded market action, particularly where the use of land is involved. There is no way, most observers feel, that a decent outcome can eventuate from the workings of selfish motives through an undisciplined mechanism. In short, there is considerable ignorance; and it is in the interest of academics, intellectuals, and politicians to foster mistrust and ignorance regarding uncontrolled institutions like markets: they, after all, are the potential controllers.

Second, much of mankind apparently is very "conservative" (in the sense of nostal-

gic, or resistant to change). Much of the apparent larger concern for the environment or for the fate of the poor which is raised against plans for development is a simple rationalization of resistance to change in familiar surroundings.

What does all of this bode for the development of areas like Orange County? At this writing, attempts are under way (via the creation of a California Coastal Commission) to protect the entire California coastline from "unplanned, chaotic, ruinous" development. Myriad interests are to be served by the coastal controllers. Conflicting interests among residential, agricultural, conservationist, and recreational claims are to be resolved in the public interest. Wetlands are to be preserved in the interest of fostering numerous lesser animal and plant species; and cleanliness, beauty, and accessibility for use are to be preserved for future generations.

Is such a plan workable? Experience elsewhere with zoning and other far less ambitious control programs suggests that (a) the bureaucracy which will be founded will add to the cost of doing business in, or simply of living in, the zone of the Commission's control; persons of limited vision and understanding (albeit of the best will) will be put in charge of disposing of matters and issues that they barely comprehend; (b) individuals will be encouraged to mount support among other individuals in coming before the Commission with plans for use of the coast of benefit to themselves, and the overriding consideration in determining whether they will be successful is the number of the right kinds of votes that they represent; and (c) *at best*, the visible effects of the Commission, compared to what would have happened in its absence, will be negligible.

But what about the poor? Won't the

efforts of the Commission to prevent urban sprawl, preserve farm land, and extend recreational opportunity help them? It appears, in fact, that the poor are the group least helped (or most injured) by such control programs. The imposition of land use controls, and the erection of barriers of bureaucratic harassment to developers, slows down the rate of increase in the supply of housing, and leads to a higher price that the poor must pay for this important good. (It matters little that the coastal zone housing typically is costly, and hence requires high income for occupancy. Persons moving into new coastal housing vacate housing elsewhere, which is occupied by others who vacate housing; and so on, until low-income people are given a wider array of more affordable choices.) Controls also slow down the rate at which more demanding and better-paying jobs are created. In short, to the extent that such intervention is impelled by egalitarian sentiment, it is misguided.

The record of past experience, then, makes it appear that large-scale intervention in land use, motivated by concern over the impact of developmental "destruction" on the environment and on the poorer members of the society, will retard the creation of privately owned wealth without distributing existing wealth more equally; and it is also likely to delay or even to prevent finding the best patterns of resource use for the future in the protected areas.

We can, of course, make planning and control more palatable and successful by agreeing that it is planners' preferences and not individual preferences that should be served; once that has been achieved, it will remain only to eliminate all competition and dissent among planners, and tranquility, harmony, and the maximum of social welfare will be ours. *Any* problem can be thus defined right out of existence, by a citizenry willing to pay a high enough price.

KEY CONCEPTS

market competition

market exchange process

political allocation process

scarcity

ROBERT H. NELSON
_____

9 New Local Growth Controls

Robert H. Nelson, a member of the economics staff at the Office of Policy Analysis of the U.S. Department of the Interior, discusses the purposes, methods, and effects of growth controls by local governments and surveys the legal status of various growth-control restrictions.

LOCAL OPPOSITION TO GROWTH

In recent years, intense local opposition to further growth has sprung up in many communities, in substantial part as a result of the environmental movement. Environmental concerns have caused new development to be perceived as less beneficial (or more damaging) by communities; it is therefore less likely to be permitted. Communities have become much more concerned about avoiding air and water pollution, noise, and other adverse consequences of growth. Forests, fields, farmland, parks, and other open spaces free from development have become more valued. Attention focused on the general quality of the environment has stimulated new planning proposals. Because a community cannot build itself, it must depend upon development projects presented in accordance with its plans. The more exact and detailed the plans are, the longer they take to prepare and the longer the wait is

likely to be before project proposals consistent with the plans can be expected.

The environmental movement has also directly challenged the traditional American regard for continual economic growth and the related willingness to accept the verdict of market demands. In the past, many communities accepted a certain amount of development that was to some degree detrimental. In many cases, communities realized that there were certain disadvantages, but because of the overriding consideration of economic growth, the detrimental consequences had to be significant—and there was always a substantial amount of that kind also—before it would be excluded. With the validity of market verdicts and the desirability of economic growth now in question, many communities have become much less willing to accept growth that involves even very minor fiscal and social disadvantages. The practical consequence is that large amounts of previously acceptable development are now unacceptable.

In England, there has been a long tradition of opposition to any growth that would alter the open countryside, perhaps because land is much scarcer there. In 1962, Delafons could observe (in something of an overstatement even then): "Despite ... rampant growth, it is very rare in America to encounter any antipathy to new development. Quite the opposite is usually the case."[1] But, by 1973, the Task Force on Land Use and Urban Growth reported:

> There is a new mood in America. Increasingly, citizens are asking what urban growth will add to the quality of their lives. ...
>
> Today, the repeated questioning of what was once generally unquestioned—that growth is good, that growth is inevitable—is so widespread that it seems to us to signal a remarkable change in attitudes in this nation.[2]

Under the influence of the "new mood," communities are now looking at the costs and benefits of growth with a skeptical eye. In the past, the consequences of development were often only very roughly evaluated. But with new questioning attitudes, a number of communities have introduced modern management techniques of analysis in order better to evaluate the impact of development.

The fiscal consequences of development are receiving close scrutiny under the formal procedures of fiscal-impact analysis. Such an analysis often shows that new residential development will cost a community more than the revenue it will generate. In some instances, even quite expensive residential projects have adverse fiscal consequences. One 1970 fiscal analysis, done for the suburban community of Barrington, Illi-

nois, showed that the development of a 50-acre parcel of land with $40,000 homes on one-half-acre lots would result in annual school costs to Barrington almost $100,000 more than would be generated in school revenues.[3] Even more surprisingly, the study asserted that the development of $100,000 homes on five-acre lots would fall just short of breaking even. The only residential development that showed a positive impact on education finance was apartment development. Mainly because fewer school children would occupy them, high-rise apartments with primarily one- and two-bedroom units could be expected to produce an annual educational surplus of $270,000. Another much-noted fiscal-impact analysis showed that a proposed 800-unit residential development (with some commercial facilities) in a fast-growing suburban area outside of Charlottesville, Virginia, would produce an overall fiscal deficit for local government of more than $100,000 annually.[4]

To determine the overall desirability of development, a community needs a comprehensive environmental-impact analysis. In California, a 1971 Palo Alto–commissioned study attempted to estimate the overall impact of different kinds of development of the foothills section. Fiscal, social, ecological, visual, geological, hydrological, and other impacts were all considered. The study concluded:

> Development at 3 units per acre (the density proposed by Land Resources Corporation) would cost 10 percent less cumulatively over

[1] John Delafons, Land-Use Controls in the United States (Cambridge, Mass.: Joint Center for Urban Studies of the Massachusetts Institute of Technology and Harvard University, 1962), p. 5.

[2] Task Force on Land Use and Urban Growth, The Use of Land: A Citizen's Policy Guide to Urban Growth, ed. William Reilly (New York: Thomas Y. Crowell, 1973), p. 33.

[3] Barton-Aschman Association, Inc., The Barrington, Illinois Area: A Cost-Revenue Analysis of Land Use Alternatives, prepared for the Barrington Area Development Council, February 1970, p. 48.

[4] Thomas Muller and Grace Dawson, The Fiscal Impact of Residential and Commercial Development: A Case Study (Washington, D.C.: Urban Institute, 1972), p. 86.

20 years than City acquisition [by public purchase with funds from bond sales]; but when the bonds were paid off, the continuing cost of the residential development would be far higher. . . .

Other factors weigh more heavily than [public] costs against development [of the area under study]. . . . none of the alternatives studied would have any great social utility except those that include low-moderate income housing (Alternatives 4 and 8) and these would have significant disadvantages in other respects. . . . Any of the development alternatives would do major ecological and visual damage to the area. . . .

In light of all these considerations, it is strongly recommended that the City deny approval to all development proposals in the area below the park and be prepared to purchase the land when necessary to prevent development. . . .[5]

Instead of purchasing the land, Palo Alto chose a less costly and more traditional approach—rezoning the land to ten-acre minimum-lot-size zoning. Predictably, this action was contested in court by property owners in the area.

Communities are increasingly excluding growth for general environmental reasons. The Levitt Corporation was interested in building a $125 million planned community for over 10,000 people in Loudoun County, Virginia, on the outskirts of the Washington, D.C., metropolitan area. When it encountered difficulty in obtaining the required zoning approvals, Levitt offered to pay $900 per dwelling unit to the county to cover public-service costs. With fiscal burdens largely eliminated, Loudoun County, in 1972, still refused the planned community, primarily because of the effects that such a large influx of people would have on the environment of a little-developed county.

Under the new attitudes toward growth, only development for upper-middle or higher-income residents is likely to be welcome in existing moderate-income communities. In high-income, high-quality communities such as Palo Alto, virtually all development, except perhaps a scientific-research park, is likely to be considered undesirable. A 1973 article in the *Christian Science Monitor* reported on the growing inclination in communities across the United States to slow or stop development altogether:

New restrictive laws, zoning actions, moratoriums on building permits, density limitations, size or height limitations, or bans on septic tanks, are sprouting all over. They are accompanied by citizen lawsuits to prevent development. Once-tranquil city council or county commission meetings have become arenas of protest, overflowing with citizens seeking to block new subdivisions or factories or amusement parks.[6]

A 1974 *New York Times* article indicated an accelerating trend: "Growth controls have erupted . . . at a rate that has reached epidemic proportions."[7]

The most intense opposition to rapid rates of development is usually found in transitional communities that have been expanding the most rapidly. Nationally, population increase was 13.3 percent from 1960 to 1970, down substantially from the

---

[5] Livingston and Blayney, *Open Space vs. Development*, Final Report to the City of Palo Alto, 1971, p. 139.

[6] Robert Cahn, "Mr. Developer, Someone Is Watching You," in *Where Do We Grow From Here?* (Boston: Christian Science Publishing Co., 1973), pp. 4–5, reprinted from *Christian Science Monitor*.

[7] Gladwin Hill, "Nation's Cities Fighting to Stem Growth," *New York Times*, July 28, 1974, pp. 1, 30.

18.8 percent between 1950 and 1960.[8] But the forces of growth in the United States do not distribute growth equally among geographic areas or in proportion to existing population; rather, at any moment, expansion is concentrated in areas that have reached a stage where they are ripe for it.

In the 1960s, the most rapidly growing sections of the United States were Florida (its population increased 37.1 percent from 1960 to 1970), followed by California and the rest of the Southwest (26.8 percent), and, largely because of growth of the federal government, Delaware, Maryland, and the District of Columbia (21.2 percent). Given long-standing national trends toward greater metropolitan concentration of population, those metropolitan areas located in growing sections of the country are often faced with particularly rapid growth. The National Commission on Population Growth and the American Future projected that if recent trends were to continue, three major metropolitan areas in Florida could be expected to double in population between 1970 and 2000, the San Diego area would more than double, and the Los Angeles area almost double. Among others, the Denver, Houston, San Francisco–Oakland, Atlanta, Dallas–Ft. Worth, and Washington, D.C. metropolitan areas would each grow by more than 50 percent, compared with a likely national population increase of about 30 percent.

A third critical trend for growth patterns has been the massive population movement from the central cities to the suburbs. Between 1960 and 1970, while central-city population rose by 5 percent, the suburban parts of metropolitan areas grew 25 percent.

Much of suburban development has occurred on metropolitan fringes in communities where population increases of 100 percent or more per decade have been common. For example, in 1930, the Washington, D.C. suburb of Fairfax County, Virginia had had a population of around 25,000 for many years. By 1973, its population had shot up to 530,000. During the decades 1940-50, 1950-60, and 1960-70, population had risen by 141 percent, 158 percent, and 83 percent respectively.

Communities that have introduced new methods of growth control include Ramapo, New York; Boulder, Colorado; Boca Raton, Florida; and Petaluma, California. All are on the fringes of major metropolitan areas and all have had very rapid population increases, rates of 119 percent, 77 percent, 310 percent, and 77 percent, respectively, for the 1960s. Except for Ramapo, all are also located in fast-growing regions of the United States, compounding pressures on metropolitan fringes even in slow-growing sections. Mount Laurel, the community involved in the recent and much-noted New Jersey Supreme Court decision on zoning, had grown 114 percent during the 1960s.

LOCAL GROWTH-CONTROL METHODS

In response to strong popular pressures, many communities with rapid recent expansion have taken steps to restrict further growth.[9] The most widely used method has been to increase the restrictiveness of traditional zoning practices.

---

[8] See U.S. Commission on Population Growth and the American Future, *Population Distribution and Policy*, ed. Sara Mills Mazie, Commission Research Reports, 5 (Washington, D.C., 1972).

[9] For a comprehensive selection of articles on growth controls, see Randall Scott, ed., *Management and Control of Growth*, 1, 2, 3 (Washington, D.C.: Urban Land Institute, 1975).

Communities refuse applications for zoning changes necessary for development that would have been granted earlier, or they enact larger minimum-lot-size requirements. One example occurred in Sanbornton, New Hampshire, which received wide attention when a federal district court upheld the town's actions.[10] Shortly after a developer purchased a tract for 500 vacation homes, Sanbornton rezoned the area to a combination of three- and six-acre minimum-lot sizes, and this prevented its development. With better timing, before any specific development proposal has been received, many other communities have similarly increased minimum-lot-size requirements.

While large lot sizes are an old fixture of restrictive zoning, in a few places these sizes have become astronomical. In 1971, in Marin County, just north of San Francisco, zoning requirements of 60 acres per dwelling unit were created in agricultural areas. Forty-acre minimum-lot sizes were required in Monterey County farther south of San Francisco. Other communities are more directly zoning areas for agriculture, forests, or simply as environmentally too fragile to allow development. Communities are zoning out development altogether throughout flood-endangered areas, confident that this action will be legally sustainable. (A 1973 consultant report on open-space preservation to the town of Medford, New Jersey, proposed extensive flood-plain zoning as the cheapest way of obtaining open spaces.)[11] Some communities are imposing higher minimum-quality standards in addition to minimum-lot sizes. Although eventually defeated in court, in 1970, the town of Glassboro, New Jersey, tried to require swimming pools, tennis courts, air conditioning, and garbage-disposal units, among other features, in apartment units.[12]

Under existing federal and state water-quality standards, a given sewage treatment plant can accommodate only so much development without violating standards for effluent discharge. Many community plants currently fall far short of meeting these standards, a situation that ultimately must be rectified. In such communities, more development would cause a more severe violation. For this reason, a substantial number of communities have imposed restrictions on new development, ranging from limits on the number of building permits or sewer connections per year to total bans until increased sewage-treatment capacity is obtained. Some 1974 estimates of the number of communities with these "sewer moratoria" were 160 in Illinois and Ohio, 40 in Florida, and 74 in New Jersey.[13] A major part of the suburban areas surrounding Washington, D.C., have been under sewer moratoria at one time or another since 1970. While no one seems to have any exact figures, sewer moratoria are clearly being widely employed. In parts of the United States such as Florida, where water is in short supply, water availability limitations have also occasionally served as a reason for restricting growth.

Public control over the sequence and timing of development has been a long-time—although almost entirely unrealized—objective of planners. According to theory, communities should plan installation of

---

[10] Steel Hill Development, Inc. v. Town of Sanbornton, 469 F.2d 956 (1st Cir., 1972).

[11] David Berry and Robert Coughlin, *Economic Implications of Preserving Ecologically Valuable Land in Medford, New Jersey,* A Report to Medford Township, New Jersey, by the Regional Science Research Institute (Philadelphia, 1973).

[12] Molino v. Borough of Glassboro, 116 N.J. 195, 281 A.2d 401 (1971).

[13] See Hill, "Nation's Cities Fighting," p. 30.

roads, sewer lines, and other necessary public facilities according to a schedule for community development. Coordinated with public-facility installation, zoning or subdivision controls would prevent development in areas not yet ready. The pace at which areas are scheduled for development in effect establishes a maximum community-growth rate. In 1969, Ramapo, New York, enacted a controversial ordinance that scheduled areas in the community for development over an 18-year period. A number of other communities are considering similar controls over the sequencing and timing of development, and thus in effect over their rate of growth.

A small number of communities have considered, and at least three have enacted, regulations that explicitly propose to control their number of housing units. The main reason more have not done so has been the possibility that such controls might be declared unconstitutional as amounting to local immigration controls regulating community population levels. But if the courts permit direct housing-unit controls, many more communities almost certainly will adopt them.

In 1972, Boca Raton, Florida, voters enacted a limit of 40,000 to the total number of housing units that could be built in the community. Calculated on the basis of an average rate of 2.5 occupants per unit, that amounts to a total population limit of about 100,000 people. Also in 1972, Petaluma, California, adopted an ordinance that established a maximum limit of 500 new housing units per year, amounting to a maximum of about 1,250 additional people per year. In 1971, Boulder, Colorado, voters nearly enacted a maximum future population limit of 100,000. Then, in 1976 they approved a limit similar to Petaluma's of 450 housing units per year.

While thus far few communities have adopted long-term controls on numbers of housing units, many have enacted temporary moratoria—typically from six months to two years—on granting building permits, or on rezoning approvals. In Orange County, New York, on the fringes of the New York metropolitan area, at least seven of the twenty communities have imposed temporary moratoria of one kind or another on new building permission since 1970. Temporary moratoria have existed in 30 of the 112 communities of New Jersey's Passaic valley. Some of these temporary moratoria are justified by the need for time to increase sewage treatment capacity, others by the need to take stock in order to plan better for future growth.

THE CONSEQUENCES OF NEW RESTRICTIONS ON GROWTH

On the face of it, new growth controls may seem more evenhanded than zoning regulations in their treatment of rich and poor because they do not involve minimum-quality standards. This feature tends to obscure the reality that they have essentially the same purposes and consequences as traditional zoning. If more people would like to live in a community than are allowed to, the resulting supply-demand pressures will drive up the price of local housing. Prices will rise until there is no longer an excess demand for local housing. Housing prices will climb to a level where most individuals cannot afford them, bringing demand for community entry into balance with the tightly restricted supply. Thus, just as in the case of zoning, local growth controls exclude less well-off people by establishing financial barriers to entry that only the better off can surmount.

The results of such supply-demand workings were described in a city-sponsored, comprehensive 1973 study of future growth possibilities in Boulder, Colorado, which examined the implications of four alternative approaches to Boulder's future growth: continuation of current policies, no growth, emphasis on environmental factors, and emphasis on social, cultural, and economic aspects:

The effect of restricted growth (Model II) will probably redistribute income upward from the 1970 level. By 1990, Boulder should be much above the State in percent of high income residents. The unsubsidized poor and lower middle income persons will probably be pressured out of the valley, and, in some instances, possibly out of the county.[14]

Housing price escalations resulting from local growth controls have already begun to be experienced in some areas. In the period from 1970 to 1974, sewer moratoria were in effect for much of the Washington, D.C., metropolitan area. An article in the *Washington Post* reported:

Environmental restrictions, which have helped to reduce the supply of new homes to a record low in the Washington metro area, have finally hit the pocketbooks of consumers in an awesome way.

The average sales price of existing homes sold in Washington jumped to $63,700 in the third quarter of 1975. . . .[15]

New local growth controls add little to the ability to control land use beyond that already established by zoning. For example, in the many communities where discretionary zoning changes have been required to gain entry, it has long been possible precisely to control the rate of community growth. The most significant aspect of local growth controls may be that they have clothed traditional zoning practices in the more respectable language of environmental protection. Local growth controls have been adopted in a number of politically liberal communities where an "exclusionary zoning" policy might have been considered irresponsible but where local "control of growth" seems a more acceptable objective.

The increasingly restrictive administration of zoning and the rapid spread of local growth controls together threaten to create a severe shortage of housing in metropolitan areas of the United States. The children of the post–World War II baby boom are now entering the ages at which households are formed and families begun. Between 1975 and 1985, the number of persons aged 30 to 40 will increase by more than 40 percent. Population composition is shifting toward growing numbers of aged and of single adults who will want their own housing units. Even though the birth rate has slowed down, population is still growing steadily, and the amount of metropolitan housing needed is sure to increase substantially. The Commission on Population Growth and the American Future projected in 1972 that metropolitan population would grow from 144 million in 1970 to 225 million in the year 2000—an increase of more than 50 percent.

Thus, at the same time that regulatory restrictions on the supply of metropolitan land are becoming tighter, housing demands are steadily growing. If reforms are not instituted, it is not only the poor who will suffer from the resulting shortage of housing. Large numbers of young mid-

[14] Boulder Area Growth Study Commission, *Exploring Options for the Future: A Study of Growth in Boulder County*, vol. 1, *Commission Final Report*, (November 1973), p. 80.

[15] Michael Sumichrast, "Area's Existing Home Sales Now Most Expensive in U.S.," *Washington Post*, November 22, 1975, Real Estate Section, p. 1.

dle-class adults and others who are seeking housing will be unable to find anything within their means in the areas they had hoped to live in. A Congressional Budget Office study found that, while median family income had risen by 39 percent from 1970 to 1975, the average price of purchasing a home had risen by more than 60 percent over this period.[16] The Federal Home Loan Bank Board reported that from February, 1975, to February, 1976, the average price of new homes in the United States rose from $38,000 to $43,000—a rate of increase in excess of 10 percent. The "continued rise in the price of buildable land in many metropolitan areas" was stated to be one factor.[17] A 1977 study by the Harvard-MIT Joint Center for Urban Studies indicated that if current trends continue the average house may cost an extraordinary $78,000 by 1981.[18] As law professor Arnold Reitze remarked of new restrictions on growth: "These attempts to protect the cultural and physical environment . . . in totality . . . threaten to leave the majority of Americans with no chance for home ownership; . . . much of the middle class is being added to the group priced out of the housing market."[19]

From 1970 to 1974, nonmetropolitan areas in the United States for the first time in decades grew more rapidly than metropolitan areas. Although a number of other influences are at work in this radical reversal of past trends, the fact that land for economical housing is increasingly unavailable over large parts of many major metropolitan areas is bound to force people to seek housing elsewhere.

LOCAL FEUDAL TENURE TRENDS

New local growth controls offer communities an advantage in that they are less overtly discriminatory than zoning. However, these growth controls may give rise to even graver legal and intellectual challenges than zoning has thus far faced. New local growth controls can be objected to on the grounds that they openly limit personal residential mobility. The feudal quality of local growth controls is thus very explicit. In recent years, a new type of legal challenge has been mounted to both zoning and local growth controls which is based on a highly feudal-sounding concern. This challenge asserts that zoning and other growth controls unconstitutionally restrict the right of individual residential mobility—in legal terminology, the "right to travel." The 1973 Task Force on Land Use and Urban Growth concluded: "Clearly, the courts are going to be asked to draw, with some precision, the line between legitimate protective regulations and improper restrictions on growth and mobility."[20]

Although there was no specific mention of it in the Constitution, it had been assumed, and the United States Supreme Court agreed in 1941, that the Founding Fathers intended that states be prohibited from regulating movement of population

---

[16] Congressional Budget Office, *Homeownership: The Changing Relationship of Costs and Incomes, and Possible Federal Roles,* budget issue paper (Washington, D.C., 1977), p. xiv.

[17] Federal Home Loan Bank Board, *Economic Briefs,* May 11, 1976, p. 3.

[18] See Bernard Frieden and Arthur Solomen, *The Nation's Housing: 1975–1985* (Cambridge, Mass.: Joint Center for Urban Studies at the Massachusetts Institute of Technology and Harvard University, 1977), p. 116.

[19] Quoted in Hill, "Nation's Cities Fighting," p. 30.

[20] Task Force on Land Use and Urban Growth, *The Use of Land,* p. 100.

among themselves. During the depression, California attempted to prevent migrants fleeing Middle Western dust bowls from taking up residence and possibly adding to welfare burdens. In overruling California's actions, the Court stated:

> But this does not mean that there are no boundaries to the permissible area of the state legislative activity. There are. And none is more certain than the prohibition against attempts on the part of a single State to isolate itself from difficulties common to all of them by restraining the transportation of persons and property across its borders. . . .[21]

The prohibition on state regulation of population movement resulted from its infringement on what has come to be called the "right to travel," which the Court has said is a basic constitutional right.

The 1965 Pennsylvania Supreme Court decision, which overturned the four-acre minimum-lot-size zoning in Easttown Township, was the first to grapple directly with the conflict between land-use regulation and residential mobility. The court saw the four-acre minimum-lot size as an unwarranted infringement on mobility. The court acknowledged that the township took the position that:

> It does not desire to accommodate those who are pressing for admittance to the township unless such admittance will not create any additional burdens upon governmental functions and services. The question posed is whether the township can stand in the way of the natural forces which send our growing population into hitherto undeveloped areas in search of a comfortable place to live. We have concluded not. A zoning ordinance whose primary purpose is to pre-

vent the entrance of newcomers in order to avoid future burdens, economic and otherwise, upon the administration of public services and facilities can not be held valid. . . .[22]

In two later important cases, the courts have again dealt with the issue of restrictions on residential mobility. The cases involved the growth controls mentioned above of Ramapo, New York, and Petaluma, California. Petaluma proposed to limit the number of building permits per year to 500 and Ramapo to schedule its future development by area over 18 years. In a split 1972 decision, the New York State Court of Appeals, the highest state court, upheld the Ramapo ordinance. However, in dissent, Justice Charles Breitel emphasized the necessity of considering interests outside the community and noted that, if Ramapo's growth controls were adopted by all suburban communities, the cumulative restrictions on mobility might well prove disastrous. The controls were "a device that maybe a few more towns like Ramapo could adopt, but not all, without destroying the economy and channelling the demographic course of the State to suit their own insular interests."[23]

Ruling on the Petaluma ordinance in 1974, Federal District Court Judge Lloyd Burke for the first time accepted the argument that a local land-use regulation could too seriously infringe on the constitutional right to travel to let it stand: "Since the population limitation policies complained of are not supported by any compelling governmental interest the exclusionary aspects of the "Petaluma Plan" must be, and are hereby declared in violation of the

---

[21] Edwards v. California, 314 U.S. at 173 (1941).

[22] National Land and Investment Company v. Kohn, 419 Pa. at 533, 215 A.2d at 612 (1965).
[23] Golden v. Planning Board of Ramapo, 30 N.Y.2d at 390, 285 N.E.2d at 309 (1972).

right to travel and, hence, are unconstitutional. . . ."[24] Although Judge Burke's decision was later reversed on appeal, the reversal was based on other grounds and did not deal with the validity of the right-to-travel argument.

In 1976, the United States Supreme Court refused to hear a further appeal on Petaluma's growth controls. In the previous few years, the establishment of similar controls in other communities has been held up to await the results of court review.

With this suggestion of possible future Supreme Court approval, the rate of introduction of new local growth controls could well escalate.

[24] Construction Industry Association of Sonoma County v. City of Petaluma, 375 F. Supp. at 586 (N.D. Cal., 1974).

KEY CONCEPTS

environmental-impact analysis

fiscal-impact analysis

minimum-lot-size zoning

restrictive/exclusionary zoning

"right to travel"

10 An Economic Appraisal of Zoning

In this selection Walter Block of the Fraser Institute examines the argument that zoning is necessary to offset market externalities in urban property markets. He finds that neither the logical nor empirical arguments support the use of extensive zoning. He also cites the city of Houston, Texas, which has no formal zoning ordinances, as a case where the lack of zoning has not created irrational patterns of urban land use.

In the view of most concerned professionals, zoning legislation is a necessary bulwark against chaos in urban land use. Without zoning, it is contended, external diseconomies will abound: pickle works will come to rest next to single-family homes, glue factories beside country clubs, and oil refineries in proximity to restaurants. Moreover, it is feared that rapacious land developers will erect, profit from, and then abandon buildings, placing undue strain on the capacities of municipal services. Further, the unzoned city will be one of haphazard construction, falling property values, instability, disregard for neighborhood "character," irrational allocation of property—and a haven for unscrupulous speculators.

Zoning is the attempt to suppress these supposed market defects by legislatively prohibiting incompatible uses of land. Under this ordinance, the pickle factory would be prohibited from residential neighborhoods and required to locate itself

Reprinted from *The Freeman* (August 1981). The original version of this article first appeared in *Zoning: Its Costs and Relevance in the 1980s* (Vancouver, Canada: The Fraser Institute, 1980). Reprinted with permission of The Fraser Institute and the author.

in a special industrial area, reserved for that kind of operation. There, surrounded by similar uses, it would presumably do little harm.

The zoning idea has a certain appeal. What, after all, could be more simple and obvious? If land usage seems imperfect, all that is needed is the enactment of a set of laws compelling proper behavior. Arguments for zoning are so widely made and frequently accepted that even those who otherwise appreciate the merits of the competitive market system have felt constrained to make an exception in this instance. In view of this state of affairs, and given the serious drawbacks in zoning which are continually making themselves felt, it is of the utmost importance to consider such legislation clearly and dispassionately.

Confronting the charge that zoning is all that stands between a viable urban environment and chaos is "Exhibit A," the City of Houston—which has never enacted such legislation. The very existence of a large North American city (an area in excess of 500 square miles and a population of 1.6 million) which can function normally and continue to grow without zoning is a major piece of evidence against the traditional view that zoning supposedly protects against chaos.

DIVERGENT TASTES

In *Zoning: Its Costs and Relevance for the 1980s* (The Fraser Institute, British Columbia, 1980) a survey is made of several empirical land use studies in Pittsburgh, Boston, Rochester, Houston, and Vancouver. The effects of "incompatible uses" on property values are traced. The overwhelming preponderance of evidence casts serious doubt upon the presence of uniform external diseconomies. (External diseconomies are said to prevail when A harms B by doing C, and B cannot collect damages nor force A to cease and desist from such activities. Uniformity would mean that all market participants view C as harmful.)

The reality appears to be that either there are few significant interdependencies and externalities in urban property markets or that "One man's meat is another man's poison." One and the same phenomenon, such as the presence of commerce in an otherwise residential neighborhood, is interpreted in a positive way by some people and in a negative way by others.

The point is that market processes exist naturally to eliminate such externalities that would arise from the proverbial glue factory on the corner of Park Avenue and East 65th Street. In a system based on the inviolability of private property rights, the laws of nuisance would prevent the dispersion of invasive odors, or dust particles. But the market process functions even without this protection. Quite simply, land prices in the residential or business neighborhoods are too expensive for the glue factory; they effectively prohibit any but the most valuable, concentrated uses—such as large office buildings or high-rise residential dwellings.

This view is supported by Roscoe H. Jones, Houston's Director of City Planning. In his opinion the market "has tended to create a reasonably well-ordered pattern. Because of private 'marketplace zoning,' we find no filling stations at the end of cul-de-sacs; ship channel industries are, naturally, located along the Ship Channel, and so on."

The natural proclivities of the market would also protect against the "hit and run" land developer who is said to leave an excessive population in his wake, swamping municipal services.

A developer who tried to pack too many people into an office building would have difficulty finding mortgage assistance. Lenders would realize that such compressed conditions would overload services, resulting in tenant dissatisfaction, lower rents, and the possibility of mortgage default. It is of course true that builders and lenders can make mistakes, and that some overcrowded structures might be built, but the inexorable forces of profit and loss would ensure that such errors were few in number. Zoners are likewise subject to miscalculation; the problem is that there are no automatic bankruptcy procedures to weed out bureaucrats with poor judgment. One of the most persuasive arguments against zoning is the fact that it institutionalizes errors. In effect, planners do not have the incentives to "get it right," nor do they suffer the consequences of "getting it wrong." The competitive system thus can obviate the need for building height restrictions, set back requirements, floor space ratios, and other bureaucratic measures which artificially attempt to limit density.

UNDUE STRAIN ON PUBLIC SERVICES

The typical pro-zoning argument is couched not in terms of undue strain on halls and elevators, which are internal to the building, but rather in terms of the effects of high density on social overhead capital: electricity, gas, water, sewers, roads, sidewalks, parking, public transit, parks—all of which are external to the subject premises, i.e., externalities.

But this should give us pause for thought. For surely there are other amenities necessary for the successful functioning of a large office building, which are or can be considered externalities, but which do not concern the city planner nor unduly worry anyone else: for example, restaurants, barber shops, banks, jewelry stores, pharmacies, stationers, and the like. One reason may be that every member of the former category is run by public or quasi public enterprises while the latter are all managed privately.

When the excavation for a new office building is begun, the small merchants in the neighborhood roll up their sleeves in anticipation of the new customers and additional profits likely to come their way. Their first thoughts are concerned with physical expansion, adding extra shifts, providing more services. The contrast with the bureaucratic orientation is stark indeed. At the prospect of new building, the bureaucratic tendency is to ponder the "strain" additional hordes of people will place on public services. Their answer is to place a myriad of zoning restrictions on the new builders, instead of encouraging coordinated expansion.

Thus it appears that if error and hence the need for correction lies anywhere, it is not with the "rapacious builder" who places "strains" on public services, but rather with those charged with the provision of the infrastructure: those in the government sector. Perhaps the answer lies in improving the provision of these services, not in holding down new construction.

THE CASE OF HOUSTON

A useful comparison is the case of Houston. Here the practice is not to hem in the private market with a bewildering array of complex zoning restrictions, but rather to *cooperate* with the land developer by forecasting the growth patterns in order that the city government may supply the necessary municipal facilities and services. It must be emphasized that zoning is only one weapon in the planning arsenal: even were these restrictions scrapped in their entirety, the public authorities would still exercise great control over land use patterns through (1) provision of infrastructure and amenities, such as parks, water mains, sewer placements, and the layout of freeway and major arterial streets; and (2) direct land use controls concerning building heights, set backs, floor space ratios, and the like, but applied uniformly to an entire city, and not differentially to districts within its boundaries.

This does indeed undercut much of the case for zoning. But in the interest of creating further discussion, one might even question whether government has a comparative advantage, vis-a-vis the market, in the creation of such products and controls. Without a market-created price system, it is extremely difficult for the public official to rationally allocate resources. Moreover, no profit or loss automatically accrues to him as a spur in decision making. He risks none of his own money, and can earn no honest profit from correct choices.

DECLINING PROPERTY VALUES

There are few things feared more by the average urban property owner than declining residential values. This is understandable, for much of the real savings of the typical citizen is tied up in a single-family house. Perhaps this is the most important explanation for the high regard with which many citizens hold zoning legislation—it is supposed to protect property values.

But the view that zoning is the best guarantee of stability is inconsistent with the evidence: The stability of neighborhoods that zoning seeks to protect thus appears to be endangered by the rezoning that is part and parcel of the enactment of zoning by-laws in the first place. What security can zoning provide against the possible ravages of the glue factory if its provisions can be rescinded at any time?

Of far greater reliability may be the system of deed restrictions, or restrictive covenants, as practiced in Houston, whereby the property owner may contract with his neighbors concerning the uses to which land may subsequently be put. Alternatively, land developers may require, as a condition of sale, that all purchasers agree to continued land usage, either for a stipulated (long) period of time or until a majority vote of such buyers overturns the agreement.

This system is far more flexible. Even the maintenance of single-family neighborhoods by zoning statutes is questionable: by keeping land and buildings in the same use over time, zoning can promote neighborhood decay and speed the demise of the single-family neighborhood. Zoning is a rigid control, and is likely to fracture during times of change in consumer tastes, neighborhood demographic structure, urban growth, and transportation and building technologies.

NO GUARANTEE OF VALUES

Ultimately, of course, there can be no absolute guarantee against declining property values. A fall in the price of wood, an increase in the market rate of interest, the sale of publicly held lands, technological improvements in prefabrication methods can all reduce housing prices. One might perhaps contract with an insurance company for the preservation of home values, but the cost of the premium payments would have to be subtracted, thus defeating the plan.

Value preservation is a will-o'-the-wisp, for price is a manifestation of the worth placed on an item not by one person, but by two groups: potential sellers and potential buyers of items like the one in question. We can not speak with certainty of the value an owner will place on his home in the future; it is even less possible to assess the worth a future hypothetical buyer will give it. It is clear, moreover, that that which is owned is the physical house, and not its value. For while the owner has a right to collect damages from the boy who breaks a window with a ball, he has no such right with respect to the man who invented prefabricated housing—even though the latter might well have been responsible for a greater drop in the value of his house than the former.

While citizens have a clear and obvious right to have their homes protected from physical damage, this does not apply to the *value* of their property. Yet this is precisely what zoning seeks to preserve. Thus not only must such legislation fail to accomplish this task—it would be improper even if it could do so.

UNIFORMITY

Another shortcoming associated with zoning is the uniformity it engenders. And this is not surprising: to divide all building into residential, commercial, and industrial, as the early enactments did, and then to impose these three categories upon the entire pattern of future construction, is hardly likely to foster architectural innovation.

This rigidity soon became evident, and an effort was made to become more "flexible." The zoning codes added variances, exceptions, Planned Unit Developments (any excess building in one parcel is to be offset by a reduction in another within the planning district), mixed-use zones, performance zoning systems, land use contracts, and development permits. In one respect these reforms were a plus, for the system became less rigid. But this change ushered in a new crop of problems. For one thing, the system became even more complex. Literally dozens of districts have been defined; what may and may not be done with each is subject to a bewildering and growing number of regulations. The days of three-district zoning with two or three pages of regulations have long since passed. Today's ordinances are continually growing to accommodate more detailed regulations of use, lot size, building height and bulk; more reasons for granting variances, bonuses, and special exceptions; and much more complicated procedures for appeals and reviews. Today few sets of zoning regulations appear in tomes of fewer than 500 pages.

A system with so many complications, exceptions and changes could no longer be governed by any clear set of rules or principles. The procedure instead became one of "judging each case on its merits" in an ad hoc manner.

Although this might appear to some as fair and judicious, the flaws in it are grave. First, it is a clear retreat from the idea of zoning itself. According to this philosophy, urban planners were assumed to have enough wisdom to forecast, at least in broad brush strokes, the future spatial organization of the city. But the very need to grant numerous exceptions, as a continuing institutionalized process, has belied this claim. Ability to incorporate the needs of a changing future is simply incompatible with patchwork changes as reality confronts the master plan. It is akin to claiming the ability to forecast inflation for the next five years—and then changing the prognostication each week.

Secondly, as Nobel Laureates Milton Friedman and Friedrich Hayek have so eloquently shown, "judging each case on its merits" is the absence of lawfulness—not its presence. Each has demonstrated (the former in his analysis of "rules not authorities" in monetary policy; the latter in his work on the "rule of law") that to consider matters on a "case by case" basis is to color the judicial process with stultifying arbitrariness.

THE RULE OF LAW

The proper scope of government, in this view, is to set down the rules of the game, clearly, and before the contest begins—and then not to continually alter them in the midst of the fray. Under these conditions, the individual is free to pursue his lawful ends, secure in the reasonable knowledge that the government powers will not suddenly be used to frustrate him at every turn. But a zoning system, especially a "flexible" or "reformed" one, can change the uses to which a land parcel may be put at any time. It is thus clearly destructive of these ends.

Thirdly, zoning complexity and change-ability have spawned graft and corruption. The reason for this is easy to discern: a less restrictive variance may be worth millions of dollars to the land developer. Be the bureaucrat ever so honest, he will be sorely tempted by a share in these gains—especially in an era where rezoning is an easily contrived and commonplace occurrence. Paradoxically, this is not necessarily all to the bad. If a bribe can convert a land parcel to a use more highly prized by consumers, wealth and the allocation of resources will have been much more nearly optimized. This is not the first case on record attesting to the benefits of black markets. The great loss, however, is the general disrespect for the law engendered by this practice.

PRIVATE ZONING

If zoning can be defined as matching specific areas of land with particular uses, then nothing said above should be interpreted as opposing *private* zoning. Indeed, it is impossible for any rational land developer to act in any other way. He must, if he is to function at all, decide to place the garage here, the house there, and the backyard elsewhere. How else could he conceivably operate? But this is all that is meant by private zoning.

The case is an exact parallel to the planning debate. As has been said many times before, people must plan if they are to act rationally. The debate, then, is not between planning and non-planning. It is between

central planning, on the part of the government, and individual planning, as coordinated through the marketplace. Similarly the real issue here is not the choice between zoning and non-zoning; it is between private and governmental zoning. What has been criticized above is *governmental* zoning, not the private variety.

What is private zoning? The most well-known example is, of course, Houston's system of deed restrictions. Private zoning also takes place every time a glue factory is priced out of a residential neighborhood, or whenever the gas station locates on a major thoroughfare, not in a side street. But it also includes such prosaic activities as the individual's arrangement of household furniture, the office's placement of desks and room dividers, the factory's disposition of machines and guardrails, and the shopping mall's apportionment of its tenants.

Items for sale must be deployed in the most advantageous manner possible. Thus merchants match store areas to particular uses. The success of each enterprise rests, in great part, upon the skill in such "zoning." If the grocer discovers, for example, that apples and oranges sell better in close proximity, or that the juxtaposition of corn and peas detracts from the sale of both, without any offsetting benefits on the remainder of the stock, he can profit by incorporating this information into his "zoning" decision making. He will gain a competitive advantage over those of his colleagues who are not similarly skilled. It is in this way that the market promotes efficient zoning.

The same process is at work in shopping centers and malls. Since the various tenants are contractually unrelated to one another, the situation is closely analogous to governmental zoning. Private entrepreneurs, however, are judged, in their profit and loss accounts, by how well they promote positive externalities and repress negative ones. And, in fact, it is difficult to imagine two "incompatible" tenants adjacent to each other in a shopping mall. Any such mal-zoning would only, in the long run, reduce the landlords' total receipts.

There is a vast reservoir of private zoning efforts operating in the economy, unreported, under-publicized. This brief discussion has barely scratched the surface. But it can be viewed as one more aspect of the case against public zoning efforts.

What public policy recommendations follow? Although one must always be cautious and realize that no one solution can offer a total panacea, there is a strong presumption toward the non-zoning extreme of the spectrum. After all, zoning has not worked very well. The externalities that it is designed to ameliorate have been shown to be minimal or nonexistent. The maintenance of single-family neighborhoods by zoning statutes is also questionable.

One might even take an extreme position here, and advocate abolishing the system of government zoning—root and branch.

KEY CONCEPTS

externalities

laws of nuisance

private property rights

private marketplace zoning

restrictive covenants

rule of law

THOMAS MULLER   GRACE DAWSON

11 The Fiscal Impact of Residential and Commercial Development

Fiscal-impact analyses have become very popular for gauging the effects on local-government revenues and expenditures of proposed developments. They have also proven to be somewhat controversial since they consider only the service costs and revenues to local government and not the full range of social benefits and costs generated by new developments. Thomas Muller and Grace Dawson of the Urban Institute present the main ingredients of a fiscal-impact study.

THE NEED FOR FISCAL-IMPACT STUDIES

The fiscal impact of residential and commercial development on the local public sector has been the subject of considerable discussion and recent litigation.[1] Measuring the difference between expected revenues from proposed development and anticipated expenditures incurred as a result of growth has become increasingly important as the nation's metropolitan areas continue to expand.

Suburbs, in which a large share of national growth has taken place, are particularly concerned that the cost of providing public services to new residents may contribute to rapid property tax increases and/or deterioration in the level and quality of public services. During the last decade the national population increased by 23.8 million. Of this total, suburbs accounted for 80 percent of the growth, central cities for less than 3 percent, while rural areas lost population.[2]

Unfortunately, objective analyses of the fiscal impact of growth have been scarce. This study presents a general methodology for evaluating the fiscal effect on a county of proposed residential and nonresidential development which can also be applied to other political jurisdictions with appropriate adjustments. It should be noted that while the net fiscal effect of development should be taken into account in land-use decisions, it is only one of a number of issues which should be examined. The impact of new development on the physical and social environment, as well as on the private sector of the economy, should also be considered. In addition, the equity issues raised by the existing tax structure,

From Thomas Muller and Grace Dawson, "Introduction," *The Fiscal Impact of Residential and Commercial Development* (Washington, D.C.: The Urban Institute, 1972), pp. 1–12. Reprinted with permission of the Urban Institute.

[1] For example, *Golden v. Planning Board*, N.Y. Ct. App., 5/3/72, cert. denied, U.S. 41 LW 3268, 11/14/72; and *Lee Jackson Development Corporation and Levitt and Sons, Inc. v. The Board of Supervisors of Loudoun County, Va.*, Cir. Ct. Loudoun Cty., Va., 3/22/72.

[2] For a discussion of government policies which influence growth patterns, see Executive Office of the President, *Report on National Growth—1972*, Washington, DC., 1972.

the secondary fiscal effect of nonresidential development,[3] and the current distribution of public services should also be weighed. Because these are complex issues and beyond the purpose of this study, they will not be examined.

This study ... presents a general framework for evaluating county revenues and expenditures associated with proposed residential and nonresidential development and discusses how this framework can be used.

OUTLINE OF METHODOLOGY

Background Profiles

Prior to undertaking the actual revenue-expenditure analysis of a proposed development project, it is useful to compile two county profiles.

First, a general profile of changes in the social and economic characteristics of the county over the past decade should be made. This should include the following items:

Population and Demography. What is the county population, growth rate, rate of mobility, fertility rate, etc.? Are these rates increasing or decreasing?

Income of County Residents. What is the median family income of the county as compared with the state and other counties of similar character? At what rate has it been increasing or decreasing?

Cost of Housing. What is the median cost of different types of housing in the county as compared with similar types of housing throughout the state and in other similar counties? Is housing primarily renter- or owner-occupied?

Special Group Impact. Does any population subgroup exist in abnormal proportion in the county? Does this subgroup have an impact on the fiscal structure of the county? (E.g., a large student population may affect the cost of housing or wage rates, or a large elderly population may result in reduced education expenditures and increased health and special transportation costs.)

The second general profile should examine the changes in the county's fiscal structure over a previous period of growth. The following items should be considered:

Changes in Local Revenue. What are the basic sources of local revenue? What new sources (new sales taxes, utility taxes, etc.) have been added during the growth period? What is the amount of total local revenue derived from households and business enterprises, and at what rate have revenues increased?

Changes in Local Expenditures. At what rate have total population and number of school children increased, implying increased capital costs for education? What wage increases have occurred? What changes have occurred in the general level and quality of public services? Has the increased population created the demand for new and expanded public services? Has the share of the budget allocated for capital expenditures and debt service remained relatively constant?

---

[3]The secondary fiscal effect occurs as follows: commercial development increases the demand for housing, thereby inducing residential development which in turn increases the demand for goods and services.

The analysis of the fiscal impact of a specific proposed residential and/or nonresidential development falls under three major headings. Estimates should be computed of: (1) revenues from the development; (2) operating expenditures incurred by the development; and (3) capital expenditures incurred by the development.

Revenue Estimates

Local revenue can be grouped into four categories: (1) revenues associated with property wealth (which in most jurisdictions represents the largest revenue source); (2) revenues associated with income and level of consumption, which is comprised primarily of local sales and utility taxes; (3) per capita revenues, which are derived from either a per capita tax or total population; and (4) miscellaneous revenues, which include fees, fines, licenses, and other minor items.[4]

Revenues Related to Property. Both real and personal property are generally taxed at the local level; however, in several states, including New York and Delaware, only real property is taxed. In general, the same tax rate applies to both residential and nonresidential property.[5] In many jurisdictions, income-producing property, including apartments, is taxed on the basis of gross or net income, rather than on the basis of the value of property.

In almost all communities, the effective tax rate is lower than the assessed tax rate.

Therefore, in computing likely revenues from real property, one has to determine the effective tax rate based on recent property sales. Frequently, it is assumed that the "adjusted" tax rate, which is in theory the rate applied to property, yields an estimate of likely taxes from real property. However, because of the time lag in assessment, as well as other factors, the adjusted tax rate is, with few exceptions, higher than the effective tax rate.[6]

In about 15 states, such as Maryland, Virginia, and North Carolina, school districts are fiscally dependent as part of the local budget. In other states, school districts can levy their own property tax independently of other political jurisdictions.[7]

Property taxes on personal property of households are most frequently on automobiles, and, in some areas, on household goods. Business personal property taxes may include taxes on machinery and inventory.

Revenues Related to Income. Revenues linked to income include local sales and income taxes, utility taxes (insofar as higher-income households consume utilities more intensively) and occasionally excise taxes on specific goods. In general, however, taxes on beer, alcoholic beverages, gasoline, cigarettes, and related items are not subject to county taxes. Gift and estate taxes related to wealth are generally the prerogative of state and federal governments.

[4]For the purposes of analysis, revenues from business enterprises should be identified separately from revenues collected from households. It is also useful, when proposed residential development includes different types of housing units, to estimate revenues (and expenditures) for each type of unit such as single-family, townhouse, apartment.

[5]There are exceptions to this, including Minnesota which taxes industrial and commercial property at a higher rate than residential property.

[6]In evaluating new development, the likely market value of land and structures is usually provided by the developer. The values can be compared to similar property to determine if they reasonably reflect the local market.

[7]For school district revenue by source of funding, see B. Levin, T. Muller, and W. Scanlon, *Public School Finance: Present Disparities and Fiscal Alternatives* (Washington, D.C.: The Urban Institute, 1972).

In view of the importance of income-related taxes in many jurisdictions, it is necessary to estimate the likely household income of new residents. One approach is to estimate the income of potential residents, based on the relationship between property value and income.[8] ... If monthly rent payments for apartment units are known, annual rents can be computed and income estimates can be derived by taking rent payments as a share of income.[9] It should be noted that the type of housing (owner-occupied or rented) as well as the share of income allocated for each type of housing varies by location, age, race, and size of the household.

A more direct method for estimating income of new residents is to examine applications to mortgage institutions and apartment managers. However, access to these data is difficult because of confidentiality. Given data on income, likely receipts from various sales and excise taxes can be approximated from various surveys on expenditures by income class, region, and metropolitan area.[10]

Per Capita Revenue. Local government occasionally, as in parts of Delaware, administers a per capita or "head" tax on all adults. More frequently, local government is the recipient of state or county revenues distributed on the basis of the number of residents or the number of students. For example, profits from the alcoholic beverage sales by the state are distributed to local jurisdictions in Virginia based on population. As a result, per capita revenues vary in proportion to changes in population. Federal revenue sharing for local jurisdictions as presently legislated uses population as one criterion.[11]

Miscellaneous Revenue. Other sources of revenue, such as automobile license tags, can also be estimated on the basis of income (higher-income households tend to have more cars per dwelling unit compared to lower-income households). Fines and other minor sources can be approximated on the basis of per capita receipts from these sources by the jurisdiction.

Local revenue sources may vary within states. Among states there are considerable tax structure differences. Examples of local taxes...include taxes on payrolls and state income tax surtaxes. Both of these taxes, however, can be estimated utilizing the methodology suggested.

Operating Expenditure Estimates

The importance and scope of public services which are the responsibility of local government can differ sharply among and within states. In some communities, utilities such as water and sewerage are part of the municipal budget; certain roads and highways are built as well as maintained by many localities. In addition, while expenditures for health and welfare may be small items in some county budgets, they are

---

[8]For a discussion of the demand for housing as a function of income, see F. deLeeuw, "The Demand for Housing: A Review of Cross Section Evidence," *The Review of Economics and Statistics,* Vol. 53, February 1971, pp. 1–10.

[9]A number of government publications discuss these proportions. For example, see U.S. Department of Labor, *Three Standards of Living for Urban Families,* Bulletin No. 1570-5, 1969.

[10]U.S. Department of Labor, Bureau of Labor Statistics, *Survey of Consumer Expenditures,* Report No. 237-88 (Washington, D.C.: U.S. Government Printing Office, 1965).

[11]Per capita income and tax effort are the other criteria. As a result, affluent Fairfax County, Virginia, receives only $8.18 per capita while adjoining Loudoun County receives $16.01.

major expenditure items in cities such as New York and Detroit.

Local operating expenditures can be grouped into (1) those incurred in supplying services used primarily by households, such as education, libraries, health and welfare, and recreation, and (2) those incurred in supplying services used by both business enterprises and households, such as fire and police services, utilities, and general government.

Operating Expenditures Related to Households. In most local jurisdictions, public education is the largest expenditure item. In suburban areas of states other than those which have large state funding for education, such as North Carolina and Delaware, education accounts for 40 to 80 percent of local current expenditures. As a result, a reliable estimate of additional school population resulting from development is a critical variable in estimating the fiscal impact of new development. Factors which affect the number of students attending public schools include type of housing, demographic and socioeconomic characteristics of households, the availability of private and parochial schools, value of new housing, and prior residence of new households in a community. The grade distribution of students is frequently a function of housing type, and since per student costs are higher in upper grades, the use of average per student cost values may be misleading.

In recent years, many communities have come to support junior colleges and other post-high school educational facilities. The demand for these facilities, which frequently have open enrollment policies, needs to be estimated, together with the likely demand for adult education.

Household-related expenditures, other than education, can be categorized[12] according to whether:

> *demand is concentrated among low-income households:* e.g., public health services aimed at indigents and low-income households, and welfare services;
> *demand increases with income:* e.g., libraries, recreation, and waste collection;
> *demand increases with size of property or structure:* e.g., water, sewerage, storm drains, and road repavement; or
> *demand is generally invariable:* e.g., police, fire, and general government.

In the revenue expenditure analysis discussed here, only demand for services which is most likely to result in increased spending is considered. The demand may exist for special expenditures for education or health care in low-income areas; however, unless past trends indicate that this demand is likely to be met by additional spending, no potential expenditure will be considered in the calculation.

It should be recognized that increases in the demand for services, as a result of either small increases in population or change in taste, do not necessarily result in an immediate increase in expenditures. For example, five new households are not likely to result in an increase in public safety, recreation, or other public service

[12]These categories are only general guides. For example, part of a county health budget serves the entire population independent of income. Library and recreation facility use increase with income, but may decline at very high incomes, where the public service is replaced by private facilities. High-income households are likely to utilize private rather than public golf courses and tennis courts, and are likely to purchase books rather than borrow them from public libraries.

Certain crimes and the frequency of fires tend to increase in low-income areas. However, this does not necessarily result in a level of expenditures for public safety which reduces crime and fire incidence to a level comparable with more affluent areas of a jurisdiction.

personnel. Thus, costs that remain fixed for a small increment in demand, rise sharply as the demand reaches a critical point, and remain fixed until demand again reaches a threshold value. In the absence of data on these threshold values, costs can frequently be averaged, rather than attributing the total incremental cost to the marginal unit which triggered the additional expenditure. Changes in local spending which are attributable to changes in population should be distinguished from those attributable to other factors.[13]

Operating Expenditures Related to Residents and Business Enterprises. Public services used by both households and business enterprises include utilities, transportation facilities, police and fire protection, the judicial system, and general government functions. In many cases, it is difficult to isolate the household demand from that of commercial or industrial enterprises, such as special equipment for fighting industrial fires, or police patrols in industrial parks. Alternative techniques for allocating operating expenditures among enterprises and households can be based on level of employment in commercial and industrial facilities as compared to number of household units, or the ratio of the property value of such facilities to residential property value.

Capital Expenditure Estimates
Capital expenditures associated with new development include: (1) facilities linked directly with the proposed development, such as new schools, sewer lines, fire stations, and other new facilities; and (2) facilities to be constructed as part of a capital improvement plan which will be shared by existing residents or enterprises in the jurisdiction as well as those from the new development, such as junior colleges, new sewage and/or water treatment plants, and health care centers. Facilities in the second category are not usually triggered by a single new development project, but may be designed to incorporate increases in demand from projected development.

In order to determine whether a capital expenditure should be allocated to the existing residents exclusively or jointly to existing and new residents, the following questions should be answered:

Would the facilities be built regardless of the approval of a proposed development?

Would the proposed size of the facilities remain constant regardless of population increase resulting from new development?

Would new residents be users, and thus beneficiaries, of the proposed facilities?

If the response to the first two questions is yes, and to the third no, then the project is unrelated to an increase in population. It is more likely, however, that the size of projects, such as schools, are based on projected growth in population. In this situation, the incremental (rather than average) cost should be allocated to the new development, if the data are available.[14] It may

---

[13]Whether unit costs of public services increase faster in an area of rapid development compared to areas with stable population requires further study. It has been shown that jurisdictions with rapid growth have higher property taxes, which could be attributable to one or more of the following factors: (1) the necessity for large capital outlays; (2) diseconomies of scale; and/or (3) rapidly increasing salaries for public employees.

[14]In some instances, the incremental cost of increasing capital outlays is below average cost, as in the case of certain educational facilities; to build a high school for 2,000 students, other factors being equal, is less expensive, on a per student basis, than a high school designed to facilitate 800 students. However, the per unit cost of providing highways and certain utilities can increase as the number of units increases.

TABLE 1

County Revenue-Expenditure Summary

Development Type	Development-Linked Revenue to County	Development-Linked County Operating Expenditures	County Capital Expenditures	
			Development-Linked	Related to Entire County
Residential				
Nonresidential				
Subtotal				
Less: Existing Land Use				
Total	$W	$X	$Y	$Z

$$W - (\$X + \$Y + \$Z) = \pm \$ \text{ Net Fiscal Effect}$$

be argued that since growth is already projected and thus a built-in factor, the approval of a specific development results in the addition of only part of the projected population. Thus, unless the population increment from new development does not exceed the projected level, the decision to provide the facility is independent of the approval of a request for new development.

Net Fiscal Effect

The revenue and expenditure estimates discussed in the preceding sections can be aggregated as in Table 1 to obtain the net fiscal impact on a county of a proposed development. It should be noted that the revenues and expenditures from the existing land use functions should be subtracted from the totals to obtain the net effect of the development.

KEY CONCEPTS

background profiles

business-related expenditures

capital expenditure estimates

fiscal-impact analysis

household-related expenditures

income-related revenues

property-related revenues

WILLIAM ALONSO

12 The Economics of Urban Size

Implicit in many public policy issues, such as local growth control and the development of new towns, is the concept of an ideal size of city. William Alonso of Harvard University uses economic analysis to examine the issue of optimum city size.

INTRODUCTION

At least since Aristotle, men have wondered about the best size for cities.[1] In the last decades developed and developing nations, capitalist and socialist, have increasingly adopted more or less explicit policies on urbanization with special reference to city sizes. Most typically, these policies assume that the big cities of the nation are too big, and therefore try to disperse growth. Complementarily, in recent years such dispersal policies, and policies addressed to distressed or backward regions, have recognized that these alternative centers must be of a certain minimum size, however ill-defined, in order to be viable. In its simplest sense, the question of urban size consists of symmetric parts: how big is too big? and, how big is big enough?

Theory and fact on these issues are scarce and poor, and they swim in an ocean of opinion, much of it highly emotional. For instance, recent American aca-

demic opinion, see Berry [6], Thompson [24], places the minimum size in the area of 250,000 to 500,000 inhabitants, which is about what the Soviet Union regards as the maximum tolerable size. The designation of "growth centers" has been awarded to settlements ranging in population from less than a handful of thousands to more than 1 million. Here we will present an aggregative economic approach to the theory of city size, and some empirical findings which suggest that even the largest cities have not yet reached excessive sizes from the point of view of growth and productivity.

THE DIFFICULTY OF DEFINING URBAN SIZE

Urban magnitude is no simple one-dimensional phenomenon. For instance, an Asian metropolis of 5,000,000 inhabitants with a gross regional product per capita of $100.00 has an economic magnitude equivalent to that of a modest American metropolis of 100,000, and is far smaller for income-elastic goods and services. Nor is the definition of population size unequivocal. Modern urban centers are surrounded by very large, diffuse zonal boundaries, within which there are marked variations in the proportion of firms and people associated with

From William Alonso, "The Economics of Urban Size," *Papers and Proceedings of the Regional Science Association* 26 (1971): 67–71. Reprinted by permission of the Regional Science Association and the author.

[1]The author wishes to thank the Centre for Environmental Studies, London, for their help. Research for this paper was supported by a grant from the Economic Development Administration, U.S. Department of Commerce.

103

that center, and in the intensity of the association. Thus, population does not constitute a conventional countable set, where people are unequivocally members or not. The situation is closer to that of "fuzzy sets," in which an element's membership in a set is a matter of degree. See Zadeh [28]. A number as a measure of population is thus gross oversimplification. The situation is further complicated in the frequent case of conurbations or megalopolitan areas, where the zonal boundaries of diverse centers overlap in complex patterns, and a person may be a member of two functional cities. In order to avoid the problem of the definition of boundaries (if not that of determining the degree of membership), some scholars have used density rather than size, but density is only a measure of local intensity of a ratio which misses the crucial aspect of the extension (or scale) of the system of interrelated elements. Certain villages of medieval origin have higher densities than giant metropoles or even their central cities. In general, we will ignore these problems, considering population as the basic magnitude and as a conventionally definable number, although some of the evidence to be cited is based on density measures; and towards the end I will consider some effects of adjacency of urban areas, although not the overlapping of their boundaries. Economic magnitude will be treated as an endogenous variable, basically a function of population.

THE MINIMUM COSTS APPROACH

Most approaches to city size have stressed the presumed diseconomies of urban scale, and have sought to establish that population at which costs per capita are least, regarding this as optimal. Although I shall argue that both the logic and the factual basis of this approach are faulty, it will be useful to review them briefly since they are so widely accepted by scholars and policy makers. Traditional studies of urban economies, going back to the turn of the century, have focused on how public costs vary as a function of population size using cross-section data. In general they have found them U-shaped, with the bottom of the curve occurring variously between 10,000 and 250,000 population. This literature is well known and has been supported by a few studies based on engineering calculations. Recent useful reviews are given by Cameron [8], Hirsch [12], Kain [14]. But the matter is not so simple, and these findings cannot be accepted at face value. Three principal difficulties may be mentioned. First, these measures of cost measure only inputs, and implicitly assume that outputs are constant. If the demand for public goods and services is at all income-elastic, cities with higher incomes would be spending more to get more, so that rising expenditures are not strong evidence of rising expensiveness. Indeed, the few studies based on multivariate techniques find no significant correlation of size and public cost after other variables are taken into account. See, for example, Schmandt and Stephens [22]. Second, the division between private and public costs is very much a matter of institutional convention. Most automobiles are private, but buses may be private or public. The production and distribution of electricity may be public or private. The sewer and waterpipes that vein a suburban residential district are public, but their exact equivalents, running vertically within a large apartment house, are private. In brief, the category of public costs is neither well-defined nor stable. Third, many of the components of costs may not be real economic costs. For instance, suppose a teacher receives a higher salary in a large city because teachers there are unionized; the difference in his salary represents a transfer payment within the city rather than a true resource cost. It is unclear, in fact, how much of education is a production cost (training people) and how much of it is a form of consumption (educating people). Similarly, the treatment of land costs is ambiguous in the cost-benefit literature.

In contrast to the extensive literature on the costs of infrastructure and municipal operation, there is only a very slender literature on the variation in producers' costs with city size. No general study of the variation in producers' costs with city size appears to exist. A recent study by Morse [17] in an Indian context finds no substantial variation (and a possible small decline) in a range from very small cities to rather large ones. In the case of consumers' costs, it appears that these vary only slightly with urban size. See Alonso and Fajans [4]. The association is weak even for the housing and transportation components, which from theory might be expected to be strongly associated with urban size. The association disappears if other factors such as local climate and income are taken into account. Subjective estimates show, however, a sharp rise in the level of income that people think is needed for adequate levels of living in larger cities. See Gallup [11]. It is popular opinion, of course, that big cities are more expensive. It appears that one can live as cheaply in big cities as in small ones, but that the more varied opportunities of large cities raise expectations.

The most sophisticated explanation of the excessive growth of cities runs as follows: where costs are rising, a new industry (or inhabitant) makes its location decision on the prevailing (average) costs, including such factors as congestion and local taxes. However, since costs are rising, marginal costs are greater than average costs. Marginal costs are borne by the urban body as a whole, and the differences between average and marginal costs are the negative externalities. For instance, a plant considering locating in a large city will take into account existing (average) levels of congestion, but does not consider the increased congestion and travel costs that would be borne by the whole population as a result of its coming. By this argument, then, this divergence between private and social costs permits the city to grow beyond its best size.

It would be clearly impossible in real life to apply to each firm and citizen in order of arrival, such a differential tax, corresponding to the difference between marginal and average costs. Nonetheless, this view is reflected in the tax policies of many countries, such as Great Britain and France, which impose surtaxes on capital and/or labor in locations which are thought to be congested. Although such taxes operate on the average value for wages, they approximate a marginal approach for capital when they are levied on new investment. In many cases, of course, governments do not trust such uncertain subtleties of pricing, and public policy manifests itself through direct command on industry and population, denying them some locations or even ordering them to others.

AN AGGREGATE THEORY OF CITY SIZE

The argument of minimum costs is insufficient in its own terms. Such an objective is sensible only if output per capita is constant. But, in fact, it appears that output per capita is an increasing function of urban size. In that case, a more sensible objective of public policy would deal with the relation of outputs and inputs, rather than only with inputs. Before going on to spell out this simple point, we must return to definitional difficulties. It is in many cases most difficult to determine whether something is an input or an output. We have already raised this question with respect to education. But examples abound: for instance, are the expensive tie and suit that a businessman wears to his office production costs, or are they a form of consumption? Such problems, which had troubled early theorists of national income accounting, have been largely ignored by consensus in recent years. Yet they constitute a crucial area of ambiguity in the type of theory with which we are dealing, because they raise fundamental questions as to which human activities are instrumental and which are ends in themselves. For our purposes we will consider that urban output is the value of the total product of the urban area. Urban costs are harder to define, and would include quantity and price effects in the costs of infrastructure and municipal operation, in the costs of exogenous inputs other than human ones into the city's economic activity, and in private consumption. Thus, we regard the city as an aggregate productive unit.

Figure 1 shows a possible set of cost and product curves, and is akin to the traditional diagram of costs and revenues for the firm. The key difference is that the horizontal axis is in terms of population rather than of quantity produced. While the usual theory of the firm treats labor as an input whose price is exogenously determined,

here labor is excluded from consideration in the construction of the cost curve, and the return to labor (in the broad sense of the total urban population) is the difference between the value of total output and total costs. Here I exclude from consideration colonial situations, in which part of this output is alienated by others elsewhere. The difference between costs and the value of output is thus available to the local population for investment or direct consumption, either directly from the city's production or through trade with others.

The average cost curve, AC in Figure 1, is shown as rising after a certain population level, both because this is generally believed to be the case (although the factual basis was questioned above) and because it weakens and therefore tests more sharply the argument being presented. The average product per capita curve, AP, is shown rising monotonically,

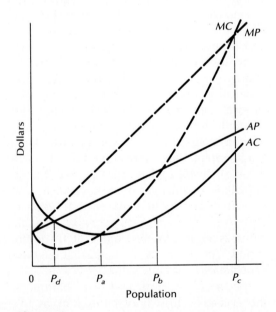

Figure 1.

partly to simplify the argument at this stage and partly because this is what most of the empirical evidence suggests. Later on we will consider the possibility of its turning down after some point.

If the general formulation is accepted, the rest is simple. The point of minimum per capita cost, P_a is uninteresting. The point of maximum local contribution to national income occurs at P_c, where marginal cost, MC, is equal to marginal product, MP. There is, of course, no need for this point to exist, in the sense that MP may remain higher than MC for the relevant range of population, but if it does exist, beyond this point further population costs more than it is worth. A national government interested exclusively in maximizing total product under conditions of labor surplus, would use such a population as its target. However, if there is not an unlimited supply of labor, the population size that would maximize national product would be smaller and would occur where the difference between MP and MC is equal to the opportunity costs similarly defined at alternative locations. From the point of view of the inhabitants of the city, however, a more sensible objective would be the maximization of the difference between average product, AP, and average cost, AC. This difference may be regarded as a per capita disposable income, and it will be maximized, of course, where the rate of increase of AP and AC are equal $(dAP/dP = dAC/dP)$.[2] Since average product is increasing with population, this must occur at a size P_b which is greater than that of minimum costs. In brief, the optimal population will differ according to whether a national or a local viewpoint is assumed,

but in neither case will it coincide with the point of minimum costs.

From the point of view of policy, in trying to bring private costs and benefits into line with social costs and benefits, the same logic that leads minimum-cost theorists to argue for taxes on new arrivals based on the difference between social cost, MC, and private cost, AC, would argue here as well for subsidies based on the positive externalities produced by the new arrival. Thus, the net tax for subsidy would be based on a calculation of $(MP-AP) - (MC-AC)$, which may be positive or negative. Needless to say, these numbers are very elusive ones, and no operational tax could be based on such arithmetic.

There is no attempt here to develop a theory to explain the increase in production with population size. Pieces of such a theory exist in the literature and they stress economies of scale, advantages of specialization, agglomeration economies, probabilistic needs for lower relative reserves of inventories and labor, ease of communication, the richness of opportunities and the adaptability of large and complex systems, and so forth. See Thompson [25] and Alonso [1], [3]. Within the dishevelled theory of externalities, they suggest that positive external economies exceed the negative ones, principally by modifying the production functions of the component activities so that inputs are used more effectively. Without trying to formulate a general theory of causes, we pass to an examination of the empirical evidence.

EMPIRICAL EVIDENCE

In every country for which I have found evidence, local product per capita (or some index for it, such as income or wages) rises

[2]This would have no meaningful equivalent in the context of the theory of the firm. It would amount to maximizing net revenue per unit product.

with urban size, and where comparable figures on cost are available, these rise far more slowly if at all. . . .

Many studies over the years have established that in the United States, for data grouped by city size, there is a strong and steady rise in income of about 30 percent depending on the size of classes and the income definition used. Fuchs [10] found a steady rise of about 40 percent in hourly earnings with urban size after discounting the effects of labor composition by color, age, sex, and education. If, by traditional economic theory, we equate wages to the marginal productivity of labor, the conclusion is that, for a given type and quality of labor, the rise in wages indicates that productivity rises with urban size. . . .

PROBLEMS IN THE INTERPRETATION OF THE CURVES

It would be well to end this discussion with an upbeat note, but it must be concluded with further cavils of interpretation and definition. Curves such as those in Figure 1 will vary from city to city, from society to society, and within a society with its evolution through time. Even after the improvement of the contextual variable of income potential, the population variable accounts for only part of the variation in local incomes. Further, while the empirical data shows substantial consistency across the arrays of cities of particular nations, it is based primarily on cross-sectional data. One might ask what is the meaning for a city of 20,000 of curves extending into the tens of millions; or, conversely, what is the meaning for a great metropolis like New York or Tokyo of the range of the curve at the 20,000 level.

It must be granted that the relation of

size to time is far from clear in these arguments. Surely it is not the same to grow tenfold in a decade as in a century, and movements along the population axis in Figure 1 would take place in real time and in particular circumstances. One might ask, further, whether paths of expansion coincide with paths of retrenchment, whether a city grown too big can regain paradise by shedding its excess population. In brief, the analysis admittedly suffers from the common limitations of the application of static theory to a dynamic process. Most particularly, there is no suggestion here that a static general equilibrium approach can serve to model a nation's system of cities because the movements of people, capital, ideas and institutional forms are slow and evolutionary, and while they change, other things are changing. Issues such as these have more to do with the dynamics of fluids than with the mechanics of solids.

REFERENCES

(1) Alonso, W. "Industrial Location and Regional Policy," Working Paper No. 74, Center for Planning and Development Research, University of California, Berkeley, 1968.

(2) _____. "Equity and Its Relation to Efficiency in Urbanization," in J. F. Kain (Ed.), *Essays in Regional Economics.* Cambridge: Harvard University Press, forthcoming.

(3) _____. "Urban and Regional Imbalances," *Economic Development and Cultural Change* Vol. 17 (October 1968), pp. 1–14.

(4) _____ and M. Fajans. "Cost of Living and Income by Urban Size," Working Paper No. 128, Center for Planning and Development Research, University of California, Berkeley, 1970.

(5) _____ and E. Medrich. "Spontaneous Growth Centers in Twentieth Century American Urbanization," in N. Hansen (Ed.),

Growth Centers and Regional Development.
New York: The Free Press, forthcoming.

(6) Berry, B. J. L. and E. Neils. "Location, Size, and Shape of Cities as Influenced by Environmental Factors: The Urban Environment Writ Large," in H. Perloff (Ed.), *The Quality of the Urban Environment.* Baltimore: The Johns Hopkins Press, 1969.

(7) Burns, L. S. "The Intra-Urban Income Distribution," Paper presented at the Annual Conference, British Section of the Regional Science Association, London, 1968.

(8) Cameron, G. C. "Growth Areas, Growth Centres, and Regional Conversion," *Scottish Journal of Political Economy,* Vol. 17 (February 1970), pp. 19–38.

(9) Douglas, R. "Selected Indices of Industrial Characteristics for U.S. Standard Metropolitan Statistical Areas, 1963," Discussion Paper No. 20, Regional Science Research Institute, Philadelphia, 1967.

(10) Fuchs, V. R. *Differentials in Hourly Earnings by Regional and City Size, 1959.* New York: National Bureau of Economic Research, Occasional Paper No. 101, 1967.

(11) Gallup, G. *Typical U.S. Family of Four Needs $120 per Week to Make Ends Meet.* Princeton, N.J.: American Institute of Public Opinion, 1970.

(12) Hirsch, W. Z. "The Supply of Urban Public Services," in H. Perloff and L. Wingo (Eds.), *Issues in Urban Economics.* Baltimore: The Johns Hopkins Press, 1968.

(13) Hirschman, A. O. *The Strategy of Economic Development.* New Haven: Yale University Press, 1958.

(14) Kain, J. F. "Urban Form and the Cost of Urban Services," Discussion Paper No. 6, Program on Regional and Urban Economics, Harvard University, 1966.

(15) Khorev, B. "What Kind of City is Needed," *Literaturnaya gazeta,* No. 14, 1969, as reported in *The Current Digest of the Soviet Press,* Vol. 21 (April 23, 1969), p. 14 and p. 27.

(16) Mera, K. "On the Concentration of Urbanization and Economic Efficiency," Economics Department Working Paper No. 74, International Bank for Reconstruction and Development, Washington, D.C., 1970.

(17) Morse, R. *et al.* "Costs of Urban Infrastructure as Related to City Size in Developing Countries: India Case Study," Stanford Research Institute, Menlo Park, California, 1968.

(18) Ornati, O. A. "Poverty in Cities," in H. Perloff and L. Wingo (Eds.), *Issues in Urban Economics.* Baltimore: The Johns Hopkins Press, 1968.

(19) Perevedentsev, V. "Cities and Years," *Literaturnaya gazeta,* No. 9, 1969, as reported in *The Current Digest of the Soviet Press,* Vol. 21 (March 19, 1969), pp. 6–9.

(20) Pred, A. *The Spatial Dynamics of U.S. Urban and Industrial Growth, 1814–1900.* Cambridge: M.I.T. Press, 1966.

(21) Regional Plan Association (New York). "The Atlantic Urban Seaboard: Development Issues and Strategies," *Regional Plan News,* No. 90 (September 1969), pp. 1–33.

(22) Schmandt, H. J. and G. R. Stephens. "Local Government Expenditure Patterns in the U.S.," *Land Economics,* Vol. 39 (November 1963), pp. 395–406.

(23) Schnore, L. "Some Correlates of Urban Size: A Replication," *American Journal of Sociology,* Vol. 69 (September 1963), pp. 185–193.

(24) Thompson, W. R. *A Preface to Urban Economics.* Baltimore: The Johns Hopkins Press, 1965.

(25) ———. "Internal and External Factors in the Development of Urban Economies," In H. Perloff and L. Wingo (Eds.), *Issues in Urban Economics.* Baltimore: The Johns Hopkins Press, 1968.

(26) Vernon, R. *Metropolis 1985.* New York: Doubleday, 1963.

(27) Williamson, J. "Regional Inequality and the Process of National Development," *Economic Development and Cultural Change,* Vol. 13 (July 1965), Part 2.

(28) Zadeh, L. A. "Toward a Theory of Fuzzy Systems," Report No. ELR–69–2, Electronics Research Laboratory, University of California, Berkeley, 1969.

KEY CONCEPTS

average cost

average product per capita

diseconomies of scale

income elasticity of demand

marginal cost

marginal product

minimum costs approach

negative externalities

positive external economies

PART *4*

THE METROPOLITAN HOUSING MARKET

Urban housing markets in the United States are shaped not only by market forces but also by government policies. The Federal government began intervening in housing markets in the 1930s, and today all levels of government have gotten into the act. Foremost among government programs are direct subsidies that may be granted either to housing producers or to buyers. Perhaps even more important than subsidies, however, in terms of their impact on resource allocation, are local-government regulations, such as zoning ordinances, building codes, and rent and condominium-conversion controls. The commonly held view that housing is a "necessity " may explain why government intervention is so extensive. Unfortunately, government policy has often either attacked the wrong causes of a housing problem or enacted programs that simply proved ineffective.

One important target of public policy is slums and blighted housing. Here, public policy must determine whether dilapidated housing results entirely from market inefficiencies or from other causes. Lower-quality housing exists partly because of the demands of lower-income buyers. Hence, an obvious starting point for government policy is to enact programs to alleviate poverty, the root cause of poor-quality housing. However, instead of attacking poverty, many programs are designed to intervene directly in the housing market and, consequently, often create market distortions and resource misallocations.

Edgar O. Olsen offers a theoretical model to interpret and explain housing-market processes. One noteworthy prediction of Olsen's model is that slum-clearance and urban-renewal programs do not eliminate slums but merely tend to shift their location. The demise of the ineffective urban-renewal program seems to have verified this prediction. Olsen argues that the most economical method of helping the poor is to offer housing vouchers that can be spent on any qualified private housing.

In a second selection, Olsen shifts attention to the economics of housing subsidies. He outlines seven necessary conditions for these programs to be effective, equitable, and efficient. Olsen finds that most current housing programs—especially public housing—violate these simple criteria. Again he suggests that a housing-allowance (voucher) program would provide more benefits to more poor people at lower costs than do existing programs.

Economics has not neglected the imperfections in the housing markets that can also create housing problems. Virtually every market found in urban areas is affected by externalities, and housing markets are no exception. External effects arise because the value of a particular dwelling can be affected by the condition of neighboring properties. Unfortunately, a property owner who contemplates improvements to his or her property will consider only the private return on the investment, not the external benefits bestowed upon his or her neighbors. As a result, the rate of return to the private owner will be below the full (or social) return. This externality might disappear if the private investor could charge owners of neighboring properties for making their properties more valuable. Otherwise, private individuals tend to invest too few resources in housing improvements. This inefficiency can be particularly serious in a blighted neighborhood.

Government urban renewal programs originally were proposed to correct externalities and to combat the flight of middle- and upper-income residents from decaying central cities. However, the importance of externalities in creating slum housing is difficult to assess. Other factors, such as local property-tax-assessment practices, have been shown also to contribute to the problem. Even if market failure is found to underlie slum-housing problems, urban renewal is an inappropriate remedy. Urban renewal creates incentives for local governments to replace slum housing with projects that generate revenue to the city—such as shopping and convention centers or luxury apartments. Because little low-income housing is built, the poor are made worse off.

Today one frequently hears mention of housing crises of one type or another, normally either shortages, high prices, or blight. While some observers are convinced that these problems are caused by market failures and require government intervention, others point out that many crises are created by the government's own policies. Roger Starr demonstrates that the good intentions of rent control—holding down rents and helping the poor—are seldom matched by the law's performance. In the long run, rent control impairs the supply and quality of rental housing, thereby harming, not benefiting, the poor. Further problems unfold when cities attempt to prop up their rent-control laws by restricting condominium conversions. Such restrictions cause would-be investors in new apartment buildings to flee in droves, further restricting the supply of rental housing.

Another example of government good intentions gone awry is municipal building codes. Building codes, it is argued, eliminate the risks of unsafe construction by specifying acceptable construction techniques and materials. If all consumers were well informed, building codes would be unnecessary;

buildings that failed to satisfy consumer preferences for safety and workmanship would be unable to compete with those satisfying these preferences. Because consumers are not perfectly informed, however, a case can be made for government intervention. The relevant question is what type of intervention would be best to deal with the information problem.

A major disadvantage of most current local building codes is their rigidity and inflexibility. The President's Commission on Neighborhoods reports that building codes retard technological innovation, deter rehabilitation of old structures, encourage demolition of existing structures, and inflate the cost of new homes and apartments. The social costs of local building codes appear to exceed the benefits. The commission recommends an alternative approach that would place legal liability for poor quality construction on the contractor.

Racial discrimination in housing markets has also become an important target of public policy. Housing segregation may impose information and transportation costs on workers who are restricted to ghetto housing and, consequently, reduce their employment opportunities. Several alternative policies to improve job opportunities for ghetto workers have heen proposed, one of which is to subsidize firms that locate in ghetto areas. An alternative is to rely upon open housing and other policies to disperse ghetto residents and reduce their information and transportation costs. Which policy would be more effective depends upon the particular causes of low employment among ghetto workers. Samuel L. Myers and Kenneth E. Phillips examine this question and provide a theoretical analysis based on a labor-market perspective. While they reach no definite conclusions as to which policy should prevail, their work addresses the issues that must be resolved in the ghetto-dispersal-versus-ghetto-development debate.

13   A Competitive Theory of the Housing Market

Edgar O. Olsen, of the University of Virginia, here develops a perfectly competitive theory of the housing market and derives implications of the model for government housing policy. It is shown that government sponsored slum-clearance and urban renewal programs will not reduce the social costs of slums or the occupancy of slum dwellings. Olsen's approach permits precise definitions of commonly used housing terms. Filtering, for example, is defined as a change in the number of housing services in a particular dwelling unit.

In his article on the demand for nonfarm housing, Richard Muth [11] rigorously developed a competitive theory of the housing market.[1] Muth used this theory in the statistical estimation of the demand function for housing service and of the speed of adjustment to long-run equilibrium in this market. His theory also makes possible the translation of some of the idiosyncratic concepts used by housing specialists in the familiar terms of microeconomic theory. A secondary purpose of this

article is to make these translations. More importantly, this theory has implications for a number of crucial issues in government housing policy. The primary purpose of this article is to derive these implications, and use them to suggest additional tests of the competitive theory of the housing market. In order to achieve these purposes, it is first necessary to explain the crucial simplifying assumption which makes it possible to view the market for housing service as a competitive market in which a homogeneous good is sold.

THE ASSUMPTIONS

Let us assume that the following conditions are satisfied in markets for housing service: (1) both buyers and sellers of housing service are numerous, (2) the sales or purchases of each individual unit are small in relation to the aggregate volume of transactions, (3) neither buyers nor sellers collude, (4) entry into and exit from the market are free for both producers and consumers, (5) both producers and consumers possess perfect knowledge about the prevailing price and current bids, and they take advantage of every opportunity

From Edgar O. Olsen, "A Competitive Theory of the Housing Market," *American Economic Review* 59, 4 (September 1969): 612–22. Reprinted with permission from the *American Economic Review* and the author.

[1] There are clearly two housing markets. There is a demand for and supply of a consumer good which we shall call housing service. There is also a derived demand for and supply of an investment good which we shall call housing stock. These two markets are integrally related. Indeed, Muth [11, p. 32] defines one unit of housing service to be that quantity of service yielded by one unit of housing stock per unit of time. Thus, he assumes that housing stock is the only input in the production of housing service. Although all buyers of housing stock are also sellers of housing service, there are many people who participate in one market but not in the other. Consumers who occupy rental housing are not typically in the market for housing stock. They are not buyers or sellers of this capital asset. Builders who construct housing for sale are sellers of housing stock but not of housing service. This paper will focus primarily on the market for housing service. Finally, it must be emphasized at the outset that this paper abstracts from consideration of the land on which dwelling units stand.

to increase profits and utility respectively, (6) no artificial restrictions are placed on demands for, supplies of, and prices of housing service and the resources used to produce housing service, and (7) housing service is a homogeneous commodity.

This set of conditions is nothing other than a conventional statement of one set of conditions sufficient for a perfectly competitive market.[2] While objections to all of these assumptions can be found in the housing literature, most scholars would probably find (7) to be the least plausible assumption. Noting the great variations among residential structures as to size, type of construction, and other characteristics to which consumers attach value, many presume that a very heterogeneous good is traded in the housing market. This paper presents a theory with a very different view of the good being traded. An understanding of this theory of the housing market requires an elaboration on its conception of housing. Therefore, we will now focus our attention on this crucial simplifying assumption.

In order to view the housing market as one in which a homogeneous commodity is bought and sold, an unobservable theoretical entity called housing service is introduced.[3] Each dwelling (or housing) unit is presumed to yield some quantity of this good during each time period. It is assumed to be the only thing in a dwelling unit to which consumers attach value. Consequently, in this theory there is no distinction between the quantity and quality of a dwelling unit as these terms are customarily used.

This conception of housing is bound to raise objections. It will be argued that housing is a complex bundle of technically independent attributes. However, since housing service is not observable directly, it is not possible to argue for or against this assumption directly.[4] Hence, it is not possible to test this theory other than by reference to its implications. The competitive theory of the housing market does contain bridge principles which relate housing service to observable phenomena and it does have testable implications in terms of these phenomena. Muth [11] has already tested some of these implications. Other implications will be derived in this paper. Eyesight is not a satisfactory judge of the question of homogeneity. The assumption of a homogeneous good called housing service can only be rejected if theories of the housing market without this assumption have greater explanatory power.

THE TRANSLATION OF CONCEPTS

Based on the assumptions of the preceding section, four concepts—dwelling unit, slum, filtering, and shortage—traditionally used in housing market analysis, can be translated into the jargon of conventional microeconomic theory.

What is a dwelling unit? A *dwelling unit* is a package composed of a certain quantity of a capital asset called housing stock. Some dwelling units will contain 10 units of housing stock, other dwelling units will

---

[2] This set is a composite taken from three standard price theory textbooks. See Leftwich [7, pp. 23–25], Stigler [14, pp. 87–89], and Henderson and Quandt [6, pp. 86–89]. As Stigler clearly explains, this is by no means the weakest set of assumptions sufficient for perfect competition. A strong set of assumptions is used in order to obtain clear-cut implications of the competitive theory.

[3] Hempel [5, pp. 70–84] gives an elementary but lucid explanation of the role of unobservable theoretical entities in scientific theories.

[4] Intuitively, it does seem more reasonable to conceive of the difference between an apartment renting for $50 and one renting for $100 in the same city as more akin to the difference between $50 and $100 worth of oranges than to the difference between $50 worth of oranges and $100 worth of golf balls. However, arguments of this sort are not scientific.

contain 20 units of housing stock. By definition, these dwelling units will be said to yield 10 and 20 units of housing service per time period respectively.[5] In long-run competitive equilibrium only one price per unit applies to all units of housing stock and another price to all units of housing service regardless of the size of the package in which these goods come. Hence, if we observe that one dwelling unit sells for twice the amount of another dwelling unit in the same market, then we say that the more expensive unit contains twice the quantity of housing stock and, hence, involves twice the total expenditure. This distinction between price, quantity, and total expenditure is not usually made in housing market analysis where it is simply said that the price of the one dwelling unit is twice that of the other dwelling unit. Similarly, if we observe that one dwelling unit rents for twice the amount of another dwelling unit, then we say that the more expensive dwelling unit yields twice the quantity of housing service per time period and, hence, involves twice the total expenditure per time period. Here again, traditional housing market analysis uses a price theory concept, in this case "rent," in a way far removed from its original meaning. Despite the fact that housing service and housing stock are not directly observable, the competitive theory of the housing market contains bridge principles which permit us to compare the relative amounts of housing service yielded by different dwelling units.

What is a slum dwelling unit? A *slum dwelling unit* is one which yields less than some arbitrary quantity of housing service per time period. Using the relationship established between total expenditure and quantity, we might decide to call all dwelling units in a particular locality renting for less than $60 per month slum dwelling units. What is a slum area? A *slum area* is a contiguous area which contains a high (but arbitrary) percentage of slum dwelling units.

It would be possible to give the word "slum" a welfare economics definition in which a slum dwelling unit would necessarily represent suboptimal resource allocation. Otto Davis and Andrew Whinston [3, pp. 111-112] have provided such a definition. At least one other distinctly different definition of this sort is possible.[6] However, the definition provided above is more in keeping with the use of this word in both popular and scholarly writings.

What is a housing shortage? The most frequently used unit of quantity for housing market analysis has been the dwelling unit. As a result, a housing shortage has usually been defined as a situation in which everyone who is willing to pay the market price for a separate dwelling unit is not able to obtain a separate dwelling unit. This is an unnecessarily narrow definition of a shortage which results from the acceptance of the dwelling unit as the unit of quantity. The unit of quantity introduced by Muth allows us to take a broader view of a housing shortage. To be precise, a *short-run housing shortage* is said to exist if, and only if, the quantity of housing service demanded at the existing market price is greater than the quantity of housing

---

[5] Dwelling unit means the same thing as housing unit. Therefore, a housing unit is quite different from a unit or housing stock or housing service. The term dwelling unit is used throughout this article to avoid this natural confusion.

[6] Some people care about the housing occupied by low-income families for altruistic and more selfish reasons. The market will not properly account for these preferences and, hence, low-income families may consume too little housing service by the criterion of efficiency. We might call the dwelling units occupied by these low-income families slum dwelling units. Clearly, with this definition slumness is not a characteristic of the housing alone.

service supplied. Short-run shortages will be eliminated by a rise in the price of housing service for bundles of the size which are in excess demand initially. A *long-run housing shortage* is said to exist if, and only if, the quantity of housing service demanded at the long-run equilibrium price is greater than the quantity of housing service supplied. Long-run shortages are eliminated by maintenance, repairs, alterations, and additions as well as by new construction. Clearly, a housing shortage can exist by these definitions even if everyone who wants to occupy a separate dwelling unit at the relevant price is doing so because everyone may want to occupy better housing (that is, to consume a greater quantity of housing service) at this price than they presently occupy and none may be available.

Although the concept of filtering has been used in housing economics for many years, a rigorous definition of this term has only recently been proposed. Ira Lowry [8, p. 363] defines filtering as "... a change in the real value (price in constant dollars) of an existing dwelling unit." Lowry uses this definition together with a theory of the housing market to demonstrate that filtering is not a process which necessarily results in all families occupying housing above certain minimum standards. With the competitive theory of the housing market, it is possible to define filtering slightly more rigorously and in a manner which significantly clarifies the meaning of the concept and the method of detecting the process. Using this new definition and a competitive theory of the housing market, it is easy to demonstrate the result which Lowry showed with great difficulty.

A dwelling unit has *filtered* if, and only if, the quantity of housing stock contained in this unit has changed. A dwelling unit has *filtered up* if, and only if, the quantity

of housing stock contained in this unit has increased. A dwelling unit has *filtered down* if, and only if, the quantity of housing stock contained in this unit has decreased.[7] Within the theory presented in this paper, Lowry's definition is the same as the new definition if he intended to deflate money values by the cost of construction. This is true because in a perfectly competitive housing market in long-run equilibrium the price per unit of housing stock equals the minimum long-run average cost of production and, hence, the quantity of housing stock contained in a particular dwelling unit is equal to the market value of this dwelling unit divided by the cost of production.[8] For example, if the cost-of-construction index was 100 in 1960 and 110 in 1962 and if a particular dwelling unit sold for $6000 in 1960 and $6050 in 1962, then we would say that this particular unit has filtered down between 1960 and 1962 because our index of quantity of housing stock fell from 60 to 55.[9]

To determine whether particular dwelling units have filtered is of far less importance than understanding the function of filtering in the operation of the housing market. In essence, Lowry set out to demonstrate that filtering is not a process that insures that all consumers will purchase greater than an arbitrarily chosen

---

[7] In these definitions, "housing stock contained in" could be replaced by "housing service yielded per time period by." These definitions are stated in stock terms to facilitate the comparison with Lowry's definition.

[8] Lowry does not say what he intends to use as a deflator.

[9] This method abstracts from changes in the price paid for a particular structure attributable to changes in the relative desirability of its location. Since I do not want to include these changes in my concept of filtering, the market value of the land must be subtracted from the total price of structure and land in determining whether a dwelling unit has filtered. Practically, this might be done by observing the sale price per square foot of nearby vacant land and assuming that the land containing the structure of interest has the same market value per square foot.

quantity of housing service per time period. If the housing market is perfectly competitive, then this result is trivial since there is nothing in the operation of such a market which insures that all individuals will consume greater than an arbitrary quantity of the good.[10] As will be shown in the next section, filtering is a process by which the quantity of housing service yielded by particular dwelling units is adjusted to conform to the pattern of consumer demand. The profit incentive leads producers to make these adjustments.

None of the definitions in this section corresponds exactly with previous usage of the terms. No simple definitions could. These definitions have been offered in order to bring housing market analysis within the realm of standard microeconomic theory where advantage can be taken of the accumulated knowledge in this field. The value of this transformation should be strongly emphasized. Even as eminent a price theorist as Milton Friedman [4, pp. 178-180] reaches an undoubtedly fallacious conclusion about public housing simply because he did not apply the conventional distinction between the very short run and the long run to the housing market.[11]

---

[10] For any given positive quantity, there exists a set of admissible indifference curves, relative prices, and income such that the consumer associated with these will choose less than the given quantity.

[11] Friedman [4, p. 179] concludes that "... far from improving the housing of the poor, as its proponents expected, public housing has done just the reverse. The number of dwelling units destroyed in the course of erecting public housing projects has been far larger than the number of new units constructed." Aside from the factual question of whether far more units have been destroyed than constructed and aside from Friedman's use of numbers of gainers and losers rather than the values of gains and losses, Friedman ignores the fact that the displaced families will lose over a few years while housed families will gain over the much longer physical life of the project. As will be demonstrated in the pages that follow, in long-run equilibrium the displaced families will occupy the same type of housing and pay the same rent as prior to the public housing project. According to Muth [11, pp. 49–52],

THE WORKINGS OF THE MARKET

The workings of the market for housing service under the set of assumptions introduced in Section 1 can best be illustrated by beginning from a situation in which the price per unit of housing service for bundles of all sizes but one is equal to the long-run average cost of production. For the one bundle size, the price is assumed to be greater than the long-run average cost. In this situation, producers will be making profits (that is, they will be making more than a normal rate of return on capital) only on this one size bundle of housing service.

Owners of housing stock can change the quantity of housing stock contained in and, hence, the quantity of housing service yielded by their dwelling units through maintenance, repair, alteration, and addition.[12] In the absence of maintenance, dwelling units deteriorate with use and over time which means that they yield smaller and smaller quantities of housing service per time period. Normally, producers of housing service find it profitable to invest in maintenance (although not enough to halt deterioration completely). If bundles of some particular size become more profitable than bundles of other sizes, then some producers with larger bundles of housing service will allow their

---

the market for housing service adjusts at a rate of one-third of the difference between the present situation and long-run equilibrium each year. Hence, there is a 90 percent adjustment in six years. By comparison, the physical life of public housing projects is likely to be far in excess of 50 years. From Olsen's calculations [12, pp. 83–87] it can be estimated that the average public housing tenant received benefits from public housing which he valued at $263 in 1965. This benefit would be received each year by some poor family during the entire physical life of the project.

[12] In the remainder of this article, the word "maintenance" will be used to denote all four of these phenomena.

housing units to deteriorate more than they would otherwise. That is, they will allow their dwelling units to filter down to the bundle size which is most profitable. This is accomplished by following a lower maintenance policy than would had been followed had all bundle sizes been equally profitable. By the same token, some producers of smaller bundles of housing service will follow a higher maintenance policy than otherwise resulting in a filtering up of their dwelling units.

The supply of the most profitable size bundle having increased, the price per unit of housing service for bundles of this size will decrease. Since initially there were zero profits for bundles of housing service slightly greater and slightly less than the profitable size bundle, the filtering down of larger bundles and the filtering up of smaller bundles will create short-run shortages, higher prices, and profits for bundles of these sizes. This will result in filtering down of still larger bundles and filtering up of smaller bundles. Eventually the process will reach bundles of sizes which can be provided by the construction of new dwelling units. This new construction will continue until there are no profits to be made on bundles of any size. This requires the price per unit of housing service for bundles of all sizes to be the same.

THE POOR-PAY-MORE HYPOTHESIS

A popular claim in current policy discussions is that the poor pay more for many goods including housing. If the housing markets are perfectly competitive and if it is neither more costly to provide small quantities of housing service nor to provide housing service to low-income families, then the poor will not pay more for housing service. It is instructive of the workings of a perfectly competitive housing market to demonstrate this result.

We begin by interpreting the poor-pay-more hypothesis in terms of the theory presented in this article. For some reason the price per unit of housing service is greater for dwelling units yielding small quantities of housing service than for dwelling units yielding large quantities. This price difference is not attributable to differences in cost.[13] For large bundles of housing service, the market works efficiently. The price of housing service tends towards the minimum long-run average cost of production of housing service. Consequently, the price per unit of housing service for small bundles exceeds the minimum average cost. As a result, owners of dwelling units yielding small quantities of housing service make economic profits. For some reason, these profits do not stimulate an increase in the supply of these small bundles of housing service. As a result, the consumers of these small bundles (that is, primarily the poor) consume a smaller quantity of housing service than required for efficient resource allocation.

Participants in a competitive housing market would not allow this situation to persist. Suppose that owners of bundles of housing stock yielding quantities of housing service less than x received a higher price per unit for their production than owners of bundles which yield greater than x units of housing service. These slum landlords would be making higher profits per dollar invested than other landlords. In this case, some owners of dwelling units yielding slightly more than x units will fol-

---

[13] If the price difference is solely attributable to differences in cost, then no market imperfection is involved and government action on grounds of efficiency is not required. A recent study by the U.S. Bureau of Labor Statistics [15] has shown that the poor do pay more for food, but that this difference is fully explained by difference in cost. The poor tend to shop in small stores where merchandising cost per unit is high.

low a lower maintenance policy than otherwise, allowing the quantity of housing service yielded by their units per time period to fall below x. The supply of dwelling units yielding less than x units of housing service per time period will increase and the price per unit for these small bundles will fall. Eventually, new construction will be induced. Only when the price per unit of housing service for bundles of all sizes is equal to the minimum long-run average cost of production will there be no incentive for change.

If we actually observe that the poor consistently pay more per unit of housing service than the rich and that it is not more expensive per unit to provide small packages of housing service or to provide housing service to low-income families, then we have evidence contrary to the assumption that the housing market is competitive. This is one of the testable implications of the competitive theory.[14]

WILL SLUM CLEARANCE AND URBAN RENEWAL RESULT IN A NET REDUCTION IN SLUMS?

Slum clearance is the destruction of slum dwelling units by government with or

without compensation to the owner. It is required by the Housing Act of 1937 as part of the public housing program. It is undertaken independently by many local governments. Finally, slum clearance is the first stage of urban renewal. Slum clearance and urban renewal have been premised in large part on the naive belief that the physical destruction of slum dwelling units results in a net reduction in the number of families occupying such units. Many writers have questioned this presumption and have suggested that slum clearance merely results in the transfer of slums from one location to another.[15] Indeed, this argument should suggest itself to all economists since slum clearance does not increase the incomes of or decrease the prices of any goods to the former residents of the cleared areas. If the market for housing service is perfectly competitive, then this argument can be made completely rigorous.

We have defined a slum dwelling unit as a dwelling unit yielding a flow of less than x units of housing service. Starting from a situation of long-run equilibrium in the housing market with normal vacancy rates, the immediate effect of slum clearance is to decrease the supply of slum dwelling units. Some of the former residents of the destroyed dwelling units will move into vacant dwelling units providing the same quantity of housing service. Others will have to move into dwelling units which provide slightly more or slightly less housing service than they prefer to buy at the long-run equilibrium price. The owners of slum dwelling units will realize that they can both charge higher prices and have lower vacancy rates than before slum clearance. They will take advantage of the

---

[14] A recent study by the BLS [16] has shown that the quality of housing occupied by richer families is superior to that occupied by poorer people in the same rent range. Unfortunately, it is almost certainly true that within each rent range the higher the income range, the higher the average rent. The higher rent may completely explain the differences in quality. This author is trying to obtain the BLS data to check this possibility with regression analysis. Finally, the BLS study does not consider the possibility that it is more costly per unit of housing service either to provide small bundles or to sell to low-income families. For example, it is reputed to be much more difficult to collect rents from low-income tenants. This involves extra costs in time and nonpayment. Furthermore, the existence and enforcement of building and occupancy codes with penalties for violations increase the long-run equilibrium price of low-quantity housing in a competitive market because there exist some producers and consumers who will have an incentive to violate the code. (I owe this point to Richard Muth.)

[15] For example, see Bailey [2, p. 291], Davis and Whinston [3, p. 112], and Anderson [1, pp. 8–9].

short-run shortage to raise prices in order to increase their profits. This, however, is only the very short-run impact of slum clearance.

In the long run, the owners of slightly better than slum dwelling units will allow their dwelling units to filter down to the level of slum dwelling units in order to take advantage of the profits to be made on such units. This adjustment will continue until the rate of return on capital invested in bundles of housing stock of all sizes is the same. In long-run equilibrium the price per unit of housing service must be the same for bundles of all sizes. Since neither slum clearance nor urban renewal subsidizes housing consumption by low-income families, and since neither results in a lower cost of production of housing service, therefore, neither results in a lower price of housing service to the former residents of slum clearance or urban renewal sites in the long run. Neither slum clearance nor urban renewal results in change in the incomes of or the prices paid for nonhousing goods by the former residents. Consequently, the former residents of the cleared area will, in long-run equilibrium, consume exactly the same quantity of housing service as before slum clearance or urban renewal. Slum clearance and urban renewal do not result in a net reduction in the occupancy of slums in the long run.

This implication of the competitive theory is testable. To conduct this test, we might observe the characteristics of the housing occupied by former residents of slum clearance sites and their incomes just prior to slum clearance and for 6 years afterwards. With respect to each characteristic, we shall probably observe that the percentage of families occupying housing with that characteristic is different immediately after slum clearance from what it was

immediately before. For example, the percentage of families in dilapidated dwelling units might have been 90 percent before slum clearance and 50 percent afterwards. The competitive theory suggests that in long-run equilibrium, we will again find 90 percent of these families in dilapidated dwelling units if these families experience no change in real income. Therefore, if we determine the percentage of families occupying dwelling units with each particular characteristic by income groups, then we should observe that within each income group the percentage of families occupying housing having the particular characteristic should, over time, approach the before-slum-clearance percentage. This convergence provides a weak test of the competitive hypothesis. As mentioned before, Muth [11, pp. 49-52] estimates that we get a 90 percent adjustment in the housing market in six years.[16] Consequently, we expect that the difference between the percentage at the end of six years and the percentage immediately after slum clearance will be roughly 90 percent of the difference between the percentage immediately before slum clearance and the percentage immediately afterwards. A test of the statistical significance of the difference between these two variables is a strong test of the competitive theory.[17]

There have been, and continue to be, many instances of slum clearance, especially associated with urban renewal. It is

[16] Specifically, Muth's estimates indicate that individuals seek to add about one-third of the difference between desired and actual stock during a year, which implies that for the adjustment of the actual housing stock to be 90 percent completed, six years are required.

[17] If there is much variation in the speed of adjustment among the housing markets in the United States, then it would be desirable to estimate Muth's equation with data from the particular local housing market to obtain the speed of adjustment for that market and to use this estimate for our test.

quite feasible to conduct studies of displaced families at least partly for the purpose of testing this implication of the competitive theory of the housing market. Since the nature of the housing market is very relevant to the choice of government housing policies, these data might reasonably be collected by the U.S. Department of Housing and Urban Development in conjunction with urban renewal and public housing.

If the housing market is perfectly competitive, then slum clearance and urban renewal result only in a shift in the location of slums rather than in a net reduction in slums. Consequently, we should expect neither urban renewal nor slum clearance to lead to a reduction in the social costs of slum living or to net beneficial spillover effects for properties not on the slum clearance site. Cost-benefit analyses of urban renewal typically find that measured benefits are far less than measured costs.[18] The authors of these studies usually do not attempt to calculate the alleged benefits from these two sources, but they claim that the benefits from the reduction in social costs of slums and the net beneficial spillover effects on neighboring properties might well overcome the excess of measured costs over measured benefits.[19] If the housing market were perfectly competitive, then the expected value of these alleged benefits would be zero and, hence, almost all slum clearance and urban renewal projects would be extremely wasteful.

THE EFFECT OF RENT CERTIFICATES ON THE HOUSING OCCUPIED BY THEIR RECIPIENTS

If it is desired either to decrease the number of occupied slum dwelling units or to improve the housing occupied by low-income families and if the housing market is competitive, then slum clearance and urban renewal are not the answers. They would have neither of these effects. The most direct ways of obtaining these results are to tax (or prohibit) the occupation of slum dwelling units or to subsidize the housing of low-income families. The former method would make the occupants of slum dwelling units worse off as they judge their own well-being. Consequently, to the extent that the desire to decrease the amount of slum housing and to increase the housing consumption of low-income families is motivated by a desire to help these people, to that extent the tax (or prohibition) alternative can be dropped from consideration.

Probably the most efficient method of subsidizing the housing of low-income families is to allow these families to buy certificates which they could use to pay the rent or make mortgage payments up to an amount equal to the face value of the certificate.[20] The low-income family would purchase this certificate for an amount less than the face value.[21] These certificates would be redeemed by the government

[18] For example, see Rothenberg [13, p. 341, Table 4] and Messner [9, p. 78, Table 13]. In each study, costs and benefits for three projects were calculated. Total benefits for the six projects were only 27 percent of total costs. The highest benefit-cost ratio was 0.37 and the lowest was 0.05. Rothenberg's calculations were intended to be illustrative only, but Messner's calculations based on Rothenberg's framework are very careful and detailed.

[19] See Rothenberg [13, p. 340]. Messner [9, p. 78] takes a much more guarded view of the likelihood of significant benefits from these two sources.

[20] Olsen [12, pp. 69–116] has made estimates which strongly suggest the rent certificate plan to be significantly more efficient than public housing.

[21] Under the principle of benefit taxation, each recipient should be charged an amount equal to average expenditure on housing service prior to the program by families of the same size and with the same income. See Olsen [12, pp. 110–116]. This result follows primarily from Muth's finding [11] that the price elasticity of demand for housing service is roughly constant and unitary.

from sellers of housing service. It would be illegal to exchange these certificates for other than housing service.

Given the amount of public money likely to be spent for such a program and the amount that might be reasonably charged for these certificates, the face values of rent certificates will not be large enough to induce many low-income families to move to newly produced housing because new housing typically comes in relatively large bundles of housing stock. Since a rent certificate plan does not directly increase the supply of newly constructed housing and since few of the recipients are likely to demand new housing, many people wonder how a rent certificate plan could result in an increase in the total quantity of housing stock. They suggest that since there will be no increase in housing stock, the only result of the increase in demand stemming from the rent certificate plan will be higher prices for housing service purchased by the low-income families who use rent certificates.[22]

By now it should be clear that if the market for housing service is perfectly competitive, then this is only the very short-run effect of a rent certificate plan.[23] In the long run, the owners of the smallest bundles of housing stock will either increase their maintenance expenditures (and thereby increase the quantity of housing service yielded by their units) or convert their buildings to other uses. There would no longer be any demand for dwelling units which provide less housing service than can be purchased with rent certificates of the smallest face values.

Some owners of dwelling units presently providing bundles of housing service larger than could be purchased with rent certificates of the highest face value will allow their units to filter down to the relatively more profitable sectors initially affected by rent certificates. As a result, there will be shortages and, hence, economic profits for these larger bundles of housing service. Owners of dwelling units yielding still larger quantities of housing service will allow their units to filter down. Eventually shortages will result for bundles of housing stock which can be provided by new construction. Construction of new dwelling units will continue until there are no more excess profits in the market for housing service. In long-run competitive equilibrium all consumers must pay the same price per unit of housing service. Consequently, purchasers of rent certificates with a face value of x dollars per month should be able to consume the same quantity of housing service as individuals who spent this much per month for housing service prior to the program.

This result leads to yet another testable implication of the competitive theory of the housing market. If the competitive theory is correct, then we should observe that the buyers of rent certificates with a face value of x dollars will occupy housing as good as the housing which rented for x dollars prior to the rent certificate plan.[24] This is the long-run equilibrium situation. The adjustment of this equilibrium will

---

[22] For a lucid statement of this position taken by many housing specialists, see Meyerson, Terrett, and Wheaton [10, pp. 71–72].

[23] Indeed, since a rent certificate plan would undoubtedly be discussed by Congress for some time before passage, it would be anticipated by sellers of housing service who would find it profitable to adjust their maintenance policy in advance of passage. Consequently, there might be little price inflation immediately after implementation.

[24] It would be necessary to correct for changes in the general price level, but we should not expect the relative price of housing to rise in the long run because of the increase in the total demand for housing service which is a result of the rent certificate plan. Muth [11, pp. 42–46] finds the supply curve to be perfectly elastic.

take several years. As already pointed out, Muth's evidence suggests a 90 percent adjustment in six years. Hence, we should observe that the characteristics of the housing occupied by recipients (for example, whether the dwelling unit has hot and cold running water) should approach the characteristics of the housing occupied by individuals who spent the same amount on housing prior to the program.

It should not be necessary to wait until a national rent certificate plan is adopted to test this implication. According to Meyerson, Terrett, and Wheaton [10, p. 71], "... welfare agencies in many states in this country do issue rent certificates to families on relief. During the Depression, millions of families received such payments." There may already be data from these experiences to test this implication of the competitive theory of the housing market. Given the demonstrated inefficiency of urban renewal and public housing, it would also seem reasonable for a city to propose and the Federal Government to accept a rent certificate plan in place of the two other programs on a demonstration basis. The experience of the buyers of rent certificates in this city could be used to test the competitive theory.

CONCLUSION

In this article, the assumptions of Muth's competitive theory of the housing market are stated and the nature of the good called housing service is elaborated upon. This theory is used to translate 4 familiar terms of housing market analysis—dwelling unit, slum, shortage, and filtering—into the standard concepts of microeconomic theory. If the housing market is perfectly competitive and if it is not more costly per unit

to provide housing to low-income families or to provide small packages of housing service, then (1) the poor would not pay more per unit for housing, (2) slum clearance and urban renewal would not result in a net reduction in the number of occupied substandard units, and (3) the recipients of rent certificates would enjoy housing just as good as the housing occupied by others who spent as much on housing as the face value of the certificates. These results and their implications for government policy are deduced. In each of the three cases, testable implications of the assumptions are derived and the nature of the test made explicit. It is hoped that this article will serve to bring housing market analysis within the realm of conventional economic theory and to suggest additional tests of one particular conventional economic theory of markets.

REFERENCES

1. M. Anderson, *The Federal Bulldozer* (Cambridge, Mass.: MIT Press, 1964).
2. M. J. Bailey, "Note on the Economics of Residential Zoning and Urban Renewal," *Land Economics* 35 (August 1959), pp. 288–292.
3. O. A. Davis and A. B. Whinston, "Economics of Urban Renewal," *Law and Contemporary Problems* 26 (Winter 1961), pp. 105–117.
4. M. Friedman, *Capitalism and Freedom* (Chicago: University of Chicago Press, 1964).
5. C. G. Hempel, *Philosophy of Natural Science* (Englewood Cliffs, N.J.: Prentice-Hall, 1966).
6. J. M. Henderson and R. E. Quandt, *Microeconomic Theory* (New York: McGraw-Hill, 1958).
7. R. H. Leftwich, *The Price System and Resource Allocation* (New York: Holt, Rinehart & Winston, 1961).
8. I. S. Lowry, "Filtering and Housing Standards: A Conceptual Analysis," *Land Economics* 36 (Nov. 1960), pp. 362–370.

9. S. D. Messner, *A Benefit Cost Analysis of Urban Redevelopment,* Bureau of Business Research (Bloomington: Indiana University, 1967).

10. M. Meyerson, B. Terrett, and W. L. C. Wheaton, *Housing, People, and Cities* (New York: McGraw-Hill, 1962).

11. R. F. Muth, "The Demand for Non-Farm Housing," in A. C. Harberger, ed., *The Demand for Durable Goods* (Chicago: University of Chicago Press, 1960), pp. 29–96.

12. E. O. Olsen, "A Welfare Economic Evaluation of Public Housing," unpublished Ph.D. dissertation, Rice University, 1968.

13. J. Rothenberg, "Urban Renewal Programs," in R. Dorfman, ed., *Measuring Benefits of Government Investments* (Washington, D.C.: Brookings, 1966), pp. 292–341.

14. G. J. Stigler, *The Theory of Price* (New York: Macmillan, 1966).

15. U.S. Bureau of Labor Statistics, "A Study of Prices Charged in Food Stores Located in Low and High Income Areas of Six Large Cities, February 1966," mimeographed, June 12, 1966.

16. U.S. Bureau of Labor Statistics, "Differences in the Characteristics of Rental Housing Occupied by Families in Three Income Ranges Paying Approximately the Same Rent in Six Cities," mimeographed, Sept. 1966.

KEY CONCEPTS

dwelling unit

economic profits

filtering

housing shortage

long-run equilibrium price

rent certificates

slum dwelling unit

EDGAR O. OLSEN

14   Housing Programs and the Forgotten Taxpayer

Government has pursued housing policies that, according to Edgar O. Olsen, are a "chamber of horrors" when examined from the viewpoint of taxpayers. He shows that existing housing programs, with one notable exception, fail to meet even rudimentary efficiency standards and also are seriously deficient on equity grounds. The single exception is the housing-allowance program, which gives cash grants to low-income families who then freely choose qualified housing in the private market.

This evaluation of housing programs is conducted from an unusual perspective, namely, the preferences of taxpayers who are neither receipients of housing subsidies nor involved in the provision of housing for these families. Most discussions of housing policy, especially among active participants in the policy-making process, ignore the interests of such taxpayers, even though they bear almost all of the costs of the programs. The traditional explanation is that members of special interest groups have a much larger stake in housing policy than other taxpayers do. Although this is surely true, it seems clear that if any substantial proportion of the electorate understood existing federal housing programs, politicians would find it in their interest to change them radically. As Irving Welfeld has remarked, the more these programs are understood, the less they are admired.

Despite their dominance in the policy-making process, I believe that the prefer-

ences of recipients and suppliers have little relevance to the formulation of good housing programs. This heresy requires an explanation.

Recipients prefer a cash grant without any strings attached, rather than any other type of subsidy having the same cost, and they want the grant to be as large as possible. The second statement is self-evident, and the first is a proposition accepted by virtually every economist and supported by a large body of empirical evidence. For example, it has been estimated that the typical family in public housing would be willing to move out in return for an unrestricted cash grant costing taxpayers only 60 percent of the public housing subsidy. If only the preferences of recipients mattered, cash grants would replace housing programs. Consequently, their preferences provide little guidance in the design of these programs.

The interests of housing suppliers are also irrelevant. Naturally, any group of suppliers would like to see the demand for its product increased. People in the construc-

Reprinted with permission of the author from *The Public Interest*, No. 66 (Winter 1982), pp. 97-109. Copyright 1982 by National Affairs, Inc.

tion industry would be delighted with a program in which the federal government purchased and destroyed all housing put up for sale. (Industry spokesmen would, of course, deny this because such a program is so outrageous that it would attract the notice of the electorate and perhaps direct attention to other programs which do the same thing in more subtle ways and on a smaller scale. Even urban renewal, which involved housing destruction on a less massive scale, attracted sufficient public attention to force its termination.) Unfortunately, it is impossible to provide a net subsidy to every producing sector of the economy. Every additional subsidy must be accompanied by additional taxes, possibly in the form of monetary expansion. After all taxes and subsidies, the demands for some products will be larger and the demands for other products smaller. Since it is impossible to increase the demand for all products, the desire of producers in each sector for government programs to stimulate the demand for their product provides no guidance for government policy.

Taxpayers who are neither participants in HUD's housing programs nor suppliers of housing provide the lion's share of the money for housing subsidies. Since they are the primary purchasers of these programs, their preferences should be, but have not been, decisive in designing them. Of course such taxpayers are not of one mind. Some are unconcerned about the plight of the poor, and their preferences are relevant to the magnitude of assistance to these families but not to its form. Taxpayers who are concerned about needy families have an interest in the design of housing programs, though their interest is rarely sufficient to justify active involvement. Even people who have no special interest in the *housing* of needy families have an interest in housing policy because housing programs typically affect recipients' consumption of other goods and services.

TAXPAYER PREFERENCES

What then are the preferences of a typical taxpayer with respect to housing policy? The truth of the matter is that no serious attempt has been made to find out, and attempts to discover these preferences with a few quick questions are not likely to yield satisfactory results because few people have thought much about it. While ordinary politicians are content to act on popular whims, a leader who respects his fellow citizens would want to know what housing policy they would favor if they were to consider the matter carefully. In the absence of credible information about taxpayer preferences, the best that can be done is to offer some conjectures about features of housing programs that would, on reflection, appeal to almost all taxpayers. If these conjectures are at all close to the mark, HUD's major housing programs, with one exception, are seriously deficient.

1. *Housing assistance should be limited to the neediest families.* The natural place to begin a discussion of housing policy is with the question of who should be subsidized. The first thing to realize is that it is not in the interest of taxpayers to provide housing subsidies to everyone....

While it is possible to reduce the price of housing relative to other goods for everyone, and in this sense to give everyone a housing subsidy, it is impossible to provide everyone with a *net* subsidy. The taxes to finance the housing subsidies must come from someone. If some people receive subsidies in excess of the additional taxes they pay on account of the program, the opposite must be true for others.

A family that receives a housing subsidy in an amount equal to its additional tax eventually will be induced to occupy better housing and spend less on other goods. Since the net subsidy to this family is zero, its total spending is unchanged. Therefore, the new combination of goods could have been (but was not) chosen prior to the program, which means that the family considers the new mix inferior to the original combination. In short, a family that gets back as much as it pays in taxes is made worse off. The typical family will do even less well because the average tax payment will exceed the average subsidy due to administrative cost.

Since it is impossible to make taxpayers better off by giving them housing subsidies financed by a tax of the same magnitude, it seems reasonable to limit housing subsidies to people whom other taxpayers want to help. There is inevitably a divergence of opinion concerning this matter. To some, the neediest families are those with the lowest income, at least among families of the same size, and this concept of need is used in many welfare programs to determine both eligibility and the magnitude of the subsidy. This definition of need clearly does not do justice to all taxpayers' preferences.

For example, consider how taxpayers are likely to feel about the following two people. One is intelligent, well-educated, but lazy. This person could be highly productive but has instead chosen to take an undemanding part-time job paying $2000 per year. The other person has been handicapped from birth, but by virtue of a tremendous effort is able to earn $3000 per year without private charity. There can be little doubt that the overwhelming majority of taxpayers would consider the handicapped person more deserving of help even though his income is higher. Clearly, the willingness of taxpayers to sacrifice their own consumption for others depends upon many characteristics of potential recipients. In practice some characteristics will have to be ignored because they are too difficult to observe, and program operation would be based on a small number of characteristics that are relatively easy to observe.

2. *Families that are generally the same should be offered the same assistance.* Once it has been decided which characteristics of potential recipients are of interest to taxpayers, it is difficult to understand how anyone could argue for different treatment of households that are the same in all these respects. This implies that we should not offer subsidies to some, but not all, similarly situated families. It is often argued that we are not willing to spend enough to serve all families eligible for housing subsidies. If this argument is correct, it means that we should either make fewer people eligible or reduce the subsidies for which they are eligible.

3. *Among eligible families that are the same in other respects, those with the lowest income should receive the largest subsidy.* After taking account of other relevant differences between families, income is probably the best available measure of productive ability and hence provides the best way of directing the most aid to the neediest people. It is all right to say, for example, that we should provide more assistance to a six-person household with an income of $4000 than to a two-person household with an income of $3000, because these two families are not the same in several respects. This preference

implies that it is undesirable to deny subsidies to poorer families while providing them to richer families who are otherwise similar.

4. *The subsidy should be zero at the upper-income limit for eligibility.* If the subsidy is zero at a lower income, then some eligible families will not participate. If the subsidy is positive for families at the upper-income limit, then subsidized families with incomes below the limit will be able to consume more than some ineligible families. For example, suppose that the upper-income limit for eligibility is $4000, that the subsidy is $1000 for a family at this limit, and that the subsidy increases by 50 cents for every dollar decrease in income. In this case, a family that earns $3000 will receive a subsidy of $1500 and thus be able to consume more than a family that earns between $4000 and $4500. Many welfare programs have this feature, and it is greatly resented by many middle-income families.

5. *A housing program should not subsidize housing that is better than the housing typical of families just above the upper-income limit for eligibility.* Since the desirability of income limits presumably reflects a judgment that no public purpose is served by changing the consumption patterns of richer families, this preference is simply a corollary of the preceding one. It does not imply that subsidized families should be prevented from occupying such housing but rather that their subsidy should not be greater if they do. If a subsidized family is willing to sacrifice one dollar's worth of nonhousing goods and services to spend an additional dollar on housing, there seems no reason to object.

6. *Housing subsidies should induce the worst-housed families at each income level to occupy better housing than they would choose were they given cash grants.*

If we simply want to help low-income families and if we think that they know better than others what is good for themselves, we should give them cash grants with no strings attached. Presumably we have housing subsidies either because we do not think that the heads of these households are acting in the best interests of their families or because better housing for these families confers more tangible benefits on others.

However, it is difficult to argue for *housing* subsidies to all low-income families. There is great variance in the housing of families of the same size and income who are facing the same set of prices. Many low-income families occupy housing which meets the standards that have been used in housing programs. Typically this is achieved by spending a large proportion of income on housing or, more precisely, on those attributes of housing covered by the standards. Do we want these families to occupy better housing than they would choose in response to an equally costly unrestricted cash grant? The often-expressed concern about excessive rent burden suggests that we do not. The collective judgment of taxpayers appears to be that these families spend too much of their income on housing. That is, we want to provide them with special incentives to consume more non-housing goods.

7. *The housing occupied by program participants should be produced at the lowest possible cost consistent with its other characteristics.* This is a necessary condition for achieving program outcomes at the smallest possible expense to taxpayers. Most government officials state this goal but few pursue it with any vigor.

It is easy to show that HUD's major housing programs are far from satisfying even these basic taxpayer preferences for equity, effectiveness, and efficiency. It has become fashionable to believe that trade-offs between goals such as these are inevitable, but there *is* one housing program, with which we have had considerable experience and which has been carefully studied, that has all seven desired properties.

A SHORT HISTORY OF
U.S. HOUSING POLICY

For more than 40 years, federal housing policy has been dominated by the construction of new units. It began in the 1930s with the public housing program under which local housing authorities commissioned the building of projects funded primarily by the federal government. Tenants and local governments paid the cost of operating these projects. With the surge in redistributive programs in the 1960s and the weakening of support for public housing, two programs emphasizing the construction of new units were inaugurated. Section 235 of the National Housing Act authorized homeownership subsidies for the richest of the poor; Section 236 authorized rent subsidies for low-income families in privately owned units. A few years earlier Congress had authorized the Section 23 Housing Assistance Payments Program which was intended to use the existing stock of standard units to house subsidized families. Within a few years the HUD bureaucracy had subverted it: By the early 1970s half of its participants lived in units built for the program.

When scandals and high default rates brought Sections 235 and 236 to the attention of the press, President Nixon ordered a halt to additional commitments under all housing programs pending a thorough review of their performance. In response to a negative evaluation of these programs, HUD developed new programs, known collectively as the Section 8 Housing Assistance Payments Program, that were intended eventually to replace all other housing programs. The new programs all involved the leasing of privately owned housing. Some were newly built for the program, others were substantially rehabilitated as a condition for participation, and still others were existing units meeting program housing standards. The existing component grew most rapidly in the early years. By 1978 there were 580,000 families in Section 8 existing units, 70,000 in Section 8 new units, and 15,000 in Section 8 rehabilitated units. Since then the new and "rehab" components have more than tripled in size while the existing component has stayed about the same. Furthermore, a substantial proportion of the budget of the Section 8 existing program is now used to bail out projects under the older new-construction programs that are on the verge of default. Of the more 3 million families receiving housing assistance from HUD, fewer than a fifth are allowed to choose their housing.

HUD administers other small housing programs, and the programs mentioned above typically have several variants and variants within variants. However, research has shown that it is not necessary to know these intricacies to see what needs to be done to make housing policy consistent with taxpayer preferences. The fundamental distinction is between programs involving the construction of new units or the major rehabilitation of units selected by bureaucrats on the one hand, and those involving assistance to families who are free to choose any unit meeting housing standards on the other hand. The effects of programs within each category are basically the same, and the differences between programs in different categories are marked. Since the rehabilitation programs account for such a small share of HUD's budget and have been subject to much less research than the other types of programs, they will be omitted from the rest of this article.

HUD'S NEW-CONSTRUCTION PROGRAMS

What has research shown about the extent to which HUD's new-construction programs have features that are desired by ineligible taxpayers? These programs do induce a substantial majority of their participants to live in better housing than they would if they were given cash with no strings attached. However, it has not shown that these families tended to be the worst housed among those with the same income, and so we do not know whether these programs change consumption patterns in ways consistent with their rationales.

Assistance is not provided to the richest families, but one could question whether ineligible taxpayers want to provide housing subsidies to families with incomes equal to 80 percent of the local average, especially if the locality is a wealthy community such as Westchester County in New York. These are the upper-income limits for eligibility for the Section 8 program which has accounted for most additions to the stock of newly constructed subsidized units in the last few years. As a result of these high-income limits, about 40 percent of the population is eligible for this program.

In all other respects HUD's new construction programs are wildly at variance with the assumed preferences of ineligible taxpayers. In their early years these programs provide their participants with much better housing than that typical of families just above the upper-income limits of eligibility. The Section 8 new-construction program is a perfect example. The average rent paid to owners of the units added to this program in fiscal year 1978 was about $400 per month; the average rent of families with incomes just above the upper limits for eligibility was roughly $200. In other words, about 60 percent of all families are ineligible for this program but few of these families live in units renting for more than the typical program unit. Under a new-construction program there are only two ways to eliminate this defect: build units of lower quality or increase the upper-income limit for eligibility.

Recipients of Section 8 subsidies pay about 25 percent of their income for housing. This is also typical of ineligible families with incomes near the upper limit. That is, both subsidized and unsubsidized families with incomes near the limit spend about the same amount on other goods and services, but the subsidized families who live in new units get much better housing. Under the Section 8 new-construction program, the subsidy to families near the upper income limit certainly exceeds $1000 per year. This grossly violates the assumed taxpayer preference for equity between eligible and ineligible families. The inequity could be removed by either raising rents or building housing of lower quality.

Due to the high per-unit cost of the new-construction programs, Congress has never been willing to appropriate enough money to serve all eligible households. It would have been possible to focus the available funds on the neediest, but this has not been done. One study estimated the percentage of eligible families in each income and family size class that are assisted by any of HUD's housing programs. It found that this percentage was highest among families with five members and incomes between $4000 and $4999. About 28 percent of these families received housing subsidies. In contrast, only 18 percent of five-person households with incomes between $3000 and $3999 are aided. Even if one believes that ineligible taxpayers have a stronger desire to help five-person households with incomes between $4000 and $4999 than other types of household, the distribution of assistance is indefensible. Almost three-fourths of these households receive no subsidy, even though this could easily be done with the available funds. Studies that consider other characteristics in addition to income and family size reveal the same general pattern. The majority of families of each type receive nothing, while the fortunate minority receive larger subsidies. Housing assistance could be concentrated on the neediest families by either lowering the income limits for eligibility for families of each type or requiring that local housing authorities select these families. In either case the effective income limit is lowered. No estimate has been make of how much the limit would have to be reduced but clearly the required reductions would be substantial.

The failure to concentrate aid on the neediest families under HUD's new-construction programs has been defended on the grounds that it is undesirable to concentrate such families in high-density projects. Correctly understood this is an argument against subsidizing the building of projects. Experience with housing allowances and the Section 8 existing program has shown that it is possible to induce large numbers of low-income families to occupy acceptable housing, and owners to upgrade their units to meet reasonable standards, without subsidizing new construction or major rehabilitation.

As a new-construction program matures, some of the preceding deficiencies become more, and others less, important. Units constructed during the early years deteriorate. As a result, the difference between the average quality of program units and that typical of families at the income limit declines. At the same time, the variance in subsidy among recipients increases because occupants of old poorly maintained units receive much smaller subsidies than occupants of new units. This is the situation today in public housing. The only ways to prevent unequal treatment of equals in a mature new-construction program are to maintain the units as good as new, which is undoubtedly inefficient, or to vary rents with the desirability of the housing, which is difficult.

SUBSIDIZED WASTE

To this point the deficiencies of HUD's new-construction programs can be remedied by changes, albeit massive ones, in their regulations. However, there is one crucial deficiency that cannot be remedied except by termination. These programs are grossly inefficient in that the housing they provide costs far more than equally satisfactory housing in the private market.

Many explanations of this finding have been suggested. Some involve program features that provide incentives for inefficiency. For example, until 1970 the federal government paid the development costs of public housing projects while tenants and local taxpayers paid the operating costs. It is reasonable to believe that local housing authorities are sensitive to costs borne by local residents but insensitive to costs borne by other taxpayers. If so, local authorities would build housing as maintenance-free as possible, even though the extra development cost is much greater than the present value of the savings in maintenance costs. In 1970 the Congress authorized HUD to reimburse housing authorities for the excess of their operating costs over their revenues. This reduced the price of maintenance and rehabilitation faced by housing authorities to zero. Much to the surprise of Congress and HUD, the operating costs of these authorities shot upward. By 1976 federal operating subsidies amounted to about 40 percent of the operating costs of public housing units, even though Congress had placed a cap on federal operating subsidies. Since maintenance and rehabilitation were free to local authorities during the early 1970s, it is reasonable to believe that they did much that was not worth its cost.

The preceding causes of inefficiency could be remedied by a radical redesign of the new-construction programs, namely, recipients could be given cash grants conditional on occupying *newly built* housing meeting the usual housing standards. This would immediately raise the unanswerable question of why low-income families should be required to live in newly built housing.

Another explanation of the estimated inefficiency of the new-construction programs involves the state of the housing market at the time that the subsidized units are built. If comparable unsubsidized units are not being built at this time, it is because they cannot compete with existing units. That is, their costs, including a competitive rate of return, cannot be recouped at existing and expected future rent levels. This indicates that the vacancy rate among

units of this overall quality is high, and therefore public construction makes no more sense than private construction.

One explanation of the inefficiency is common to all public production of goods and services. If a businessman finds a way to produce the same output at a lower cost, he gets to keep the difference. If an administrator of a housing program does the same, he does not get to keep the difference. Similar statements can be made about producing a better product at the same cost. The effect of this difference in incentives between private and public providers of housing is obvious.

Although the importance of different explanations for the inefficiency is not known, its existence is now well documented using data going back to the 1930s. It is not equally well documented for all programs and times, but the consistency across programs is marked. The smallest estimate of inefficiency is 10 percent and the most meticulous study estimated it to be 100 percent. That is, the cost of providing housing under these programs excluding administrative cost exceeds the cost of equally satisfactory housing in the private market by at least 10 percent and probably by much more.

HUD's traditional housing programs are grossly inconsistent with plausible taxpayer preferences concerning equity and efficiency. Even a radical redesign of these programs would undoubtedly leave substantial inefficiency, and if the past is any guide, much political energy would have to be expended to achieve each of the required changes. What then should we do? The answer is remarkably simple. Replace all current programs that subsidize the housing of low-income families with a housing-allowance program. Under this program, low-income families would be given a cash grant on the condition that they occupy housing meeting certain standards. The amount of the grant would be greater for families with lower incomes and more members.

This type of program involves the minimum government interference in the lives of recipients and housing suppliers consistent with providing housing subsidies. Removal of the housing standards converts the program into one of unrestricted cash grants often called a negative income tax. It may well be desirable to use the money currently devoted to housing subsidies to expand cash assistance to the needy or to provide relief to taxpayers or both. However, the issues raised here are largely irrelevant to this decision. This article addresses the question of how housing subsidies should be delivered if we are to have them at all.

A housing-allowance program avoids the inefficiencies of the new-construction programs by subsidizing households and not requiring them to occupy newly built units. It reduces the inequities of these programs substantially by offering equally situated households the same grant under the same conditions and providing a subsidy to all eligible families who wish to participate.

WOULD IT WORK?

It is only natural to ask why anyone should believe that this program will actually perform any better than its predecessors. There is a good answer. We have had considerable experience with housing allowances; this experience has been the subject of an enormous quantity of research including a comparison with HUD's current programs; and there are other high-quality studies of the current programs.

The Experimental Housing Allowance Program is the largest social experiment (in the true sense of the word) ever undertaken by the federal government. During the 1970s over 30,000 households in 12 different locations across the nation were involved. Over 300 technical reports have been produced. Full-scale programs were conducted in two urban areas. Based on evidence from this experiment, we can be confident that housing allowances could have been used to induce participants in HUD's new-construction programs to occupy units as satisfactory as their program units at a much lower cost to taxpayers. This could be achieved without forcing them to reduce their spending on other things.

Of course, we would not want to have a housing-allowance program that had the same effects as the new-construction programs because they are highly inequitable. The housing-allowance programs that have been proposed are much more equitable than one that would simply reproduce the effects of HUD's current programs. The major objections to a housing-allowance program have been that it would result in higher rents without leading to better housing and that it would be too costly. Evidence from the experiment is inconsistent with these views. The full-scale housing-allowance programs conducted by HUD in two urban areas did not result in perceptibly higher rents for units that were not improved. For units that were upgraded, increases in rents were commensurate with the extent of the improvements. Furthermore, the average subsidy under the housing-allowance programs tested at the two sites is far less than that under the new-construction programs. In 1978 the annual subsidy was about $900 per household for the housing-allowance program and $3800 for the Section 8 new-construction program.

One great virtue of a housing-allowance program in addition to its superior efficiency and equity is the ease with which program outcomes can be changed. If the total cost of a new housing-allowance program is unexpectedly large, the size of the grant could be reduced proportionally for all families. Indeed, a program can be designed to have any cost desired. If the extent of housing improvement is not satisfactory, more stringent standards can be used and larger grants offered to prevent dropouts.

For almost 50 years the federal government has pursued a housing policy that is a chamber of horrors from the viewpoint of the preferences of taxpayers who are neither recipients of housing subsidies nor involved in providing housing for these families. Anyone who believes that the preferences of such taxpayers should be decisive in designing housing programs must take one of two positions. Either we should do more and improved studies comparing alternative housing programs in order to confirm or refute beyond reasonable doubt the findings of the past decade, or we should replace HUD's current housing programs with a housing-allowance program.

KEY CONCEPTS

housing allowances

local housing authorities

public housing

urban renewal

15 Controlling Rents, Razing Cities

New York City has imposed rent controls since World War II. Using New York's experience, Roger Starr evaluates arguments for and against rent controls. Starr is uniquely qualified for this task, having served as Executive Director of the Citizen's Housing and Planning Council of New York City and as Chairman of the New York City Rent Guidelines Board. Starr is also on the editorial board of the New York Times.

Everybody hates to pay rent. No other expenditure—except perhaps alimony—returns so little satisfaction to the spender. No matter how absurd inflated prices seem to someone who must buy clothes, food, or any of the other necessities or pleasures of life, he can assuage his pain with the prospect of getting something he never had before: a new suit, shining on the rack; a new piece of meat to chew on; a new trip; a new broom. But every month the rent-payers of the world find themselves forced to pay once again for what they already have. Even the owner of a house, making a mortgage payment on the home he has been living in for years, derives some satisfaction from the knowledge that he has reduced his debt and increased what he calls his "equity" in the house. The rent-payer has none.

Years ago, on behalf of a non-profit group interested in proving that decent housing could be provided in old tenements by an owner content with moderate profits, I supervised the rehabilitation of such a tenement. We raised rents barely enough to pay back the cost of improve-

ments over a 20-year period. A tenant complained about the increase that brought his rent to $60 a month. I pointed to the improvements we had made in his apartment: a bathroom, for the first time; oil heat; a modern kitchen; new window frames—didn't he like all this? Oh, yes, he said, he liked it, but, after all, the apartment didn't belong to him, it belonged to me. Why should he pay for it? I have struggled all these years to find a pithy answer.

If no one likes to pay rent, why shouldn't it be regulated by law so that politicians can take credit for the largesse? One reason only. It doesn't work.

Unfortunately, the apparent immediate benefits of rent control are obvious to a large number of people, while its destructiveness takes longer to notice. As a result, rent control appears to be not only a supremely popular government activity where there are large numbers of tenants; it even, and perhaps more dangerously, offers the satisfaction of high morality to the legislators who support it. They believe they are fighting inflation, and helping poor tenants against rich landlords, although, ironically, rent control is never—to my knowledge—based on the tenant's ability to pay (far too complicated even for

Reprinted by permission from *The American Spectator*, October 1978, pp. 38–42. Copyright 1978 *The American Spectator*, P.O. Box 1969, Bloomington, Indiana 47402.

the hungriest bureaucracy to administer). Thus, protected tenants may be richer than the owners of the buildings in which they rent.

The immediate peril of the rent control fallacy is that it seems to be spreading. For years, New York was alone among big cities with rent control. This distinction is now shared by Washington and Boston. Newark has rent control. Miami Beach has it. The New Jersey legislature is now debating a statewide bill establishing rent control standards to guide localities—which in many cases have leaped ahead to install their own versions. Los Angeles held an unofficial "Town Hall" meeting to discuss rent control in December of last year; the interest in rent control in California will surely be stimulated by the passage of Proposition 13. The reduction in real property taxes will inspire a demand that government ensure that the tax savings be passed on to the tenant. Anyone who understands the economics of housing would expect that lower real property taxes will inevitably produce lower rents because of their stimulation of construction and rehabilitation and ensuing competition; but no one ever wants to wait for natural processes when there's a laxative handy for landlords.

Thus, my tenant who didn't want to pay for improvements to the apartment he merely lived in, did not want to be told that it would take years for the owner to recoup what had been put into rehabilitation, without which the house would soon have crumbled completely. He preferred to assume that the cost of fixing his apartment was somehow "over" when the reconstruction was complete and the last painter had rolled up his dropcloths and gone home.

Most of us forget that the new costs of a home last as long as it does. Installing the oil burner in the tenement house was a one-time capital expense—but to buy oil, to service the radiators, pipes, and boiler, to check the bills from the oil company, and to pay the electricity bill for driving the atomizer and blower, the owner spends continuously—more, as prices rise. If I owned the whole world, I could, like the Soviet government, increase the prices of clothing, food, and automobiles to cover my losses on rent. Soviet citizens always boast about their low rents, and refuse to draw the connection between the low price of rent and the high price of all other government-furnished goods and services.

One need not be ruler of the world to establish low rents. A simpler method is to repeal all laws mandating housing safety and health standards. Wealthy tenants would still be able to demand quality housing as a condition of moving in, just as they do now. Poor tenants would get cheap rents, but their housing would probably be miserable, as it was when the first housing laws were passed more than 100 years ago: no heat, no light, no air, no bathrooms, insufficient space to live decently. Tenants would get the impression that they were paying low rents, but if they wanted to stay warm, dry, and healthy, they would have to supply these qualities for themselves. The cost of supplying them would have to be added to the payments to the landlord to get the true rental cost, which would end up exactly where it is now—too high for may low-income families to afford.

Thus, rent control is meaningless unless it forces owners of buildings to maintain the quality of their apartments. This is much harder even than controlling prices, but the two—price and quality—are integrally connected, as the reformers discovered when they started passing laws raising the minimum standards of housing quality. One of the earliest housing reforms by American city governments was the requirement that every room people lived in (technically called a "living room," but not in the sense in which that term is used today) have a window to the outside air. This made housing more expensive because it cut down the number of living rooms in buildings or the size of the building that could be put on a fixed amount of ground (because the inside of the structure could no longer be used for living rooms). The reformers believed that rents would not necessarily rise because of the rise in costs; they believed that the increased cost would simply reduce the monopolistic profits which landlords got from their tenants.

Rent control today is based, though perhaps not explicitly, on the same two premises. First, that tenants are the victims of a monopoly pricing system which rent control corrects, and second, that without rent control, large numbers of apartments that meet housing standards would be priced out of the reach of moderate- and low-income families. We should examine each proposition.

The hypothesis that rental housing is controlled by a monopoly simply does not square with the facts in American cities. By far the largest single owner of apartment houses in New York City is the New York City Housing Authority, an agency of the municipal government. It owns less than 10 percent of the rental apartments in the city. No private owner owns as many as 5 percent. Nor do the apartments of the city resemble a monopoly: They differ widely in age, size, style of construction, and location. The thousands of individual owners vary in wealth, professional skill, ownership motive, and access to capital. This is true in every American city.

Those who claim rent control is necessary supplement the imaginary owning monopoly with the allegation that a "real estate lobby" must be held in check. It is true that owners of real estate—the source of most cities' tax revenue—were able to dominate the courts for many years. They established a form of lease that was very favorable to the landlord, and correspondingly unfavorable to the tenant. Subsequent to the days when the real estate lobbies overwhelmed local legislatures, changes occurred. Real estate taxes were reduced to a much smaller part of the total city revenue. Tenant and public-interest groups became active and politically powerful. And, most important, the pace of apartment-house construction quickened to the point at which monopolistic control over prices became a practical impossibility.

Rent control came to almost all major American cities during World War II when the Office of Price Administration was controlling all prices. War made housing a natural monopoly because the government decreed that no manpower or material resources coud be used for any construction not directly related to military needs. In most cities, except New York, the end of the war marked the end of rent control. Restrictive situations other than war—as when American blacks faced serious discrimination in obtaining housing in white areas—subjected rents to monopolistic manipulation. Like war, they made rent control seem a reasonable effort to protect tenants from exploitation. But that rarely remains its sole or its major objective; instead, its objective becomes the perpetuation of low rents and unchallengeable tenure for those tenants who happen to be protected by it, usually those tenants who have moved least often, or not at all, and who thus constitute a firm political power base for elected legislators and administrators.

The bias in favor of protecting tenants who have not moved is perfectly natural: It is always easier, politically, to permit rents to rise when an apartment becomes vacant; like the high price of shoes in Russia, the high rent of a vacant apartment makes up for part of the losses on continuously occupied apartments. All rent control systems, therefore, depend on a change of tenancy to provide the owner relief from the squeeze of increased costs against fixed rental income.

Favoritism toward the tenant-in-occupancy (who, as we shall see, is in a weaker position than the prospective tenant looking for an apartment) has two very unfortunate results. First, it does not relate economic need to the benefit conferred by rent control. People who remain in their apartments without moving for the longest period of time are not necessarily those of lowest income and greatest financial need. In an industrial city, the highest turnover rates are usually found among the poorest people who are most likely to have to move in pursuit of work, or because they can't pay rent, or because the building in which they live becomes so unprofitable that its owner abandons it. Under New York's venerable rent control system, it became clear long ago that the *top floor* apartments in six-story, walk-up tenements had higher legal rent ceilings than all other apartments in the buildings. This happened because top floor apartments were the worst, occupied by the poorest tenants. Consequently, they turned over most frequently. The better apartments could not legally be rented at market rents, while the

worse apartments could not be marketed at the rents to which they were legally eligible, a topsy-turvy consequence of rent control.

The second defect that follows inevitably from favoring the tenant-in-residence is the gross misallocation of housing space. Few tenants go through life without changing their need for space. Younger people marry, and have children. When they are very young, boys and girls occupy the same room. As the family grows, it should move to larger quarters. But the economic benefit of staying in one's original rent-controlled apartment tends to slow down the move to new quarters despite the desire for a larger apartment. In the very same building as the growing family, there may live a shrinking family, whose children have left to live on their own. The parents now rattle about in an apartment for which they have no use because their continued occupancy makes it a bargain. Rent control has encouraged families to occupy space which does not suit them, and which can only be duplicated at the far greater cost of new construction.

Somewhat less poignant for individual families, but of even greater significance to the city as a whole, is the waste of *public* space which rent control entails. To understand it, we should ask what governments seek to accomplish when they regulate the prices of monopolies like power utilities. Because in distributing electric power the cost of competition is prohibitive, or nearly so, the regulatory authorities ideally seek to establish by administrative action a fair price per kilowatt/hour. Usually, this is deemed to be the lowest price at which the service can be sold while covering all costs of operation with a profit large enough to attract needed new capital. The pricing process is filled with pitfalls and argumentative issues even in the case of electricity.

Defining the price for a rent-controlled apartment is even more difficult. Electricity can be measured by instruments. It is uniform. Because of the diversity and imprecision in defining housing quality, there can be no standard rent per room/month. Rent control law usually assumes that the price of an apartment at the time it came into effect is a fair basic price. At their most theoretical, rent regulators claim to modify the base price of each apartment as operating costs vary—raising it as costs rise, lowering it as services are cut in a specific building. In practice, their attempts to modify the legal rent for tenants in continuing possession *always* fall short of the reality of increased costs, and *always* result in diminished services in a period of inflation. But even if rising costs of operation were covered by rent increases, no rent control scheme can provide for the increased value of the land on which an apartment house is built, as some areas of a city inevitably become more attractive while others decline.

Having started with the claim that it is directed against a landlord monopoly, rent control creates instead a tenant monopoly that distorts land value downward or, at best, prevents a municipality from taking advantage of its major economic asset, the value of locations that are in high demand.

Thus, when a section of the city becomes popular, attracting people who would cheerfully pay higher rents to live there, the apartments remain instead in the hands of tenants who are forbidden to pay a market rent, even if they wished to. Inevitably, the city loses the tax revenues it could charge on a more profitable property, unless it permits someone to demolish the building, replacing it with a larger one containing far more expensive accommodations.

Even if its owner decides to demolish an old building on valuable land, however, rent control regulations discourage him. Rent-controlled tenants are specially protected against having to move. Even if rent controls are not imposed on new construction, the delays met in the course of finding new apartments for rent-controlled tenants from the older building encourage landlords to keep apartments empty as they become vacant. The underutilization that results from this is grossly against the general interest. Ultimately, the losers include not only those who would move into the apartments now vacant, and the owner of the building who sacrifices rents to make his building more saleable, but also the city as a whole and those who require its services, paid in large part by the tax revenues derived from the value of land in great demand. Since those who need the most municipal services are poor, the misuse of land value is one more indication of the way in which rent control serves people who do not need its help at the expense of the poor. It tends to be a middle-class subsidy.

Proponents of rent control argue both that their laws shield tenants from monopolistic exploitation and that they are necessary because government standards for housing have destroyed a free market in any case. It is now time to examine this second hypothesis.

From the simplest of requirements—like the insistence on a window in every room—government housing standards have been built into an immense structure of law. Its provisions govern the dimensions of buildings and their component parts like hallways, doorways, and fire escapes. They govern maintenance procedures like winter temperature and painting. They govern administrative procedures like the posting of owners' and agents' names in public spaces. They may soon be expanded to include the licensing of owners and agents everywhere, a requirement that has already been imposed in some cities.

All of these standards make housing more expensive to build and operate, but the process of raising them still higher is extremely seductive to state and city lawmakers. They believe that the passing of laws like these really helps tenants by making their homes more habitable. But because they make housing more expensive, they succeed in pricing new housing, that fully conforms with all the new standards, out of reach of a continually growing number of tenants. Because the constant rise in cost makes new housing prohibitively expensive for moderate-income tenants, the older housing that provides lower-cost rentals becomes a precious asset. We must, say the rent control advocates, protect the older housing by rent control so that this precious asset will be saved.

The responsibility for doing something to ensure that everyone has access to housing that meets its standards is unquestionably a government responsibility. Properly, if it takes its standards seriously, government should tax everyone to enable those who need financial help to enjoy the same standards as anyone else. Expecting rent control to be a cheap way to provide standard housing for the needy is as absurd as using great white sharks for lifeguards: They are cheaper than people, but they destroy the drowning. While rent control keeps down the rents in older buildings that originally met the standards imposed by law, it also slows the flow of capital into these buildings that is needed to keep them well maintained. The lower the original rents, the faster the deterioration. Using rent control as a substitute for governmental subsidies is simply a perverse, regressive way of enabling better-off tenants to escape the taxation necessary to pay such subsidies while accelerating the decay of the housing in which all tenants live; and the housing of the poorer tenants, likely not to be fully standard in the first place, deteriorates more quickly than that of the middle-income tenants. To the extent that landlords are unwilling to throw new money into a deteriorating building, the quality standards that rent control allegedly protects are, instead, slowly destroyed. Rent control does not replace the marketplace which quality standards impair; it merely proffers a false solution to the real question of how much government money should be spent to raise housing standards for those who cannot afford housing without help.

There is, however, one respect in which the market for rental housing does not work, and this is the area in which some government action is indicated, even wise. While rent control *overprotects* the tenant-in-occupancy, there nevertheless is a basic justification for protecting him to a reasonable extent. In the nature of things, the tenant whose lease expires is at a serious disadvantage compared with the tenant who is on the outside looking for an apartment. Only the tenant-in-occupancy is put to extraordinary expense when he turns down the landlord's offer of a new lease. While the shopper looking for a new suit or a steak can simply look elsewhere if the price he is asked is unsatisfactory, the tenant-in-occupancy must move his home. Always an expensive process, moving may involve re-cutting carpets, draperies, and bookcases. The tenant-in-occupancy, at a time of housing shortage, tends to accept a new rent which the tenant outside would not. Sometimes he will refuse to accept a rent asked by the owner, who will then find himself with an empty apartment because he has overestimated the demand for his apartments.

A sensible program to strengthen the natural rental market would offer the tenant-in-occupancy enough protection to put him in the same position as the tenant outside. One suggestion has been to require an owner to offer the tenant-in-occupancy a new lease 90 days before the expiration of his current lease. The owner would be allowed to ask whatever rent he chooses, but the figure would become a matter of public record with an appropriate governmental board. The board would also set, each year, a figure for the "normal" rent increase, based on the general increase of housing costs within the past twelve months. If the owner decided to ask no more than the "normal" increase, the tenant would have to accept a new lease at that figure, or move. But if the owner asked more than the "normal" increase, the tenant could choose, instead, to remain at his present rental until the owner finds someone willing to pay at least the rent that he had asked of the tenant. Faced by the possibility of forgoing any increase at all for a long period of time, the landlord would presumably ask for more than the "normal" increase only in areas of great market strength. But the final decision would be left to him, giving him the opportunity to run his own business without allowing him to exact from the tenant-in-possession any more than he could get from the tenant outside.

Naturally, tenant groups object to this procedure because it does not give absolute renewal rights to the tenant-in-posses-

sion. The resistance of these groups indicates that, for them, the real purpose of rent control is not to provide a real market in the face of monopolistic interference, but to provide cheap rents for tenants who already have apartments and to assure their permanent tenure wherever they happen to live.

This motive is not in the public interest, but it is politically very attractive in areas with many rental apartments. What must be examined is its costs.

The first cost is the diversion of a very large sum of money from the hands of the owners of rental property into the pockets of tenants, without reference to whether or not the tenants need this form of subsidization. The question which immediately rises, but cannot so readily be answered, is how much damage this diversion of income does to the quality and supply of rental housing.

Advocates of rent control insist that no one has proved that it is this deprivation of income that has caused the deterioration and abandonment of rental housing properties in New York City, which has had rent control since 1947. A tremendous amount of housing has been abandoned in New York City, and over a million violations of the housing codes are on record in other buildings. It is true that abandonment has taken place in many other cities which have no rent control but have been subject to the same decline of economic capacity as New York has. How, then, can one say that rent control was responsible for New York's housing decay? The answer is that one can never *prove* economic events in the real world, as one can chemical reactions in a laboratory. One can't even prove that rent control alone caused the gap of about $400 million a year between the rents needed to keep housing in New York in good condition and the rents actually collected (this according to a Rand Corporation study conducted in 1970). Even without rent control, people might have been unable to pay rents adequate to maintain housing in good condition. But there is enough evidence to satisfy any objective observer that *some*, indeed a very significant part, of the deterioration in the better buildings of New York has been due to rent control.

New York differs from other older cities in the very large portion of its families who live in rental housing. While in other cities the lowest-income families and a few of the highest rent their homes, in New York apartment houses constitute a significant part of the housing lived in by the middle class. For these people, rent control offered a truly golden opportunity to cut down on their housing expenses in favor of spending their money on optional pleasures: winters in Florida, summers abroad, second homes. Draining the customary portion of current income from the buildings they lived in meant that these same buildings suffered from maintenance undone, gradual deterioration, and a desperate, but rational, move by their owners to discount the future and grab whatever instant return was available—through renting to welfare families, for example. This had the effect of hastening turnover. Rent control advocates, who are quick to counsel their followers to take advantage of every opportunity the law offers them to minimize housing costs, pretend that the owners of buildings should be motivated by something other than economics. In fact, the combination of rent control and natural cupidity produced the deterioration of middle-class areas at the same time that it stimulated a demand for government intervention to produce new housing for the very people who should

have been living in the formerly middle-class apartments.

Rent control, then, produced a political demand for massive state and city investment in mortgages to build new housing to replace deteriorating older housing. Between the state and city governments as much as $3 billion has been invested in so-called Mitchell Lama Housing in New York City since 1955. The great majority of these buildings are now in arrears on their mortgage payments. Rent control not only forced the construction of these developments—through the deterioration of the older, decent stockpile of housing and the irrational use of space—but it also remained as a formidable price competitor for the housing in which the government placed so heavy an investment. Recognizing that a government which had built housing for them would not dare to evict them, tenants and tenant co-operators in middle-income projects have refused to pay rent increases, gone on "rent strikes," and otherwise contributed to the financial pains of the state and city. "We were lured out of our rent-controlled apartment houses," said the strike leadership committee of Co-op City. Its 15,500 apartments made it the largest such project. Its mortgage of more than $400 million, borrowed by the state, is hopelessly in arrears. Rent control has not only spread disease among decent, older buildings, but has destroyed the cure which it made necessary.

Indeed, the most serious offense against the public good that rent control commits is its debasement of public discourse and corrosion of the political process. No elected official in New York City dares to admit publicly that there is a connection between housing deterioration and government control of rents. None dares to say that a government which borrows for the purpose of providing housing for middle-class families must be able to demand adequate rents from the beneficiaries of its policy. Tenant groups ritualistically publish their own newspapers, attacking the notion that rent control hurts housing. "Flight of Capital—not rent controls—causes building abandonment" trumpets a headline in the December 1977 issue of the *Heights & Valley Free News,* published by the Columbia Tenants Union. There is no suggestion that capital flees from housing not because the owners of buildings want it to flee, but because it has been destroyed by uneconomic rental levels. As rent control becomes a permanent way of life in New York City, the political spokesmen become accustomed to pretending that no-cost economics works. No one can run for office without agreeing that the payment of rent is a surrender to the greed of landlords.

Any state or city which is persistently told by candidates for public office that the cost of capital is unreal, and that con-sumer appetites can be satisfied without pain, should expect to find itself in financial trouble. The attitudes fostered by rent control—attitudes which support the myth that social benefits cost nothing—are largely responsible for New York's financial condition today. It finds itself, like the owners of most rent-controlled apartment houses, facing the demand of citizens for services whose costs they refuse to pay, and at its back it hears from the reluctant bankers who will not continue to finance a venture whose expenses exceed its income. Cities that consider imposing rent controls as a cheap way to insure low rents will get a better idea of its real costs by studying New York—not only its towering housing, but its towering debts.

KEY CONCEPTS

rent control

tenant-in-occupancy

16 The Impact of Local Building Codes on Housing

This selection is an excerpt from a special national commission report on neighborhoods and housing. This portion concentrates on the effects of local building codes on the cost of building and rehabilitating housing, especially for lower-income groups. The commission concludes that the building-code system needs to be reformed, echoing the conclusion reached 11 years earlier in 1968 by the National Commission on Urban Problems (The Douglas Commission).

Governmental responsibility for regulating the construction industry in the interest of public health and safety extends far back into American history. The breadth of municipal police powers has been extended to include official oversight of construction practices, the installation and maintenance of plumbing and electrical systems, fire safety, and sanitation. The exercise of these powers started as a progressive social reform designed to protect public safety. Municipal codes were frequently rewritten to serve the interests of powerful commercial interests. Complex, unresponsive bureaucracies have mushroomed in many municipalities, reducing the likelihood that the law will be administered in the interests of low- and moderate-income people. Municipal code enforcement has recently come under steadily increasing attack. The Commission decided to examine in detail one of the key points of contention in which neigh-

From *People, Building Neighborhoods.* Final Report to the President and the Congress of the United States of the National Commission on Neighborhoods (Washington, D.C.: U.S. Government Printing Office, 1979, pp. 204–208).

borhood organizations are most interested—the effect of building codes on the rehabilitation of older urban housing.

A building code is a document which prescribes in detail the materials and standards that all construction must meet. There are four major model building codes in use in the United States, all drafted by private trades organizations: the BOCA Basic Building Code (Building Officials Conference of America); the Uniform Building Code (International Conference of Building Officials); the Southern Standard Building Code; and the National Building Code (American Insurance Association). There are also a number of specialized codes, such as the National Electrical Code and the National Plumbing Code. The major code-drafting organizations have reached agreement on a uniform Model Code for One- and Two-Family Residences, but there is as yet no model code adapted to the special needs of older housing rehabilitation.

Building standards have traditionally been enforced by municipalities which incorporated a code into their ordinances.

A city government may merely refer to a particular model code, but many cities have either written their own codes or added numerous amendments to the model codes. These changes in the codes are usually added at the insistence of and for the protection of local commercial interests.

The ordinance makes it a punishable offense for any person to engage in covered construction without first securing a municipal building permit. The ordinance also creates or designates a city agency to review applications for permits, perform field inspections, and issue permits. Criticism of the effect of these rules and the way they are enforced has recently come not only from builders but also from citizen groups and from neighborhood organizations seeking to rehabilitate dilapidated buildings. They argue that:

A. *Building codes have artificially increased the costs of new housing construction and rehabilitation.* The diversity of code rules from jurisdiction to jurisdiction prevents builders from achieving economies of scale in providing construction services. Builders must either accept excessive overhead costs in product design and variation of work-site techniques or concentrate within a limited number of jurisdictions where they will seek higher prices to compensate for lower volume. While the effect of code enforcement on housing rehabilitation costs is a matter of dispute, it seems reasonable to expect that current practices add as much as 10 percent to the costs of each unit. The code administration system has become so complicated, laborious and expensive that it discourages construction and rehabilitation. Frequently, a number of different permits are required. There are delays while agencies ponder plans. A study of graft in the New York

City building department revealed that most bribes to inspectors were made not to secure some exemption from code requirements, but to get permit applications up to the top of the approval pile.

B. *Building codes have inflated the costs of suburban housing.* The policy has also prevented lower-income people from purchasing homes. Some municipalities reason that low-cost housing will attract lower-income families with small children, minority families, and the poor. These potential residents are viewed as "tax eaters." Exorbitant building code requirements, coupled with exclusionary zoning rules, are used to drive up the cost of housing, tending to restrict the market to stable, middle- or upper-income families.

C. *Building codes have often inhibited innovation in construction technology.* The codes specify materials ("2 × 4 inch joists") rather than establishing performance standards for equivalent materials. Less expensive, but equally safe materials are prohibited. The use of material specifications also gives manufacturers and labor organizations an incentive to "rig" local codes to favor their products and to increase labor costs.

D. *Building codes encourage demolition rather than restoration and reuse of older urban structures.* Many buildings cannot be economically adapted to meet requirements for new construction. For example, there was a plan to convert an old five-story garment factory in Boston into apartments. The code specified a stair width far in excess of that required when the building was first built. The rule was justified when the building was first built by the argument that, in case of fire, the tenants would need to exit as rapidly as possible. However, widening the staircases would have required relocating major structural components in all five floors of the building, rebuilding the entire floor joist structure, and ripping up all the old floors. Because the building was being rehabilitated to house only ten families, the existing stairs were clearly adequate to handle emergency traffic. Yet, it was technically in violation of the code on this. In this case, the city, after lengthy negotiations, agreed to grant a special exception. In many other instances, sound structures are demolished because of the impossibility of conversion or the costliness of potential delays while exceptions are sought.

E. Building codes place impossible administrative and legal burdens on building inspectors. In some jurisdictions, the rules are so rigid that inspectors have no discretion to cope with unique situations. A former chief building official has stated to the Commission that "half of downtown Los Angeles" was demolished to build high rises under rules that discouraged renovation of older structures. On the other hand, attempts to liberalize the rules have been undercut by the imposition of personal liability on inspectors for later construction defects. There is no reason for an inspector to jeopardize his job and his income by approving materials that vary from the letter of the code.

RECOMMENDATIONS FOR IMMEDIATE ACTION

Federal, state and local officials should immediately reform the existing system to reduce the cost and problems of traditional code enforcement. For the short term, the Commission specifically endorses the recommendations on code reform made by the National Commission on Urban Problems (the Douglas Commission) in 1968 and in several subsequent studies. These recommendations include:

1. Improving national model codes by shifting from specifying materials to establishing general performance standards.

2. Consolidating the four national model codes as much as possible to assure uniformity.

3. Strengthening and accelerating the testing and approval of new materials technology by the National Institute of Building Sciences, the National Bureau of Standards, and other such bodies.

4. Drafting model rehabilitation guidelines which respond to the special needs of urban rehabilitation projects. The rules should emphasize the use of less expensive materials and permit inspectors to use reasonable discretion in approving projects. The 1971 HUD-sponsored BOCA Rehabilitation Guidelines were a failure. Section 903 of the Housing and Community Development Act of 1978 directs HUD to try again.

5. Establishing statewide building codes as a ceiling. Municipalities should be prohibited from enacting rules more restrictive than the state standards.

6. Denying federal housing subsidies to jurisdictions which maintain unreasonably restrictive building code requirements. HUD exercised this power against the city of Los Angeles, which had refused to permit Romex electrical cable in its code. The city relented.

7. Providing training courses and technical assistance to local building

code departments and their personnel.

8. Encouraging local administrative improvements, especially one-stop shopping for building permits.

9. Providing a state building code appeals board to settle disputes between builders and inspectors. This system has been established in Massachusetts.

10. Offering pre-permit counseling for builders, homeowners, and neighborhood housing corporations to familiarize them with local code requirements.

11. Creating a surety bond program to protect inspectors from liability suits in situations where they are required to use their professional judgment in interpreting the code. Alternatively, the inspector should be relieved by statute of all liability other than for gross negligence.

12. The HUD Minimum Property Standards should be amended so that they are satisfied when a building complies with an approved local building code.

RECOMMENDATIONS FOR LONG-TERM REFORM

Under the present system, the rules are essentially a checklist which can be mechanically applied by the inspector acting in a purely ministerial capacity. If the building fails to meet any specific criterion, the inspector is justified in refusing a permit. This system also tends to retard innovation in construction technology, is easily captured by special interests, and deters rehabilitation of existing structures.

A flexible code-enforcement system may seem a reasonable solution. Under the flexible approach, codes are changed from a set of detailed specifications to broad, flexible guidelines. Inspectors are given considerable discretion to use their judgment. This, however, creates a new set of problems. Rather than mechanically enforcing rules, the inspector now would have to make sophisticated judgments about the design capacity of the structure. This would require a high level of expertise, for which inspectors would have to be trained and paid. The changes would also make inspectors vulnerable to attack by irate builders demanding permits. Unless the threat of personal liability was removed, inspectors would be likely to simply apply the strictest standards. Finally, a flexible approach to code enforcement does not eliminate the incentive for powerful economic interests to shape the codes to eliminate rival products or to prevent the adoption of labor-saving techniques.

In recent years some groundwork has been laid for basic structural reform of the traditional building-code-enforcement system. The French experience, built upon the legal liability of contractors under the civil code, may offer a workable model. Both the National Association of Home Builders and the National Association of Realtors have developed and implemented warranty protection plans for home buyers. The 1977 New Jersey New Home Warranty and Builder's Registration Act provides protection to home purchasers through registration of contractors and their mandatory participation in either an approved private warranty protection plan, or a state-operated "Home Warranty Security Fund."

The Commission recommends that states build upon this experience by restructuring their building safety programs.

1. Jurisdictions should adopt a basic life safety code derived from present

codes, covering structural safety, fire safety and egress.

2. Jurisdictions should develop a set of generally accepted, performance-based guidelines for new construction and for rehabilitation of older structures. The National Conference of States on Building Codes and Standards, the National Institute of Building Sciences, the Conference of American Building Officials, and industry experts should work with HUD to discharge the mandate of Section 903 of the Housing and Urban Development Act of 1978.

3. Jurisdictions should provide for certification by licensed design professionals (architects and engineers) of compliance with, and departure from, the guidelines on all larger projects. These certificates should be filed as a matter of public record and indexed in the land record information system. The design profession should be allowed to allocate up to 15 percent of annual gross receipts to a tax-deductible loss reserve account. This would allow architectural and engineering firms to effectively self-insure against the deductible portion of their professional malpractice insurance coverage.

4. Contractors should be required to provide a ten-year warranty of the performance of major building systems and shorter warranties for other construction components.

5. Rehabilitation contractors should be registered. An information system should publicize the contractors' performance records to prospective customers, lenders, insurance carriers, and neighborhood housing sponsors. State registration agencies should suspend or cancel registration for irresponsible performance.

KEY CONCEPTS

building code

flexible code-enforcement system

inspector liability

performance standards

rehabilitation guidelines

SAMUEL L. MYERS, JR.   KENNETH E. PHILLIPS

17   Housing Segregation and Black Employment: Another Look at the Ghetto Dispersal Strategy

Samuel L. Myers, Jr., of the University of Texas–Austin, and Kenneth E. Phillips of Rand Corporation survey the debate over the most effective strategy for improving employment and income of ghetto residents: developing the ghetto versus dispersing ghetto residents into the suburbs. Opponents of development have contended that such programs do little to increase employment and constitute what has been termed "gilding" of the ghetto. Myers and Phillips discuss some of the theoretical aspects of these arguments as well as some recent empirical evidence.

There is some irony in how the debate about whether black inner-city ghettos should be dispersed or developed has been translated into public policy on revitalization of central city areas. Recall how, a decade ago, vehement defenders of ghetto dispersal were stating that black employment opportunities had been restricted because of housing segregation and suburbanization of jobs. Along with low automobile ownership among ghetto residents and declining low-skill job opportunities in the central business district, housing segregation and suburbanization of jobs were factors ranking high on the list of explanations of why gilding of ghettos should not be encouraged. The alternative offered was ghetto dispersal.

Recall, on the other hand, how opponents of ghetto dispersal denied that suburban jobs were any better, opportunities any less bleak, or labor markets any less discriminatory for blacks living in segregated ghettos than they were for blacks living in suburban areas. The advocates of developing inner-city communities proposed policies of public employment, subsidies for renovation of commercial and residential property, and relocation of businesses back to the central cities. Many of these policies have been adopted and some have been modestly successful in curtailing continued dehabilitation of our central cities. Yet, the major impact of recent urban revitalization schemes, particularly plans to renovate inner city residential property, has been massive dislocation of poor blacks. Thus, in many cities, the ghetto has indeed dispersed. Who would have guessed ten years ago that the very policies advocated by the proponents of inner-city community development would hasten ghetto dispersal?

This essay revisits the decade-old ghetto development vs. ghetto dispersal debate. Whether by design or by accident, ghetto dispersal may be a suboptimal means of improving the economic status of poor urban blacks. There are a number of theo-

From Samuel L. Myers, Jr. and Kenneth E. Phillips, "Housing Segregation and Black Employment: Another Look at the Ghetto Dispersal Strategy," *American Economic Review* 69, 2 (May 1979): 298–302. Reprinted with permission of the *American Economic Review* and the authors.

retical arguments besides those offered a decade ago for why decentralization of black residential location alone need not resolve the problems of low incomes, high unemployment, and lack of economic mobility of inner-city residents. One argument states that the observed wage differences between suburban and ghetto jobs can be attributed to the distance that workers must travel to accept these jobs and not merely to the differences in the labor market demand. Hence moving ghetto workers closer to suburban jobs, thereby reducing their travel costs, may merely reduce the premium required to attract distant workers. Another argument is based on a model of job search in which moving ghetto workers closer to suburban jobs reduces their search costs and hence their reservation wages rise. In the short run, the effect could be longer durations of unemployment. Only in a world of competitive labor markets, no business cycles, and no changes in aggregate demand could we guarantee that in the long run reemployment wages would rise.

The empirical evidence is mixed. In a number of isolated cases wages and employment really are higher in suburban labor markets. Support is found for the notion that the demand for low-skilled workers exceeds the supply in suburban areas. Moreover, poor blacks and whites appear to have similar employment experiences in the suburbs. The isolated evidence does not support the view of racial discrimination in suburban labor markets.

However, support is found for the view that there are positive externalities in employment in one's own community. The isolated evidence suggests that poor workers who both live and work in census tracts of similar racial composition have better employment experiences.

THE ORIGINAL CASE FOR GHETTO DISPERSAL

Can decentralization of residential locations improve black employment prospects? This issue, of course, is but a part of the larger "ghetto development vs. ghetto dispersal" debate. While the dispersal of the urban ghetto has been debated on a number of levels, perhaps the igniting spark, at least among economists, can be traced to John F. Kain.

Kain explored a number of hypotheses relating housing segregation to employment. A reasonably accurate premise is that job opportunities have become spatially dispersed throughout the metropolitan area since World War II. Principally, labor market opportunities have been expanding in suburban areas while blacks have remained segregated in housing centered near the urban core. The resulting spatial separation of jobs and residences, Kain contended, would impose high transportation costs on ghetto workers because of the long distance which those workers travel. The net effect of these imposed travel costs is to reduce the effective wage which central city workers receive relative to white suburban residents. Still another cost imposed by the spatial separation of jobs and residences includes the higher search costs which blacks experience in finding suburban employment and the lower quality of information about potential job opportunities.

Other issues explored by Kain included the possibilities that employers outside of the ghetto discriminate against blacks and those in the city discriminate in favor of blacks. These possibilities are offered as explanations for how residential segregation affects the spatial distribution of employment. Coupled with two additional hypotheses, 1) that residential segregation reduces black job opportunities, and 2) that suburbanization of jobs worsens the relative position of ghetto workers, Kain presents his case for dispersal of the ghetto.

THE CASE AGAINST THE CASE FOR GHETTO DISPERSAL

Kain's hypotheses have been subjected to considerable attack. Bennett Harrison argues that there is no difference in the quality of jobs held by blacks in and out of suburbs, that racial discrimination in the labor market may restrict opportunities to blacks even if they moved nearer to the jobs, and that dispersal of the ghetto may disperse the ghetto problem but would not improve black employment. Paul Offner and Daniel Saks demonstrate that removal of housing segregation may result in a loss of black jobs rather than a gain as Kain suggests. Kain's response to this is that even if creating ghetto pockets in the suburbs is needed to move blacks closer to the jobs, then this policy is to be preferred over maintaining one "gilded ghetto." Joseph Mooney contends that spatial separation of jobs and residences plays a less important role in reducing employment opportunities than Kain asserts. Both Charlotte Freemon and Wilfred Lewis have questioned Kain's hypothesis and have examined the components of industrial relocation to show that employment opportunities have not declined for ghetto residents.

A THEORETICAL PERSPECTIVE

The notion that spatial separation of jobs and residences diminishes employment opportunities suggests a job search theory of wage differentials. But such a theory could lead to just the opposite policy conclusion than that offered by defenders of ghetto dispersion. In the conventional job search model (for example, see Steven Lippman and John McCall), job searchers are assumed to be risk neutral, to maximize their expected net benefits, and decide whether or not to accept any given job offer according to a reservation wage decision rule. If the wage offer equals or exceeds the reservation wage, accept the offer; otherwise, continue to search. One important property of the reservation wage is that it declines for higher search costs. Workers with higher reservation wages can be expected to search longer and thus be frictionally unemployed longer. The longer duration of search is expected to yield the benefit, however, of higher reemployment wages. Hence, policies like ghetto dispersal which might reduce search costs (by reducing travel costs of search and improving information flows via decentralization of residences) would lead to higher short-run unemployment among the beneficiaries of the policy. Longer-run gains from higher reemployment wages may not be forthcoming if cyclical fluctuations in economic activity dictate that employers use last-hired first-fired rules.

Another contradictory result flowing from a job search view of ghetto dispersal is that reservation wages may rise not only due to lower search costs, but because of higher expectations about the opportunities in suburban labor markets. If there are serious overestimates by workers of their potential earning prospects and if through time the reservation wage is revised downward only slowly, then one consequence of ghetto dispersal could be decentralized pockets of high unemployment throughout the metropolitan area among former ghetto residents.

Wage inequality resulting from spatial separation of jobs and residences suggests another view casting doubt on the ghetto dispersal argument. Suppose that search costs are negligible, perhaps because of the existence of a costless job referral service. But suppose that travel cost, increasing in the distance between job and residence, reduces utility of jobs accepted. The risk-neutral worker's utility could be given by wage income less travel costs. If the hours worked were identical for both ghetto residents who work in the suburbs and those who work in the inner city, and if the opportunity cost of time were identical for everyone, then the requirement that all workers' utilities be equal implies the well-known result that black workers living in the ghetto, who work in the ghetto, receive lower wages than black ghetto residents working in the suburbs. However, it is easy to see in such an abstract world how moving blacks to the suburbs need not make black workers better off, unless there really are better jobs there.

Of course, the theoretical arguments in favor of ghetto dispersal rarely adopt such simple reference models. The point of looking at a model of rational job choices is, however, to present a valid challenge. If ghetto dispersal cannot be expected to work in a simple abstract model, how could it be expected to work in a complex realistic model?

EVIDENCE FROM AN ISOLATED CASE

If there is racial discrimination in suburban labor markets, or if there are substantial employment losses as a result of decentralization of black residential communities, the ghetto dispersal argument appears to degenerate into merely dispersal of the ghetto problem.

In our earlier paper, limited evidence was presented suggesting that although there may not be discrimination in suburban labor markets, living and working in neighborhoods of similar levels of segregation appears to improve one's probability of employment. The evidence is from a study of low-income job applicants who were clients of a Comprehensive Employment and Training Act (CETA) job referral service in Baltimore during 1974–75. Higher mean wages were offered to both black and white clients in suburban jobs compared to wage offers in city jobs. Similarly, job offer probabilities were higher for suburban jobs than city jobs, suggesting the often-argued point that blue collar vacancies have grown faster in the suburbs than in the city. Although blacks are less likely than whites to obtain a job offer in the suburbs, the wages of placed blacks and whites are not significantly different. Important wage disparities exist between blacks and whites in the suburban construction industry, but the low proportion of total referrals accounted for by construction leave the overall mean wages for blacks and whites about the same.

In a model predicting the probability of a job offer (controlling for age, education, race, duration of job search, and marital status) it is found that applicants who apply for jobs in the suburbs are more likely to obtain an offer than those who apply in the city. Moreover, those who travel away from the central business district to work can expect 16 cents more per hour in higher wages on the average (controlling for age, sex, race, education, duration of search, and distance travelled).

However, a different story is told by data

on racial composition of census tracts. Controlling for distance, race, and other variables, CETA clients are less likely to show up for a scheduled interview in the suburbs (where census tracts are largely nonblack). Of those that show, applicants who interview in census tracts of the same level of racial segregation as their own neighborhood generally have higher probabilities of being offered a job. For example, applicants from home tracts 0–20 percent black are more likely to be hired in tracts 0–20 percent black than those from any other area. Similarly, those from nearly all black tracts have the highest odds of being placed in a job located in an all black tract. This evidence is not inconsistent with higher probabilities of job offers in suburban locations reported earlier. It corroborates the contention that even suburban residences are highly segregated. High wages, on the other hand, are concentrated in essentially white census tracts, regardless of the census tract of the residence. While there is a gain in wages offered in suburban areas, there are losses because blacks, wherever they live, are less likely to show and less likely to be hired if they do show.

CONSEQUENCES OF URBAN REVITALIZATION

Whether because of declining tax bases, deteriorating public services, the energy crunch making housing closer to the urban core more attractive to middle-income workers, or because of a general aesthetic lure back to the cities, there has been a renewed desire to make large urban areas comfortable, safe, and convenient places to live. Either by design or consequence, black inner-city residents have been displaced and new pocket ghettos are becoming the future problems of suburban towns. For whatever reasons, the ghetto is being dispersed and it is difficult to see how poor blacks will benefit. However, more comprehensive evidence, emerging from the 1980 Census, may show that the scattered black residences, the isolated black pockets of what was once a community, indeed, have fared well.

The difficulty in assessing whether development of a centralized minority community in a large urban area is to be preferred to dispersing the residences closer to changing employment prospects goes beyond merely arguing over whether the dispersed prospects exist or are viable employment alternatives. The difficulty becomes one of comparing the welfare gains and losses of both the black community which loses a few positive externalities through dispersal, and the rest of the urban area which could obtain a few negative externalities from continued gilding of the ghetto. If factors such as crime really are more deleterious in monolithic concentrations of blacks near the urban core rather than dispersed throughout the metropolis, one must question whether the positive aspects of community given up, such as the political power generated from geographical proximity to a homogeneous constituency, outweigh the gains achieved in reducing the negative externalities.

REFERENCES

Charlotte Freemon, *The Occupational Patterns in Urban Employment Change, 1965–1967,* Washington 1970.

Bennett Harrison, *Urban Economic Development,* Washington 1974.

David T. Herbert, *Urban Geography—A Social Perspective,* New York 1973.

J. F. Kain, "Housing Segregation, Negro Employment and Metropolitan Decentralization,"

Quarterly Journal of Economics, May 1968, 82, 175–98.

W. Lewis, Jr., "Urban Growth and Suburbanization of Employment: Some New Data," unpublished manuscript, Brookings Institution, 1969.

S. A. Lippman and J. J. McCall, "The Economics of Job Search: A Survey," *Economic Inquiry,* Sept. 1976, 14, 347–67.

J. D. Mooney, "Housing Segregation, Negro Employment and Metropolitan Decentralization," *Quarterly Journal of Economics,* May 1969, 83, 299–312.

P. Offner and D. A. Saks, "A Note on John Kain's 'Housing Segregation, Negro Employment and Metropolitan Decentralization,'" *Quarterly Journal of Economics,* Feb. 1971, 85, 147–61.

K. E. Phillips and S. L. Myers, "Job Search, Spatial Separation of Jobs and Residences, and Discrimination in Suburban Labor Markets," P-6189, Rand Corporation, 1978.

KEY CONCEPTS

frictional unemployment

ghetto development

ghetto dispersal

job search costs

reservation wage

risk-neutral worker

PART 5

URBAN TRANSPORTATION

After World War II urban mass-transit ridership in the United States went into a steep decline from which it has never fully recovered. Indeed, mass-transit has failed to recover lost passengers even though recent economic trends favor the growth of public transit. Beginning about the mid-1970s, the real cost of driving began to rise rapidly while mass-transit fares either remained constant or fell. Given this promising set of circumstances, one may ask why public transit has failed to recapture a significant number of urban commuters.

The woes facing mass transit can be traced directly to the relative superiority of the automobile in the minds of individual commuters. Urban commuters are often wrongly believed to possess an irrational love affair with their cars. Far from it, the decision to drive to work springs from rational comparisons of the relative costs and benefits of alternative transportation modes.

Several economic factors heavily favor the automobile. First, the ownership costs (purchase price, taxes, license) of a car are fixed and, therefore, irrelevant to the decision of whether to use it. The actual cost of using the car consists only of the marginal (or operating) cost, which is normally a small proportion of the car's total cost. Second, the majority of commuters obtain free parking at work, subsidized by their employers. This amounts to a substantial subsidy to drivers, especially in central cities where parking prices are high. Third, and possibly most important, the time cost to complete a given trip by mass-transit modes normally far exceeds that by car.

In addition to cost factors, several nonmonetary factors, such as a car's comfort, convenience, and flexibility, also favor the car. These benefits may be so important that many commuters would still choose to drive to work even if money and time costs favored mass transit.

For years government has attempted to steer commuters out of their automobiles. The major strategy of federal policy has been to divert drivers by constructing new fixed-rail transit systems. Stephen L. Mehay evaluates the cost and demand conditions necessary for investment in rail transit to be efficient. Such investments appear to be economical only under very limited circumstances, which unfortunately are seldom met in cities where new rail systems have been constructed. The experience of the BART rail system in the

156

San Francisco area is particularly instructive. After a capital investment of over $1.6 billion, notwithstanding its chronically large operating subsidies, BART has failed to make more than a dent in the Bay Area's transportation problems. Mehay discusses several alternative transit proposals that may offer a greater chance of improving urban transportation at a reasonable cost.

Stephen F. Williams advances the case for charging peak-hour congestion tolls on urban highways. Williams appeals not so much to the efficiency arguments long embraced by economists, but to the successful experiences of a congestion pricing plan in Singapore. The Singapore plan has been effective in relieving downtown congestion and clearly demonstrates the technical feasibility of congestion tolls.

Thomas C. Peterson reveals the pitfalls of applying cost-benefit analysis to large transportation projects. Peterson examines the potential net social benefits of a proposed rail-transit system in Los Angeles. Making use of an actual cost-benefit study of the Los Angeles system conducted by a reputable consulting firm, he demonstrates how easy it is to overestimate the benefits and underestimate the costs. He also shows the sensitivity of cost-benefit studies to the numerous assumptions that must be made and to forecasts of passenger ridership.

In the final selection, C. Kenneth Orski discusses recent transportation policies in European cities. He points out that the major thrust of European policy has been to more effectively manage existing transport systems, rather than attempt to construct new ones. Orski also discusses transportation innovations in Europe that may hold some promise of adoption in U.S. cities.

STEPHEN L. MEHAY

18 Urban Transportation Problems and Policies

This selection surveys alternative policies for dealing with urban transportation problems. The cost-effectiveness of investments in new fixed-rail systems is analyzed, based on the experience of the San Francisco BART system. In addition, several innovative policies— which do not require extensive capital investment—are discussed. These include lifting the legal restrictions currently imposed on jitney operations and removing legal barriers to entry into the taxicab market.

Traffic congestion in most U.S. cities grows worse daily while public-transit systems continue to experience declining patronage. This combination of trends has produced serious smog and noise pollution and contributed to the problem of urban sprawl. The source of these trends is not difficult to pinpoint. Urban commuters have repeatedly demonstrated a marked preference for the automobile over mass transit. Although mass transit is much cheaper to ride, the convenience, speed, and comfort of the private automobile make it the preferred choice for most commuters. Studies have shown that even the elimination of fares on mass-transit systems would not divert a significant number of commuters from cars to public transit.[1]

The evidence that policies aimed at diverting automobile users to mass transit will not work seems to have been ignored by transportation planners who have favored construction of new fixed-rail systems. In the last decade, construction of new fixed-rail systems has begun in Atlanta (MARTA), Washington, D.C. (Metro), Baltimore, and Miami, is scheduled to begin in

Houston and Los Angeles, and was completed in San Francisco (BART). Many experts question whether building expensive new rail systems can attract enough former automobile users to justify the cost. A quick review of the costs and benefits of transportation improvements reveals the major sources of concern.

MASS TRANSIT INVESTMENT DECISIONS

Only when the social benefits exceed the social costs can a transportation investment be considered a sensible use of scarce public funds. The capital and operating costs of transit systems are relatively easy to measure. Measuring social benefits of transit projects, on the other hand, can be difficult and poses the major challenge to conducting an accurate cost-benefit study.

The most significant communitywide benefit of a transportation improvement is the saving in travel time to users. A new rail line, for example, saves time not only for those riders who use it, but also for those drivers using the highways and streets that become less congested as a result of the new line. Transportation analysts have estimated that the value of the

[1] For a review of the evidence on fare elasticities, see A. Largo, et al., "Transit Fare Responsiveness to Fare Changes," *Traffic Quarterly* 35 (January 1981): 117–42.

time savings is some fraction of a commuter's hourly wage rate. Assume, for example, that a commuter values his or her time at one half his or her hourly wage rate, which is, say, $9. Assume further that a new rail line diverts him or her from driving to work and saves 15 minutes on the commute. He or she would value that improvement at $1.12 (0.25 x $4.50) per trip. Summing these values for all commuters over the year who use the new line (and for those who continue to drive) would yield the total annual time-saving benefits of the line.

Cost-benefit analysis is undertaken to assess the present value of net *future* benefits. The major benefits, such as the time saving, are highly sensitive to estimates of the future patronage on the new line. For new mass transit lines, transit planners hope that most patrons will be former automobile commuters. However, it is easy to overestimate the future expected patronage on proposed new rail systems and the proportion drawn from former automobile users.[2]

The indirect or secondary benefits of transit improvements are also susceptible to exaggeration. Secondary benefits may include better air quality, fewer traffic accidents, less urban sprawl, and economic development of areas served by the new transit lines. Once again, expected secondary benefits depend on estimates of the new system's ability to attract automobile users.

Fixed Rail Systems

The major advantage of fixed-rail systems, and the major reason they are preferred by transit planners, is their ability to move a large volume of passengers along a given transportation corridor. Some rail lines can carry as many as 45,000 persons per hour. By comparison, one highway lane with each car carrying an average 1.4 passengers can carry only 2,500 persons per hour. Despite this advantage, available evidence suggests that investment in new fixed-rail systems is unlikely to generate social benefits in excess of the costs.

The major problem is the inability of new transit systems to reduce automobile usage significantly, even in cities with extensive transit systems. When new lines have been added to existing rail systems in cities such as Cleveland and Boston, ridership on the new line and the diversion of automobile users have been disappointing. The costs of constructing new fixed-rail lines can be enormous, as much as $150 million per mile in some cities. Meyer, Kain, and Wohl, in a ground-breaking study, analyzed the comparative costs of serving given transportation corridors with alternative modes. The authors distinguished between three segments of a transit system: (1) the residential collection segment, (2) the line haul, and (3) the downtown-distribution system. For the major part of a transportation system, the line haul, they concluded that cities with sufficient population density to justify rail operations already possessed rail transit.[3] Their major overall conclusion was that cost considerations, on all segments of the system, weigh heavily against the fixed-rail system.

On the Right Track with BART?

The 71-mile BART system in San Francisco is the first fixed-rail system built in the

[2] T. Peterson, "Cost-Benefit Analysis for Evaluating Transportation Proposals: Los Angeles Case Study," *Land Economics*, February 1975, pp. 72–79.

[3] J. Meyer, J. Kain, and M. Wohl. *The Urban Transportation Problem* (Cambridge, Mass.: Harvard University Press, 1965).

United States in this century. It was designed to transport suburban commuters to the central business districts of the region—San Francisco and Oakland. The original cost-benefit study of the BART system concluded that construction would be in the community's interest.[4] But a comparison of the actual performance of BART with the study's predictions proves otherwise.[5]

Ridership on BART was predicted to reach 258,496 daily trips by 1975. But by 1981, after nearly 10 years of operation, the actual number of trips had reached only 160,000. The original cost-benefit study predicted that 61 percent of BART's patrons would be diverted from automobiles. The actual figure is only about 35 percent; moreover, most of BART's riders formerly rode the bus. A study by the U.S. Department of Transportation concluded that BART had reduced neither traffic volumes nor highway travel times nor congestion. One of the major social benefits of a transportation improvement—the time saving to nondiverted commuters—is almost entirely absent in the case of BART. On the cost side, both the capital and operating costs of the system were underestimated—operating expenses by about 500 percent. It is clear in retrospect that the positive net social benefits of the study were derived by exaggerating the system's benefits and by underestimating its costs.

BART's cost figures become more meaningful when they are compared to the costs of alternative modes. One analyst has concluded that when BART is compared to buses and subcompact cars, the bus is consistently more cost-effective at almost all traffic densities.[6] Even a subcompact car is cheaper than BART for commuting, except at very high passenger densities. In fact, the benefits generated by BART may not be sufficient to justify even the operating costs, let alone the capital costs. John Kain estimated that converting existing freeways to express-bus systems could have achieved the same performance as BART at a cost of between $15 to $50 million. This represents about 1 to 3 percent of the capital cost of BART.[7] These results have prompted at least one observer to suggest that the best use of BART would be to pave over the rails and use them for express buses.[8]

BART is questionable not only on economic grounds, but also because of equity considerations. The distribution of the costs and benefits of the system are not spread evenly across income groups. Because fare revenues cover only about one third of the operating expenses, BART patrons receive a substantial in-kind subsidy. The subsidy, including annualized capital costs, amounted to $3.76 per trip in 1976. Much of BART's funding is drawn from sales and property taxes, which are generally assumed to be borne disproportionately by lower-income persons. BART's patrons receiving the in-kind subsidy, however, tend to be young, educated, affluent suburbanites who commute to the central business districts. Melvin Webber's description that "the poor are paying and the rich are riding" appears to be accurate.[9]

[4] Parsons, Brinckerhoff, Tudor, Bechtel, *The Composite Report: Bay Area Rapid Transit* (San Francisco, May 1962).

[5] Unless otherwise stated, the remaining data on BART are from: U.S. Department of Transportation, *BART in the San Francisco Bay Area: The Final Report of the BART Impact Program* (Washington, D.C.: U.S. Government Printing Office, 1979).

[6] Melvin Webber, "The BART Experience—What Have We Learned?" *Public Interest,* Fall 1976.

[7] John F. Kain, "How to Improve Urban Transportation at Practically No Cost," *Economic Analysis and the Efficiency of Government.* Hearings before Subcommittee on Economy in Government of the Joint Economic Committee, U.S. Congress, May 6, 1970.

[8] "BART's Many Woes Affecting Growth of Rail Mass Transit," *Wall Street Journal,* June 29, 1977, p. 1.

[9] Webber, "The BART Experience," p. 22.

Finally, BART has generated few secondary benefits to the Bay Area. Because it has dislodged few commuters from their cars, the impact on regional air quality has been practically nil.[10] In addition, after 10 years of operation, neither regional development nor population patterns (that is, sprawl) have been altered measurably by BART.

URBAN TRANSPORTATION POLICIES— PAST AND FUTURE

Since fixed-rail transit is clearly not the panacea many have claimed, public policy has increasingly considered other solutions to solve the problems faced by urban commuters. Much of the impetus for new policy directions in urban transportation is provided by the Urban Mass Transportation Administration (UMTA) of the U.S. Department of Transportation. The policy shifts that have taken place since the inception of UMTA (in 1965) suggest some future directions urban transportation policy might take.

Annual federal subsidies to mass transit grew rapidly during the 1970s and reached $4 billion by 1979. Most federal subsidies are given in the form of matching capital grants. Smaller amounts are devoted to subsidizing the operating expenses of local transit systems.[11] These policies have had the effect of reducing the relative price of new equipment, which qualifies for capital grants, and of increasing the relative price of maintenance and repair. It is not surprising, therefore, to find that local bus systems tend to underinvest in the maintenance and repair of buses and to replace them more frequently than is economically justified.[12]

Early UMTA programs proceeded without requiring local governments to conduct cost-benefit analyses. Fortunately, this is no longer the case. Cities must now carry out cost-benefit analyses of various transportation alternatives—especially when the request is for assistance to build a new fixed-rail system. Because numerous studies have found that several alternatives are more cost-effective than rail systems, UMTA's goals consequently have shifted away from rail in recent years to alternative modes.

Transportation Options

One alternative that has been rediscovered in the United States is the trolley, or light-rail transit. Light rail has several advantages over heavy rail. When built on exclusive right-of-way, light rail's speed and carrying capacity compares favorably with heavy rail. However, light rail has much lower construction costs and wider coverage than heavy rail. Compared to buses, light rail generally creates less noise and air pollution. In addition, by attaching several cars that can be operated by a single driver, operating costs can be held below either heavy rail or buses.[13] Currently, several cities are constructing or expanding existing light-rail lines. San Diego completed a new light-rail line in 1981 at a cost of only $5 million per mile. This figure compares with the per-mile construction costs of $35 million for BART, $34 million for Washington's Metro, and $42 million for Atlanta's MARTA.

---

[10] The U.S. Department of Transportation estimates that even if BART were to operate at full capacity only a 3 percent reduction in air pollution could be expected.

[11] In 1979 about three fourths of federal assistance was in the form of capital grants. See U.S. Department of Transportation, *Thirteenth Annual Report*, 1979.

[12] George Hilton, *Federal Transit Subsidies* (Washington, D.C.: American Enterprise Institute, 1974), pp. 56–59.

[13] For a fuller cost analysis of light-rail transit, see Hans Brems, "Light Rail Transit: Cost and Output," *Journal of Urban Economics* 7 (1980): 20–30.

Studies also have shown that express bus service may be far more effective than fixed-rail transit. One UMTA proposal that has been adopted in some cities is to reserve special highway lanes for express buses. Under certain conditions, a reserved bus lane can carry as many as 25,000 persons per hour. This volume is comparable to rail and far exceeds that of a highway with lanes devoted solely to automobiles. Also, express buses eliminate the problem of multiple stops, which impose the greatest time cost on users and present the biggest obstacle to attracting riders who value their time.

Improved bus systems must be combined with other policies that increase the efficiency of the existing transport capacity. One promising alternative is to increase highway efficiency by levying congestion tolls during rush hours. The economic basis for such tolls is that the marginal social costs that the peak-hour driver creates in terms of extra travel time (and pollution) imposed on all drivers exceeds the average private cost paid by the last driver. The objective of congestion tolls would be to induce some drivers to shift to less crowded, off-peak hours, or else to shift to alternative modes such as car pools or mass transit. In this way the efficiency of the existing capacity could be improved, and the need for expensive additions to capacity perhaps could be avoided.

An alternative method of reducing highway congestion is to use signal lights on freeway on-ramps during peak hours. Metering, by regulating the number of cars entering the freeway, can achieve the optimal flow rate of cars per lane per hour. Even though the commuter will spend some time waiting to enter the freeway, total trip time should fall because of reduced congestion *on* the freeway. Also,

express buses and car pools can be given priority access to the freeway.

The elimination of free parking for employees—perhaps through higher parking taxes—would serve to correct a current price distortion. Free parking makes auto commuting artificially cheap so that private costs of driving to work are less than social costs. Full-cost parking would discourage driving to work alone during the most congested hours. If the number of persons per car could be doubled, highway capacity would double without necessitating any increase in investment. Initial evidence indicates that the demand for parking may be very sensitive to price increases.[14] If so, one would expect higher parking charges to lead to more car pooling and bus riding and less driving to work alone.

Developing Paratransit

In recent years UMTA has stressed development of so-called paratransit modes: jitneys, dial-a-ride, car pools, shared taxicabs, and subscription bus service. Paratransit modes offer two advantages over traditional public transit systems. The traditional suburb-to-downtown commute is rapidly being replaced in most urban areas by increasingly diverse trip patterns. Almost all public transit systems follow fixed routes that are unable to accommodate these new urban trip patterns. Paratransit modes offer the flexibility and scheduling convenience to accommodate the changing trip patterns.

A second advantage is that paratransit modes would enable suppliers to offer a greater variety of service quality levels to fill the untapped market for quality differentiation. Public transit in the United States typically offers only a single class of ser-

[14] U.S. Department of Transportation, Urban Mass Transportation Administration, *Financing Transit: Alternatives for Local Government,* 1979.

vice, which is usually of the lowest quality. In contrast, many European systems offer riders the alternative of higher quality service (such as first class) at a higher fare.

Jitneys. The term *jitney*[15] refers to a type of service rather than to a type of vehicle. Jitneys operate along any route pattern that maximizes the private owner's income. Jitneys emerged about 1914 in many U.S. cities and became very popular, partly because they provided a flexible and inexpensive alternative to trolleys. Soon trolley companies began suffering substantial losses, and they retaliated by obtaining legislation in most cities prohibiting jitney operations.

Today jitneys operate legally in only a few cities (notably San Francisco, Atlantic City, and Miami), while illegal jitneys operate in a few others (New York, Chicago, and Pittsburgh among others). In many instances jitneys serve minority residents who are poorly served by the bus and taxi monopolies. In many foreign nations, jitneys constitute a major segment of the transportation system.

Legalization of private jitneys in the United States would fill a large gap the urban transport market. Jitneys provide an intermediate flexible mode between fixed-route, low-quality buses and the individually hired cabs. They would offer convenient transportation to low-income city residents whose trip patterns are not well served by existing public transit.

Jitney owners, seeking to maximize their income, could be expected to adjust their route patterns to meet demand. Competition can be expected to keep fares low,

perhaps to no more than a regular bus fare. In addition, the capital investment required for jitneys is minimal and would require no government subsidies.

Deregulating Taxicabs. The advantages of jitneys—flexibility, low capital and operating costs, and convenience—are shared by taxicabs. Unfortunately, taxicabs in most U.S. cities are often considered to be a luxury. Fares are high because most cities restrict entry into the taxicab market, limiting either the number of cabs or the number of firms allowed to operate. Table 1 shows how these restrictions have reduced the number of cabs available. The three cities with a significant number of cabs per 1,000 residents—Washington, Atlanta and Honolulu—are the only cities without entry restrictions. It is easy to see why studies have found that cities with entry restrictions tend to have lower service levels and higher prices.[16] Low-income residents of restricted-entry cities are often especially poorly served by the monopoly cab companies. As is true in the case of jitneys, entry restrictions have led to the appearance of illegal or "gypsy" cabs to serve the unfilled demand for service. The gypsy cabs often serve mostly minority areas where legal service is inadequate. Taxicabs historically were regulated to reduce competition and protect the mass-transit operators.

Deregulating taxicab markets would seem to be a simple step to increase the availability, quality, and convenience of urban transportation. The greatest beneficiaries might be the poor, the aged, and the handicapped, who are not well served

---

[15] This section and the following section rely on material from Robert Poole, Jr., *Cutting Back City Hall* (New York: Universe Books, 1980).

[16] E. Kitch, M. Issacson, and D. Kasper, "The Regulation of Taxicabs in Chicago," *Journal of Law and Economics* 14 (October 1971).

TABLE 1

Number of Taxis Per Thousand Population, Selected Cities, 1970

City	Restrictions on the Number of:	Number of Taxis	Taxis per 1,000 Population
New York	Firms	11,722	1.5
Chicago	Firms	4,600	1.4
Los Angeles	Cabs	885	0.3
Philadelphia	Cabs	1,480	0.8
Detroit	Firms	1,310	0.9
Houston	Cabs	473	0.3
Washington, D.C.	No restriction	19,144	10.2
San Francisco	Firms	798	1.2
Boston	Firms	1,525	2.3
Phoenix	Cabs	99	0.2
Pittsburgh	Cabs	600	1.2
Atlanta	No restriction	1,900	3.9
Minneapolis	Firms	248	0.8
Miami	Firms	431	1.0
Honolulu	No restriction	1,400	4.3
Birmingham	Cabs	245	0.8

Source: Sandi Rosenbloom, "Taxis and Jitneys: The Case for Deregulation," *Reason* 3 (February 1972).

by public transit. Some transportation experts have concluded that changes in taxicab regulation would probably do as much as any other single policy to lure auto users from their cars and to improve public transportation.[17]

CONCLUSIONS

No single policy will solve once and for all the problems of urban transportation. BART fell victim to the thinking that fixed-rail transit with spectacular new space-age technology would provide a solution. Unfortunately, going to the moon and transporting urban residents in a cost-effi-

cient manner do not seem to be comparable tasks. Transport policies that appear economically feasible are those that improve the efficiency of existing transport systems. In some cases improving efficiency means removing legal impediments to greater competition and experimentation in transportation markets. Many transit planners until recently have ignored the characteristics of urban transportation markets and instead sought glamorous, high-technology solutions. Few of the new policy directions that appear promising require major investments in new capital equipment or new technology. It is the distortive effects of incorrect prices, together with laws that abet monopoly and stifle innovation that are the main problems in urban transportation today.

[17] Martin Wohl, "Increasing the Taxi's Role in Urban America," *Technology Review*, July-August 1976.

KEY CONCEPTS

congestion tolls

cost-benefit analysis

fixed-rail transit

freeway metering system

jitneys

light-rail transit

net social benefits

paratransit modes

STEPHEN F. WILLIAMS

19   Getting Downtown:
Relief of Highway Congestion through Pricing

Economists have long favored levying tolls during peak commuting hours to reduce congestion on urban highways. Stephen F. Williams of the University of Colorado describes how such a scheme actually works in Singapore. He also details the efficiency and equity gains from congestion tolls. However, he notes the formidable political problems currently blocking implementation of such a plan in U.S. cities.

Each morning a Chicago radio station presents a bulletin of traffic conditions on the major expressways in the area. On bad days, the network announces running times, such as "It's 90 minutes on the Kennedy from Mannheim to Ohio," a distance of only 14 miles. The waste of time is staggering. Surely, one thinks, there must be ways of getting better value out of Chicago's imposing expressway system.

Two approaches are especially congenial to politicians and administrators—building more highways and managing traffic more effectively. But there is a third—making drivers pay for using the highways at peak hours of congestion. This approach is a stepsister, languishing in learned journals where equations outnumber sentences. Yet here and there it is attracting glimmers of interest. Singapore has actually put peak-hour pricing into practice, and the Urban Mass Transportation Administration is

scheduled to subsidize some small experiments this summer. It is time the idea enjoyed the whirl of public discussion.

THE SINGAPORE EXPERIENCE

Singapore instituted its present pricing system in June 1975. Officials designated a downtown zone of about 25 square miles, with 22 entry points. During the morning rush hour from 7:30 to 10:15 A.M., passenger cars and vans could enter the zone only if they displayed special licenses. These sold for $33 a month or $1.67 a day.[1] Car pools of four people or more were exempt. The government's purpose was to bring about a 25-30 percent reduction in peak-hour traffic. What happened was a good deal more dramatic. According to a before-and-after study by the World Bank ("Relieving Traffic Congestion: The Singapore Area License Scheme," June 1978), overall traffic in the priced period fell about 40 percent, car traffic 65 percent.

From Stephen F. Williams, "Getting Downtown: Relief of Highway Congestion through Pricing," *Regulation*, March/April 1981, pp. 45–50. Reprinted with permission from the American Enterprise Institute for Public Policy Research, copyright 1981.

[1] The charges were set slightly lower initially, but raised to these levels in December 1975.

What happened to all the people? Car pooling increased sharply. The number of vehicles qualifying for the car pool exemption doubled, while smaller car pools also rose in number as people sought to cut the burden of the license fee by splitting it with others. Bus ridership increased too, and buses were able to move a bit faster through the less congested streets.

As the World Bank study showed, however, not all the peak-hour reduction took such a welcome form. Far too many travelers simply changed the time of their trips to just before or just after the priced period. A bit of this would have been all to the good—spreading the peak travel across a longer period and reducing the valuable time consumed by congestion. But so much of it occurred that traffic bulges appeared on either side of the former rush hour. Thus, traffic in the worst half-hour (10:15 to 10:45 A.M.) was only 7 percent less than it had been in what was formerly the worst half-hour (8 to 8:30 A.M.), and the old rush hour became relatively deserted. Similarly, far too many travelers simply changed their routes. Indeed, enough people whose destinations were on the far sides of the priced zone shifted to "free" roads around it to produce considerable congestion on those roads.

These not altogether expected responses provide a dramatic demonstration of what economists call "edge effects": distortions that occur when people flee a priced zone and pile up its unpriced borders. The edge can be one of time or geography. The Singapore system obviously has both—leading to the traffic bulges around the restricted morning period and around the restricted area. The system also has a combined time-and-geographic edge. To simplify monitoring, the designers did not place a charge on exit from the core, expecting the evening traffic to mirror the morning's. This did not happen. Evening traffic fell only trivially. Evidently many travelers who were headed for places across the restricted zone would skirt it in the morning but cut through it when returning in the evening.

The flaws in Singapore's scheme demonstrate the major difficulty facing the designer of a congestion pricing system: how to make it simple enough to be workable without creating too many harmful side effects.

THE BASIC CONCEPT

The Singapore system, warts and all, works well enough to have lasted. But a pricing scheme, some might argue, could do little to solve U.S. traffic problems because American drivers are hopelessly addicted to their cars. There is growing evidence, however, that price matters, even here. For example, as U.S. gasoline prices increased in the 1970s, gasoline demand responded, first rising more slowly than before and then in the last two years actually falling. For another example, the initiation last year of monthly parking fees of $10 to $30 for federal employees in Washington, D.C., has caused, according to preliminary reports, a 3 to 10 percent drop in employee car use. This drop is especially impressive, given that agencies had already induced a good deal of car pooling by regulatory measures.

The simple idea underlying a congestion charge is that, because price does matter, people will tend to overuse a resource when they do not have to pay the full cost of each use. Peak-hour travelers impose delay costs on one another. Of course each traveler takes his own time into account. But on an urban expressway a driver often inflicts costs on other drivers that are several times greater than those he suffers himself. Just as the failure of society to price air and water causes these resources to be overused (polluted) and imposes costs on others, so the lack of congestion pricing leads to overuse of highways at rush hours. By making travelers bear these costs, congestion pricing persuades some of them to switch to car pooling, public transportation, and travel at less congested hours. Without prices, many a traveler is now making solo journeys whose value is not worth the total costs imposed—that is, the "private" costs of his time and vehicle operating expenses, plus the "social" costs of others' time.

In an ideal congestion pricing system every vehicle would be charged exactly the costs that it imposed on others at any particular time and place. Thus for each morning and evening period there would be matching prices, at every stage, with the most popular times having the highest prices and the surrounding times having prices that were gradually lower, but still high enough to prevent bulges. Geographically, too, prices would shade off smoothly from the routes of the highest traffic density.

Oddly enough, the technology for such an ideal system may be available at reasonable cost. Two schemes stand out. The first is an in-car meter that would run up charges based on electric impulses from control points in the streets. The other is an in-car identification device that would trigger a mechanism in the street, which would register the information necessary to charge each owner on, say, a monthly basis.

At present, however, these schemes appear unnecessarily radical. For one thing,

people are not at all used to being charged for something historically provided "free," especially when it cannot be explained that the revenue is needed to pay for construction costs. With all that conceptual novelty, congestion pricing probably cannot afford to be saddled with a Buck Rogers technology. In any event, more conventional devices can probably come close enough to curing the edge problems. But first let us look at the main alternatives to congestion pricing.

MORE HIGHWAYS AND BETTER TRAFFIC MANAGEMENT

Highway building and traffic management may well have some place in a program for curing urban highway congestion. But neither is a substitute for pricing.

To try to solve the congestion problem exclusively by building more highways is like trying to solve water pollution exclusively by increasing stream flows. It increases the supply of the resource but does nothing to ensure that the amount supplied is used intelligently. The result is enormous waste. As early as 1963 the estimated cost of building enough extra lanes to meet rush-hour traffic loads had risen, for some urban expressways, to $23,000 per regular commuter. It is no wonder that urban highway construction has dwindled (by 37 percent in the 1970-75 period, to take one figure).

In the face of such enormous construction costs, highway engineers have accepted the idea of managing *demand* more effectively. But to date, they have gone no further than to give "high occupancy vehicles" (HOVs) a preferred status in the queue. For example, where entry ramps are metered to improve expressway flow, highway engineers are willing to accept ramp designs that enable HOVs to bypass the main access lanes. Where there are tolls, they may allow HOVs less congested access to the tolled facility or even exempt them from the toll (as on the San Francisco-Oakland Bay Bridge). And occasionally they will go so far as to assign an entire lane to HOVs (or even two lanes, as on the Shirley Highway into Washington, D.C.).

All of these devices retain queuing as the basic method for allocating highway use. And there is a crucial difference between queuing and a price system: Queuing rations access to users who are most willing to *throw away* a valuable resource (time). A price system, on the other hand, requires users only to *transfer* a claim on resources (money); and the resources need not be wasted because the recipient of the claims, here the government, can use them to reduce taxes or improve services.

Within the framework of queuing, one can reduce the waste of time only by increasing some other real loss. To illustrate the point with a rather extreme example, queuing time on entry ramps could be reduced by directing noise at the unfortunate waiters and increasing it gradually to the ear-splitting point where enough people are driven out of the queue (to HOVs or other times of travel) that congestion falls to the economically ideal level. But the social cost, which would then take the form of discomfort and hearing loss as well as waiting time, would have to equal the value of the loss that formerly consisted exclusively of wasted time. By contrast, prices can bring demand into line with supply without inflicting a loss on society as a whole.

The demand management devices now used by highway engineers, like command-and-control regulatory systems in general, sort out high-value and low-value uses crudely and at unnecessary social costs. They make some choices conditional on the chooser's accepting burdens that are intrinsically unrelated to his choice. The people for whom car pooling is relatively costly (because of their location, their tastes, or the value of their time) can persist in travel as single occupants only by continuing to throw away their time and that of others in delay on the ramp, on the highway, or in the toll lane. Under a pricing system, people pay for their choice, but since they pay in cash, society can use the payments for worthy purposes.

WINNERS AND LOSERS

Thus peak-hour pricing, well conceived and well executed, should increase the size of the social "pie" in the city adopting it. Although fewer vehicles would be traveling on urban highways, the net value that the highway contributed to society would be greater. Just as pollution charges can lead to more highly valued uses of air and water by eliminating the emissions whose value to the emitter is less than the damage they cause to others, so highway charges would make the highway network more valuable by eliminating auto use with a value less than the delay costs it inflicts.

But a change that increases total wealth may also redistribute wealth among individuals. Who would win and who would lose under congestion pricing?

Winners
Urban taxpayers would win because the introduction of a pricing scheme shifts de

facto ownership of the highway from users to the entity that receives the revenues—the city. Again the analogy to air pollution is instructive. Without charges, the air is in effect owned collectively by users—polluters and breathers—and, being owned collectively, it is abused and its value reduced. Pollution fees transfer the polluters' ownership to whatever unit of government collects the fees. Congestion pricing has the same effect.

Car poolers and bus riders would also win because they would enjoy the benefits of less congestion at relatively little extra charge—or none if car pools and buses were exempt. Finally, some people, perhaps a surprisingly large number, would find the time they saved more valuable to them than the charges. Estimates of the ideal charge for an urban expressway tend to run about $.30 a mile. If a $4.50 charge on a fifteen-mile commute saves 15 minutes, a commuter can be a winner without placing a desperately high value on his time.

Losers

At first glance, the most obvious candidates for grand losers would seem to be the poor. The reason for this is that congestion pricing shifts the basis for allocating the highway from readiness to spend time to readiness to spend money, and the poor typically assign a lower dollar value to their time than the rich.

In fact, however, many of the poor would unequivocally gain. Because traffic would move more quickly, current car poolers and current bus users, who include disproportionate numbers of the poor, would enjoy a pure gain in saved time. Beyond that, if buses became more crowded (in Singapore the reverse actually

happened), the city could readily correct this loss of amenity—either by taking advantage of the lighter traffic to coax more trips out of the same number of buses and driver-hours, or by using the pricing proceeds to improve service.

But what of the poor person who lives in an area with little public transportation, or none, and who works in the priced zone? Happily, congestion pricing has a peculiarly mild impact even on this apparent victim. The very fact that stirs our concern for him—the low dollar value he sets on his time—suggests a way for him to mitigate the burden of the price. Time, after all, is the major cost of the several alternatives to a solo peak-hour trip. Merely by taking the time to recruit *one* fellow car pooler, a commuter can cut the money price in half; and if larger car pools are exempt (as in Singapore), the commuter can eliminate the money price altogether merely by finding three kindred spirits. Finally, anyone can cut the price by incurring the inconvenience costs (mainly time) of traveling at off-peak hours.

Thus, the poor as a group would not necessarily do badly under peak-hour pricing, even when we view them only as travelers. But the poor are also urban taxpayers and recipients of urban services. As such they would stand to gain from tax reductions or service increases made possible by the pricing revenues. And the poor would probably also gain as consumers. If freight shipments were exempt (as in Singapore), shipping costs would fall, producing a decline in commodity prices. Even if freight were not exempt, the savings in wage and vehicle expenses resulting from speedier deliveries might more than offset the cost of the congestion charge, and, again, commodity prices would fall.

The other principal candidates for losers would seem, again at first glance, to be central-city firms and landowners. Some point out, for example, that any program that increases the out-of-pocket costs of access to the central city, *without changing anything else*, makes it more difficult for central-city firms to attract employees, clients, and customers. Thus, under congestion pricing, firms desiring to hold employee compensation constant would have to offset the congestion price with a pay increase, and firms desiring to remain competitive would have to reduce prices on their products and services.

But all that overlooks the gains from pricing. For peak-hour travelers who save more in time than they pay in charges (whether driving alone, car pooling, or using buses), the central city becomes more attractive. And for those going downtown in off-peak hours—probably the bulk of shoppers—the charge does not apply. In general, the central city benefits by becoming more efficient as a commercial and shopping center and more aesthetically appealing. Air pollution levels should fall and pedestrian amenities should rise, as they have in Singapore. Finally, there is the added municipal revenue. Real estate or sales tax reductions financed out of the pricing revenues could considerably sweeten the deal.

POSSIBLE FORMS OF CONGESTION PRICING

If we put aside the high-technology metering systems, the leading techniques for implementing congestion pricing are toll systems, area charges, and parking charges.

Toll systems have two advantages. First, they use a small number of entry points—those where the expressway disgorges its burden into the city. Second, they provide an easy solution to the time edge effect because they can accommodate a variable charge—a high rate for the peak and lower rates for the one or two time zones on either side.

But the ease with which tolls can cure the time edge effect is likely to be offset, in many cities, by unfortunate geographic edge effects. Motorists could duck off the expressway just before the toll, with the result that congestion is preserved on all but the last segment of the expressway and increased on the nonexpressway streets in the core. Further, the toll collection process would itself consume some of the time that pricing is intended to save. Finally, toll systems would entail a large capital investment in the collection areas, an investment politically difficult to justify for a system launched as an experiment.

Area charges—which price access to an area by the sale of permits, as in Singapore—avoid many of the inconveniences of toll collection. Persons entering the priced zone would have to display the correct sticker, presumably sold by mail or in stores or vending machines. The last-minute escape to arterials would become irrelevant, and the scheme's flexibility would be plain for all to see.

Besides, area pricing has the advantage of being able to handle both time and geographic edge effects, by having more than one concentric geographic zone and several time zones. But the system mounts to unrealistic complexity fairly quickly. For instance, a plan with daily and monthly stickers, three geographic zones, and two time zones would require twelve different stickers. If the system is to rely on visual monitoring as cars flow along, it must not overstrain the human capacity to distinguish symbols quickly.

Singapore's experience with monitoring is encouraging, in that only one or two extra policemen have been needed to monitor each of 22 entry points. But this ease of enforcement was obtained at the cost of having only two sticker types (daily and monthly), with severe edge effects as a consequence. In other words, the smaller the edge effects, the higher the monitoring costs.

Parking surcharges possess the important advantage of piggybacking on an existing transaction, the driver's payment at the parking lot. And because the transaction is a more or less sedentary one, it can easily handle enough pricing variety to deal well with edge effects. Commuters can be charged differential rates, with the highest rates applied to peak-hour arrivals and to parking in the downtown center. The main flaw of a surcharge system is that it cannot catch vehicles moving through the center city to destinations on the other side. If there is heavy through traffic, or if heavy through traffic develops once the surcharges have cut back traffic headed into the core, commuters will suffer a cash burden without enjoying faster traveling time.

The parking surcharge's greatest appeal over other pricing systems is, perhaps, that it seems to involve the least assault on established institutions. Thus it is not surprising that the Urban Mass Transportation Administration (UMTA) is using this approach in the experimental pricing programs it plans to start this year. The sites of the experiments—beach areas in Hermosa Beach and Santa Cruz, California—enjoy the key preconditions for the success of parking charges: there is little or no through traffic, and little or no chance that lessened congestion will attract any new through traffic.

POLITICAL HAZARDS

Like many policy innovations, congestion pricing is not perfect. Its practical problems—edge effects, de facto shifts in property rights, and possible impact on the poor and the central city—are real. Nevertheless, they are probably manageable, at least if the pricing scheme is carefully tailored to the particular area.

But when citizens are asked about congestion pricing they often reply that they have already paid once for the highway—through taxes—and that once is enough. To the travelers who fear they would lose from the program (because, for them, the time gains would be worth less than the charges paid), the argument may seem powerful. The answer, of course, is that peak-hour travelers have not paid for one of the inputs to their trips: the time of other travelers. Apart from that answer, the only way to secure their political support is by a shrewd program for distributing the revenue (possibly even a simple per capita rebate).

The real problem is a political one, of the sort that inheres in so many market solutions. Indirect payment through such forms as queuing is typically much more palatable than direct payment. Our very language illustrates the depth of the problem. Throughout this article I have used the term "expressway" for something that people normally call a "freeway." On a moment's reflection the ordinary "freeway" user will acknowledge that the road is not free, that it is financed by taxpayers. Still, the difference between direct and indirect payment seems to be enough for the indirect method to have captured the semantic advantage of the word "free."

Yet there are grounds for hope. An ancillary benefit from congestion pricing is reduced air pollution. As the high costs of present pollution control strategies become more obvious, congestion pricing may win friends as a thrifty weapon in that battle. Another appealing side effect is reduced energy consumption. Finally, history offers some encouragement. Radical ideas that have merit do eventually become settled policy. With luck, Singapore and UMTA's forthcoming experiments may speed the process.

KEY CONCEPTS

edge effects

high-occupancy vehicles (HOVs)

peak-hour pricing

private costs

rationing by queuing

rationing by pricing

social costs

THOMAS C. PETERSON

20 Cost-Benefit Analysis for Evaluating Transportation Proposals: Los Angeles Case Study

Thomas C. Peterson of Central Michigan University analyzes in some detail a cost-benefit study that was used to justify construction of a fixed-rail transit system in Los Angeles. His critique discusses in general the various types of social benefits that can justifiably be attributed to a transportation improvement and those that cannot. He discovers numerous instances where social benefits were either significantly exaggerated or attributed incorrectly to the proposed rail system. His article illuminates the hazards and pitfalls in cost-benefit analysis, particularly for transportation investments.

Although most economists and public officials understand the theory of cost-benefit analysis, there seems to be great difficulty when it comes to applying this technique to "real world" problems. This article critically examines a cost-benefit study undertaken for a proposed rapid transit system in the Los Angeles metropolitan area in order to illustrate the problems and to suggest alternative methods for treating them.[1] For the proposed Los Angeles rapid transit system, the benefit cost ratio is favorable (exceeds unity) only because: (1) many benefits are incorrectly calculated due to such factors as inflation, anticipated unemployment reductions and expenditure decreases, along with double counting and the inclusion of nonquantifiable benefits; (2) many costs are understated or omitted entirely; and (3) the passenger estimates are overly optimistic. This last point is particularly important since passenger estimates are crucial to a cost-benefit study of any rapid transit system.[2]

In 1968 the voters of the Southern California Rapid Transit District (hereinafter referred to as SCRTD) rejected a $2.5 billion fixed rail transit system. The rejected proposal was an 89-mile, 66-station, 5-corridor rapid transit system.[3] ... The recommended system included the inauguration of 250 miles of express feeder bus route and 300 miles of local feeder bus service. The estimated cost—$2,514,861,000—was almost equal to the maximum debt limit the SCRTD could incur.

The SCRTD paid Stanford Research Insti-

From Thomas C. Peterson, "Cost-Benefit Analysis for Evaluating Transportation Proposals: Los Angeles Case Study," *Land Economics* February 1975, pp. 72–79. Reprinted with permission of The University of Wisconsin Press, copyright 1975.

[1] I would like to acknowledge the helpful comments on an earlier draft by Jeffrey Barbour, anonymous reviewers, and the editors of *Land Economics*.

[2] This article is a revised section of the author's doctoral dissertation. Peterson [1970].

[3] See SCRTD [1968].

tute (hereinafter referred to as SRI) $68,000 to undertake a cost-benefit analysis of its proposed rapid transit system [SRI 1968]. Specifically, SRI was commissioned to: (1) evaluate the traveler benefits accruing to both rapid transit users and automobile travelers, (2) identify and appraise the community benefits accruing to the public, (3) compare traveler and community benefits with system costs, and (4) appraise the overall feasibility of the system.

TRAVELER BENEFITS

Travel time savings, based on 1980 trip patterns, are estimated by comparing trip travel times both with and without rapid transit. The difference in travel time . . . is valued at $39.5 million per year [SRI 1968, p. 15]. Travel time saving for airport patrons is valued at $3.05 million per year. Since no airport study was undertaken, these savings are based on the 1.4 million airport patrons required for the airport route to break even. The decrease in vehicle operating costs for motorists who switch to rapid transit and for those who continue to use the less congested street and freeway facilities is valued at $46.5 million annually.

The system would also reduce required parking spaces. SRI reported: "Rapid transit will result in an estimated reduction of 117,770 parking spaces needed, at an annual saving of $22.7 million in the cost of providing these spaces" [1968, p. 18]. The cost of providing parking spaces at the transit stations is included in the system's cost. SRI asserted that automobiles no longer needed for commuting are a benefit assigned to the rapid transit system. This benefit is due to the availability of rapid transit, which would allow some former automobile users to sell their cars or use them for other purposes. SRI valued the decrease of 10,000 automobiles at $3.4 million per year. Use of rapid transit is likewise expected to decrease the number of vehicle miles driven per year, which would decrease the number of automobile accidents. The decrease in accidents is valued at $4.7 million per year. Also included under traveler benefits by SRI was a $14.9 million yearly "revenue surplus" used to improve bus service and to avoid fare increases. This alleged "benefit" is merely an income transfer payment because it is not generated from the investment in rapid transit.

The total value of all traveler benefits estimated by SRI is $134.8 million per year [1968, p. 25]. These benefits are greatly dependent on the number of passengers carried. If passenger estimates are not achieved, then these traveler benefits must likewise be reduced.

COMMUNITY BENEFITS

The second classification of benefits from the system are those that accrue to the population as a whole as a by-product or consequence of traveler benefits. Community benefits result from: (1) structural and functional unemployment reductions, (2) construction unemployment reductions, (3) improved business productivity, (4) improved government productivity, and (5) improvements in life style.

SRI estimated that by 1980 rapid transit improvements to labor mobility could reduce the monthly jobless total by 4,200 through improved access to areas of labor shortage. This benefit is questionable since rapid transit alone is not expected to have a major impact on the hard-core unemployment problem in the poverty areas of Los Angeles County. Improved transportation does not by itself increase job opportunities.[4] There are other equal or greater controlling factors. In other words, lack of public transportation may not be the major cause of unemployment in poverty areas of Los Angeles. SRI valued a permanent reduction in unemployment due to improvements in labor mobility at $30 million per year. SRI asserted that the construction of the rapid transit system would have a major impact on unemployment in the construction industry. The construction program was estimated to provide an average of 5,300 jobs for construction workers over a seven-year period, with one-half of the workers coming from the unemployed ranks. The increase in construction employment valued at $24 million per year is open to question since it is difficult to predict the level of unemployment that would exist without the project.[5]

If the employment of one-half of the workers who construct the system is counted as a benefit, one can ask why the decrease in parking space expense, valued at $22.7 million per year, is also counted as a benefit. Even if the gain from increased construction activity due to the rapid transit were counted, other individuals would be laid off—for example, gas station attendants and others associated with automotive transport, including insurance claim adjusters and freeway fence repairmen. In other words, why does SRI count only the positive effect on employment and not the negative effect? To solve this difficulty, the

effect on employment due to construction and operation of the system should not be counted in a cost-benefit analysis. SRI also mentioned that millions of dollars of local expenditures for materials, machinery and services will be a further short-term aid to employment demand and a major boon to local industry. This erroneous statement of a secondary benefit is a superb example of what McKean meant when he wrote about multiple counting: "Right before our eyes . . . the project's costs . . . have suddenly turned into gains" [1958, p. 157].

A third source of benefits to the community from the system is an increase in business productivity. This benefit, estimated at $15 million per year, results from improved labor supply, so-called environmental factors, and business profit on increased labor employment. SRI admitted that most of these benefits are not susceptible to measurement, but wrote that "one indication of their value is the fact that the Los Angeles Chamber of Commerce publicly registered strong support for an extensive rapid transit system" [1968, p. 39]. However, if the gain to merchants located in the central district is at the expense of outlying business districts, then the system only provides an income transfer payment from merchants outside the central area to those located in the central area.

Another $15 million yearly benefit results from improved government productivity. Part of this productivity improvement was derived by SRI based on a "hypothetical city structure." SRI also estimated that the efficiencies through a mass improvement in labor supply would result in a cost reduction of 0.1 percent, which would produce $3 million in savings annually. SRI concluded that the ". . . dollar value of $15 million per year in increased government productivity . . . is believed defendable

---

[4] *Los Angeles Times*, July 1, 1968. The federally funded transportation-employment project director for Los Angeles ". . . found evidence that car ownership is a prime condition of employment regardless of job." See *Los Angeles Times*, February 24, 1969, and Wohl [1970], p. 23.

[5] See Haveman and Krutilla [1968], for further discussion on this topic.

because it is so conservative" [1968, p. 183].

SRI asserted that there "... are a number of non-monetary improvements that rapid transit will bring to many District residents to broaden their range of choice of mobility as well as residential possibilities that will enrich their 'style of urban life'" [1968, p. 43]. This benefit was estimated by SRI at $25 million annually. After the SCRTD *Final Report* was issued, an SRI representative, when questioned about the value of this benefit, answered that "... others were entitled to their opinion of the value of this particular benefit."[6] Indeed, opinions may differ but there is no way to quantify these benefits to the satisfaction of all voters.

The quantifiable community benefits estimated at $109 million-plus per year by SRI are reduced to only $60 million when the construction employment and "life-style" benefits, valued at $24 million and $25 million per year, respectively, are eliminated. These benefits are correctly excluded because the construction employment benefit, as pointed out, is erroneous and the "life-style" benefit is highly subjective and left for each individual to quantify himself.

COMPARISON OF COSTS AND BENEFITS OF SCRTD'S PROPOSAL

The SCRTD estimated the "equivalent annual cost" of the investment at $140.2 million [SRI 1968, p. 99]. In an attempt to reconcile the difference in the value of costs and benefits which accrue in different years, SRI took the estimated 1980 benefits of $194 million and assumed they would extend until 2016. The benefits were

[6] *Los Angeles Times*, October 6, 1968.

first expressed as constant in real terms to the end of the study period, but " ... because the purchasing power of the dollar is expected to change the benefits are adjusted for *anticipated* inflation" [1968, p. 54]. (Emphasis added.) This annual adjustment was estimated at $58.5 million per year.

SRI reasoned that: "The amount required to pay the interest and principal may decline in value by today's standards because of the decreased purchasing power of the dollars used to make these payments. We have therefore increased the benefits at a constant annual rate to measure the value of the benefits and the amount of money paid for bond service in any year in equivalent dollars" [1968, p. 54]. This procedure is incorrect since bondholders would anticipate the inflation, as did SRI, and therefore demand higher bond payments. If the inflation were unanticipated, then the SCRTD or taxpayers would gain as SRI indicates since the amount of interest and principal would decline in real terms as the purchasing power of the dollar declines. However, from a social point of view the inflation does not produce a net gain since the gain incurred by the SCRTD is exactly offset by the losses incurred by the bondholders or creditors. To avoid the inflation problem the entire comparison of costs and revenues should be calculated in constant dollars of the present period and the discount rate adjusted to what would be the ruling rate if, in fact, people were confident that dollars would have constant purchasing power.

A cost overlooked by SRI is the increase in police costs required to provide safety for users. An indication of this cost can be gained by considering the subway system of New York, where $11 million were spent in fiscal 1964–65 policing its trains and stations.[7] Another cost of the system which must always be considered when a public service replaces a private one is the forgone taxes that a private undertaking would pay, not only on the land right-of-way, but also on the equipment and on all the income earned from operations.

An important factor to consider in the rapid transit proposal is that it was to be financed entirely by bonds. This means that some allowance for risk should be calculated in the SCRTD's proposal, because a similar private undertaking could not be financed entirely by bonds. The riskiness of the project would require that there be some equity financing, the return on which is heavily taxed. As Hirshleifer et al. so clearly put it: "If this interaction is ignored ... any shoe store or macaroni factory could be shown to be more 'profitable' if government owned since the enterprise could be entirely debt financed escaping the corporate income tax" [1960, p. 142].

In summary, even when SRI's optimistic traffic estimates are used, the annual equivalent cost of the system, as computed by Carlin and Wohl, is still greater than the annual equivalent benefit [1968, p. 115]. Table 1, which compares the costs and benefits of the 89-mile system, shows that the estimated net annual benefit of $117.1 million calculated by SRI becomes a negative $10.8 million when recalculated.

PASSENGER ESTIMATES

Since the benefits estimated depend heavily on the level of system patronage, these passenger estimates must be examined very closely. The number of passengers using the 89-mile rapid transit system was esti-

[7] Assembly Interim Committee [1965], p. 155.

TABLE 1

Comparison of Net Equivalent Annual Benefits of Proposed Rapid Transit System (millions of 1968 dollars)

	SCRTD Final Report	Carlin and Wohl
1. Traveler benefits	$ 85.3	$119.9
2. Community benefits	109.0	60.0
3. Adjustment for inflation . . .	58.5	–
4. Equivalent annual benefits	252.8	179.9
5. Annual operating costs	–	49.2
6. Equivalent annual capital costs	140.2	146.0
7. Less equivalent annual value of $700 million salvage value of ROW and structures received in 2017	–4.5	–4.5
8. Equivalent annual costs	135.7	190.7
9. Net equivalent annual benefits	117.1	–10.8

Source: Carlin and Wohl [1968], p. 15.

mated by forecasting the 1980 travel demands in a band surrounding the rail system called the "service area."[8] The 1980 travel demands, based on data provided by the Los Angeles Regional Transportation Study and private surveys, were estimated through the use of a transportation model.[9] Table 2, which summarizes the results of this model, shows that in the service area there are 5.7 million potential rapid transit users, and that 1.7 million of these poten-

[8] The service area is defined as an area "extending 10 minutes in travel time outward from the stations except for the terminal stations which will draw from a more limited area" [Coverdale and Colpitts 1968, p. III–1].

[9] For a discussion of the factors that were assumed to affect future travel demands and the development of the transportation model, see Coverdale and Colpitts [1968], p. 71, and Los Angeles Regional Transportation Study, *Base Year Report*, 1960, vol. 1.

TABLE 2

Projected Source of 1980 Rapid Transit Revenue Passengers (1980 average weekday)

	Potential Service Area Trips	Trips Diverted to Rapid Transit	Percentage of Service Area Trips Diverted to Rapid Transit
Trips via bus			
Peak	96,200	70,000	72.8%
Off-peak	100,000	61,000	61.0
All day	196,200	131,000	66.8%
Trips via auto			
Peak	1,604,800	307,000	19.1%
Off-peak	3,911,100	39,000	1.0
All-day	5,515,900	346,000	6.3%
Trips via bus and auto combined			
Peak	1,701,000	377,000	22.2%
Off-peak	4,011,000	100,000	1.5
All day	5,712,000	477,000	8.4%

Source: Reproduced verbatim from the SCRTD, *Final Report,* p. CC–4.

tial trips would take place during the peak hours.

From the estimate of potential riders, Coverdale and Colpitts estimated the number that would be diverted to the rapid transit system during both the peak and off-peak hours.

The SCRTD's passenger estimates are used to show that even with their optimistic estimates the rapid transit system will not have much effect on traffic congestion in the Los Angeles area.

Table 2 shows that during the peak hours the rapid transit system is expected to carry 307,000 former automobile passengers on an average weekday, which is less than 20 percent of the potential automobile trips that take place in the service area during the peak hours. In other words, the system's greatest effect will be in the service area during peak hours. The benefits

from this passenger switch have been discussed earlier. When the county is considered rather than the smaller service area, these passengers reduce the number of automobiles from the county's streets by about 5 percent during the peak hours.[10] Table 2 also shows that during the peak hours the bus and transit system will carry 377,000 passengers, roughly 80 percent of its passengers, with almost three-fourths of them being diverted from the bus system.

During the off-peak hours, when approximately two-thirds of the average daily trips

[10] This figure is determined by assuming that the 307,000 weekday passengers using rapid transit results in 256,000 automobiles being removed during the peak hours. The 1980 employment in Los Angeles County is expected to be 3,512,250. Using the information from the 1958 Coverdale and Colpitts Report which showed that 80 percent of those employed in the Los Angeles area travel by automobile during the peak hours and that each automobile carries 1.2 passengers, the number of autos on the streets during the 1980 peak hours is estimated at 4,683,000.

take place, the rapid transit system will divert only 1 percent of the automobile passengers from the service area. The total system, both rapid transit and bus, is expected to carry slightly over 8 percent of the total number of daily trips in the county.

The rapid transit system is expected to remove 74,327,000 automobiles per year from the streets and freeways during the peak hours, at a cost of at least $1.80 per peak automobile per weekday.[11] The total number of automobiles removed by the rapid transit system on an average weekday in 1980 is 288,833—with 256,333 removed during peak hours and 32,500 during the remaining 20 hours. By 1980, an estimated 4,683,000 autos will be used during the peak hours.[12] If the number of automobiles used during the *peak* hours increases at 3 percent per year, the rapid transit system will remove less than two years' automobile growth.[13] Less than 50,000 peak-hour automobiles would be diverted from the central business district, since only 23 per-

cent of the peak-hour automobile trips diverted to transit have the central area as their destination.[14]

EVALUATION OF PASSENGER ESTIMATES

The passenger estimates made by Coverdale and Colpitts are extremely optimistic, as are most passenger and revenue estimates made for other transit systems. For example, before the Oakland–Fremont line opened in the San Francisco Metropolitan Area, the management of the Bay Area Rapid Transit System (BART) estimated that the line would carry 26,000 passengers per day. By November 1972 the line carried only one-half that number.[15]

One method of analyzing the SCRTD passenger estimates is to compare the proposed system with current traffic patterns. This method was used by Coverdale and Colpitts in 1968, when they likened the traffic pattern of the proposed rail system to be more " ... comparable to a commuter railroad than to a conventional rapid transit system as now exists in other cities in that a high degree of travel occurs in rush hours and the average trip length is longer" [SRI 1968, p. IV–ii]. This confirmed their previous study, completed in 1959, where they found that five out of every six bus riders to and from the CBD came from within a 10-mile circle and 20 percent of all riders came from within a 5-mile circle

---

[11] The SCRTD estimated the yearly cost of the complete bus and rail system at $135,700,000.

[12] Employment in Los Angeles County is estimated at 3,512,250 for 1980. Eighty percent travel during the peak hours by automobiles, and average automobile occupancy is 1.2 people: 1980 employment times the number who travel by automobile during peak hours (0.80) divided by people per automobile (1.2) times the number of trips (2).

[13] In Chicago the Dan Ryan and Kennedy rail lines opened in late 1969 and early 1970, respectively. Their opening did not significantly reduce the number of cars from the parallel freeways, as the following table (average daily vehicle counts at peak points) shows:

Year	Dan Ryan	Kennedy
1968	122,300	103,000
1969	126,100	108,200
1970	121,500	104,300
1971	144,100	109,200
1972	159,000	117,000

Source: Hilton [1974], p. 69. See this source for similar results in other cities.

[14] SCRTD, "Appendix B to the Final Report," Table IV–B. The net number of automobiles diverted from the CBD may be less than zero because, "If the mass transit favored downtown disproportionately, it will induce such a rate of development within downtown ... that the effect of mass transit in reducing travel to downtown by private vehicle will be more than offset by the increase of total trip demands" [Contini 1969, p. 6].

[15] Hilton [1974], p. 73.

centered on Broadway and 7th Streets [Coverdale and Colpitts 1959, p. A–II].

In light of these data, the DeLeuw Report correctly concluded in 1964 that although "rail rapid transit may be appropriate for the inner areas, it is clear that beyond the 10-mile circle the number of rush hour trips to and from the CBD at the present time is too small and too widely dispersed geographically to justify a high type of rapid transit service" [DeLeuw 1964, p. 15]. Given this pattern of short-length trips to the CBD, the SCRTD five-corridor system, with its focus on the CBD and routes longer than 10 miles, seems designed for a nonexisting passenger demand. This conclusion is further supported by the fact that in 1967 all but two SCRTD bus lines in the San Fernando Valley were losing money. Most bus lines in the outlying areas were unprofitable [Citizens' Advisory Council 1968, p. 69].

The SCRTD estimated that 72.5 percent of its rapid-transit passengers will be former automobile users. This figure is extremely high in light of the experience of other transit systems. The Yonge Street subway in Toronto and the Congress Street Rapid Transit in Chicago which were opened in the 1950s diverted less than 13 percent of their passengers from automobiles [Meyer et al. 1965, p. 100]. No other rapid transit system has had the passenger diversion from autos that the SCRTD expects. Even the BART system expects to attract only 30.3 percent of its passengers from automobiles. The small role that public transit plays in the Los Angeles area, where over 95 percent of the daily trips are taken by automobile, is another reason for doubting the SCRTD's passenger estimates.

Since the rail system is more nearly comparable to a commuter railroad than to a conventional rapid transit system, and since the users of North American suburban commuter railroads tend to have higher incomes than other travelers and residents of a region, one could question the welfare implications of having lower-income groups subsidize the high-income group's transportation. The Los Angeles system was to be financed by a one-half of 1 percent sales tax which would last for almost 50 years. This tax stream, discounted at 6 percent, would have a present value of $400–$2,000 for families with yearly taxable expenditures of $5,000–$25,000, regardless of whether or not they used the service.

CONCLUSION

Because of the interest in rapid transit for solving a city's transportation problems, a detailed investigation of the cost-benefit study computed for Los Angeles can provide valuable insight to an agency contemplating such a system for its own area. The Stanford Research Institute demonstrates that the benefits are often incorrectly calculated, while not all costs are considered. Further investigation is also needed to estimate passenger demand, since the number of passengers greatly influences the benefits to be derived from the system.

If Los Angeles, or any other city, is planning to introduce a rapid transit system, the difficulties of using cost-benefit analysis raised in this article must be faced.

REFERENCES

Assembly Interim Committee on Transportation and Commerce. 1965. *Southern California Rapid Transit Financing.* State of California. September 15–16, 1965.

Carlin, Alan, and Wohl, Martin. 1968. *An Eco-*

nomic Re-Evaluation of the Proposed Los Angeles Rapid Transit System. Santa Monica, California, Rand Corporation, September 1968.

Citizens' Advisory Council on Public Transportation. 1968. *Improving Public Transportation in Los Angeles.* Los Angeles.

Contini, E. 1969. "Transportation." In *Agenda for Los Angeles Area in 1970,* W. Hirch and Samuel Hale. Los Angeles: Institute of Government and Public Affairs, University of California.

Coverdale and Colpitts. 1959. "A Study of Public Transportation Needs in the Area Served by the Los Angeles Mass Transit Authority." Los Angeles, May 5, 1959.

——— and ———. 1968. "Estimates of Traffic Revenues and Expenses." Appendix B to the *Final Report.* SCRTD, Los Angeles.

DeLeuw, Cather and Company. 1964. "Report of Automobile Club of Southern California on Public Transportation in Los Angeles." San Francisco.

Haveman, R. H., and Krutilla, J. V. 1968. *Unemployment, Idle Capacity and the Evaluation of Public Expenditures.* Baltimore: Johns Hopkins Press.

Hilton, George W. 1974. *Federal Transit Subsidies.* Washington, D.C.: American Enterprise Institute.

Hirshleifer, Jack, et al. 1960. *Water Supply: Economics, Technology, and Policy.* Chicago: University of Chicago Press.

McKean, Roland N. 1958. *Efficiency in Government through Systems Analysis.* New York: Wiley.

Meyer, John, et al. 1965. *The Urban Transportation Problem.* Cambridge: Harvard University Press.

Peterson, Thomas C. 1970. "An Economic Evaluation of the Southern California Rapid Transit District: Its Proposed Solution to the Transportation Problem in Los Angeles." Ph.D. thesis, University of California, Los Angeles.

Southern California Rapid Transit District. 1968. *Final Report.* Los Angeles, May 1968.

Stanford Research Institute. 1968. "Benefit/Cost Analysis of the Five-Corridor Rapid Transit System for Los Angeles." Prepared for Southern California Rapid Transit District. Menlo Park, California, May 1968, mimeo.

Wohl, Martin. 1970. "Users of Urban Transportation and Their Income Circumstances." *Traffic Quarterly* 24, No. 1 (January 1970).

KEY CONCEPTS

anticipated inflation

benefit-cost ratio

community benefits

discount rate

forecasted passenger usage

secondary benefits

travel time saving

C. KENNETH ORSKI

21 How To Improve Urban Transportation and What To Do About the Automobile

C. Kenneth Orski, of the U.S. Urban Mass Transportation Administration, presents various transportation strategies from the perspective of a federal transportation planner. Orski surveys recent developments in urban transportation planning in European cities and discusses which European innovations might be feasible for American cities.

As a backdrop for our understanding of how European cities view these issues it would be useful to recall briefly the events of the past 30 years. Europe emerged from World War II with a shattered economy and with many of its cities in ruin. Its energies during the immediate postwar years were devoted to rebuilding its industries, reconstructing its cities and modernizing its basic infrastructure. Consumer products, including automobiles, took second place to the basic task of rebuilding the economy.

Automobile production thus increased slowly during the early postwar years, and this meant that the cities of Europe remained heavily transit-dependent through the 1950s. Automobile ownership and new highway construction did not become widespread until the 1960s. However, already in the mid-1960s, there were danger signals that the rising level of automobile use was taking its toll. The narrow streets of old European cities were never designed to accommodate large numbers

of automobiles. By the late 1960s traffic congestion had become endemic in Paris, London, Rome, Madrid, and many other urban centers. Air pollution worsened and parking became a nightmare. At the same time, efforts to build new urban expressways were running into mounting opposition from a large and vocal public bent on preserving the historic quality of the medieval cities. One need only recall the reaction to the proposed Left Bank Expressway in Paris or to the "motorway box" in London to appreciate the depth of the antihighway feeling.

Then came the Arab oil embargo with its traumatic shock of skyrocketing gas prices, gasless weekends, and the discovery of how dependent on the automobile European cities had become. Coupled with the energy crunch was the economic recession and double-digit inflation which swept Western European in the early 1970s. Governments no longer found it possible to finance massive capital projects. There was a new inclination to make do with what was already there and to proceed cautiously with major new investments.

Three sets of constraints thus came to influence the urban transportation policies

Reprinted from U.S. House of Representatives, Committee on Banking, Finance and Urban Affairs, Subcommittee on the City, *Toward a National Urban Policy* (95th Congress, First Session, September 28, 1977).

183

of European cities in the mid-1970s. They were (1) the rapidly rising gasoline prices and the desire to limit dependency on foreign oil supplies; (2) the growing public perception and concern over the disruptive effects of automobiles and highways, especially on the historic city centers; and (3) the shrinking availability of investment capital for new public projects.

In many ways these same concerns have come to dominate our own thinking. It is particularly instructive, therefore, to examine how public policy in Europe has responded to the new constraints, and to what extent these responses may also be applicable in this country.

I find it convenient to discuss these issues under two headings. The first is the changing philosophy of transit planning and implementation; the second is the new emphasis on more effective management of the existing transportation system.

TRANSIT PLANNING AND IMPLEMENTATION

Incremental Development

Traditionally, transit construction has been viewed in Europe as an incremental, open-ended process. Typically, the initial segment of a rail transit system was built in the central portion of a city, where traffic density was already high enough to justify high-capacity service. Progessively, the initial rail segment would be lengthened and connecting branch lines added, until eventually a rail network was created covering the entire central city.

Over the years, the network would be extended, usually a few miles at a time, into newly developing suburbs. After several decades of this incremental process, a full-scale, regionwide rail system would

emerge, by then organically imbedded into the fabric of the metropolitan area.

This is the way all the great European underground rail transit networks have evolved. London, for example, began its District and Circle Lines in 1865. In 1900 the underground system was still only some 50 miles long. During the next 50 years the network grew progressively, reaching some 240 miles by 1940. In the late 1960s the Victoria Line was added to the system. Today, over 100 years later, the system is still being expanded with the construction of the Fleet Line and the Heathrow Extension.

This, incidentally, is also the manner in which the great subway networks of this country have been built. Construction of the New York subway, for example, began in 1900 with the first IRT lines totaling 23 miles. The system, as we know it today, was not completed until 1940. In the intervening three decades some 200 miles of rapid transit lines were added to New York's metropolitan transit network.

Somewhere after the war, however, the transit planning style changed. Partly to compensate for the many years of neglect and partly, perhaps, because this was the way highways always had been planned, cities began to come up with ambitious master plans for massive, regionwide rail systems and with construction schedules that would bring the systems into operation so as to provide service to an entire metropolitan area more or less simultaneously. This is how the postwar rapid transit systems of Stockholm, Milan, and Munich were built; this was also the way the San Francisco BART and the Washington Metro systems came into being.

Today, the scarcity of investment capital in Europe is once again forcing transit planning into the classic mold. Plans for ambitious new rapid transit systems and for major expansion of existing networks are being reassessed and drastically scaled down or stretched out. Phased, incremental construction has once again become the conventional wisdom.

Multimodal Planning

There is also a growing recognition in European transportation planning that single-mode transportation systems are no longer capable of coping with the travel needs of large metropolitan areas. The land uses, ridership densities, and travel patterns of today's cities have become simply too diverse to be served efficiently by a transportation system of a single kind, be it an all-bus, an all-rail or an all-automobile system. Each of these modes has certain unique attributes which enable it to perform well only under certain conditions. Thus, there is a growing tendency in European transit planning to match the modes and technologies closely to the service requirements and traffic volumes which prevail in specific corridors. Instead of a massive network of fixed guideways of one particular kind, a transit development strategy for a large metropolitan area might involve a rail rapid transit line in a corridor of heavy demand, a light rail network in lower density portions of the urban area, and buses serving as suburban feeders to the rail system—all working cooperatively as elements of one integrated, interconnected and coordinated metropolitanwide transportation system.

Light Rail Transit

This brings me to the subject of light rail transit, a mode which embodies many of the planning concepts I have just referred to. Unlike American cities, most European cities never abandoned their streetcars. Today, these trolley networks are being converted into modern "light rail" systems. The conversion involves placing the lines underground in the congested city centers and providing separate surface rights-of-way elsewhere, with grade separation at major intersections. Some cities are also closing off certain downtown streets and turning them into transitway malls as a less costly alternative to subway construction. The upgraded light rail transit systems are being equipped with attractive modern vehicles of different sizes and capacity. A number of cities—including Antwerp, Brussels, Cologne, Zurich, Bern, Gothenburg, Frankfurt, Bonn, Stuttgart, Ghent, and Geneva are thus turning their existing streetcar networks into modern, high-performance rail transit systems at a relatively low cost. The trend toward light rail transit is not limited to cities that still possess operational streetcar systems. A number of European cities—Hanover, Milan, and Amsterdam, for example—which had originally planned to build heavy rail rapid transit lines, have reconsidered their decision in favor of light rail technology. Several other cities—including Utrecht, Tyneside, Edmonton, and Vancouver—have opted for new light rail systems as the preferred technology.

How can we explain the growing popularity of light rail transit? The main reason, I suspect, is the dramatic difference in cost. A recent study has estimated the average cost of construction of a light rail system at $5 to $20 million per mile; by contrast, the cost of heavy rapid transit can reach $50 to $60 million per mile.

Light rail has other advantages. It can be built in stages, a few miles at a time; it can be converted to higher capacity rapid transit once the traffic warrants the additional investment; it can serve as an internal circulation system in the central city as well as connect outlying suburban communities with the city center; and its unobtrusive vehicles and guideways enable light rail transit to penetrate into residential areas at grade with a minimum of environmental disturbance.

Most importantly, light rail transit is well suited to the evolving urban patterns. Traditional transit planning concentrated on accommodating travel demands in high-volume radial corridors that typically were found in the older, densely developed metropolitan areas. But such corridors represent a relatively small and shrinking share of the total urban travel market. A growing proportion of metropolitan travel—in the United States as well as in Europe—takes place in low- and medium-density areas that have sprung up on the fringes of our metropolitan areas, and that characterize the newer, automobile-age cities.

In these areas, trip patterns are too diffuse and travel volumes too small to justify high-capacity transit systems. The need is for public transportation that can function efficiently and economically in conditions of low- and medium-trip density and still provide a level of service that will attract people out of their automobiles. There is a growing body of opinion that light rail transit is the mode that best satisfies that need.

TRANSPORTATION SYSTEM MANAGEMENT

The new constraints have not only taught European cities to think smaller in terms of new infrastructure, but also to better manage the existing transportation system. Cities are discovering that innovative operation of buses and automobile traffic pays off in terms of improved public transportation service, less congestion, and more pleasant pedestrian environment—without any sacrifice in mobility.

Improvements in Bus Service

New imaginative ways are being used to improve existing bus service. Special bus-lanes have been set aside in city streets in some 30 European cities, including Paris, Hamburg, London, Bologna, Madrid, Lille, Marseilles, and Toulouse. These exclusive lanes have improved the speed and reliability of bus service by up to 25 percent, and have led to increased bus patronage.

In some cities, bus-only streets have been established. The best known European example is Oxford Street, a busy shopping street in central London, which has been closed to all auto traffic since November 1972. Where bus flows do not justify the allocation of an exclusive lane or an entire street, priority can be given to buses at signalized intersections. This technique is, in effect, an extension to bus transit of the priority treatment that has always been granted to trains at grade crossings. Bus priority at traffic signals exists in Glasgow, Bern, Paris, Gothenburg, and several other cities.

The concept of giving buses and other high-occupancy vehicles preferential treatment over the rest of the traffic has been widely embraced in the United States. Over 50 urban areas have introduced some form of bus priority over portions of their highway networks. Most of these schemes involve setting aside reserved bus and carpool lanes on urban freeways and giving buses preferential access at toll plazas and on freeway access ramps. Less frequent are schemes involving exclusive bus lanes on city streets. Yet, it is precisely in dense, congested central urban areas that buses need and can benefit most from preferential treatment. Foreign experience suggests that such schemes are technically and operationally feasible and can substantially improve the speed and reliability of city bus sevice.

Management of the Automobile

The search for an appropriate urban transportation strategy in America is often hampered by our unwillingness to decide on the appropriate role of the automobile and of public transportation, and then to execute that policy in some consistent way.

European cities are less circumspect in that regard. In Hamburg, for example, transportation planning is based on a zone concept of concentric rings around the city. In the most central zone pedestrian movement is favored and automobile traffic is actively discouraged. As one moves outward, the use of the automobile is given higher prominence.

This policy has been adopted de facto in a large number of other European cities. The city center is being increasingly dedicated to pedestrians and transit vehicles, while private auto use is either discouraged, restricted, or banned. In the inner suburbs transit and automobiles are given equal role, while in the outlying areas the automobile clearly predominates.

Vehicle-free zones, together with the designation of certain streets for transit and pedestrians only, have had an impressive effect on both mobility and the environment in the center city. Over 100 cities in

Europe have excluded automobiles from portions of their central shopping districts—a move that European merchants and shoppers now consider as an essential element in preserving the vitality of the downtown areas. Land uses and property values within these car-free zones have been invariably improved after their conversion to pedestrian use.

Other approaches to automobile management include parking restrictions, diversion of through traffic, restrictions on daytime truck deliveries, and deliberate automobile "restraints." One type of restraint, adopted in a number of European cities (Bremen, Gothenburg, Stockholm, Besancon, Bologna, Nottingham), involves dividing the city center into sectors. A system of pedestrian streets, transitways, and one-way streets prevents automobile traffic from crossing directly from one sector to another. Instead, cars are required to return to the periphery and use a designated circumferential route in order to travel to another sector. This type of traffic management scheme has resulted in greatly improved speed and regularity of public transit and vastly improved environment for pedestrians and central area residents.

Another type of restraint, adopted in Nottingham and Southampton, involves "metering" of downtown-bound automobile traffic. The intent is to impose time delays on private automobiles during the morning peak, and thus promote a modal shift to buses. Traffic signals are used to meter autos at exits from residential areas onto radial routes. Buses enjoy preferential passage through the zone exits.

Perhaps the most important lesson European cities have learned from all this experience is that the individual measures must not be used in isolation but should be combined into a comprehensive and coordinated transportation management strategy. Such a strategy might involve the establishment of reserved lanes for buses, downtown parking prohibitions, car-free zones and pedestrian streets, diversion of through traffic away from the center, provision of park-and-ride facilities on access roads to the city, fare policies to stimulate off-peak use of transit, staggered work hours, and so forth.

Conclusion

I now come to the key question: How relevant are any of these policies for the United States? How much of the European experience is transferrable to our own cities? In answering these questions we must be mindful of the considerable differences in the physical and institutional organization of European and American cities.

First, European cities have retained to this date relatively compact, thriving centers with diverse land uses and activities that make for constant movement throughout the day and evening.

Secondly, because the automobile came relatively late upon the scene, the European city dweller never lost the "transit habit," and the public transportation systems were never allowed to deteriorate. Quite the contrary, the urban transit systems and suburban railways enjoyed sustained support and infusion of funds throughout the postwar period and are today in a better physical shape than ever.

Thirdly, the cities of Europe grew and were formed long before the advent of the automobile. Their streets were never designed to accommodate heavy traffic. Quite the contrary, the city centers were built around the pedestrian, a feature which is discernible even today as one walks through the teeming streets of Cologne Brussels, Amsterdam, Zurich, or Bologna. Few of our cities were designed with the pedestrian in mind.

Finally, suburbanization never became quite as chaotic in Europe as it has in the United States. Even today, suburban growth in Europe is occurring largely in established suburban centers situated along rail lines. Much of the residential development takes place within walking distance of rail stations or else clusters in self-contained settlements connected to the centers of suburban communities with frequent bus service.

Given these differences in urban character, it is obvious that we cannot blindly transplant every transportation innovation that has succeeded in Europe. Our downtowns are not compact enough, for example, to allow us to pedestrianize them on a scale attempted in Nottingham, Besancon, or Munich. Excluding cars may make sense in medieval town centers but not in spread out central business districts of American cities. Road pricing may work in Singapore, but this is no guarantee that it will be politically acceptable in Cincinnati.

However, there is much that we can learn from our European friends.

We can learn to build rail transit systems incrementally—one line at a time—instead of bringing massive regional systems into operation all at once.

We can learn to adopt a multimodal approach to transportation development: To consider transportation needs on a corridor-by-corridor basis instead of building vast networks of highways or guideways without consideration of whether adequate densities exist to justify all that heavy capital investment. In this connection we can learn to pay more attention to light rail transit as an alternative to heavy rapid transit or to multilane freeways.

And finally, we can learn from European cities to be more sensitive to the needs of pedestrians and to manage our existing transportation system more efficiently with the help of such measures as reserved bus lanes, parking management, transit malls, pedestrian streets, and staggered work hours.

KEY CONCEPTS

guideways

high-occupancy vehicles

incremental development

light rail transit

multimodal planning

trip density patterns

PART 6

URBAN PUBLIC FINANCE

State- and local-government expenditures have risen rapidly in recent years, more than doubling in per capita terms during the 1970s. Spending by municipal governments has also grown rapidly even though many major cities have lost population. Per capita spending in New York City, for example, doubled from 1970 to 1978 even though the city lost population and experienced a fiscal crisis of unprecedented proportions.

It may seem reasonable that this growth of local government revenue and spending would have helped both the quantity and quality of municipal government services. Yet, despite this tremendous growth in the commitment of resources to local government, there is evidence that the quality of public services has deteriorated. The performance of public schools reportedly sags every year; urban crime continues to mount; pollution and congestion worsen in many cities; public transit falls into disrepair; basic sanitation services are performed badly and occasionally not at all. Citizen discontent with the way public services are provided and financed has been registered in numerous ways, not least of which is the tax revolt that began with Proposition 13 in California in 1978.

Many major central cities in the United States, despite tremendous increases in taxes and financial aid from state and federal government, remarkably are beset by recurring fiscal crises. The causes of these crises vary from city to city, but certain common elements can be detected. One factor contributing to core-city fiscal distress, as Anthony M. Rufolo points out, is the attempt by central-city governments to redistribute income. When undertaken by a single city, redistributive programs are likely to be self-defeating in the long run because groups who are net gainers (generally the poor) tend to migrate to that city while groups who are net losers (upper- and middle-income groups) tend to migrate out. The exodus of higher-income residents leaves the central city with a diminished tax base and a disproportionately poor population who impose high service demands on the city. The task of financing services that involve significant redistribution should be left to state and federal government. Local government should concentrate on improving efficiency and seeing that the costs of public services are borne by those who receive the benefits.

One of the causes of New York City's fiscal crisis in the mid-1970s was the

190

effort by the city to preserve and enlarge extensive redistributional programs, including welfare, health, higher education, and public housing. Because of New York's relatively generous welfare programs (as well as high unemployment rate), public-assistance rolls burgeoned to more than 1 million during 1975. At the same time, the flight to the suburbs from the city was in full swing. This problem and others contributing to New York's financial plight are discussed by Edward M. Gramlich.

New York's fiscal downfall was precipitated when it began issuing long-term bonds to finance current-account deficits. Generally, such bonds are justifiably used only to finance long-term capital projects. This use of bonds allows the costs of a project, which will yield revenues for many years, to be spread evenly over the project's life. By using bond financing to cover operating expenses, however, the interest burden of the debt mounted until New York could not raise sufficient tax revenue to meet its obligations.

One source of core-city fiscal problems is the oft-repeated claim that central cities are fiscally exploited by their suburbs. While suburbanites often work in the central city and impose demands on city services, their residential tax base lies beyond the city's reach. On balance, suburban commuters are said to impose a net fiscal drain on the city. Believing this claim to be valid, numerous cities have sought to impose municipal payroll taxes on employees who work in the central city, regardless of their residence.

Only a careful analysis of the statistical evidence can resolve this controversy and David F. Bradford and Wallace E. Oates critically review the studies that have analyzed this question. They discover little evidence of central-city exploitation in the literature. The weight of the evidence seems to be that efforts by central cities to impose payroll taxes are unjustified. Such taxes may also be misguided because their main effect may be to drive businesses from the city.

What has caused the rapid growth of government spending in recent years? One explanation is that the growth simply reflects rising demands by urban residents for city services. Some economists argue that the external diseconomies of city life—especially crime, congestion, and pollution—rise exponentially with population density. As a result, the demand for government services to deal with such problems may also rise disproportionately with urban growth.

An entirely different explanation for the growth of local government is offered by William J. Baumol. According to Baumol, local public services can be characterized as labor-intensive and "technologically backward." Under these conditions the growth of labor productivity tends to be sporadic and slow. If, as seems likely, local labor markets are relatively competitive, local governments must pay prevailing wages to attract the necessary labor skills. However, these wages will be determined in the private sector, which can be characterized as "technologically progressive," with high rates of productivity growth. Consequently, cost increases in local government tend to consistently outpace productivity advances. And because public services are highly labor-intensive, the overall cost of government will continue to rise over time, requiring ever-higher taxes and spending just to maintain services at a constant level.

Baumol's "cost disease" hypothesis, as it has come to be known, poses difficult choices for local government. The familiar methods of raising productivity in the private sector—such as improved management techniques or technological innovations—are less effective in government because services are so labor-intensive. Cities must look to alternative approaches to improving public-sector productivity, such as contracting out government services to private suppliers.

Selma Mushkin, Frank Sandifer, Charles Vehorn, and Charlie Turner examine the economic arguments for greater emphasis on user charges in financing local government services. They analyze the numerous services that could be financed, at least in part, by user fees but are currently tax-financed. They argue that not only would applying user charges—where it is feasible to do so—improve efficiency, it would also improve equity in the financing of local government services.

ANTHONY M. RUFOLO

22 Anatomy of a Fiscal Crisis

Anthony M. Rufolo, of Portland State University, argues that attempts by central-city governments to redistribute income may account in part for their fiscal problems. Redistributive programs may induce higher-income residents to relocate to the suburbs. As a result, lower-income people in the central city may lose more from this loss of tax base than they gain from the redistribution itself. The author also discusses various proposed solutions, including metropolitan consolidation and revenue sharing.

Although the fiscal plight of New York City has been making headlines, most local governments now complain that expenditures are growing faster than taxes. Many residents demand increased services despite rising costs, but they quickly rebel at attempts to raise more tax dollars. Nearly everyone wants more goods and services for less money, so these demands don't seem unusual. It's one way for citizens to remind City Hall that every expenditure decision involves a budget trade-off. After all, as economists never tire of pointing out, resources are limited and budgets limit their use. However, mayors in certain areas—particularly central cities—fear that if they fail to maintain the same level of services or to clamp a lid on taxes, the exodus of jobs and wealth to the suburbs may accelerate. Many of them call this a "fiscal crisis," conjuring up visions of nothing but abandoned buildings and jobless poor. Is such alarm justified, or are some city administrators simply rebelling against the constraints of their budgets?

Taxpayer Smith may forsake the paved

Reprinted from the *Business Review* of the Federal Reserve Bank of Philadelphia (June 1975), with permission.

sidewalks of the city for the manicured lawns of suburbia for any number of reasons. He may commute a greater distance for more open living space. He may want his children to attend a suburban school. If he moves from one suburb to another, generally no one would care. But a move from city to suburb makes him another statistic to furrow the city mayor's brow. The likeliest candidate for such a move is the relatively wealthy taxpayer. For example, Smith's contributions to the city's coffers may be more than it actually costs to provide him with government services, so he pays for services for relatively poor taxpayer Jones as well. This redistribution of income provides an incentive for Smith and others like him to leave the city, thereby putting increasing pressure on city budgets. Thus, income redistribution at the local level may be a major force behind the "fiscal crisis."

So far, no major cities have folded. Perhaps the danger signals were heeded before the situation became hopeless. Recently Federal revenue-sharing funds have helped relieve the pressure on city budgets. But the underlying source of the problem may still be with us. An analysis of what makes a fiscal crisis is in order, so that the pros and cons of proposed solutions can be weighed intelligently. Perhaps there is a solution which attacks the source of the problem rather than its symptoms.

CITY VERSUS SUBURBS

Every government has budget constraints, so why must *only* major cities face crises? One reason for the difference in ability to cope is that suburban communities have been more successful in attracting the "Smiths" and banning the "Joneses." This creates a problem for the city because the poor require relatively more services from government but have less ability to pay. More low-income residents force a larger tax burden on city businesses and wealthier residents or shift services away from them, or both. Some of these businesses and individuals avoid this increased burden by just moving to the suburbs. This movement in turn leads to greater tax burdens and/or decreased services for those remaining in the city. The poor don't emigrate because of inadequate low-cost housing or poor public transportation in the suburbs as well as barriers such as zoning restrictions. This population shift then affects government budgets, and a quick review will show that cities' tax bases relative to expenditures are not keeping pace with the suburbs'.

The property tax is the primary source of most locally raised revenue. In the early '70s, property taxes accounted for 82 percent of all tax revenue of local governments in metropolitan areas and 40 percent of their total revenue from all sources. However, this important component of the tax system has its base rising more slowly in central cities than in the suburbs. . . .

Several major cities have turned to a wage or income tax to pay for services without increasing the tax burden on real estate. . . . Unfortunately, however, shifting to a different tax is not likely to alleviate the problem. City residents paying more in total local taxes than it costs to serve them are still likely to have an incentive to move to the suburbs. It is this incentive that is at least partially behind the fiscal plight of many major cities.

LOCAL INCOME REDISTRIBUTION: AN INCENTIVE TO MOVE?

Most people consider political factors as the primary determinants of the tax rates and services provided by a local community. Residents as voters register their desires through elections, and the elected representatives try to coordinate the often conflicting goals of various groups. Some economists, however, emphasize a rather different aspect of this process. They point out that communities can be considered as sellers of a package of goods and services who charge a certain tax-price for the package. So while a resident/voter can try to influence what local government does, he can also decide to move to a community more tailored to his preferences. Consumers in a sense "shop" among communities much as they shop among stores for goods.

Unfortunately, though, this analogy has its limitations. There are easily recognizable differences between the way stores sell and the way local governments "sell." Stores charge directly for the items bought while governments charge indirectly by taxing sources such as property or income. This difference affects people when they are "community shopping."

The major effect is that people do not necessarily contribute equally to the cost of public goods and services, even if they receive the same benefits. For example, with a property tax, a person with a small house might pay much less in taxes than a neighbor with a big house although both may send the same number of children to the same school. This local redistribution of income may be desirable on equity grounds (if we accept "ability to pay" as our equity criterion), since presumably the resident of the larger house is wealthier. However, such a situation motivates the person paying higher taxes to try isolating himself from the person paying lower taxes, since the wealthier resident is, in a sense, paying part of the poorer person's bill. Each person has an incentive to live in a community in which he has less property (and hence lower tax payments) than anyone else in the community. Of course, everyone cannot have less than the average amount. The only stable solution to this type of system would seem to be one in which each resident of a community has approximately the same amount of property and makes similar tax payments. All persons who want smaller houses or apartments would be kept out by zoning laws or similar arrangements.

Redistribution and Efficiency

Economics tells us that if the price of something corresponds to the costs of providing it, then our scarce resources will be channeled to their most highly valued uses. When local governments charge tax "prices" unrelated to the costs of the services they provide, these resources may end up in inefficient uses. For example, consider our friend Smith's decision to move from the city to the suburbs. Suppose he

was entirely happy with the services he received but discovered the same services could be received in suburbia for lower taxes. If the cost were the same in the two places, but taxes were higher because of local income redistribution, then Smith's move would waste both the resources involved in the actual move and those used in his daily commuting. However, if taxes were different because the suburban government had lower costs, then Smith's move would result in the saving of resources employed in providing the services. This saving would be balanced against the cost of Smith's moving and commuting. In this case moving would mean not only a cost saving to him, but more efficient use of society's resources would result.

If suburban communities succeed in keeping out low-income residents, they reduce the incentive for *current suburbanites* to move around. This can cut the loss of resources resulting from a game of "musical chairs" among communities. However, this cannot reduce the loss of resources because of excess movements out of the city, and it reinforces the result of little or no income redistribution at the local level.

This description of how people choose a community may seem an extreme case, and it certainly omits other important factors which shape a location decision. However, tax-benefit considerations may have significantly influenced the movement to suburbia and may have helped create communities where all the residents have very similar characteristics. To the extent that this process really operates, it can thwart the attempt of cities to pay for the services they provide by redistributing income through taxes. In fact, attempts to redistribute income locally through taxes can not only influence the movement of people and jobs out of the city, but can also backfire and deepen the plight of the poor.

Redistribution and Low-Income Residents

If attempts to redistribute income lead to separation of families by income class, then the poor could be worse off than if no income redistribution were attempted. This is because current financing only allows communities with a large tax base per person to provide large amounts of goods and services per person. Thus, it is usually necessary for each resident of such a community to buy a large house or rent an expensive apartment. A poor family desiring high levels of some public services (education, for example) would then have to pay for large amounts of housing as well as for the services they desire. While low-income families might be able to afford payments for the services, they obviously cannot also afford large payments for housing. Efforts to encourage low-income housing in the suburbs have encountered stiff opposition, with income redistribution probably a major objection. The likely outcome is that the poor with their demand for services are "locked" into the central city. And, there's the heart of a "fiscal crisis."

So, cities face the problem of providing goods and services which are increasingly more costly to a population which has a growing percentage of those with the least ability to pay. This leads to high-tax and low-service levels for those who can pay. To avoid income redistribution payments at the local level, some people who would otherwise have stayed in the city may incur the costs of moving and commuting. They might also move to a community which provides a different amount of public services than they would choose if they were bearing the direct cost.

The net result is likely to be some waste of society's resources, very little actual income redistribution at the local level, and forces continuing to militate against locating in the central city. While there are many factors creating fiscal pressure on the city, this one may truly be called a "fiscal crisis," for the situation cannot be controlled from within the city. However, this does not imply that all cries of "crisis" should be treated the same. If the city is driving away jobs and residents because it has high production costs or is inefficient, the situation should be labeled an internal management problem, not a crisis.

PROPOSED SOLUTIONS

Two often-proposed methods of aiding the central city are the formation of a metropolitan or regional government and the sharing of revenue by the state or Federal Government. Either method can achieve the goal of relieving the fiscal pressure on central cities, but each also has shortcomings.

Metropolitan Government: A Loss of Competition

A metropolitan government consists of a central city and all of its suburbs replacing many local governments. Proponents of this approach argue that it would eliminate competition for the tax base at the local level. Individuals or businesses would have to move outside the metropolitan area to escape paying their share of taxes. The problem with this solution is that local government competition can be desirable.

Local government, locally financed, is

beneficial in two important respects. The first is that to some extent it forces people to reveal what they are willing to pay for government services. Suppose property taxes were used only to finance goods and services whose costs are approximately proportional to the amount of property people own. It is then likely that the "shopping" element of community choice would direct people with similar preferences for government services to the same communities. They would not have any incentive to move to communities that provided more of these services than they wanted because they would have to pay the cost. Similarly, people would not have an incentive to move to communities providing too little of these services because the resultant tax savings would not compensate them for having less of these services.

The second benefit (and perhaps that which advocates of local government stress most) is the wider range of choice which results from many "suppliers" (governmental units). For example, suppose that Jones would like more police protection than would Smith. If they live in the same community, both cannot be satisfied. Voting may lead to some compromise, perhaps less than Jones would like to "purchase," but more than Smith wants to pay for. However, if Jones and Smith each move to other communities populated with residents of similar tastes, each may be able to achieve his desired level of police protection. A more inclusive metropolitan government is not likely to offer as much variety.

This is not meant to imply that local government would not have fiscal pressures in the absence of local income redistribution. Most economists now agree that suburbanization would have occurred even if

central cities had had no fiscal or social problems. Also, people in every community will want to minimize their costs for particular services. But this type of incentive serves to inform government of what the residents want. In this case, a community may lose residents by not providing the desired level of services or by being inefficient, but it will not lose residents because another community is a "tax haven."

Sharing Revenue Distorts "Prices"

The sharing-revenues approach leaves government units unchanged but provides funds from state or Federal sources to relieve the fiscal pressure on local government. Tax collections are made from all over the state or even the country, making tax avoidance very difficult.

Sharing revenue has been with us for some time, although large-scale transfers of unconditional funds are relatively recent occurrences. . . . Sharing revenue has, indeed, relieved some of the fiscal pressure on central cities and other local governments. However, this solution also has a drawback.

Revenue sharing does not force people to relate their tax payments to the cost of providing services. If one community should consistently get more in transfer funds than another, it will become more attractive relative to the second community. In addition, each community will still have incentives to attract businesses and individuals who pay more in taxes than it costs to serve them and to keep others out. Because the "prices" of services in one community versus another still do not reflect the cost of resources used in providing these services, people will expend time and money in relocating. Moreover, they will not move to the community which can best satisfy their preferences with the least use of resources.

LOCAL FINANCING WITHOUT INCENTIVES TO MOVE

It may sound like local tax financing will always create incentives for people to separate into similar income goups, but this is not true. This result arises from attempts to redistribute income locally through the tax process. If Smith's taxes represent the cost of serving him, then it doesn't matter much to the community whether or not he lives there. Neither a new rich neighbor nor a new poor one would alter the taxes or benefits for current residents of the community. For example, if the property tax were restricted to financing services whose cost is approximately proportional to the amounts of property in the community just as the property tax is, then people with large houses would have no *tax* incentive to bar construction of small houses. Such services as fire protection are likely to fit into this category. Thus, owners of large houses on large lots (which are likely to require more fire equipment and create a bigger area to cover than do small houses on small lots) would pay higher taxes to offset the higher costs imposed on the community. No doubt there are other reasons why people might want similar houses in the same community (such as aesthetic appeal and a desire to socialize with people of similar income), but such considerations often relate more to an immediate neighborhood than to an entire town.

When a government service has costs which are not related to property, then the property tax should not be used for financing. Similarly, if the cost of serving some-

one is not related to his income, then a local income tax should not be used to finance that service. Certainly, we would seldom expect to find an exact correspondence between a certain tax and the cost of providing a particular service. But now taxes and services are usually completely unrelated. Take welfare as an example. Most people agree that society has some obligation to care for the indigent, but why should the burden fall on property owners in a particular community? This is definitely an area where direct payments from the Federal Government would lead to more equal treatment for the poor in different communities and would relieve an unfair burden on city property owners. This proposal would, in turn, reduce the incentive to move strictly to avoid local tax payments aimed at redistributing income.

Another benefit of such a system is that the range of choices available to many people would increase. Education is a good example. "Charging" on the basis of the number of school children avoids income redistribution at the local level. Given that government has assumed the financing of the service, the funds should come from state or Federal sources. One way would be for the state to issue a voucher which would be used to "pay" for schooling. Each student would receive a voucher and present it to the school he attends. The school would then redeem the voucher with the state or Federal government for its operating funds. Local communities might continue to *provide* school services, but there would no longer be any reason to restrict entrance to local residents. Thus, a family would not have to relocate to obtain the educational services it desires.

In short, let local government continue to finance those services which do no result in significant income redistribution. And, whenever possible do this with taxes that closely reflect the costs of providing services. Let the state and Federal governments finance services which entail significant income redistribution. Income redistribution can be more effectively administered at these higher levels of government. The difficulty in avoiding broader-based taxes will reduce the amount of resources spent in trying to avoid them. At the same time, the benefits of local choice can be maintained or increased.

SUMMING UP

Now, what about that "fiscal crisis"? To the extent that such a crisis exists, it is at least partly caused by communities using local taxes to finance public goods and services in such a way that some redistribution of income results. When this effect is large, communities are forced both to compete for citizens who make a net contribution to the local treasury and to keep out those who are a net drain. This can lead to segregation by income, and it's possible for this to make everyone, including the poor, worse off than if no such attempt were made.

The benefits of many communities offering a range of services are very real. Financing the wrong services—ones where taxes are not linked to costs—by means of local taxes is likely to cause inefficient use of resources and excessive decentralization of people and businesses. It is time for a rational approach to financing government expenditures, and this includes a recognition that efficiency and equity may require one level of government to raise taxes while another provides goods or services. However, it also requires the recognition that competition at the local level can be beneficial. There is no reason for city governments to be spared from having to accept the trade-off of taxes and services faced by other governments. But there is also no reason for them to shoulder most of the burden of financing services for the poor.

KEY CONCEPTS

efficiency

local income redistribution

metropolitan government

revenue sharing

tax prices

EDWARD M. GRAMLICH

23   The New York City Fiscal Crisis:
What Happened and What Is To Be Done?

New York City's recent flirtation with bankruptcy is a source of many lessons for handling the fiscal problems faced by many older central cities. Edward M. Gramlich of the University of Michigan analyzes the causes of New York's fiscal plight and the likely economic effects of default. As a side issue, he examines the performance of the municipal bond rating system and its role in New York's problems.

The New York City fiscal crisis as it was played out in the nation's newspapers had all the elements of a first class drama. There was first of all the tension—would the city make it through its periodic financial hurdles ... what would happen if the city defaulted? Then there were the accusations—was it the fault of Wagner, Lindsay, Beame, Rockefeller, Ford, the unions, or economic and social forces beyond the city's control? Then the controversy—the issue seemed ideally suited to split deficit spenders from budget balancers, soft-headed liberals from hardheaded accountants, eastern establishment intellectuals from the silent majority. Finally ... the crisis also graphically illustrated several basic issues in the economics of federalism that are now creeping into public finance textbooks—the proper role of local and national governments in stabilizing the economy and redistributing income, whether the federal or the state government has an obligation to protect the financial integrity of local governments,

whether public expenditures can be effectively controlled in the short run. This article discusses the city's fiscal plight in the context of all of these issues.

HOW BIG ARE THE DEFICITS?

Local governments borrow for three reasons, two of which are generally acceptable to bondholders and one dangerous. The first acceptable reason is to finance long-term capital investment projects—if a locality is building a school that will last for many years, it does not have to pay the entire bill in any one year but can spread the cost over the lifetime of the school by floating long-term debt. The second acceptable reason is to smooth out seasonal fluctuations in revenues and expenditures by short-term borrowing. The final reason, which generally is not acceptable either by a city's laws or in the eyes of bondholders, is to cover a current account deficit.

The first fact to recognize about the New York City fiscal plight is that unfortunately the city has borrowed to cover current account deficits continuously ever

Reprinted with permission from the *American Economic Review* 66, 2 (May 1976): 415-29 and the author.

since fiscal 1960-61. How this was allowed to happen is still something of a mystery, but the relevant data, from the official U.S. Census figures, are given in Table 1. The first column lists the gross revenue of the city—taxes, charges and fees, grants from the federal government and New York State, and revenue from the water and transit authorities.... The second column lists the current general government expenditures for all functions.... The deficits are in the third column, the level of capital expenditures in the fourth, and net borrowing in the fifth. The large current account borrowing, particularly in recent years, was not backed up by capital formation; as a consequence it had to be done in the short-term market, and the city now has both extraordinary levels of outstanding short-term debt and extraordinarily high "uncontrollable" expenses simply to roll over this short-term debt every year. In 1973—74, for example, the outstanding short-term debt was $485 per capita, much higher than any other large city, and it would now claim 32 percent of current expenditures—almost the entire controllable portion of the expenditure budget—to pay it off if new lenders cannot be found.... The general picture is one of large and growing current account deficits, persisting for long periods of time, and bound to frighten prospective lenders and threaten default sooner or later.

THE COMPOSITION AND GROWTH OF THE DEFICITS

The hypotheses that have been advanced to explain these deficits can be divided loosely into two groups. One type of explanation focuses on the power of the

TABLE 1

New York City Budget Data, Fiscal 1960–1974
(millions of current dollars)

Date	Revenue	Current Expenditures Plus Debt Retirement	Current Account Surplus	Capital Expenditures	Net Borrowing
1960	2,769.6	2,726.5	43.1	528.3	485.2
1961	2,901.0	2,948.2	− 47.2	542.0	589.2
1962	3,119.5	3,170.0	− 50.5	582.0	632.5
1963	3,408.4	3,459.0	− 50.6	667.4	718.0
1964	3,688.8	3,788.5	− 99.7	657.6	757.3
1965	3,961.1	4,015.4	− 54.3	657.7	712.0
1966	4,367.5	4,537.0	−169.5	561.3	730.8
1967	5,174.8	5,176.0	− 1.2	554.8	556.0
1968	6,085.8	6,144.1	− 58.3	658.0	716.3
1969	6,864.7	6,945.6	− 80.9	698.3	779.2
1970	7,233.9	7,775.4	−541.5	797.0	1,338.5
1971	8,274.8	9,053.9	−779.1	1,135.1	1,914.2
1972	9,501.5	10,119.6	−618.1	1,192.9	1,811.0
1973	10,774.9	10,807.2	− 32.3	1,371.5	1,403.8
1974	11,291.5	11,779.1	−487.6	1,709.6	2,197.2

Source: U.S. Bureau of the Census, *City Government Finances;* various issues.

public employee unions in New York City, the bargaining concessions that have been won over the years, and the sheer size and ability to control votes of public employee unions.[1] A second focuses on the fact that the city finances an ambitious social welfare program on its own—it funds expensive welfare, higher education, public hospital, and public housing programs, along with a persistently large transit deficit and generous contributions to employee pension funds. In other large cities these programs are either not undertaken at all by the public sector, completely financed by grants or user charges, financed by the tax revenues of independent special districts, done by an overlapping county government or done by the state. Though all programs might be desirable at the national level, and in fact many argue that the city is doing a job made necessary by the lack of adequate national or state policies in these areas, it remains an inescapable fact of federalism that if localities try to redistribute income to a much greater extent than the other localities, or if they run abnormally large deficits and incur subsequent high interest and debt retirement costs, there is a good risk that the taxpaying population will simply pick up stakes and leave the locality in a fiscal situation that much more precarious.

These competing hypotheses can be tested very loosely by examining the city's budget in more detail. Table 2 decomposes expenditures into a normal component—expenditures for functions normally undertaken by city governments, school expenditures—which are usually financed out of the budgets of independent school districts in other large cities, and the net deficit of each of these six "marginal functions"—marginal in the sense that they do not normally drain revenue from the city government. The total deficit on these marginal functions came to the enormous total of $2,492 million in 1973–74, almost five times the measured current account deficit. It is of course true that often the deficits in the accounts of these marginal programs are related to union pressure, particularly in the case of pensions but also in the case of transit, hospitals, and higher education, but as an overall impression it does appear that the city's problems stem more from the fact that it subsidizes a broad array of functions than from the fact that the employees are gaining very high wages for performing normal public services.

This point is reinforced by examining growth rates over the 1960–74 period. Over this time the net marginal functions deficit has grown by 11.1 percent per annum, more than expenditures either on the normal functions or on schools. Normal expenditures have grown by 8.4 percent, roughly 2.1 percent of which is a growth in employment, 2.4 percent is a growth in real wages per employee, and 4.0 percent is a growth in prices in New York City. School expenditures have grown by 10.3 percent— 3.7 percent employment, 2.6 percent real wages, and 4.0 percent prices.

COMPARISON WITH OTHER CITIES

It is also instructive to compare the New York City budget with that of the 29 other largest cities. This comparison can illustrate first the degree to which New York City is

---

[1] A long catalogue of the bargaining concessions is given by Raymond D. Horton. An indication of the sheer size effect is given by the fact that there are now about 450,000 full and part-time city government employees in New York City. If each was married, lived in the city, and had one close friend or relative who would vote alike on city issues, conceivably 1,350,000 votes, 30 percent of the entire voting age population and roughly half of the probable number of voters, could be marshalled in favor of making some strategic concession to, or dealing leniently with, unions.

TABLE 2

Composition of New York City Budget Deficit, Fiscal 1974
(millions of current dollars)

Revenues	11,291.5	Current expenditures	11,779.1
Grants	5,076.3	Normal functions	3,769.5
Normal functions plus untied	1,442.2	Schools	1,726.3
Schools	872.4	Marginal functions	6,283.3
Marginal functions	2,761.7	Welfare	2,587.4
Welfare	2,393.1	Higher education	490.1
Higher education	196.0	Transit	989.7
Public hospitals	135.5	Public hospitals	1,088.1
Public housing	37.1	Public housing	294.3
Own revenues	6,215.2	Pension contributions	833.7
Taxes plus normal charges	5,186.0		
Marginal functions	1,029.2		
Higher education	72.0		
Transit	629.5		
Public hospitals	147.3		
Public housing	180.4		
Current account deficit	487.6		
Normal revenues	6,628.2	Normal expenditures	3,769.5
School grants	872.4	School expenditures	1,726.3
Current account deficit	487.6	Marginal functions deficit	2,492.4
		Welfare	194.3
		Higher education	222.1
		Transit	360.2
		Public hospitals	805.3
		Public housing	76.8
		Pension contributions	833.7

Source: U.S. Bureau of the Census, *City Government Finances,* 1973–74.

unique, and secondly the risk that the New York fiscal disease may spread to other cities.

Budget data for the general governments of the 30 largest *U.S.* cities for 1973–74 are given in Table 3. The budgetary items are grouped into normal and marginal functions categories, as was done in the bottom panel of Table 2, and are all expressed in per capita terms. Per capita expenditures on schools in the city are also shown in the table, even though New York City, Washington, Buffalo, Baltimore, Boston, and Memphis are the only other cities

where school expenditures are actually in the general government budget.[2]

The table indicates first that only two large cities had current account deficits in 1973–74—New York City and Washington. But where New York City had to finance its deficit by borrowing from the bond market, Washington did not at the time have home rule and could borrow with federal guarantees (though this situation has changed as of January 1, 1976). Of the

[2] In the remaining cities schools are financed by an independent school authority.

other cities, only Philadelphia had a current surplus that was small enough relative to revenues that it would have been converted to a deficit had the city's 1973–74 unemployment rate been as high as it is now.

In terms of composition, it is again the marginal functions where New York City stands out. The net deficit on these margi-

nal functions was $326 per capita in New York City, roughly the same as Washington, which is also a state government and therefore has a large budget for welfare, higher education, and public hospitals. The only other cities that have marginal functions deficits of more than $60 per capita are San Francisco (large transit subsidies and pension contributions), Boston (large

TABLE 3

Comparative Budgets, 30 Largest U.S. Cities, Fiscal 1973–74
(dollars per capita)

	Normal Revenue	Normal Expenditures	School Expenditures	Marginal Functions Deficit	Current Account Surplus
New York City	$ 962.1	$493.0	$207.0	$325.9	$ −63.8
Buffalo	660.3	318.0	272.0	17.1	53.2
Baltimore	796.1	358.6	207.9	40.6	189.0
Boston	835.8	487.3	188.1	117.4	43.0
Philadelphia	637.4	369.5	202.5	54.0	11.4
Pittsburgh	523.9	233.9	220.6	13.7	55.7
Washington	1,223.4	823.1	227.7	324.1	−151.5
Chicago	512.2	247.1	219.0	20.9	25.2
Cleveland	628.7	350.7	214.0	8.3	55.7
Columbus	423.8	225.6	160.2	0.5	37.5
Detroit	702.9	334.2	219.9	98.4	50.4
Indianapolis	450.4	177.7	191.4	40.4	40.9
Milwaukee	564.2	260.9	217.0	25.3	61.0
St. Louis	572.3	299.1	173.3	60.3	39.6
Kansas City	568.3	292.1	173.4	38.0	64.8
Atlanta	674.8	294.8	204.2	25.9	149.9
Jacksonville	561.6	208.4	199.8	27.7	125.7
Memphis	489.8	204.4	168.0	20.4	97.0
New Orleans	487.7	253.0	138.8	24.1	71.8
Dallas	474.5	236.4	167.9	13.1	57.1
Houston	366.9	178.1	158.1	8.7	22.0
San Antonio	342.0	128.8	136.5	6.1	70.6
Denver	723.0	350.1	208.0	50.3	114.6
Los Angeles	607.4	242.5	224.7	50.9	89.3
San Francisco	956.4	466.2	194.7	225.0	70.5
San Diego	467.3	181.2	217.9	23.4	44.8
San Jose	492.4	163.1	282.0	14.4	32.9
Phoenix	480.1	210.0	208.8	5.9	55.4
Seattle	672.7	314.9	250.9	36.7	70.2
Honolulu	304.6	242.5	—	2.5	59.6

Source: U.S. Bureau of the Census, *City Government Finances*, 1973–74.

pensions and public housing), and Detroit (large pensions).

Table 4 makes this comparison more systematically. The top panel compares New York's per capita budget figures with the mean for the 27 other large cities. . . . New York's normal expenditures are $219 more than average, school expenditures are above average, and the marginal functions deficit is $286 more than average. Revenues are fortunately also $382 more than average, but the current account deficit is still $130 more than average.

It can be argued that these comparisons are misleading because New York City is not an average large city. Its racial composition, income levels, employment growth, and age are not extraordinary as cities go, but its population size and density clearly are (the population density in New York City of 25,000 per square mile is 2.5 times as great as the next highest). One way to correct for those factors in making budgetary comparisons is to run regressions for

the 27-city sample, explaining budgetary variables as a function of independent variables such as population size and density, income and poverty levels, federal and state grants, and regional and governmental structure dummy variables. Values for New York City can then be inserted in the regressions and budgetary totals "predicted" for a hypothetical city with all of New York's properties.

When this comparison is made, it cuts down but does not eliminate the deviations of New York's actual budgetary values from their predicted values. Information in the second panel of Table 4, based on regressions explaining the four right-hand budgetary variables, leads to a positive residual of $121 for normal expenditures, $228 for marginal functions, and $62 for the current account deficit. Information based on regressions for all five budgetary variables, estimated in a way that insures the budget identity is preserved, leads to positive residuals of $132 for normal

TABLE 4

New York City Budget in Relation to That of 27 Other Large Cities
(dollars per capita)

	Normal Revenue	Normal Expenditures	School Expenditures	Marginal Functions Deficit	Current Account Surplus
New York City	962.1	493.0	207.0	325.9	− 63.8
Mean of 27 cities[a]	580.5	273.6	200.8	39.5	66.6
NYC—Mean	381.6	219.4	6.2	286.4	−130.4
New York City	962.1	493.0	207.0	325.9	− 63.8
Unconstrained regression prediction[a]	681.1	372.0	213.3	97.8	− 2.0
NYC—Reg. Pred.	281.0	121.0	−6.3	228.1	− 61.8
New York City	962.1	493.0	207.0	325.9	− 63.8
Constrained regression prediction[a]	758.3	361.5	225.9	98.6	72.3
NYC—Reg. Pred.	203.8	131.5	−18.9	227.3	−136.1

[a] Excluding New York City, Washington, and Honolulu from sample.
Source: U.S. Bureau of the Census, *City Government Finances*, 1973–74.

expenditures, $227 for marginal functions, and $136 for the current account deficit. However this comparison is made, New York runs a substantially greater current account deficit than is predicted on the basis of other cities, has somewhat greater expenditures on normal functions, virtually no greater expenditures on schools, and much greater deficits for marginal functions.

THE BOND RATINGS

One of the interesting sidelights in the gradual progression of the city toward default was that an investor looking solely at the ratings of New York City bonds would have gotten rather misleading information. Back in the early 1960s, when the city first experimented with current account deficit spending, the city's bonds were rated *A* by both Moody's and Standard and Poor's Investors Services—of "upper medium" quality. In 1965–66, when the deficits had persisted for five years, both services downgraded the city's bond rating to *Baa*—of "lower medium" quality (the classification is labelled *BBB* by Standard and Poor's, but it means the same as *Baa* for Moody's). This caused a 50 to 75 basis point increase in borrowing costs and raised a continuing popular outcry by city officials and congressmen against the private rating services.... The lengthy political compaign eventually seemed to pay off and in December 1972, Moody's upgraded the city bonds again to *A*, despite the fact that the very large current account deficits were just then beginning. Standard and Poor's behaved even more curiously, holding out against upgrading the city until December 1974, but then upgraded the city's bonds to *A* just as the early signs of a potential default were being raised.

The rating services are private agencies, and though they publish voluminous information on the budgets of borrowing governments, it is impossible to tell exactly how they arrive at their ratings. A statistical attempt to explain their ratings by Carleton and Lerner turned up population size, the debt-assessed value ratio, the average tax collection rate, and whether or not the borrowing agency was a school district as statistically significant independent variables, but still left a large random component to the ratings.... It is difficult and possibly unfair to make a very forceful criticism of the rating services—no general obligation bonds rated by the services have defaulted in the postwar period, and their information and stamp of approval has surely played a role in that good record. As the New York City case illustrates, however, there is always a first time, and in retrospect the information provided by the rating services in this particular case was not so good. They correctly penalized the city in the 1965–72 period, but incorrectly backed down in 1972. This faulty information may reflect a possible weakness in the criteria apparently used by the rating services—specifically, the fact that the deficit position of the current account budget appears to have little or no direct role in the ratings—or it could also reflect the possibility that the ratings may have been influenced by political pressures from city officials.

IMPACT ON THE ECONOMY

The present fiscal difficulties of New York and other cities arise in part because of the economic recession, but there is also some reverse feedback. If the city defaults, or flirts with default, this may set in motion a chain of events that will threaten the recovery from the recession. It then becomes important to try to determine whether there are any such multiplier effects for the New York situation.

The most immediate problem is the capital losses on bonds in default. If the city were to be unable to meet all its obligations, in all likelihood bondholders would be the ones to take the first losses. A large share of the outstanding bonds are held by banks in New York, and there was for a time thought to be a risk that the losses would be so great as to trigger a flight of deposits from the city banks. Most of the risk from this quarter seems to have passed, however. It never was highly likely, and now that the federal government has agreed to make short-term loans to the city, and the Federal Reserve to make discount loans to any banks in difficulty, the risk of a chain reaction collapse of banks because of the New York fiscal crisis is relatively slight.

A second possible way in which the New York fiscal situation could retard the recovery is through the direct cutbacks or tax increases required to balance the city's budget. The New York State Emergency Financial Control Board plan for balancing the city's budget calls for expenditure cutbacks of about $100 million in fiscal 1975–76, $500 million in fiscal 1976–77, and $700 million in fiscal 1977–78. This comes on top of a previous 6 percent expenditure cutback and 7 percent revenue increase already made by the city, and a further $200 million tax increase as part of the package which induced the Administration to agree to short-term federal loans to the city. New York State, with its own financial problems, has also recently raised taxes by $600 million. The net effect of all of these actions seems likely to reduce the aggregate demand stimulus contributed by state and local governments by about $2 billion, leading to a reduction in GNP of approximately $4 billion below what would otherwise be the case.

A third factor that must be considered is the impact on the state and local bond rate. This impact can be tested as follows. A regression was fit of the form

$$CORP\ (l-t)\ -\ RATE\ =\\ a_o +\ a_1 U\ +\ a_2 TIME,$$

where CORP is the corporate Aaa rate, RATE is the municipal bond rate in the appropriate risk class (Aaa, Aa, A, or Baa), t is the estimated average personal and corporate marginal tax rate among state and local bondholders, U is the unemployment rate, and TIME is a time trend. The regression explains the rate differential between the after-tax corporate bond rate and the relevant municipal rate as a function of the unemployment rate (since state and local governments must borrow relatively more in a recession, their rate would rise relative to the corporate rate) and time (since municipal rates have been falling relative to the corporate rate over time). The equation was fit to halfyear data from 1955–74, and then extrapolated to 1975 to see how values predicted by the regression compare with actual municipal rates in 1975.

For the Aaa rate, the actual municipal rate averaged 13 basis points above the predicted rate throughout 1975. . . .

It is not clear whether the entire residual in 1975 actual municipal bond yields can be blamed on New York City, but it seems likely that a large component can. . . . If we make the extreme assumptions that the entire residual is caused by the New York situation and that the corporate rate is not *lowered* by these troubles in the municipal market, the New York situation will reduce

the extent to which state and local governments borrow to finance capital construction projects. Weighting the third quarter
residuals by the proportion of borrowing in
each risk class leads to an increase in the
state and local bond rate of 63 basis points,
which should by itself reduce state and
local construction by about $4.5 billion.
The *GNP* impact of this would be about $9
billion in the first year or two, and when
added to the impact of the direct cuts discussed above, both together would reduce
GNP by .7 percent and raise the unemployment rate by about .25 percentage points
over what it would otherwise be. This is
quite a large effect for the fiscal difficulties
of just one city. . . .

Moreover, focusing only on this surprisingly large macroeconomic impact can
obscure two points. The first is that if the
city does default, and if that default does
threaten the solvency of major New York
banks and cause a loss of deposits, the situation becomes much more uncertain and
the risk of a general collapse of borrowing
and investment much greater. In this context, one greater advantage of bailing out
the city is precisely this—it keeps the general economic risks predictable and
manageable.

The second point is that this estimate of
the impact of any New York default is only
manageable for the country as a whole—
the impact on the economy and the citizens of the city itself will be extremely
painful. Table 4 showed that per capita
taxes are already much higher in New York
than in other cities, and the measures
taken to put the city on a sounder fiscal
footing will raise them further, increasing
the risk of a flight of the taxpaying businesses and households to other localities.
On the expenditure side, the *MAC* figures
project that by fiscal 1978 55 percent of the

city's expenditures will be "uncontrollable"—mandated for interest, debt service,
welfare, and pension payments. This forces
very deep cutbacks in the remaining controllable portion. . . .

WHAT IS TO BE DONE
IN THE SHORT RUN?

It is generally easier to analyze what went
wrong than to say what to do about it.
Several principles do emerge from the preceding facts, however, and I will try to
highlight the pertinent ones.

The first is that the city itself is ultimately responsible for its financial woes—
the budget deficits started long ago, in part
because of official underestimates of the
severity of the problem. . . . The second is
that even though the problem is of the
city's own making, things have reached
such a point that now the city simply cannot correct the problem by itself—tax burdens in the city and state are already
extremely high, uncontrollable expenditures are extremely high, and the cash
expenses necessary to roll over the short-
term debt, when the market will not, are
excruciating. Even with the severe cuts in
expenditures mandated by the Emergency
Financial Control Board, it will take the city
three years to restore balance in its budget,
and only then under relatively optimistic
assumptions regarding future revenues.

The question facing the national government is whether to take steps to avoid the
city's having to default on the bonds it
must retire in the near future. If this were
not done, there is at least some chance
that a financial panic could develop, and
some chance that the economic recovery
could be aborted even if a panic did not
develop. There is also an excellent chance
that the delivery of vital services in the

city—police, fire, sanitation, health, education—could be temporarily or permanently disrupted by default, and that it would be very difficult to pick up the pieces. Minimizing each of these fears is essentially the rationale for not allowing the city to default.

On the other side, the advantage of a default is that the city has in fact signed certain contracts that it is simply unable to meet, it has to improve its budget process and reduce its deficits, and it never will unless it is forced to go through the default process. The last assumption is the key one—by this time the state itself and through its Emergency Financial Central Board has exerted so much control on the city that it effectively lost its budgetary autonomy and will have to abrogate some contracts, whether or not there is a default. Given this, these marginal benefits of a default are probably unimportant and it seems almost foolish to risk the possible severe dangers of allowing the city to go under. . . .

LONG-TERM MEASURES

The city's plight does illustrate several more long-term issues, however, and it is well to emphasize them before such crises recur. The first is that better state and local financial accounting is urgently needed. There is no obvious reason why the budgets of large state and local governments could not be more quickly made available to the financial community, tabulated in standard form, using official conventions on what is current and what capital spending, on the increase in pension fund liabilities, on the size and maturity of outstanding debt. . . . There should also be much more explicit statement of why bonds are rated as they are, the criteria used, and the data behind these criteria. As a specific suggestion, the rating agencies have apparently relied solely on stock figures such as the ratio of debt to assessed property values; it would seem that flow figures such as the recent size of current account surplus, the controllable portion of the budget, and the dangers in not being able to roll over short-term debt should also enter in.

A second point regards the intrinsic financial difficulties of state and local governments when macroeconomic conditions change. State and local revenues are now composed largely of income and sales taxes—those two sources comprised 60 percent of own revenue in 1973—and net expenditures for welfare and medicaid have also become very large. When aggregate conditions change, state and local budgets will tend to operate in an automatically stabilizing manner just as will the federal budget. The only difference is that the inability to run current account deficits at the state and local level forces the stabilizers to be offset by other spending costs or tax increases. It can, of course, be argued that governments should have had the foresight to build up a stock of liquid assets for just such an emergency. . . . To illustrate the problem, a special Joint Economic Committee survey of eighteen large cities found only five that did not raise taxes or cut spending in the past year. This is both counterproductive from a macro standpoint and, more importantly, it leads to instability in the delivery of services at the state and local level. A sensible remedy would be to give out revenue sharing money on a countercyclical basis. It was emphasized above that the recession was not at the heart of New York's woes, and these woes would have only been modestly ameliorated by a countercyclical revenue sharing program, but they would have been ameliorated and the program would still seem to have appeal in a cyclical economy.

A final point involves the redistributive nature of the city's social programs. As was argued earlier, New York's difficulties can in large part be traced to the fact that it was doing too much on its own. In some cases—pension contributions, higher education, transit subsidies, public hospitals—the choice was the city's own; in others—welfare and medicaid—the choice was made by the state and mandated on the city's budget. Laudable as these choices may be from a social standpoint, local governments do have to be careful in a federal system, first, not to laden taxpayers with too much debt and forced debt service payments, and, second, not to undertake too much redistribution at the local level. If these programs are to be done, they must at least be financed on a national scale. In this sense, the New York experience can also be interpreted as something of a setback for the new federalism, which some advocates interpret as turning functions such as income redistribution back to the states and localities.

REFERENCES

W. T. Carleton and E. M. Lerner, "Statistical Credit Scoring of Municipal Bonds," *J. Money, Credit, Banking,* Nov. 1969.

R. D. Horton, *Municipal Labor Relations in New York City: Lessons of the Lindsay-Wagner Years,* 1973.

KEY CONCEPTS

bond rating system

current account deficit

general obligation bonds

marginal functions

marginal tax rates

normal expenditures

regression analysis

short-term debt

uncontrollable expenditures

DAVID F. BRADFORD   WALLACE E. OATES

24   Suburban Exploitation of Central Cities and Governmental Structure

David F. Bradford and Wallace E. Oates, of Princeton University, review the claim that central cities are fiscally exploited by suburban commuters who work in the city and impose demands on central-city services but live in the suburbs and pay taxes there. This claim has come to be known as the central-city exploitation hypothesis, and its acceptance by government officials has led them to levy taxes aimed at reaching nonresident workers in the city. Bradford and Oates indicate that the empirical evidence does not lend much support to this hypothesis.

The fiscal difficulties of the central cities and, in fact, the whole host of social and economic problems that contribute to our so-called urban crisis are largely the result, according to some observers, of a systematic "exploitation" of the cities by residents of suburban municipalities. The precise form this exploitation takes is often not made explicit, but at any rate the assertion is that the suburbanites are in large measure to blame for the deterioration in the quality of life in the cities.

The term "exploitation" typically refers to an "unjust relationship" between one individual (or group of individuals) and another. It is therefore a normative concept and can take on a precise operational meaning only when a just relationship is defined. Unfortunately, there seems to be no generally accepted definition of such a relationship between residents of cities and

suburbs, with the result that exploitation of central cities by their suburbs has been given a number of different interpretations.

In some of the public-finance literature, for example, the term has been used to describe a process in which suburban commuters utilize the public services provided by the cities but then return home to their residential communities to pay (at least the bulk of) their local taxes. The suburbanites thus exploit the central-city residents who must, willy-nilly, support public services for the commuters in order to have any themselves. This we shall call the "narrow" public-finance version of the exploitation thesis.

In the writings of more popular commentators on the plight of American cities, however, quite another set of issues dominates the discussion. Here the sin of the suburbanites is said to be their clustering in homogeneous settlements from which the poor are "walled out" by zoning and other devices, there to enjoy public-service

Reprinted with permission from *Redistribution Through Public Choice*, Harold Hochman and George Peterson, editors, pp. 43–48. Copyright 1974 Columbia University Press.

standards higher than those maintained in the central city while paying less in local taxes. This situation describes exploitation of the central city, and more generally of the poor, in a rather odd sense. It appears that the tax instruments available to local governments, taken together with the package of services normally provided by them and with the rules for local political procedures, tend to produce local public budgets that are somewhat redistributive toward the poorer residents of the jurisdiction.[1] A local governmental system that allows formation of jurisdictions uniform in income composition thus allows the upper-income families of a metropolitan area to avoid "exploitation" by the poorer families of the area. By taking away their ability to exploit the rich through the local fiscal system, the suburban governmental system exploits the poor!

Whichever of these notions of exploitation is accepted, there is little doubt that the system wherein public services are provided by relatively small and autonomous local-government jurisdictions in the suburbs has important implications for the distribution of welfare when compared to the obvious alternative of a unified metropolitan jurisdiction or the transfer of public functions to even higher (state or federal) levels of government. Particularly in view of the California and New Jersey court decisions that the finance of public schools through local property taxes is incompatible with the equal service provisions of the state constitutions, there is a pressing need

for analyses of the distributive and allocative effects of the enlargement of fiscal jurisdictions.

THE NARROW PUBLIC-FINANCE EXPLOITATION THESIS

Some 20 years ago Amos Hawley found that local public spending per capita in 76 cities, each with a population in excess of 100,000, showed a positive correlation to the proportion of the population in the metropolitan area living outside the central city. From this finding Hawley concluded that central cities were being exploited by the suburbs in the sense that residents of the cities ". . . are carrying the financial burden of an elaborate and costly service installation, i.e., the central city, which is used daily by a noncontributing population in some instances more than twice the size of the contributing population."[2] Hawley used 1940 data for his study. A number of later studies using more recent fiscal and population figures, notably studies by Harvey Brazer and Julius Margolis, found this same type of empirical relationship, but these authors were far more cautious about drawing the type of inference Hawley drew from this phenomenon.[3] In particular, it is clear that suburban commuters do make some positive contributions to the fiscal well-being of the city. Many cities, such as Philadelphia, Detroit, and New York, have local income or wage taxes levied on income earned in the city. In addition,

---

[1] In his comprehensive study of the redistributive effects of governmental budgets, W. Irwin Gillespie found that, in the United States for 1960, state-local budgets were redistributive in favor of families with incomes under $5,000. See his "Effect of Public Expenditures on the Distribution of Income," in R. A. Musgrave, ed., *Essays in Fiscal Federalism* (Washington, D.C.: Brookings Institution, 1965). pp. 164–66.

[2] Amos Hawley, "Metropolitan Population and Municipal Government Expenditures in Central Cities," *Journal of Social Issues* (1951), p. 107.

[3] Harvey Brazer, *City Expenditures in the United States* (New York: National Bureau of Economic Research, 1959); Julius Margolis, "Metropolitan Finance Problems: Territories, Functions, and Growth," in James Buchanan, ed., *Public Finances: Needs, Sources, and Utilization* (Princeton: Princeton University Press, 1961), pp. 229–93.

most cities levy sales taxes and, in some cases, a variety of user charges, including such things as tolls on bridges and tunnels leading into the city. Less directly, but perhaps at least as important, the use of city facilities by a greater number of suburban residents may increase the level of economic activity in the city and thereby enhance city property values with a corresponding stimulus to city receipts from property taxation. In fact, residential suburbs have been known to claim that the cities take advantage of them by reaping the tax benefits from a high concentration of commercial-industrial property, whereas the suburbs must service the population (particularly the heavy expense of providing public education). The existence of a positive correlation between central-city expenditures per capita and fraction of the population living in the suburbs is not convincing evidence for the exploitation thesis. The suburban commuters may even more than pay for the extra costs of the public services that the city must provide.

A few studies have been undertaken to attempt to settle this issue by measuring both the fiscal contribution and the fiscal costs that suburban residents bring to the city. The approach has typically been to allocate the costs of city services on a per capita basis between city and suburban users of city services and to estimate the fiscal receipts to the city that come from the pockets of suburban residents. The difference between costs imposed and revenues generated by suburban users of city services is then calculated. Such studies have generally found little in the way of fiscal exploitation one way or the other. William Neenan, for example, notes the findings of James Banovetz in a study of the Twin Cities metropolitan area.

Banovetz's results indicate that "... no conclusive evidence can be found to support charges that either the core cities of Minneapolis and St. Paul or their suburbs in Hennepin or Ramsey Counties, respectively, are subsidizing the other to any appreciable extent."[4]

Neenan himself is the author of a recent study of suburban exploitation in the Detroit metropolitan area.[5] In comprehensiveness of services included and in the care with which measurements of service flows are carried out, Neenan's analysis probably represents about the best that can be done. We shall therefore review briefly his procedures and findings.

Neenan's approach differs from that of earlier studies. Rather than simply allocating costs on a per capita basis, he develops indices of "willingness-to-pay." Assuming the benefits (that is, the willingness to pay) to vary proportionately with income, Neenan allocates the benefits from city services among city and suburban residents according to their relative income levels. An example may be helpful here. Suppose that the cost per visit (total cost per number of visits) of operating the city's museum is one dollar. If a suburban resident has twice the level of income as that of a city resident, Neenan would attribute a benefit of two dollars per visit to the suburban user of the city museum and a benefit of only one dollar to a city resident. Since, in Neenan's sample of seven suburban communities, income levels in the suburbs are generally higher than those of city residents, this approach naturally has the effect of placing a relatively high

---

[4] William Neenan, "Suburban-Central City Exploitation Thesis: One City's Tale," *National Tax Journal* (June, 1970), p. 119.

[5] *Ibid.*, pp. 117–39.

value on city services consumed by suburbanites.

Neenan's procedure is biased in two ways toward a finding of positive exploitation. First, because of higher suburban incomes, his technique generates a value of city services to all users that exceeds their cost; thus a suburbanite may well pay the costs he imposes on city residents and yet realize a "consumer surplus" when these costs are compared to his willingness-to-pay. But Neenan assumes that the suburban resident "exploits" the city if he does not contribute to the city treasury the full benefits from any city services he consumes. This is somewhat like saying that the purchaser of a commodity exploits the seller because he gets more in satisfaction than he gives up in terms of his payment (that is, he realizes a consumer surplus). Now surely an ethical question exists as to how these "gains-from-trade" should be allocated between city dwellers and suburbanites, but it does seem somewhat questionable to insist, as Neenan in effect does, that they should all accrue to the residents of the city.[6] It would seem to make just as much sense to argue that city residents should be fully compensated for the costs imposed by suburban users of city services, but that there is no compelling reason why they should receive payments in excess of these costs. At any rate, Neenan's approach is surely favorable to obtaining results indicating suburban exploitation of the city.

Second, it should be noted that the particular assumption made by Neenan, namely, valuation proportional to income, does not seem to be derivable from any

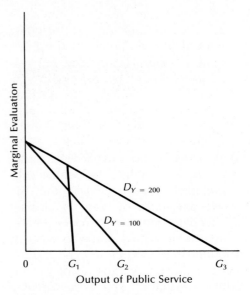

Figure 1.

more fundamental assumptions about the underlying demand functions. Figure 1 illustrates what happens to the total valuation of a given output as income varies for the simple case where demand is linear and unit income elastic.[7] At output G_1, a doubling of income leads to considerably less than a doubling of total valuation (as measured by the areas under the demand curves). As a little experimentation should convince the reader, as long as we are operating in a region in which the lower-income citizen positively values increments in G (that is, to the left of G_2), no income elasticity would be large enough to produce a doubling of total valuation with a doubling of income, if the underlying demand curves are linear. All this says is that it is difficult to know whether Neenan's particular assumption is reasona-

[6] In one Detroit suburb, Grosse Point Park, Neenan in fact finds that the residents contribute more in revenues to Detroit than they impose on the city in terms of costs, but yet "exploit" the city because these payments fall short of their measured willingness-to-pay.

[7] We assume here that these are "income-compensated" demand curves, so they indicate the marginal valuation of each additional unit of output.

ble or not; we suspect that his willingness-to-pay factor is high.

In spite of these procedures, which favor the exploitation thesis, Neenan finds it to be of minor quantitative significance. The net subsidy from Detroit to the seven suburban communities ranges from $1.73 per capita to $12.58 per capita, with a median value of only $6.78. This compares with an average level of local spending per capita in the United States in 1966 (the year of Neenan's data) of roughly $200. Neenan's study, like the others, thus suggests that the narrow public-finance version of the suburban exploitation thesis is of little moment.

KEY CONCEPTS

allocative effects

correlation

distribution effects

exploitation

linear demand

willingness to pay

WILLIAM J. BAUMOL

25   Macroeconomics of Unbalanced Growth: The Anatomy of Urban Crisis

William J. Baumol, of Princeton University, shows why we should expect government to grow over time relative to the private sector. His argument is based on the technological characteristics of government production, not on its bureaucratic features. Costs increase because labor's productivity in government-service provision tends to remain constant over time.

There are some economic forces so powerful that they constantly break through all barriers erected for their suppression. Such, for example, are the forces of supply and demand which have resisted alike medieval efforts to abolish usury and contemporary attempts to control prices. In this paper I discuss what I believe to be another such mechanism which has colored the past and seems likely to stamp its character on the future. It helps us to understand the prospective roles of a wide variety of economic services: municipal government, education, the performing arts, restaurants, and leisure time activity. I will argue that inherent in the technological structure of each of these activities are forces working almost unavoidably for progressive and cumulative increases in the real costs incurred in supplying them. As a consequence, efforts to offset these cost increases, while they may succeed temporarily, in the long run are merely palliatives which can have no significant effect on the underlying trends. . . .

Reprinted with permission from the *American Economic Review*, 57, 3 (June 1967): 415–26, and the author.

PREMISES

Our model will proceed on several assumptions, only one of which is really essential. This basic premise asserts that economic activities can . . . be grouped into two types: technologically progressive activities in which innovations, capital accumulation, and economies of large scale all make for a cumulative rise in output per man hour and activities which, by their very nature, permit only sporadic increases in productivity.

Of course, one would expect that productivity would not grow at a uniform rate throughout the economy so it is hardly surprising that, given any arbitrarily chosen dividing line, one can fit all goods and services into one or the other of two such categories in whatever way the dividing line is drawn. I am, however, making a much stronger assertion: that the place of any particular activity in this classification is not primarily a fortuitous matter determined by the particulars of its history, but rather that it is a manifestation of the activity's technological structure, which determines quite definitely whether the productivity of its labor inputs will grow slowly or rapidly.

The basic source of differentiation resides in the role played by labor in the activity. In some cases labor is primarily an instrument—an incidental requisite for the attainment of the final product, while in other fields of endeavor, for all practical purposes the labor is itself the end product. Manufacturing encompasses the most obvious examples of the former type of activity. When someone purchases an air conditioner he neither knows nor cares how much labor went into it. He is not concerned one way or the other with an innovation that reduces the manpower requirements for the production of his purchase by 10 per cent if the price and the quality of the. product are unaffected. Thus it has been possible, as it were, behind the scenes, to effect successive and cumulative decreases in the labor input coefficient for most manufactured goods, often along with some degree of improvement in the quality of the product.

On the other hand there are a number of services in which the labor is an end in itself, in which quality is judged directly in terms of amount of labor. Teaching is a clear-cut example, where class size (number of teaching hours expended per student) is often taken as a critical index of quality. Here, despite the invention of teaching machines and the use of closed circuit television and a variety of other innovations, there still seem to be fairly firm limits to class size. We are deeply concerned when elementary school classes grow to 50 pupils and are disquieted by the idea of college lectures attended by 2000 underclassmen. Without a complete revolution in our approach to teaching there is no prospect that we can ever go beyond these levels (or even up to them) with any degree of equanimity. . . .

In addition to the separability of activities into our two basic categories I shall utilize three other assumptions, two of them primarily for ease of exposition. The reader will recognize, as we proceed, that neither is essential to the argument. The first of the incidental premises consists simply in the assertion that all outlays other than labor costs can be ignored. This assertion is patently unrealistic but it simplifies greatly our . . . model. A second, far more important, and more realistic assumption is that wages in the two sectors of the economy go up and down together. In the long run there is some degree of mobility in all labor markets and consequently, while wages in one activity can lag behind those in another, unless the former is in process of disappearing altogether we cannot expect the disparity to continue indefinitely. For simplicity I will . . . take hourly wages to be precisely the same in both sectors, but the model is easily complicated to allow for some diversity in wage levels and their movements.

A final inessential assumption which is, however, not altogether unrealistic, asserts that money wages will rise as rapidly as output per man hour in the sector where productivity is increasing. Since organized labor is not slow to learn of increases in its productivity it is likely to adjust its wage demands accordingly. This assumption affects only the magnitude of the absolute price level in our model, and does not influence the relative costs and prices that are the critical elements in the analysis. . . .

DISCUSSION OF THE PROPOSITIONS

The logic of the . . . analysis can be restated rather simply in intuitive terms. If productivity per man hour rises cumulatively in one sector relative to its rate of growth elsewhere in the economy, while wages rise commensurately in all areas, then relative costs in the nonprogressive sectors must inevitably rise, *and these costs will rise cumulatively and without limit*. For while in the progressive sector productivity increases will serve as an off-set to rising wages, this offset must be smaller in the nonprogressive sectors. For example (ignoring nonwage costs) if wages and productivity in the progressive sector both go up 2 per cent per year, costs there will not rise at all. On the other hand, if in the nonprogressive sector productivity is constant, every rise in wages must yield a corresponding addition to costs—a 2 per cent cumulative rise in wages means that, year in year out, costs must be 2 per cent above those of the preceding year. Thus, the very progress of the technologically progressive sectors inevitably adds to the costs of the technologically unchanging sectors of the economy, unless somehow the labor markets in these areas can be sealed off and wages held absolutely constant, a most unlikely possibility.

We see then that costs in many sectors of the economy will rise relentlessly, and will do so for reasons that are for all practical purposes beyond the control of those involved. The consequence is that the outputs of these sectors may in some cases tend to be driven from the market. If their relative outputs are maintained, an ever increasing proportion of the labor force must be channeled into these activities and the rate of growth of the economy must be slowed correspondingly.

SOME APPLICATIONS

These observations can be used at once to explain a number of observed phenomena.[1]

---

[1] Some of the ideas in this section arose out of discussions with Eugene Beem of Sperry and Hutchinson.

For example, there is evidence that an ever increasing portion of the nation's labor force has been going into retailing and that a rising portion of the cost of commodities is accounted for by outlays on marketing. Now there have been several pronounced changes in the technology of marketing in recent decades: self service, the supermar-ket, and prewrapping have all increased the productivity per man hour of the retailing personnel. But ultimately, the activity involved is in the nature of a service and it does not allow for constant and cumulative increases in productivity through capital accumulation, innovation, or economics of large-scale operation. Hence it is neither mismanagement nor lack of ingenuity that accounts for the relatively constant produc-tivity of this sector. Since some sort of mar-keting effort is an inescapable element in economic activity, demand for this service is quite income elastic. Our model tells us what to expect in this case—cumulatively increasing costs relative to those of other economic activities, and the absorption of an ever growing proportion of society's resources by this sector—precisely what seems to have been observed.

Higher education is another activity the demand for whose product seems to be relatively income elastic and price inelastic. Higher tuition charges undoubtedly impose serious hardships on lower-income stu-dents. But, because a college degree seems increasingly to be a necessary condition for employment in a variety of attractive occu-pations, most families have apparently been prepared to pay the ever larger fees instituted in recent years. As a result higher education has been absorbing a constantly increasing proportion of per capita income. And the relatively constant productivity of college teaching leads our model to predict that rising educational costs are no tempo-rary phenomenon.... Rather, it suggests that, as productivity in the remainder of the economy continues to increase, costs of running the educational organizations will mount correspondingly, so that whatever the magnitude of the funds they need today, we can be reasonably certain that they will require more tomorrow, and even more on the day after that.

But not all services in the relatively constant productivity sector of the economy face inelastic demands. Many of them are more readily dispensable than retailing and education as far as individual consumers are concerned. As their costs increase, their utilization tends therefore to decrease and they retreat into the category of luxury goods with very limited markets or disappear almost completely. Fine pottery and glassware produced by the careful labor of skilled craftsmen sell at astronomical prices, though I am told the firms that produce them earn relatively little profit from these product lines which they turn out primarily for prestige and publicity, obtaining the bulk of their earnings from their mass production activities. Fine restaurants and theaters are forced to keep raising their prices, and at least in the case of the latter we know that volume is dwindling while it becomes ever more difficult for suppliers (the producers) to make ends meet.

An extreme example of an activity that has virtually disappeared is the construction (and, indeed, the utilization) of the large and stately houses whose operation even more than their construction allows for little in the way of enhanced productivity, and whose rising costs of operation have apparently decreased their salability even to the wealthy.

These observations suggest something about the likely shape of our economy in the future. Our model tells us that manufactures are likely to continue to decline in relative cost and, unless the income elasticity of demand for manufactured goods is very large, they may absorb an ever smaller proportion of the labor force, which, if it transpires, may make it more difficult for our economy to maintain its overall rate of output growth.

The analysis also suggests that real cost in the "nonprogressive" sectors of the economy may be expected to go on increasing. Some of the services involved—those whose demands are inelastic—may continue viable on the free market. Some, like the theater, may be forced to leave this market and may have to depend on voluntary public support for their survival. Our hospitals, our institutions of private education and a variety of other nonprofit organizations have already long survived on this basis, and can continue to do so if the magnitude of contributions keeps up with costs. Some activities will either disappear or retreat to a small scale of operation catering primarily to a luxury trade. This fate may be in store for restaurants offering true *haute cuisine* and it is already the case for fine hand-worked furniture and for clothes made to measure. Some activities, perhaps many of the preceding among them, will fall increasingly into the hands of the amateurs who already play a considerable role in theatrical and orchestral performances, in gastronomy, in crafts such as woodworking and pottery. Finally, there is a considerable segment of nonprogressive activity that is dependent on tax support. Some of the problems that go with this position will be considered in the remainder of this article. . . .

ON THE FINANCIAL PROBLEM OF THE CITIES

One of the major economic problems of our times is the crisis of the larger cities.

Together with their suburban periphery the cities are attracting ever greater segments of our population. Yet at least the core of the metropolis is plagued by a variety of ills including spreading blight as entire neighborhoods deteriorate, increasing pollution of its atmosphere, worsening traffic, critical educational problems, and, above all, mounting fiscal pressures. The financial troubles are perhaps central to the entire issue because without adequate funds one cannot hope to mount an effective attack on the other difficulties. More than one reform mayor has taken office determined to undertake a radical program to deal with the city's difficulties and found himself baffled and stymied by the monstrous deficit which he discovered to be hanging over him, a deficit whose source appeared to have no reasonable explanation. There seems in these cases to be no way to account for the growth in the city's financial needs—for the fact that a municipal budget far above that which was roughly adequate a decade earlier threatens to disrupt seriously the city's most vital services today. Where the political process is involved it is easy to blame growing costs on inefficiency and corruption but when they take office, reform administrations seem consistently puzzled by their inability to wring out the funds they require through the elimination of these abuses.

A critical element in the explanation becomes clear when we recognize how large a proportion of the services provided by the city are activities falling in the relatively nonprogressive sector of the economy. The bulk of our municipal expenditures is devoted to education which, as we have already seen, offers very limited scope for cumulative increases in productivity. The same is true of police, of hospitals, of social services, and of a variety of inspec-

tion services. Despite the use of the computer in medicine and in traffic planning, despite the use of closed circuit television and a variety of other devices, there is no substitute for the personal attention of a physician or the presence of a police patrol in a crime-ridden neighborhood. The bulk of municipal services is, in fact, of this general stamp and our model tells us clearly what can be expected as a result. Since there is no reason to anticipate a cessation of capital accumulation or innovation in the progressive sectors of the economy, the upward trend in the real costs of municipal services cannot be expected to halt; inexorably and cumulatively, whether or not there is inflation, administrative mismanagement or malfeasance, municipal budgets will almost certainly continue to mount in the future, just as they have been doing in the past. This is a trend for which no man and no group should be blamed, for there is nothing that can be done to stop it.

THE ROLE OF STATIC EXTERNALITIES

Though these may be troubles enough for the municipal administrator, there are other compelling forces that plague him simultaneously. Among them are the general class of externality problems which have so long been the welfare economist's stock in trade.

Since the appearance of Marshall's and Pigou's basic writing in the area a most significant development has been the growing impact of external costs on urban living. No longer are road crowding and smoke nuisance only quaint cases serving primarily as textbook illustrations. Rather, they have become pressing issues of public concern—matters discussed heatedly in the daily press and accorded serious attention by practical politicians. Newspapers devote headlines to an engineer's prediction that the human race is more likely to succumb to its own pollutants than through a nuclear holocaust, and report with glee the quip that Los Angeles is the city in which one is wakened by the sound of birds coughing.

Now there are undoubtedly many reasons for the explosion in external costs but there is a pertinent observation about the relationship between population size in a given area and the cost of externalities that seems not to be obvious. It is easy to assume that these costs will rise roughly in proportion with population but I shall argue now that a much more natural premise is that they will rise more rapidly—perhaps roughly as the square of the number of inhabitants. For example, consider the amount of dirt that falls into the house of a typical urban resident as a result of air pollution, and suppose that this is equal to kn where n is the number of residents in the area. Since the number of homes in the area, $an,$ is also roughly proportionate to population size, total domestic sootfall will be equal to soot per home times number of homes = $kn \cdot an = akn^2$. Similarly, if delays on a crowded road are roughly proportionate to n, the number of vehicles traversing it, the total number of man hours lost thereby will increase roughly as n^2, since the number of passengers also grows roughly as the number of cars. The logic of the argument is simple and perhaps rather general: if each inhabitant in an area imposes external costs on every other, and if the magnitude of the costs borne by each individual is roughly proportionate to population size (density) then since these costs are borne by each of the n persons involved, the total external costs will vary

not in proportion with n but with n^2. Of course I do not maintain that such a relationship is universal or even that it is ever satisfied more than approximately. Rather I am suggesting that, typically, increases in population size may plausibly be expected to produce disproportionate increases in external costs—thus pressures on the municipality to do something about these costs may then grow correspondingly.

CUMULATIVE DECAY AND DYNAMIC PARETO OPTIMALITY

Economic theory indicates yet another source of mounting urban problems. These are the processes of cumulative urban decay which once set in motion induce matters to go from bad to worse. Since I have discussed these elsewhere I can illustrate the central proposition rather briefly. Public transportation is an important example. In many urban areas with declining utilization, frequency of service has been sharply reduced and fares have been increased. But these price rises have only served to produce a further decline in traffic, leading in turn to yet another deterioration in schedules and another fare increase and so on, apparently *ad infinitum*. More important, perhaps, is the logic of the continued flight to the suburbs in which many persons who apparently would otherwise wish to remain in the city are driven out by growing urban deterioration—rising crime rates, a growing number of blighted neighborhoods, etc. Once again, the individuals' remedy intensifies the community's problems and each feeds upon the other. Those who leave the city are usually the very persons who care and can afford to care—the ones who maintain their houses, who do not commit crimes, and who are most capable of providing the taxes needed to arrest the process of urban decay. Their exodus therefore leads to further deterioration in urban conditions and so induces yet another wave of emigration, and so on.

It is clear that these cumulative processes can greatly increase the financial pressures besetting a municipality and can do so in a variety of ways: they can increase directly municipal costs by adding to the real quantities of inputs required for the upkeep of buildings, to maintain levels of urban sanitation, to preserve the level of education attained by an average resident, etc; they can reduce the tax base—the exodus of more affluent urban inhabitants causes a decline in the financial resources available to the city; and with the passage of time the magnitude of the resources necessary to arrest and reverse the cumulative processes itself is likely to grow so that the city may find it increasingly difficult to go beyond programs that slow the processes slightly.

CONCLUSION—
THE FINANCIAL PROBLEMS OF THE LARGE CITY

The story is perhaps completed if we add to the preceding observations the fact that each city is in competition with others and with its own surrounding areas for industry and for people with the wherewithal to pay taxes. No city government acting alone can afford to raise its tax rates indefinitely. Even if they were politically feasible, mounting tax rates must eventually produce diminishing and perhaps even negative returns as they depress the tax base further.

We can now quickly pull the pieces of our story together. We have just seen that our municipalities are perhaps unavoidably subject to a variety of growing financial pressures: the limited sources of tax funds, the pressures imposed by several processes of cumulative decay, the costs of externalities which seem to have a built-in tendency to rise more rapidly than the population. These phenomena imply that the activities of the municipality will have to be expanded if standards of city life are to be maintained. But the funds available for the purpose are extremely limited. And over all this hangs the shadow cast by our model of unbalanced growth which has shown that the costs of even a constant level of activity on the part of a municipal government can be expected to grow constantly higher.

The picture that has been painted is bleak. It suggests strongly that self-help offers no way out for our cities. All of this would then appear to offer stronger theoretical support for the Heller-Pechman proposal that the federal government can provide the resources necessary to prevent the serious crisis that threatens our larger urban communities and whose effects on the quality of life in our society may become one of the nation's most serious economic problems.

KEY CONCEPTS

capital accumulation

cumulative urban decay

dynamic optimality

economies of scale

labor productivity

static externalities

SELMA MUSHKIN   FRANK SANDIFER   CHARLES VEHORN   CHARLIE TURNER

26   The Taxpayer Revolt: An Opportunity to Make Positive Changes in Local Government

Selma Mushkin, Frank Sandifer, Charles Vehorn, and Charlie Turner of Georgetown University make the case for greater reliance on user charges by local governments to finance services. They contend that both efficiency and equity can be improved if user charges are employed more widely.

There are three major sources of local government revenue: local taxation, intergovernmental grants, and user charges. When the public revolts against property taxes and forces a reduction in that source of revenue, local-government officials can either reduce their expenditures proportionately, look to higher-level governments for larger grants, establish or raise nonproperty taxes, or place public prices on public products. Not all local government services, however, are amenable to the pricing mechanism. Some public services have a redistributive characteristic; it would be inappropriate to charge the poor for consumption of services designed explicitly for their benefit. Some public services have characteristics that prevent exclusion of nonpayers. Control of communicable diseases and the maintenance of public safety are examples of such services. When bene-

ficiaries can be identified, however, user charges provide a means of rationing government output, while allocating the burden of payment to those desiring the service.

RATIONALE FOR MORE RELIANCE ON USER CHARGES

Most economists have long been in favor of giving greater emphasis to user fees and charges. Three of the major reasons are the following:

> They can improve efficiency in choice and public resource allocation.
> They can improve government structure.
> They can be more, rather than less, equitable in certain cases.

In each community, citizens now express their demands for local public goods through the voting mechanism. But this mechanism results in a supply of public services that is not sensitive to variations in demand by individual citizens. For example, there are often divergent interests

From *Local Distress, State Surpluses, Proposition 13: Prelude to Fiscal Crisis or New Opportunities?* Hearings before the Subcommittee on the City of the Committee on Banking, Finance, and Urban Affairs (U.S. House of Representatives, 95th Congress, 2nd Session, July 1978).

between the elderly and families with young children. Some divergences among individual citizens do not yield efficient outcomes, except in very special circumstances. A price for a public service, in contrast, permits different citizens to record their preferences by purchases of the quantity and quality of services desired.

Under present public-resource allocation practices, the wrong product is sometimes produced in the wrong quantity, and with inappropriate quality differentiation. "Wrong" is used here with the special meaning of different in type, quantity, and quality from that which would be produced if rigorous analysis were made of comparative effectiveness at the given budget level. It is also being used to describe the volume and quality of production that is lower than it would be at market prices under competitive conditions.

Analysis of a public service or activity may give new emphasis to uncertainty about the consumer's or voter's response to the public product being produced. If the government sets a price on the product—thereby opening up a market through which consumers can register their vote for or against, by either paying the price or not consuming the product—this could help guide the city in the production of its services.

Local governments currently are structured in ways that centralize authority for spending decisions. But there are many enterprises under the local-government umbrella. Conceptually, it could be more efficient to decentralize by allowing various enterprises to operate on a fee-for-service basis. This structure would be beneficial to consumers because it would give the government enterprises the opportunity to compete with enterprises that privately provide similar services. Such competition should foster greater efficiency.

Decentralization would allow public enterprises to operate as separate entities, generate their own funds through user charges, and place only their profits into the local-government general fund. Rates for fire protection, for example, could be based on a variety of pricing rules that take into account property value and fire hazards on the property, with lower rates for less hazardous occupancies. Part of the monies paid in as fees could be set aside in a separate account to provide low or no-interest loans to property owners for improving the fire risk of their structures.

GREATER FAIRNESS

A fee or public price could be a fairer source of revenue than the property tax, since it may be that poor families now pay more through the economic effects of the property tax than under some alternative arrangement. If prices were used instead of the tax, some of the poor families might choose not to have the priced services, and those who did presumably would benefit in proportion to the prices. Analysis of current "use" of a service by income class or age may disclose a heavy concentration among middle-income individuals, rather than poor individuals. In this case, the low-income families would be partially subsidizing the middle-income families under the present financing system. Relative income effects are at issue, as well as the distribution of benefits among age groups.

Prices for services may also achieve greater fairness because payment would be made only by those who benefit. Prices can be used to discourage some users and to encourage others (for example, by negative prices). If uniform charges would be more regressive than an alternative revenue system, it is possible to devise a fair pricing method by use of eligibility tests to determine ability to pay. This method typically has been used in financing health-care service, in financing certain welfare services, such as family counseling, and in school meal programs. Such a technique gives the subsidy to those who need it, while making the benefits of the service available to all those who desire to purchase it.

LIMITATIONS TO INCREASING USER CHARGES

One difficulty in extending user charges is that many fiscal officers feel the political constraints are too binding; another is determining the appropriate price to charge. Local policymakers who indicate a political reluctance to extend user charges may be doing so because they are unaware of the potential of public prices. A recent Rand report suggests that policymakers, many of whom have been schooled in the judiciary process, are more familiar with regulation as a tool. However, public pricing can alter people's behavior, perhaps even more efficiently than regulation. For example, charging for a public service can discourage misuse of that service.

A good illustration is the fees for emergency ambulance services that some local governments, including the District of Columbia, now impose. Part of what the fee does is to discourage requests for ambulances in situations that are not really emergencies.

Once a decision is made to rely more on public pricing, the next complication is in establishing the appropriate price for a given service. When a price less than the appropriate price is charged, a subsidy is given to the person purchasing the service. The Advisory Commission on Intergovernmental Relations has suggested that states provide consultants and technical assistance to local governments to determine the appropriate price to charge. However, many states currently do not possess a capability to offer soundly based advice on the pricing of public services. Even with this limitation, it would be possible to set a price, assess demand, and then reset the price if the first price was inappropriate. This incremental procedure could help in overcoming the difficulties in determining price elasticities for public goods.

KEY CONCEPTS

ability to pay

allocative efficiency

decentralization

intergovernmental grants

market prices

rationing

user charges

PART 7

LOCAL GOVERNMENT SERVICES

Pure public goods represent one type of market failure. Such goods, once produced, bestow equal benefits on everyone in the community; one person's consumption of the service does not reduce the amount available to others. An example is a lighthouse, which benefits equally every ship that uses the harbor. If the costs of the lighthouse are to be assigned on the basis of benefits received, then shipowners have no incentive to reveal their true preferences, for the benefits of the service—once the lighthouse is built—will be received regardless of whether they share in the cost. Because of this "free rider" problem, it is doubtful that the private provision of a public good will achieve the efficient level of service, and involuntary tax collections may be necessary to promote efficiency.

Local governments often provide some services that contain at least some elements of pure public goods. Police patrol and fire protection, for example, provide collective benefits to the entire community. An important question in urban economics is whether public services that have characteristics of public goods can be efficiently produced. Is there any mechanism that forces residents to reveal their preferences for public goods and to pay a tax price that is based on their preferences and that is sufficient to cover the cost?

Charles M. Tiebout suggests that such a mechanism exists in metropolitan areas. His article is a classic in urban public finance. It has spawned an enormous volume of theoretical and empirical research on the nature of the market for local public services.

The Tiebout model gives the conditions for efficient public-goods provision in metropolitan areas containing a large number of communities. Consumer-voters are assumed to be mobile in choosing where to live, to possess full information about local tax and expenditure patterns, and to be unaffected in their residential choice by their job location. Each community is assumed to seek the lowest point on a U-shaped average cost function, while the migration of residents across communities pushes these communities toward or away from the optimum size.

In brief, Tiebout develops a model whereby consumer-voters choose communities on the basis of the tax and expenditure package offered to residents. This spatial movement of residents—called "voting with one's feet"—

reveals their true preferences for local public goods and results in efficiency in the public sector. Consumers maximize their well-being, and local public services are provided at least cost.

Subsequent research has attempted to empirically test the Tiebout model. Wallace E. Oates[1] interpreted the Tiebout hypothesis to mean that consumer-voters choose residences on the basis of the fiscal residual afforded—the difference between public-service benefits and tax costs. In Oates's model, communities offering more attractive fiscal packages experience greater demand for sites located there, and property values are bid up to reflect these fiscal advantages. That is, fiscal factors—taxes and local spending—are capitalized into the value of land and housing.

Oates attempted to test this hypothesis statistically. He found that, everything else equal, communities with greater school spending had higher house values and communities with higher tax rates also had lower property values. While a vigorous debate has emerged concerning Oates's research methodology and results, its major contribution is that it suggested how the Tiebout model could be tested empirically.

The Tiebout model offers numerous important insights about the local public sector. Conceptualizing the metropolitan area as a local-government-services market has completely changed the way urban analysts now approach public-sector efficiency questions. Also, the drive to consolidate local government that characterizes the political reform movement now must face the question of whether decentralized local government is not actually more efficient than consolidated government.

The general question of which level of government can best undertake various government services is addressed by George J. Stigler. One argument he raises against small local jurisdictions is that if one community imposes an inordinately high standard on some activity, say environmental quality, this standard can be defeated by communities with lower standards. Industry will move away from the high-standard area and toward the low-standard area. Stigler, echoing Tiebout, makes a case for why individual local standards may not be inefficient. The major exception would be income-redistribution programs, which should be conducted at the national level.

Werner Z. Hirsch addresses the issue of the optimum city size for providing local public services. Hirsch proposes several criteria to assess whether a particular public service should be provided at the local or the areawide (regional) level. His two major criteria are economies of scale and people-government proximity. For many services these two criteria will conflict. For

---

[1] Wallace E. Oates, "The Effects of Property Taxes and Local Spending on Property Values," *Journal of Political Economy,* vol. 77, 1969.

example, schools may be subject to economies of scale in their operation, suggesting that large jurisdictions should be preferred; on the other hand, to maximize citizen control and input, school districts should be as small as possible.

Hirsch also introduces the concept of spatial spillovers as a factor in determining the optimum size of local jurisdictions. Spillovers occur whenever the costs or the benefits of a service accrue to residents living outside the jurisdiction. In principle, each jurisdiction should be large enough to capture all of these spillovers, otherwise inefficient decisions will be made regarding what level of service to provide.

27 A Pure Theory of Local Expenditures[1]

Charles M. Tiebout presents a simple analysis of local government that has become a classic known simply as The Tiebout Model. Tiebout develops the conditions necessary for local-government expenditures on pure public goods to be efficient. A large body of literature has been inspired by this initial study. Part of the ensuing literature has attempted to test empirically the implications of Tiebout's model.

One of the most important recent developments in the area of "applied economic theory" has been the work of Musgrave and Samuelson in public finance theory.[2] The two writers agree on what is probably the major point under investigation, namely, that no "market type" solution exists to determine the level of expenditures on public goods. Seemingly, we are faced with the problem of having a rather large portion of our national income allocated in a "non-optimal" way when compared with the private sector.

This discussion will show that the Musgrave-Samuelson analysis, which is valid for federal expenditures, need not apply to local expenditures. The plan of the discussion is first to restate the assumptions made by Musgrave and Samuelson and the central problems with which they deal. After looking at a key difference between the federal versus local cases, I shall present a simple model. This model yields a solution for the level of expenditures for local public goods which reflects the preferences of the population more adequately than they can be reflected at the national level. The assumptions of the model will then be relaxed to see what implications are involved. Finally, policy considerations will be discussed.

THE THEORETICAL ISSUE

Samuelson has defined public goods as "*collective consumption goods* ($X_n + 1$, ..., $X_n + n$) which all enjoy in common in the sense that each individual's consumption of such a good leads to no subtraction from any other individual's consumption of that good, so that $X_n + j = X_n^i + j$ simultaneously for each and every *i*th individual and each collective good."[3] While defini-

Reprinted from Charles M. Tiebout, "A Pure Theory of Local Expenditures," *Journal of Political Economy* 64 (October 1956): 416-24 by permission of The University of Chicago Press. Copyright 1956 by the University of Chicago.

[1] I am grateful for the comments of my colleagues Karl de Schweinitz, Robert Eisner, and Robert Strotz, and those of Martin Bailey, of the University of Chicago.

[2] Richard A. Musgrave, "The Voluntary Exchange Theory of Public Economy," *Quarterly Journal of Economics*, LII (February, 1939), 213-17; "A Multiple Theory of the Budget," paper read at the Econometric Society annual meeting (December, 1955); and his forthcoming book, *The Theory of Public Economy*; Paul A. Samuelson, "The Pure Theory of Public Expenditures," *Review of Economics and Statistics*, XXXVI, No. 4 (November, 1954), 387-89, and "Diagrammatic Exposition of a Pure Theory of Public Expenditures," *ibid.*, XXXVII, No. 4 (November, 1955), 350-56.

[3] "The Pure Theory ...," *op. cit.*, p. 387.

tions are a matter of choice, it is worth noting that "consumption" has a much broader meaning here than in the usual sense of the term. Not only does it imply that the act of consumption by one person does not diminish the opportunities for consumption by another but it also allows this consumption to be in another form. For example, while the residents of a new government housing project are made better off, benefits also accrue to other residents of the community in the form of the external economies of slum clearance.[4] Thus many goods that appear to lack the attributes of public goods may properly be considered public if consumption is defined to include these external economies.[5]

A definition alternative to Samuelson's might be simply that a public good is one which should be produced, but for which there is no feasible method of charging the consumers. This is less elegant, but has the advantage that it allows for the objections of Enke and Margolis.[6] This definition, unfortunately, does not remove any of the problems faced by Musgrave and Samuelson.

The core problem with which both Musgrave and Samuelson deal concerns the mechanism by which consumer-voters register their preferences for public goods. The consumer is, in a sense, surrounded by a government whose objective it is to ascertain his wants for public goods and tax him accordingly. To use Alchian's term, the government's revenue-expenditure pattern for goods and services is expected to "adapt to" consumers' preferences.[7] Both Musgrave and Samuelson have shown that, in the vertically additive nature of voluntary demand curves, this problem has only a conceptual solution. If all consumer-voters could somehow be forced to reveal their true preferences for public goods, then the amount of such goods to be produced and the appropriate benefits tax could be determined.[8] As things now stand, there is no mechanism to force the consumer-voter to state his true preferences; in fact, the "rational" consumer will

---

[4] Samuelson allows for this when he states that "one man's circus may be another man's poison," referring, of course, to public goods ("Diagrammatic Exposition ...," *op. cit.*, p. 351).

[5] There seems to be a problem connected with the external-economies aspect of public goods. Surely a radio broadcast, like national defense, has the attribute that A's enjoyment leaves B no worse off; yet this does not imply that broadcasting should, in a normative sense, be a public good (the arbitrary manner in which the level of radio programs is determined aside). The difference between defense and broadcasting is subtle but important. In both cases there is a problem of determining the optimal level of outputs and the corresponding level of benefits taxes. In the broadcasting case, however, A may be quite willing to pay more taxes than B, even if both have the same "ability to pay" (assuming that the benefits are determinate). Defense is another question. Here A is not content that B should pay less. A makes the *social judgment* that B's preference *should* be the same. A's preference, expressed as an annual defense expenditure such as $42.7 billion and representing the majority view, thus determines the level of defense. Here the A's may feel that the B's *should* pay the same amount of benefits tax.

If it is argued that this case is typical of public goods, then, once the level is somehow set, the voluntary exchange approach and the benefit theory associated with it do not make sense. If the preceding analysis is correct, we are now back in the area of equity in terms of ability to pay.

[6] They argue that, for most of the goods supplied by governments, increased use by some consumer-voters leaves less available for other consumer-voters. Crowded highways and schools, as contrasted with national defense, may be cited as examples (see Stephen Enke, "More on the Misuse of Mathematics in Economics: A Rejoinder," *Review of Economics and Statistics,* XXXVII [May, 1955], 131-33; and Julius Margolis, "A Comment on the Pure Theory of Public Expenditure," *Review of Economics and Statistics,* XXXVII [November, 1955], 247-49).

[7] Armen A. Alchian, "Uncertainty, Evolution, and Economic Theory," *Journal of Political Economy,* LVIII (June, 1950), 211-21.

[8] The term "benefits tax" is used in contrast to the concept of taxation based on the "ability to pay," which really reduces to a notion that there is some "proper" distribution of income. Conceptually, this issue is separate from the problem of providing public goods and services (see Musgrave, "A Multiple Theory ...," *op. cit.*).

understate his preferences and hope to enjoy the goods while avoiding the tax.

The current method of solving this problem operates, unsatisfactorily, through the political mechanism. The expenditure wants of a "typical voter" are somehow pictured. This objective on the expenditure side is then combined with an ability-to-pay principle on the revenue side, giving us our current budget. Yet in terms of a satisfactory theory of public finance, it would be desirable (1) to force the voter to reveal his preferences; (2) to be able to satisfy them in the same sense that a private goods market does; and (3) to tax him accordingly. The question arises whether there is any set of social institutions by which this goal can be approximated.

LOCAL EXPENDITURES

Musgrave and Samuelson implicitly assume that expenditures are handled at the central government level. However, the provision of such governmental services as police and fire protection, education, hospitals, and courts does not necessarily involve federal activity.[9] Many of these goods are provided by local governments. It is worthwhile to look briefly at the magnitude of these expenditures.[10]

Historically, local expenditures have exceeded those of the federal government.

---

[9] The discussion that follows applies to local governments. It will be apparent as the argument proceeds that it also applies, with less force, to state governments.

[10] A question does arise as to just what are the proper expenditures to consider. Following Musgrave, I shall consider only expenditures on goods or services (his Branch I expenditures). Thus interest on the federal debt is not included. At the local level interest payments might be included, since they are considered payments for services currently used, such as those provided by roads and schools.

The 1930s were the first peacetime years in which federal expenditures began to pull away from local expenditures. Even during the fiscal year 1954, federal expenditures on *goods and services exclusive of defense* amounted only to some 15 billions of dollars, while local expenditures during this same period amounted to some 17 billions of dollars. There is no need to quibble over which comparisons are relevant. The important point is that the often-neglected local expenditures are significant and, when viewed in terms of expenditures on goods and services only, take on even more significance. Hence an important question arises whether at this level of government any mechanism operates to insure that expenditures on these public goods approximate the proper level.

Consider for a moment the case of the city resident about to move to the suburbs. What variables will influence his choice of a municipality? If he has children, a high level of expenditures on schools may be important. Another person may prefer a community with a municipal golf course. The availability and quality of such facilities and services as beaches, parks, police protection, roads, and parking facilities will enter into the decision-making process. Of course, noneconomic variables will also be considered, but this is of no concern at this point.

The consumer-voter may be viewed as picking that community which best satisfies his preference pattern for public goods. This is a major difference between central and local provision of public goods. At the central level the preferences of the consumer-voter are given, and the government tries to adjust to the pattern of these preferences, whereas at the local level various governments have their revenue and expenditure patterns more or less set.[11] Given these revenue and expenditure patterns, the consumer-voter moves to that community whose local government best satisfies his set of preferences. The greater the number of communities and the greater the variance among them, the closer the consumer will come to fully realizing his preference position.[12]

A LOCAL GOVERNMENT MODEL

The implications of the preceding argument may be shown by postulating an extreme model. Here the following assumptions are made:

1. Consumer-voters are fully mobile and will move to that community where their preference patterns, which are set, are best satisfied.

2. Consumer-voters are assumed to have full knowledge of differences among revenue and expenditure patterns and to react to these differences.

3. There are a large number of communities in which the consumer-voters may choose to live.

4. Restrictions due to employment opportunities are not considered. It may be assumed that all persons are living on dividend income.

5. The public services supplied exhibit no external economies or diseconomies between communities.

Assumptions 6 and 7 to follow are less familiar and require brief explanations:

---

[11] This is an assumption about reality. In the extreme model that follows the patterns are assumed to be absolutely fixed.

[12] This is also true of many non-economic variables. Not only is the consumer-voter concerned with economic patterns, but he desires, for example, to associate with "nice" people. Again, the greater the number of communities, the closer he will come to satisfying his total preference function, which includes non-economic variables.

6. For every pattern of community services set by, say, a city manager who follows the preferences of the older residents of the community, there is an optimal community size. This optimum is defined in terms of the number of residents for which this bundle of services can be produced at the lowest average cost. This, of course, is closely analogous to the low point of a firm's average cost curve. Such a cost function implies that some factor or resource is fixed. If this were not so, there would be no logical reason to limit community size, given the preference patterns. In the same sense that the average cost curve has a minimum for one firm but can be reproduced by another there is seemingly no reason why a duplicate community cannot exist. The assumption that some factor is fixed explains why it is not possible for the community in question to double its size by growth. The factor may be the limited land area of a suburban community, combined with a set of zoning laws against apartment buildings. It may be the local beach, whose capacity is limited. Anything of this nature will provide a restraint.

In order to see how this restraint works, let us consider the beach problem. Suppose the preference patterns of the community are such that the optimum size population is 13,000. Within this set of preferences there is a certain demand per family for beach space. This demand is such that at 13,000 population a 500-yard beach is required. If the actual length of the beach is, say, 600 yards, then it is not possible to realize this preference pattern with twice the optimum population, since there would be too little beach space by 400 yards.

The assumption of a fixed factor is necessary, as will be shown later, in order to get a determinate number of communities. It also has the advantage of introducing a realistic restraint into the model.

7. The last assumption is that communities below the optimum size seek to attract new residents to lower average costs. Those above optimum size do just the opposite. Those at an optimum try to keep their populations constant.

This assumption needs to be amplified. Clearly, communities below the optimum size, through chambers of commerce or other agencies, seek to attract new residents. This is best exemplified by the housing developments in some suburban areas, such as Park Forest in the Chicago area and Levittown in the New York area, which need to reach an optimum size. The same is true of communities that try to attract manufacturing industries by setting up certain facilities and getting an optimum number of firms to move into the industrially zoned area.

The case of the city that is too large and tries to get rid of residents is more difficult to imagine. No alderman in his right political mind would ever admit that the city is too big. Nevertheless, economic forces are at work to push people out of it. Every resident who moves to the suburbs to find better schools, more parks, and so forth, is reacting, in part, against the pattern the city has to offer.

The case of the community which is at the optimum size and tries to remain so is not hard to visualize. Again proper zoning laws, implicit agreements among realtors, and the like are sufficient to keep the population stable.

Except when this system is in equilibrium, there will be a subset of consumer-voters who are discontented with the patterns of their community. Another set will be satisfied. Given the assumption about

mobility and the other assumptions listed previously, movement will take place out of the communities of greater than optimal size into the communities of less than optimal size. The consumer-voter moves to the community that satisfies his preference pattern.

The act of moving or failing to move is crucial. Moving or failing to move replaces the usual market test of willingness to buy a good and reveals the consumer-voter's demand for public goods. Thus each locality has a revenue and expenditure pattern that reflects the desires of its residents. The next step is to see what this implies for the allocation of public goods at the local level.

Each city manager now has a certain demand for n local public goods. In supplying these goods, he and $m - 1$ other city managers may be considered as going to a national market and bidding for the appropriate units of service of each kind: so many units of police for the ith community; twice that number for the jth community; and so on. The demand on the public goods market for each of the n commodities will be the sum of the demands of the m communities. In the limit, as shown in a less realistic model to be developed later, this total demand will approximate the demand that represents the true preferences of the consumer-voters—that is, the demand they would reveal, if they were forced, somehow, to state their true preferences.[13] In this model there is no attempt on the part of local governments to "adapt to" the preferences of consumer-voters. Instead, those local governments that attract the optimum number of residents

[13] The word "approximate" is used in recognition of the limitations of this model, and of the more severe model to be developed shortly, with respect to the cost of mobility. This issue will be discussed later.

may be viewed as being "adopted by" the economic system.[14]

A COMPARISON MODEL

It is interesting to contrast the results of the preceding model with those of an even more severe model in order to see how these results differ from the normal market result. It is convenient to look at this severe model by developing its private-market counterpart. First assume that there are no public goods, only private ones. The preferences for these goods can be expressed as one of n patterns. Let a law be passed that all persons living in any one of the communities shall spend their money in the particular pattern described for that community by law. Given our earlier assumptions 1 through 5, it follows that, if the consumers move to the community whose law happens to fit their preference pattern, they will be at their optimum. The n communities, in turn, will then send their buyers to market to purchase the goods for the consumer-voters in their community. Since this is simply a lumping together of all similar tastes for the purpose of making joint purchases, the allocation of resources will be the same as it would be if normal market forces operated. This conceptual experiment is the equivalent of substituting the city manager for the broker or middleman.

Now turn the argument around and consider only public goods. Assume with Musgrave that the costs of additional services are constant.[15] Further, assume that a doubling of the population means doubling the amount of services required. Let the number of communities be infinite and let each announce a different pattern of expenditures on public goods. Define an empty community as one that fails to satisfy anybody's preference pattern. Given these assumptions, including the earlier assumptions 1 through 5, the consumer-voters will move to that community which *exactly* satisfies their preferences. This must be true, since a one-person community is allowed. The sum of the demands of the n communities reflects the demand for local public services. In this model the demand is exactly the same as it would be if it were determined by normal market forces.

However, this severe model does not make much sense. The number of communities is indeterminate. There is no reason why the number of communities will not be equal to the population, since each voter can find the one that exactly fits his preferences. Unless some sociological variable is introduced, this may reduce the solution of the problem of allocating public goods to the trite one of making each person his own municipal government. Hence this model is not even a first approximation of reality. It is presented to show the assumptions needed in a model of local government expenditures, which yields the same optimal allocation that a private market would.

THE LOCAL GOVERNMENT MODEL RE-EXAMINED

The first model, described by the first five assumptions together with assumptions 6 and 7, falls short of this optimum. An example will serve to show why this is the case.

Let us return to the community with the 500-yard beach. By assumption, its optimum population was set at 13,000, given its preference patterns. Suppose that some people in addition to the optimal 13,000 would choose this community if it were

---

[14] See Alchian, *op. cit.*

[15] Musgrave, "Voluntary Exchange ...," *op. cit.*

available. Since they cannot move into this area, they must accept the next best substitute.[16] If a perfect substitute is found, no problem exists. If one is not found, then the failure to reach the optimal preference position and the substitution of a lower position becomes a matter of degree. In so far as there are a number of communities with similar revenue and expenditure patterns, the solution will approximate the ideal "market" solution.

Two related points need to be mentioned to show the allocative results of this model: (1) changes in the costs of one of the public services will cause changes in the quantity produced; (2) the costs of moving from community to community should be recognized. Both points can be illustrated in one example.

Suppose lifeguards throughout the country organize and succeed in raising their wages. Total taxes in communities with beaches will rise. Now residents who are largely indifferent to beaches will be forced to make a decision. Is the saving of this added tax worth the cost of moving to a community with little or no beach? Obviously, this decision depends on many factors, among which the availability of and proximity to a suitable substitute community is important. If enough people leave communities with beaches and move to communities without beaches, the total amount of lifeguard services used will fall. These models then, unlike their private-market counterpart, have mobility as a cost of registering demand. The higher this cost, *ceteris paribus*, the less optimal the allocation of resources.

This distinction should not be blown out of proportion. Actually, the cost of register-

ing demand comes through the introduction of space into the economy. Yet space affects the allocation not only of resources supplied by local governments but of those supplied by the private market as well. Every time available resources or production techniques change, a new location becomes optimal for the firm. Indeed, the very concept of the shopping trip shows that the consumer does pay a cost to register his demand for private goods. In fact, Koopmans has stated that the nature of the assignment problem is such that in a space economy with transport costs there is *no* general equilibrium solution as set by market forces.[17]

Thus the problems stated by this model are not unique; they have their counterpart in the private market. We are maximizing within the framework of the resources available. If production functions show constant returns to scale with generally diminishing factor returns, and if indifference curves are regularly convex, an optimal solution is possible. On the production side it is assumed that communities are forced to keep production costs at a minimum either through the efficiency of city managers or through competition from other communities.[18] Given this, on the demand side we may note with Samuelson that "each individual, in seeking as a competitive buyer to get to the highest level of indifference subject to given prices and *tax*, would be led as if by an Invisible

---

[16] In the constant cost model with an infinite number of communities this problem does not arise, since the number of beaches can be doubled or a person can find another community that is a duplicate of his now filled first choice.

[17] Tjalling Koopmans, "Mathematical Groundwork of Economic Optimization Theories," paper read at the annual meeting of the Econometric Society (December, 1954).

[18] In this model and in reality, the city manager or elected official who is not able to keep his costs (taxes) low compared with those of similar communities will find himself out of a job. As an institutional observation, it may well be that city managers are under greater pressure to minimize costs than their private-market counterparts—firm managers. This follows from (1) the reluctance of the public to pay taxes and, what may be more important, (2) the fact that the costs of competitors—other communities—are a matter of public record and may easily be compared.

Hand to the grand solution of the social maximum position."[19] Just as the consumer may be visualized as walking to a private market place to buy his goods, the prices of which are set, we place him in the position of walking to a community where the prices (taxes) of community services are set. Both trips take the consumer to market. There is no way in which the consumer can avoid revealing his preferences in a spatial economy. Spatial mobility provides the local public-goods counterpart to the private market's shopping trip.

EXTERNAL ECONOMIES AND MOBILITY

Relaxing assumption 5 has some interesting implications. There are obvious external economies and diseconomies between communities. My community is better off if its neighbor sprays trees to prevent Dutch elm disease. On the other hand, my community is worse off if the neighboring community has inadequate law enforcement.

In cases in which the external economies and diseconomies are of sufficient importance, some form of integration may be indicated.[20] Not all aspects of law enforcement are adequately handled at the local level. The function of the sheriff, state police, and the FBI—as contrasted with the local police—may be cited as resulting from a need for integration. In real life the diseconomies are minimized in so far as communities reflecting the same socioeconomic preferences are contiguous. Suburban agglomerations such as Westchester, the North Shore, and the Main Line are, in

part, evidence of these external economies and diseconomies.

Assumptions 1 and 2 should be checked against reality. Consumer-voters do not have perfect knowledge and set preferences, nor are they perfectly mobile. The question is how do people actually react in choosing a community. There has been very little empirical study of the motivations of people in choosing a community. Such studies as have been undertaken seem to indicate a surprising awareness of differing revenue and expenditure patterns.[21] The general disdain with which proposals to integrate municipalities are met seems to reflect, in part, the fear that local revenue-expenditure patterns will be lost as communities are merged into a metropolitan area.

POLICY IMPLICATIONS

The preceding analysis has policy implications for municipal integration, provision for mobility, and set local revenue and expenditure patterns. These implications are worth brief consideration.

On the usual economic welfare grounds, municipal integration is justified only if more of any service is forthcoming at the same total cost and without reduction of any other service. A general reduction of costs along with a reduction in one or more of the services provided cannot be justified on economic grounds unless the social welfare function is known. For example, those who argue for a metropolitan police force instead of local police cannot prove their case on purely economic

---

[19] "The Pure Theory . . .," op. cit., p. 388. (Italics mine.)

[20] I am grateful to Stanley Long and Donald Markwalder for suggesting this point.

[21] See Wendell Bell, "Familism and Suburbanization: One Test of the Choice Hypothesis," a paper read at the annual meeting of the American Sociological Society, Washington, D.C., August, 1955. Forthcoming in *Rural Sociology*, December, 1956.

grounds.[22] If one of the communities were to receive less police protection after integration than it received before, integration could be objected to as a violation of consumers' choice.

Policies that promote residential mobility and increase the knowledge of the consumer-voter will improve the allocation of government expenditures in the same sense that mobility among jobs and knowledge relevant to the location of industry and labor improve the allocation of private resources.

Finally, we may raise the normative question whether local governments *should*, to the extent possible, have a fixed revenue-expenditure pattern. In a large, dynamic metropolis this may be impossible. Perhaps it could more appropriately be considered by rural and suburban communities.

CONCLUSION

It is useful in closing to restate the problem as Samuelson sees it:

> However, no decentralized pricing system can serve to determine optimally these levels of collective consumption. Other kinds of "voting" or "signaling" would have to be tried.... Of course utopian voting and signaling schemes can be imagined.... The failure of market catallactics in no way denies the following truth: given sufficient knowledge the optimal decisions can always be found by scanning over all the attainable states of the world and selecting the one which according to the postulated ethical welfare function is best. The solution "exists"; the problem is how to "find" it.[23]

[22] For example, in Cook County—the Chicago area—Sheriff Joseph Lohman argues for such a metropolitan police force.
[23] "The Pure Theory ...," *op. cit.*, pp. 388-89.

It is the contention of this article that, for a substantial portion of collective or public goods, this problem *does have* a conceptual solution. If consumer-voters are fully mobile, the appropriate local governments, whose revenue-expenditure patterns are set, are adopted by the consumer-voters. While the solution may not be perfect because of institutional rigidities, this does not invalidate its importance. The solution, like a general equilibrium solution for a private spatial economy, is the best that can be obtained given preferences and resource endowments.

Those who are tempted to compare this model with the competitive private model may be disappointed. Those who compare the reality described by this model with the reality of the competitive model—given the degree of monopoly, friction, and so forth—*may* find that local government represents a sector where the allocation of public goods (as a reflection of the preferences of the population) need not take a back seat to the private sector.

KEY CONCEPTS

average cost function

collective consumption goods

constant returns to scale

cost of mobility

external economies

factors of production

market solution

optimum community size

production function

social welfare function

GEORGE J. STIGLER

28 The Tenable Range of Functions of Local Government

George J. Stigler, a Nobel prize laureate from the University of Chicago, analyzes the efficiency of public service provision for governmental units of different sizes. He argues that redistributional programs should be performed on a national level to avoid the inevitable competition among local communities. However, he argues that smaller-scale communities would perform better on the other economic criteria of economies of scale and satisfying voters' preferences.

The preservation of a large role in governmental activity for local governments is widely accepted as an important social goal. No one can doubt that the individual citizen gains greatly in political dignity and wisdom if he can participate in the political process beyond casting a vote periodically. It is also generally conceded that a good political system adapts itself to the differing circumstances and mores of different localities, or, as I would wish to rephrase it, the system should allow legitimate variations of types and scales of governmental activity to correspond with variations in the preferences of different groups of citizens.

Nor will it be denied that this social goal is being increasingly sacrificed. In 1900, virtually all questions of housing, public health, crime, and local transportation were dealt with exclusively by state or local governments, and the role of the federal government in education, regulation of business practices, control of natural resources, and redistribution of income was negligible. Today the federal government is very active in each of these areas, and its share of responsibility is gradually increasing.

I propose to examine some of the reasons which are given for the growing centralization of political processes. The proper range of activities of government in general will not be raised. Our question is simply this: If the people in a given community wish to embark on a particular governmental policy, when does the efficient discharge of this policy require that it be imposed by a central authority also upon other communities?

In many minor areas of governmental activity no real questions are raised, as yet, about the feasibility of local sovereignty. If a given community wishes to have superb library facilities, it can build and pay for them; if another community wishes instead a skating rink, it may so choose. If individual citizens in any community disagree strongly with the majority preferences, they may move to a more congenial community.

From George J. Stigler, "Tenable Range of Functions of Local Government," *Federal Expenditure Policies for Economic Growth and Stability,* Joint Economic Committee, Congress of the United States (Washington, D.C.: U.S. Government Printing Office, November, 1957), pp. 213-219.

Since governmental functions must often be provided upon a considerable scale to be tolerably efficient in execution, a sufficiently eccentric individual may not be able to find any community with enough like-minded individuals to be able to adopt that series of governmental policies which would exactly suit his taste. For example, he may wish to live in a community with gravel streets and a magnificent observatory, and find no community willing to provide this combination. This sort of limitation is also encountered in consuming the products of private enterprise—I may not find precisely the automobile or typewriter that suits me.

In most areas of governmental activity, however, it is increasingly felt that local governments are inefficient units. When any of three types of governmental activity are sought, it is said that the unit of effective administration must be large in scale—

1. When the object of a regulatory policy can be nullified by the competition of (including migration to) other local governmental units.
2. When the source of revenue of the activity can escape financial responsibility by migration to another unit.
3. When the policy is incapable of efficient performance upon a local scale.

We consider these problems in turn.

THE PROBLEM OF COMPETITION

Suppose that a community wishes to set a high standard of factory safety, and requires the installation of a very expensive safety device. Then the local portion of a much larger industry will be undersold in the common market by factories in other communities, provided they do not also simultaneously set as high standards of safety practices. The local branch of the industry then dies or migrates. These facts can be taken as data for our discussion.

The essence of this argument is that competition, which usually works so well in the area of private enterprise, serves to defeat desirable goals in the area of government. If every governmental unit, save one, were to desire and require elaborate safety devices in the factories of some industry, it is claimed that their desire could be stultified by the presence of the exceptional community which did not have this desire, because the regulated industry would migrate to this community and escape regulation, and the knowledge that it would do so is often enough to prevent the various communities from attempting to regulate it.

It may be remarked that a similar argument is often encountered in the private-enterprise sector. Plants with low wage rates, it is often said, force plants with high wage rates to reduce their wages in order to compete successfully in the common market. In this case the argument is reversible: the plants with high wage rates force plants with low wage rates to raise their wages in order to compete successfully for workers in the common labor market. Both formulations, however, are singularly uninformative, for they do no lead directly to the correct conclusion, which is that the wages of all (similar) workers must approach equality in all plants under competition, and the common wage rate will be governed by the value of the worker's services in those plants which can pay this rate. Can it be that some parallel obscurity attaches to the customary formulation of the unfortunate effect of competition among governments?

The governmental analysis is, in fact,

incomplete. Suppose any community set the required level of safety practices as high as it wishes, and then gave a subsidy to each enterprise in the locality equal to the additional cost that these safety devices imposed upon the enterprises. Then there would be no tendency for the local industry to be handicapped in competition with other areas with lower safety standards, and the community would enjoy more worker safety and less of other things than other communities. If 47 per cent of the localities or 99 per cent of the localities embark upon this policy, then 47 or 99 per cent of the factories will have the desired safety practices, and the nonconformist competitors will not have the slightest tendency to injure or attract these safe and expensive factories.

When a community imposes the safety regulations without giving a compensating subsidy, its troubles arise from the fact that it is seeking to push these higher costs off on consumers, and neither local nor distant consumers wish to assume this burden. The problem of competition resolves itself into an unwillingness of the community to bear the costs of its policy when they are posed as an explicit burden.

A similar analysis holds when the community wishes to require of some consumer good that it be of unusually high quality. If it specifies that only goods of this unusual quality be sold in the community, the producers will be quite eager to meet the specifications—at a remunerative price.

Although it involves a digression, it may be profitable to discuss more generally our example of factory safety devices because the discussion will serve to illuminate the workings of competition in general. If workers are faced with the choice of working in one plant, unequipped with safety devices, at an hourly rate of $1.50 but with expected losses from injuries of 5 cents per hour, and in another plant with safety devices they are offered $1.46 with no expected losses from injuries, we should expect them to choose the latter plant. If under these conditions they do not choose the safer plant, the most probable explanation is that they do not correctly appraise the expected losses from injuries and the remedy is to inform them of the consequences of working in factories unequipped with safety devices. In a fully competitive system the entrepreneurs will supply at cost all the safety devices that the workers demand, and all safety devices which return (to the worker, in terms of reduced injuries) as much or more than the cost will be adopted. It may well be that in this situation there will be safety devices which do not pay but which would reduce injuries further, and that the community as a whole sets a higher value on avoidance of these injuries than the workers themselves do. Some moral philosophers might argue that these workers should set a higher value on the avoidance of injuries, but the workers do not, and in a society with free choice of occupation they cannot be made to pay for more safety than they wish. Hence the society must bear the costs of achieving more safety, and the sole question is whether the costs be borne by consumers through compulsory installation of the safety devices and restriction of supply, or by direct grant from public funds.

The competition of other communities as tax collectors is an important form of the alleged difficulty arising out of competition. Suppose community A wishes to have splendid and expensive schools, streets, housing, poor relief, and what not. If it levies sufficient taxes to finance this elaborate program, a large portion of the tax base (industries and well-to-do individuals) will leave the community while simultaneously a large number of beneficiaries of the generous program may immigrate. The tax rates on the narrower tax base will have to be prohibitive (from the viewpoint of the remaining taxpayers) to finance the sumptuous program.

Again we can accept the facts, with one temporary amendment. Let us assume that the same income is received by every family, and no questions of income redistribution are involved. Will the presence of communities with lower tax rates defeat the ambitions of community A? The answer is clearly in the negative. There will be some redistribution of population among communities: those people who prefer cheaper public services and lower tax rates will move elsewhere, and others with opposite taste will move to A. Competition of communities offers not obstacles but opportunities to various communities to choose the types and scales of governmental functions they wish. The proviso that all family incomes are equal has a vast influence on this argument, of course, and we turn now to income redistribution as a goal.

THE DISTRIBUTION OF INCOME

If all families had equal (real) income, would there be any need for local governmental units? Why could not each city be a private corporation, supplying at a price the services its dwellers demanded? With many, many such corporations, competition would prevent monopolistic pricing, and schooling and police and fire protection would be sold at a price including a fair rate of return on investment. This scheme would obviously be inappropriate where

the service must be a monopoly (like national defense) and probably also where the community size was so large (due to the economic advantages of size) that the communities were too few to rely upon competition, but let us put these instances aside. We are not seeking to prove that there should be no government, but rather to find the logic of government at the multiunit governmental level.

A basic deficiency in this private enterprise organization of social life, we would all agree, is that it allows excessive freedom to the individual. It would allow parents to horsewhip children, and it would create communities populated chiefly with drunkards and drug addicts—although thieves would presumably prefer to live among honest men (even with their policemen) than only with other thieves. Public opinion would curb many undesirable personal actions, but the society would wish to compel observance of its basic values. As a result, we must recognize the need for political units large enough so their numbers include enough normal people to insure the imposition of the society's basic moral standards on local communities. Our states—with 1 or 2 possible western exceptions—meet this condition of statistical large numbers.

The second basic weakness—some will call it a strength—of the private enterprise organization of local government is that it would not permit price discrimination; it does not have the ability to redistribute income. The purely competitive organization of local services would make it impossible for a local government to obtain money from the rich to pay for the education of the children of the poor, except to the extent that the rich voluntarily assumed this burden.

How can local governments cope with

this problem? If 99 communities tax the rich to aid the poor, the rich may congregate in the hundredth community, so this uncooperative community sets the tune. Here competition does not perform with its usual excellence, for competition is the system calculated to organize only voluntary activity.

What is the correct amount of redistribution of income in light of the society's desires? It is more than the unrestricted competition of tax-free colonies of the rich would allow, but less than the most aggressively egalitarian community would desire. The decision must be in some sense a national decision, for the proper amount of redistribution, even if rich and poor were chained to their communities, could not depend upon the accidents of income composition of a particular community. And once this level of redistribution is set, no one community may complain if its rich citizens migrate when it seeks to go above this level of distribution unless the society is prepared to let the most egalitarian community set the scale of income redistribution.

Since redistribution is intrinsically a national policy, it should not be restricted to a community level; a community consisting only of poor people should receive the desired minimum social services. Hence, in pure principle, the federal government should collect the progressive levies and redistribute them (in whole or in part) to local units with each unit receiving an amount governed by the number of its poor and the degree of their poverty.

Given this system of tax revenue redistribution, the local governments could still be allowed to perform any function which they were competent to perform efficiently. One community might choose to spend more on schools and less on hospi-

tals than another, but this is surely an area of legitimate freedom; there is no "correct" distribution of expenditures among such functions.

In a society which has no serious program of income redistribution (even as a means to the attainment of minimum goals), local governments would face no basic revenue problems because of competition.[1] It is in keeping with this argument that a century ago almost all functions were local and the problem of competition for the tax base was negligible. With an appropriate fiscal system we could restore these revenue considerations to a position of unimportance even in an era of extensive income redistribution. There still remains the question of whether the local governments could efficiently perform the enlarged range of functions that modern governments have assumed. We turn now to this question.

THE ECONOMIES OF SCALE

How large must a governmental unit be to perform efficiently the activities which the public wishes governments to perform? This is an area which deserves much more attention than it appears to have received, and the following remarks are highly tentative.

There are a set of functions which are intrinsically national because they are indivisible. The greatest of these is national defense, and it would be ill-served if each state or local unit were to undertake the defense of its own area. One may cite also foreign relations, the national governmental

[1] Perhaps a qualification should be entered with respect to the growth of taxable wealth that escapes a general property tax. In England the desire of property owners to ease their tax burdens was a force in the emasculation of local government; see E. Cannan, *The History of Local Rates in England*, second edition, 1912, ch. VI.

machinery, and the control of relationships among lower governmental levels.

In addition to such traditional functions, one may list certain functions which are or can be performed at a local level but which must be coordinated to achieve efficiency in their design. The transportation systems of localities must take some account also of the needs of long-distance transportation. The radio and television stations of various localities must not jam one another. These are functions which in the economist's language, have large external economies or diseconomies accruing to the areas which do not participate in their execution, so it is essential that they be formulated (although not necessarily administered) on a larger area than the local government.

We should reserve for the federal government those functions which are much more efficiently discharged on the largest scale. When local performance involves large duplication, it is inefficient. Thus it seems undesirable to have 48 estimates of wholesale prices since the price movements in most regions will be parallel; on the other hand, the calculation of cost-of-living indexes might suitably be removed from the BLS to the states.

The optimum scale of performance has tacitly become identified with the national, or at least the state, scale almost without examining the nature of the governmental functions under discussion. This seems most surprising to the student of industrial organization; he is accustomed to finding that the activity in an industry with a complex technology is usually efficiently conducted by a firm smaller by almost any measure than the government of a town of 25,000. Is there some special characteristic of governmental functions that makes large units necessary to efficiency?

Only one characteristic seems a possible candidate for this role: the great variety of functions performed by even the small governmental units. The lack of specialization is pronounced even though political scientists complain of a multiplicity of overlapping local units (many of which were established to evade tax or debt limits on local units). Some of these functions can be performed efficiently on a very small scale. Many of the most distinguished private schools and colleges are much smaller than the school system of a town of 5,000 people. Others are more varied. A police department can efficiently control local traffic on a small scale; in one sense it must be worldwide to have an efficient "missing persons" bureau.

But this variety of function is not really unusual. Every enterprise must use goods and services, or produce goods or services, which must be produced or sold on a much wider scale than the enterprise itself can undertake. Even a huge department store is not large enough to make its own delivery trucks, or to print the newspapers in which it advertises. Just as cooperation in these matters is brought about by the price system, so cooperation among governmental units has been developed—and could be carried much further—to avoid the determination and execution of all public functions by that government unit which is most efficient in conducting the function with the largest scale of operation.

It happens, as we have already noticed, that one function of paramount importance must be conducted on a very large scale: the collection of revenues designed to redistribute income. Much centralization, in fact probably most centralization, has been a consequence of this situation. A central government is loathe to make grants without exercising a degree of control over the local units which disburse the funds. No degree of control less than 100 per cent, however, is sufficient to guarantee local performance exactly as the central authorities wish it, and there is no obstacle except tradition to slow down their gradual extension of controls.

The case for imposing controls over the smaller units receiving grants, however, is far from general. The central disbursing authority has no monopoly of wisdom. The state boards of education have imposed a series of certification requirements on local teachers, for example, that have done much to lower the quality of elementary education in the United States. When central governments have superior civil servants, as they often do, the cause lies more often in their control of finance and authority than in the advantages of centralization. It may be true that when most administrative units are small the ablest men cannot conduct affairs on the largest scale, but this seems an odd consideration to give weight in setting the functions of local governments in a democracy. More often the complexity of the tasks at the national level has reached such levels that not the ablest men can control them efficiently.

If grants were given to local governments without supervision, there would be some instances of gross neglect or venality and more variety in the quality of the performance of public functions. We should also expect to find that much of this variety was eminently sensible, and that many types of experimentation would constantly be embarked upon by the more venturesome and the more foolish communities—with large social benefits from both the successes and the failures.

If we give each governmental activity to the smallest governmental unit which can efficiently perform it, there will be a vast resurgence and revitalization of local government in America. A vast reservoir of ability and imagination can be found in the increasing leisure time of the population, and both public functions and private citizens would benefit from the increased participation of citizens in political life. An eminent and powerful structure of local government is a basic ingredient of a society which seeks to give to the individual the fullest possible freedom and responsibility.

KEY CONCEPTS

economies of scale

income redistribution

intercommunity competition

intergovernmental grants

WERNER Z. HIRSCH

29 Local Versus Areawide Urban Government Services

Werner Z. Hirsch, of the University of California, Los Angeles, applies several economic and political criteria—scale economies, political proximity, and geographical spillovers—to determine the optimum size of an urban governmental unit with respect to local service provision. In most cases the criteria conflict, some calling for small-scale jurisdictions, while others point to a large-scale jurisdiction. Hirsch attempts to balance the importance of each criteria and to reach some tentative conclusions concerning optimum government size.

INTRODUCTION

Urban governments provide a variety of services which are rendered by units of varying size, some having a single responsibility and others multiple responsibilities. What criteria can be advanced to help decide whether small local governments should perform a particular service or whether areawide provision should be favored? How could these criteria be applied to decide which urban government services are better performed on a local and which on an areawide basis; and which of the services that favor local operation should be given subsidies by higher levels of government, and why? These are some of the questions that I will attempt to elucidate and, in part, answer.[1]

Reprinted with permission from the *National Tax Journal* 17 (December 1964): 331-39.

[1] The author would like to express his appreciation to Drs. Norman Beckman, Marjorie C. Brazer, Lazlo Ecker-Racz, Selma J. Mushkin, Sidney Sonenblum and Charles M. Tiebout and Messrs. Clifford LaZar and Morton J. Marcus for their helpful comments and suggestions. Needless to say, all are accorded complete discharge from responsibility.

In certain respects this paper was stimulated by a report of the Advisory Commission on Inter-Governmental Relations, "Performance of Urban Functions: Local and Areawide."[2] The Report proposed the application of seven criteria to fifteen urban government services. The criteria may best be summarized in the following manner:

1. spillover minimization
2. scale economy maximization
3. geographical area sufficiency
4. legal and administrative ability
5. functional sufficiency
6. controllability and accessibility by constituents
7. maximization of citizen participation consistent with adequate performance

The Commission Report recognizes that these criteria may yield conflicting results, and it therefore states that "it is seldom

[2] Advisory Commission on Inter-Governmental Relations, *Performance of Urban Functions: Local and Areawide* (Washington, D.C., September 1963), 281 pp.

possible or desirable to weight each criterion equally in every instance. Instead they must be balanced, one with the other, to decide in each case which are important for the particular function or situation."[3]

In short, the Commission Report employs some implicit, highly subjective balancing of competing criteria to rank urban government services on a scale of "most local" through "most areawide" services.

CRITERIA AND PROCEDURE

We suggest considering separately the physical rendering of urban government services on the one hand and their financing on the other. The first is concerned with operating a program and the second with raising the funds to meet accompanying expenditures. Clearly, under political and fiscal federalism it is quite common that a given service is performed by one unit of government, while some or all of the financing is the responsibility of a larger unit. For example, in the case of public education a school district is responsible for operating the schools, while the state provides parts of the financing.

With this distinction in mind, we will first discuss three major groups of criteria which can guide in the decision whether a certain urban government service is best performed on a local or areawide basis. They are economic considerations (scale economy), political considerations (people-government proximity), and administrative considerations (multi-functional jurisdictions sufficient in scope to resolve conflicting interests).

Thereafter we will examine welfare criteria, which bear on the decision whether a

given service is to be financed locally or its tax base extended over a larger geographic area. We propose to meet welfare considerations with the aid of fiscal devices for governments of appropriate size. The optimum operational government size is determined on the basis of the other three criteria, explicitly applied in proper succession.

SCALE ECONOMY

Certain programs are carried out more efficiently on a large scale than on a small scale. In a few instances the opposite can be true, while in others scale of operation is unimportant. The scale phenomenon has been of interest to the economist for many years. Initially his concern was with economies of scale in the private sector of the economy.[4] In more recent years his interest has included the public sector.[5] Both theoretical and empirical inquiries reveal a distinct difference between the two sectors. Scale economies are much less common in the public than in the private sector for two reasons. First the location of many urban government services must be user oriented, since they cannot be rendered efficiently over large distances. Examples are fire protection, police protection, and primary education. Second, urban government services are labor intensive services so much so that wages and salaries are the

---

[3] *Ibid.*, p. 6.

[4] Arthur R. Burns, *The Decline of Competition* (New York: McGraw-Hill, 1936), 619 pp.; Joel Dean and R. Warren James, *The Long-Run Behavior of Costs in a Chain of Shoe Stores* (Chicago: University of Chicago Press, 1942); Raymond G. Bressler, "Transportation and Country Assembly of Milk," *Journal of Farm Economics* (February 1940), pp. 220-224.

[5] Werner Z. Hirsch, "Expenditure Implications of Metropolitan Growth and Consolidation," *The Review of Economics and Statistics* (August 1959), pp. 232-241; Harvey E. Brazer, "Factors Affecting City Expenditures," *Proceedings of the Fiftieth Annual Conference of the National Tax Association* (1957), pp. 437-443; Harvey Shapiro, "Economies of Scale and Local Government Finance," *Land Economies* (May 1963), pp. 175-186.

dominant budget item. But when labor is hired centrally, it does not lend itself to pecuniary economies.

From the economist's point of view, criteria 2-4 in the Commission Report involve mainly scale economy considerations. These include the effects on the shape of the long-run cost functions of physical as well as legal and administrative characteristics of an area.

Based in part on a number of economic studies, it appears that the following urban government services are likely to enjoy major economies of scale: air pollution control, sewage disposal, public transportation, power, water, public health services, hospitals and planning.[6] The other urban government services are likely to enjoy only minor, if any, economies of scale as long as we are concerned with government units of more than 50,000 inhabitants (see Table 1). This classification is not to deny the fact certain specialized higher education and library facilities can incur scale economies, which, however, appear to be the exception compared to the major education and library expenditures.

PEOPLE-GOVERNMENT PROXIMITY

In determining whether a local or areawide unit should be assigned a given urban government service, political issues loom large. In a democracy we are concerned both with active participation of citizens in the operation of government and with the need to obtain a consensus that leads to action. These two political considerations

[6] Walter Isard and Robert Loughlin, *Municipal Costs and Revenues* (Wellesley: Chandler-Davis, 1957), 111 pp.; Werner Z. Hirsch, *op. cit.*, pp. 232-241; Harvey E. Brazer, *op. cit.*, pp. 437-443; Harvey Shapiro, *op. cit.*, pp. 175-186; Marc Nerlove, *Returns to Scale in Electricity Supply* (Stanford: Institute for Mathematical Studies in the Social Sciences, 1961), 53 pp.

TABLE 1

Urban Government Services Favoring Local vs. Areawide Operation

Service	Important Scale Economies Can Be Expected	Political Proximity Is Considered Essential
Air pollution control	Yes	No
Sewage disposal	Yes	No
Transportation	Yes	Yes and No
Power	Yes	No
Water	Yes	No
Public health services	Yes	No
Hospitals	Yes	No
Planning	Yes	Yes and No
Education	No	Yes
Libraries	No	Yes
Public housing	No	Yes
Public welfare services	No	Yes
Police protection	No	Yes
Fire protection	No	Yes
Refuse collection	No	No
Neighborhood parks and recreation	No	Yes and No
Urban renewal	No	Yes and No
Street maintenance	No	No

can be inconsistent with one another. A good example is planning. Here, while an effective dialogue between citizen and official can make for enlightened and responsible government action, it can also lead to chaos and often has led to inaction.

Proximity of people to government can help in the prevention and exposure of graft; it can promote new avenues of operation, improved management practices, greater efficiency and better services. It can insure that change is evolutionary rather than revolutionary. In short, an effective citizen-consumer feedback into the government sector can produce better services for the same amount of expenditures than could be obtained in its absence.

Services for which close citizen participation is particularly important include education, libraries, public housing, welfare services, police protection and fire protection. Here the advantages of close proximity far outweigh the disadvantages. Then there is a group of services for which proximity appears of little consequence and therefore need not be assured. These are air pollution control, sewage disposal, power, water, public health services, hospitals, refuse collection and street maintenance.

Finally, with regard to a small number of services, proximity has mixed benefits, as citizen participation enriches democratic procedure but at the same time tends to prevent decisive socially desirable action from being taken. Examples are transportation, planning, parks and recreation, and urban renewal.

In Table 1 these services have been grouped in terms of whether proximity between people and government is considered essential (Yes), essential in one respect but not in another (Yes and No), or inconsequential (No).

MULTI-FUNCTIONAL JURISDICTIONS

Perhaps the separation between political proximity and administrative comprehensiveness is somewhat artificial. Both bear on effective government action. However, the Commission Report looked at the two issues separately and we find a certain advantage in doing so, too. The Report is concerned with multi-functional sufficiency of government jurisdictions and urges: "Every unit of government should be responsible for a sufficient number of functions so that its governing processes

involve a resolution of conflicting interests, with significant responsibility for balancing governmental needs and resources. Thus, in the jurisdictional allocation of individual functions, there is an ever present danger of creating so many separate entities as to result in undemocratic, inequitable, and inadequate assignment of priorities."[7]

Clearly this criterion can be inconsistent with that of scale economies, since in the abstract each and every service is likely to favor operation at different scales. Likewise, there can be some inconsistency with the "closeness of people to their government" argument. The most we can hope to do is to assign to a given government unit a number of services with similar scale-economy and political-proximity characteristics.

WELFARE CONSIDERATIONS

There are two main criteria which should help determine who should pay for urban government services. These are spatial benefit (and cost) spillovers and income redistribution.

In line with the Commission Report we propose to relate spatial benefit spillovers to the financing of services. While we will not agree to have benefit spillovers affect the choice of whether a service is rendered by a local or areawide government, we will examine spillover characteristics to determine what level of government should assume financial responsibility.

Government services differ as to their spatial cost and benefit spillovers. If any portion of the costs or benefits resulting from services provided in one urban government jurisdiction is ultimately realized

[7] Advisory Commission on Inter-Governmental Relations, *op. cit.*, p. 6.

by residents of another, we speak of spatial cost or benefit spillover. The flow can move in both directions—into the jurisdiction and out of it. In the first case we have spillins and in the second, spillouts. If major spillins and spillouts occur and are not offset by one another, welfare inequities and malallocation of resources can result.

The problem of equity and resource efficiency can be stated as follows. Inequities come about when a community's tax burdens exceed benefits or vice versa. If the net benefits do not vary inversely with income, the system does not meet the test of fiscal progressivity.

Maximizing resource allocation efficiency means that marginal social benefits should coincide approximately with marginal social cost. But social benefits or costs do not always coincide with community benefits or costs. If this happens, the community will tend to behave in a socially non-optimum manner. Specifically, the community will tend to underinvest if its ratio of marginal benefits to marginal costs is less than the corresponding ratio anticipated for the nation as a whole from expenditure in the community. Likewise, when the community's ratio of marginal benefits to costs exceeds that of the nation, there is a tendency to overinvest. Such discrepancies can result from either spatial cost or benefit spillovers, or both spillovers, at disparate rates.

Our position with regard to the equity issue will be that, as income redistribution is mainly the responsibility of the federal government, all urban government services which do not play an important income redistribution role are to be largely financed according to the benefit taxation principle. In this way, resource allocation efficiency is fostered. If benefit spillovers are such that the local tax system cannot provide a cost spillover pattern which neutralizes them, higher levels of governments can provide subsidies to correct the situation. In doing so, hopefully, we could come close to meeting the benefit taxation principle, even if local government jurisdictions are quite small.

Government units, especially if they are small, can encounter both major cost and benefit spillovers. Benefits spill over because either a beneficiary or a service crosses the boundaries of a jurisdiction; costs spill over because of a spatial tax incidence. Clearly benefit spillovers will differ depending on the services. However, this is not true in relation to spatial cost spillovers which mainly depend upon the type of taxes levied to finance them.

There is some empirical evidence that benefit spillovers can be large and do not neutralize cost spillovers.[8] Little can be done to change the spatial benefit spillover pattern, although cost spillovers can be readily affected by rearranging the intergovernmental fiscal relations. Our strategy, therefore, will be to identify those services for which major benefit spillovers can be expected, as well as identify their geographical dimensions, and suggest that fiscal arrangements be made which are consistent with equity and efficiency objectives[9]. We will consider a community of 50,000-100,000 citizens as the base unit from which major spatial spillovers do or do not occur.

Conclusions about the extent of benefit spillovers, by their very nature, are some-

[8] Werner Z. Hirsch, Elbert W. Segelhorst and Morton J. Marcus, *Spillover of Public Education Costs and Benefits* (Los Angeles: Institute of Government and Public Affairs, University of California, 1964), 465 pp.

[9] When a government is responsible for a number of services, as is favored by administrative comprehensiveness considerations, it would be sufficient to balance aggregate benefit and cost spillovers of all the services.

what subjective. We offer the following thoughts.

Relatively little, if any, spatial benefit spillover would be expected in relation to power, water, libraries, public welfare services, police protection, fire protection, refuse collection, and parks and recreation. Major benefit spillovers could be expected in relation to air pollution control, sewage disposal, transportation, public health services, planning, education, urban renewal, hospitals and street maintenance, not necessarily in that order. For example, the benefit spillovers of urban renewal, public housing and hospitals often will extend only into parts of the metropolitan complex; those resulting from air pollution control can extend into an entire basin, sometimes covering a metropolitan complex plus the surrounding countryside; and the benefit spillover of education, because of widespread migration of educated persons throughout the country, is likely to cover the entire country, if not the entire world. The size of the spillover area indicates the proper unit for fiscal interrelation.

The second major criterion for deciding on the level of government that should finance part or all of a service's costs is income redistribution. The federal government, which by a broad consensus has been assigned the income redistributing function, has pre-empted the major tax with income redistributing characteristics—the personal income tax. Of the eighteen urban government services listed, only five have important income redistributing qualities—education, public welfare, public housing, public health services and hospitals—and their financing should be delegated, at least in part, to the federal government.[10]

[10] Actually, it is debatable whether subsidized public housing offers an efficient way to bring about income redistribution.

Table 2 summarizes our tentative conclusions as to which of the eighteen urban government services can be expected to entail only few spatial benefit spillovers and which ones entail major spatial benefit spillovers. It also indicates which services have important income redistribution characteristics and which ones do not. (See above.) The spatial benefit (and cost) spillovers of urban services merely require a geographic tax base similar to the major spillover area. Except for education, this area seldom exceeds a handful of counties.

APPLYING THE CRITERIA

We have argued that under political and fiscal federalism, welfare objectives, which

TABLE 2

Urban Government Services Favoring Local vs. Areawide vs. Nationwide Financing

Service	Major Benefit Spillovers Can Be Expected	Income Redistribution Plays an Important Role
Air pollution control	Yes	No
Sewage disposal	Yes	No
Transportation	Yes	No
Power	No	No
Water	No	No
Public health services	Yes	Yes
Hospitals	Yes	Yes
Planning	Yes	No
Education	Yes	Yes
Libraries	No	No
Public housing	Yes	Yes
Public welfare services	No	Yes
Police protection	No	No
Fire protection	No	No
Refuse collection	No	No
Neighborhood parks and recreation	No	No
Urban renewal	Yes	No
Street maintenance	Yes	No

are complicated because of major spatial benefit (and cost) spillovers and income redistribution objectives, can be attained with the aid of carefully selected intergovernmental fiscal arrangements. These arrangements, however, need not be considered in the search for the proper government unit to operate service programs. We will start by concentrating on the non-welfare considerations.

Our approach will be to assign to large operating units those services which promise to benefit in a major way from economies of scale, unless we expect major losses to result from lack of people-government proximity and/or major administrative difficulties due to an insufficient number of different services controlled by that unit. Thus we will start by singling out those services for which major economies of scale can be expected, examine them in the light of the criterion of people's closeness to government and hopefully end up with a sufficient number of services favoring large government units so that the multifunctional administrative comprehensiveness criterion is met.

In a somewhat similar manner we will deal with the group of services devoid of major economies of scale. Each of them appears to meet our political criterion, and if there are enough services favoring the same size government unit, the administrative criterion is also met.

Finally, we will have a look at the financing problem. We will examine that group of services which appears to lend itself to local operation and see which of them because of benefit spillover and/or welfare considerations, deserve to be financed in part or *in toto* by larger governments.

When this procedure is applied, two groups of urban government services emerge. The first group promises to benefit from major economies of scale as the population exceeds 50,000-100,000 while the second group appears not to have such advantages. Of the first group, air pollution control, power, sewage disposal, water, public health services and hospitals do not appear to require close proximity between people and government. In the case of planning and transportation the picture is not so clear. While citizen's participation may be desirable here it can frustrate action. In the absence of clear proximity advantages, we are inclined to be guided by scale economies. Some of these eight services could be assigned to one and the same government unit and thus also meet the administrative requirement, that is, provision by a multifunctional unit which can help resolve conflicting interests. For example, planning, electric power, water, hospital and public health services can be provided by county government. Topography and population distribution may favor sewage disposal, air pollution control and transportation to be assigned to a government unit which is larger than a single county. However, each situation would have to be analyzed on its merits and the advantages and disadvantages of alternative arrangements investigated and compared. In general, financing could be done by the same unit that provides the service.

The second group appears unlikely to incur major scale economies if handled by units of more than 50,000-100,000 inhabitants. These are education, libraries, public housing, public welfare services, police protection, fire protection, refuse collection, parks and recreation, urban renewal and street maintenance. Some of them favor proximity between people and government, while others do not. However, all of these services can be provided by local governments, especially if they are not smaller than 50,000 inhabitants.

Certain problems may arise in our three-fold classification of services. There is some evidence that economic considerations favor somewhat larger high school and junior college districts over primary school districts. At the same time, there are distinct advantages in having all education vertically integrated and a compromise is needed on the district's size.

Another problem relates to refuse collection and disposal. While refuse collection appears to benefit from relatively minor economies of scale, disposal with the aid of incinerators appears to incur scale economies. Thus, while refuse collection can be provided by a local government, disposal might be on an areawide basis.

Turning next to the financing issue of the group of services which favor local operation, the following conclusions suggest themselves—education, welfare services, public housing, public health services and hospitals have considerable income redistribution characteristics and therefore should be subsidized by federal, and perhaps to a minor extent, by state, government. Benefit spillovers of urban renewal, public housing and street maintenance can extend over much of the metropolitan complex or county and they could be financed on these levels. Finally, an examination of the services favoring district financing suggests that in the case of water and air pollution the affected areas may not want to cooperate and federal funds may have to be used as an inducement.

CONCLUSION

The preceding analysis suggests that local urban governments, particularly if they serve 50,000-100,000 citizens, can effectively provide education, library service, public housing, public welfare services, fire and police protection, refuse collection, parks and recreation, urban renewal and street maintenance programs. Income redistribution considerations favor that education, welfare services, public housing, public health services and hospitals, while provided locally, be financed by governments which rely heavily on progressive income taxes—the federal government and to a minor extent, state governments.

Services which appear to be best provided on an areawide basis are air pollution control, sewage disposal, transportation, power, public health services, water, planning and hospitals. Most of these services often can be both rendered and financed by county governments, although topography and population distribution can favor the first three to be the responsibility of multi-county units, possibly in the form of multi-purpose districts. Urban renewal and street maintenance can be provided by municipalities with some subsidies from county governments.

If we compare these conclusions with the existing state of affairs in the United States, we find, surprisingly much harmony. This in itself is an astonishing conclusion. Insofar as local governments are concerned, our analysis indicates that many should become somewhat larger than they are today. This statement, however, is quite different from the call heard so frequently a few years ago urging wholesale metropolitan consolidation.

We should make a greater effort to have more of our urban governments serve no less than 50,000 residents and possibly as many as 100,000—but not more than 250,000.[11] Such an arrangement offers many economic, political and administrative

[11] The Royal Commission on local government in greater London recommended local government units with 100,000-250,000 residents (Sir Edwin Herbert, *The Reorganization of London's Government*, a paper read to the University of California Conference on the Metropolitan Future, September 26, 1963).

advantages and yet provides for a maximum of choice by citizens.

Many urban areas have not, to a sufficient extent, created those multipurpose districts advantageous for air pollution control, sewage disposal and transportation, and more ingenious federal and state inducements may have to be developed. Finally, federal subsidies to public education should be extended and preferably more federal funds directly applied to education.

Altogether, while we have still some way to go before rational assignments of local and areawide operating and financing responsibilities are completed, we appear to be well on our way. Our present system is not as illogical and irresponsive to need as is so often claimed.

KEY CONCEPTS

benefit principle of taxation

long-run cost functions

marginal social benefits (costs)

multi-functional jurisdiction

people-government proximity

scale economies

spatial spillovers

vertical integration

PART *8*

URBAN POLICY ISSUES

The readings in this section suggest the full scope and range of urban economics, a field whose boundaries are constantly being shaped. The readings were chosen because of the high level of current interest in these topics and also because they deal with troublesome public-policy issues.

Poverty was not always regarded as an exclusively urban problem, but today the incidence of poverty tends to be highest in the nation's central cities. Moreover, as the President's National Urban Policy Report shows, the incidence of poverty in central cities is growing even though it is apparently declining in other areas. The President's report attempts to analyze the causes of the growing concentration of poverty in large central cities. One contributing factor appears to be that central cities are heavily populated by minority and female-headed households, groups that tend to experience the highest unemployment rates. The report also finds a strong correlation between a city's overall employment growth rate and its poverty level. Cities with positive population growth tend to experience both a higher rate of job growth and a lower incidence of poverty.

The report poses several difficult policy issues for decision makers. For example, poor residents of central cities demonstrate no special tendency to migrate to areas where employment growth is better. This finding bears on the question of whether public policy should attempt to develop the ghetto and to bring jobs to the core city.

Equally difficult policy issues are posed by the air, water, and noise pollution afflicting many urban areas. Pollution results when markets fail to achieve efficient resource allocation due to the presence of external costs. W. Lee Hoskins poses the following question: What approach will achieve pollution-abatement goals with the minimum use of scarce resources? The normal policy approach has been for the government to impose direct regulations uniformly on all polluters. Hoskins points out the serious economic disadvantages inherent in this approach. He then presents the economic case for using the price system, where possible, to internalize the costs of pollution.

Another disturbing problem that plagues urban areas and lowers the quality of life is crime. Major crime rates in the largest metropolitan areas are often double those in smaller cities; moreover, central-city crime rates are often double those in the suburbs. Like poverty and pollution, crime has come to be identified as an urban problem.

In recent years, many urban police departments have been forced to respond to rising crime rates armed with smaller budgets. Like other local-government agencies, the police have been forced to look for ways to improve services with fixed or declining resources. Stephen L. Mehay analyzes two major approaches that are often recommended to improve the efficiency of police services. The first approach is to apply economic techniques, such as cost-benefit analysis, and then use the information gained to determine actual trade-offs confronting the police. This approach assumes that the police should analyze the full social benefits and costs of alternative methods and programs to combat crime. While in principle this approach should improve efficiency, in practice measurement problems and a lack of data pose serious obstacles. Moreover, and perhaps more important, while this approach improves the information available to decision makers, it does not compel officials to act on the information.

Mehay argues that a market approach may be necessary to alter the incentive structure facing police officials. This approach involves levying prices when feasible on police services or contracting out police services to private (or other governmental) suppliers. These techniques would introduce some of the same mechanisms that keep private firms efficient—competition, prices, markets, and profits.

Finally, Kenneth A. Small analyzes some factors affecting the future pattern of urban development. Many experts have argued that rising fuel prices will raise the cost of commuting so much that suburbanites will begin moving back to the central city. Small simulates the likely effects of dramatic increases in fuel prices and concludes that the stimulus to "recentralization" of metropolitan areas will be slight. Instead, he forsees the evolution of metropolitan areas into numerous suburban centers rather than the revival and growth of older central cities.

30   The Poor and the Jobless in the Central City

Poverty not only diminishes individual dignity and well being, but also imposes fiscal burdens on government. Poverty in the United States has continued to decline each year, except in the central cities where during the previous decade it has been growing. This excerpt from the President's National Urban Policy Report *attempts to explain why central cities that are surrounded by growing affluence contain growing proportions of poor people. The explanation focuses on shrinking economies and employment opportunities in central cities, especially for minorities and female-headed households. In addition, the reading introduces the community need index.*

Today, nearly four in every ten poor Americans live in a central city. Over one in every seven central city residents is poor—and in some of the larger cities with troubled economies, the proportion of poor persons exceeds one in five. Furthermore, these figures understate the relative severity of large city poverty. This occurs because national poverty standards don't vary by region or location, while living costs are often 10% to 25% higher in large central cities.

Why has poverty substantially increased in large central cities, particularly in those characterized as needy and declining? This is the difficult question this chapter seeks to answer. The response is framed primarily in terms of three factors: first, these cities disproportionately house minorities and female-headed households who are more often underemployed and poorly paid; second, these poverty-prone families find it especially difficult to work their way out of poverty in the shrinking job markets of

Reprinted from the U.S. Department of Housing and Urban Development, *The President's National Urban Policy Report*, 1980.

needy cities; finally, these cities continue to lose relatively affluent residents.

The standard Federal poverty measure used by the Bureau of the Census and many other Federal agencies identifies who is poor in terms of annual income for families of various sizes. The most commonly cited figure is the annual income for a family of four persons. As of 1979, non-farm families of four persons were classified as poor if their annual income fell below $7,412. This income figure includes transfer payments such as welfare but excludes the value of in-kind assistance such as food stamps.

THE GROWING CONCENTRATION OF POVERTY IN THE CENTRAL CITY

... The number of poor living in central cities rose by almost 3 percent between 1969 and 1976. In the largest central cities the rate of increase was 8 percent. These absolute increases in poor residents occurred at the same time that total central city population was declining. As a result, the poor became a significantly larger fraction of all central city residents. This was reflected in sharp increases in the poverty rate. Rising poverty rates had serious consequences for needy communities. They often faced increased social service burdens simultaneous with losses of jobs, affluent households, and tax base.

During the same period, many suburbs and non-metropolitan communities enjoyed a declining poverty population. Overall the suburbs sustained major population growth from 1969 to 1976 while the number of poor persons fell by 4 percent.

Who Are the Central City Poor?

The poor people who live in central cities are not a cross-section of all Americans. To a disturbing degree, they are:

1. *blacks and other minorities.* Although blacks make up about 22% of the population of the nation's central cities, they make up 45% of the central city poor. By 1976, central cities housed 55% of all poor blacks in the United States, up from 48% in 1969. This reflects the increasing urbanization of blacks. While the white poor living in cities declined in numbers from 1969 to 1976, the number of central city black poor rose by 12%. All of the increase in black poor took place in the central cities of metropolitan areas larger than a million population. For large central cities, the number of poor blacks increased 21% during this seven year period. Equally noteworthy, the poverty rate for blacks increased significantly (17%) for large central cities, while showing a marked decline in suburbs (−27%), non-metropolitan areas (−27%), and even in smaller central cities (−10%).

2. *families with female heads.* Families with female heads are more frequently poor than those with male heads. In 1976, nearly two in every five central city families headed by a woman fell below the poverty line. In the seven years after 1969, the number of poor female-headed families in large central cities rose by more than 50 percent. During the same time period, central city poor families headed by males declined. As a result, by 1976 female-headed families accounted for nearly two-thirds of all poor families in large cities.

The highest rates of poverty are for central city households headed by black females. Black female-headed families living in large central cities are almost twice as likely to be poor as are white female-headed families; 51% of the families headed by black women had below-poverty incomes in 1976, compared to 27% of the families headed by white women. Both the rate of poverty and the total number of black families headed by women is growing. From 1969 to 1976, the number of poor black families headed by women rose by almost two-thirds in large central cities. The 1980 census may well reveal a doubling in the number of such impoverished families over the decade.

Cities with High Poverty and Unemployment

Almost all of the growth of poverty in large central cities during the 1970s occurred among needy central cities. This is suggested by Table 1. Philadelphia, Detroit, Baltimore, New York, and Chicago—all needy central cities—experienced sharp increases in the poverty rate after 1970. On

TABLE 1

Change in Rate of Poverty for Large High- and Low-Need Central Cities: 1969 to 1976–78

| | Poverty Rate | | Average Annual Growth of: | |
	1969	1976–1978	Population, 1970–1976	Jobs, 1970–1977
High Need				
New York	14.6%	18.2%	-1.0%	-2.4%
Detroit	14.6	15.7	-2.2	-4.4
Chicago	14.3	21.0	-1.5	-2.8
Philadelphia	15.1	20.8	-1.3	-1.7
Baltimore	18.1	21.3	-1.7	-1.7
Low Need				
Dallas	13.4	11.9	0.1	2.5
Houston	14.0	12.2	3.4	6.1

| | Poverty Rate | |
	1969	1977
Type of City		
High need, population decline	15.8%	20.7%
Low-moderate need, population decline	13.1	12.0
Low-moderate need, population growth	12.2	11.7

Source: HUD Census Tapes; Special Tabulations *Current Population Survey* (March 1976, March 1977, and March 1978); employment estimates provided by Semour Sacks (HUD Urban Data Reports, Number 1).

the other hand, the poverty rate in Dallas and Houston—both low need cities—declined. As a group, high need cities with declining populations witnessed a 31% growth in the rate of poverty from 1969 to 1977, while less needy cities with expanding economies achieved reductions in poverty. By 1977, the neediest cities reflected a rate of poverty of 20.7%, about 75% above that for declining or growing cities with lesser need (see Table 1). In 1969, by contrast, disparities in poverty rates between high and low need communities were significantly smaller.

A lack of employment opportunities is closely related to central city poverty. In central cities where jobs grew more rapidly than population, the level of poverty is typ-

ically low and falling. Conversely, in cities where job opportunities shrank relative to population, poverty is usually on the rise. High unemployment is also generally associated with above-average rates of poverty. Further, most of the cities with high and increasing rates of unemployment are needy cities with shrinking job opportunities. Unemployment rates in high need central cities with relatively large poverty populations average well over one and a half times those in non-distressed cities. In 1978, for instance, unemployment rates in high need cities such as Detroit, New York, Philadelphia, and Buffalo were between 8 and 10 percent compared to rates of about 4 percent in Dallas and Houston, low need cities whose economies were expanding.

The Special Problem of Youth

Unemployment levels among urban youth, and especially among black youth, tend to be much higher than among adults. March 1977 data for central cities of metropolitan areas with over 1 million population show unemployment rates for black youth aged 16-19 at the extremely high rate of 52.6%, compared to an 18.0% rate among white youth of the same age. For blacks aged 20-24, the rate was 31.4% compared to an 11.4% rate for whites.

The causes of this serious employment problem for black youth are complex. Clearly, the decline in the availability of low and semi-skilled entry level jobs in large central cities has not helped. Further, growing competition for the available jobs from other entrants in the labor force, including illegal immigrants and adult women, has perhaps limited job opportunities. Educational inadequacies, racial discrimination, low household income, and family problems have also contributed to black-white disparities. The growing numbers of black youth in central cities probably have intensified their labor market difficulties. From 1970 to 1977 the number of central city black youth aged 18-24 grew by 27% and the number aged 14-17 rose by 16%.

THE COINCIDENCE OF PEOPLE AND PLACE POVERTY

When families who are likely to be victims of poverty live in central cities that are economically distressed, their economic opportunities are doubly constrained. As has already been shown, central city poverty is disproportionately concentrated among families that are black and whose heads are women.... Central city econo-mies have tended to lose in the job competition with suburbs and non-metropolitan areas and these losses have been most serious in the distressed central cities of the Northeast and Midwest. When the problems of people and place coincide—as they do for many poor families—opportunity is drastically foreclosed and the threat of poverty is sharply increased.

Census survey data suggest further significant differences in black poverty rates across types of city. The findings accord with the city unemployment, labor force participation, and female heads of household data reported earlier. In needy and declining cities, nearly 60% of poor blacks do not participate in the labor force. For less needy cities, 25-30% of poor blacks do not participate. Consequently, household earnings of the black poor in high need, declining cities are less than half those in less needy cities. This indicates that the poor or near poor in most needy cities are much less likely to earn their way up the income ladder than if they live in less needy central cities.

... For the largest cities the net difference in unemployment levels for blue and white collar workers tends to be greater in high need and declining cities than in low need cities. While blue collar workers tend in all cities to have higher levels of joblessness, the severe manufacturing losses of the older Northern and Midwestern industrial centers have created disproportionate employment problems for cities located in these regions. This is especially true when the surrounding metropolitan area is suffering job declines as well and where the job composition shifts from low to high technology, and from manufacturing to services.

Several studies of urban households have

found that the economic conditions of a city affect the personal economic performance of otherwise similar households. One such study related the poverty experience of families to the age, experience, and skills of the head of household as well as to the unemployment rate in the county in which they lived. For persons on the borderline of poverty, the study found that those living in high unemployment communities were significantly more likely to be poor than were similar persons living in areas with low unemployment. For instance, a household headed by a black male in a high unemployment area was two-thirds more likely to be poor than a comparable household in a low unemployment community. For households headed by females, poverty was 50% more frequent in high unemployment areas. Thus, a community's condition apparently influences the ability of otherwise similar households to escape poverty. Another analysis of welfare dependency found that controlling for household characteristics, the likelihood of a household going on welfare was much greater in areas where unemployment rates were high or where the number of unskilled jobs was less than the number of potential applicants for such jobs.

Mobility of the City Poor

Migration for increased economic opportunity is a classic American pattern. It was a major factor in building the great industrial belt cities of the nation during the nineteenth and early twentieth centuries when millions of European immigrants crowded into city slums in search of a better life. In a more recent period, millions of rural Americans moved from the South and Puerto Rico in search of urban jobs.

Unfortunately, there is little evidence at the present time that the poorest families from the most distressed central cities are migrating in large numbers to other parts of the metropolitan area or to other economically stronger areas of the nation. This is in sharp contrast to the clear evidence of major national population movements from cities to suburbs and non-metropolitan areas, and from distressed areas of the North and Midwest to the nation's growth centers in the South and West.

Illegal Immigration

During the 1970s, the most publicized group of lower income urban migrants has been illegal aliens from developing countries such as Mexico. Their numbers are estimated to be from 3 to 6 million persons and to be increasing by at least one quarter million yearly. The cities attracting great numbers of illegal aliens—Los Angeles, New York, and the border towns of Texas and California—are cities where large numbers of their fellow countrymen already resided in 1970. Some growing cities, such as Houston, do not appear to attract substantial numbers of legal or illegal aliens.

Illegal aliens are perhaps less numerous than legal resident aliens, who are estimated to total 6 million and to be increasing by 400,000 yearly. Unlike newly arrived legal immigrants, who often are sponsored by American relatives or bring professional skills to the American job market, the illegal aliens are generally poor and frequently possess few skills. Yet millions have found employment, often in large urban centers. The question, then, is do they find opportunities that their unskilled American counterparts do not seek, thereby strengthening the local economy, or do illegal aliens generate increased social burdens by displacing American citizens from low-skilled jobs, thereby increasing unemployment rates? Also, because of their relatively low incomes, do they impose a special burden on services and housing for low income residents overall?

An analysis of illegal aliens requires more than the usual caution about the quality of the data. However, the weight of the evidence indicates that illegal aliens at present provide a net benefit to local economies. Specifically, most seem to take relatively low paid jobs that many low income citizens no longer are willing to accept. Their indirect taxes and service-charge payments probably exceed the costs they impose on public services. Only if family formation increased or if illegal aliens were unable to find work would the public cost-benefit ratio shift from positive to negative. Though they might raise the price level of low income housing somewhat, they may also lessen the rate of abandonment in cities losing households and generate improvements in the "filtered out" housing stock.

CENTRAL CITY-SUBURBAN INCOME GAP

While poverty has become more concentrated in central cities, migration trends have widened the income gap between central cities and suburbs. Families moving from a central city to a suburb on the average have higher incomes ($20,770 in 1978) than those moving to a central city from a suburb ($19,410) or a nonmetropolitan area ($16,570). Over time, these differentials have widened the city-suburban income gap. In 1969, central city median family income was 83% of suburban family income; by 1977, it had decreased to 79%.

Data gathered for the 20 largest SMSAs show that high need cities with declining populations experience the largest city-suburb income gaps, and these gaps have been widening (see Table 2). In 1969 Newark's median family income was only 60% of its suburbs'; its average for the 1975-1977 period was even lower (42%). Between 1969 and 1975-1977, median family income declined as a percentage of suburban family income in St. Louis from 79% to 57%; in Philadelphia, from 89% to 71%; and in Chicago, from 76% to 66%.

Low need, stable or growing cities apparently experience smaller city-suburban income gaps, and these gaps have shown less change over time. Median family income in Houston decreased relative to that of its suburbs by only three percentage points between 1969 and 1975-1977, from 93% to 90%. In Dallas, it increased by two percentage points from 93% to 95%.

Per capita income differentials between cities and suburbs are narrower than family income differentials, but follow the same pattern, being more pronounced in high need, declining cities than low need, growing cities. They also generally showed less change in the city-suburb income gap in the 1969 to 1975-1977 period.

Median family income in central cities has failed to keep pace with inflation, unlike family income in the suburbs. Between 1969 and 1977, central city family income increased 57.1%, while the Consumer Price Index rose 65.3%. Suburban family income rose by 65.6% in the same period, just keeping pace with inflation.

These central city-suburban income differentials have serious consequences for the welfare of poor people and the cities in which they reside. Central cities experiencing declines in family income relative to their suburbs and relative to the rate of

TABLE 2

Ratio of City-to-Suburb Family Income, for the 20 Largest SMSAs: 1969, 1975 to 1977

Degree of Resident Need	Population Trend	Metropolitan Area	Ratio of City-to-Suburb Family Income		Change in Income Gap
			1969	Average 1975–1977	
High	Decreasing	Newark	.60	.42	−.18
High	Decreasing	St. Louis	.79	.57	−.22
High	Decreasing	Atlanta	.72	.62	−.10
High	Decreasing	Baltimore	.74	.63	−.11
Moderate	Decreasing	Washington, D.C.	.69	.63	−.06
High	Decreasing	Cleveland	.72	.64	−.08
High	Decreasing	New York	.71	.64	−.07
High	Decreasing	Chicago	.76	.66	−.10
Moderate	Decreasing	Milwaukee	.82	.67	−.15
High	Decreasing	Philadelphia	.89	.71	−.18
High	Decreasing	Detroit	.60	.74	+.14
Moderate	Decreasing	San Francisco-Oakland	.81	.74	−.07
Low	Decreasing	Minneapolis-St. Paul	.82	.74	−.08
Low	Decreasing	Seattle-Everett	.90	.74	−.16
High	Stable	Boston	.76	.79	+.03
Moderate	Decreasing	Pittsburgh	.88	.84	−.04
High	Stable	Los Angeles-Long Beach	.93	.90	−.03
Low	Increasing	Houston	.93	.90	−.03
Low	Increasing	Anaheim-Santa Ana-Garden Grove	.86	.95	+.09
Low	Stable	Dallas	.93	.95	+.02

Source: Larry H. Long and Donald C. Dahlmann, "The City-Suburban Income Gap: Is It Being Narrowed by the Back-to-the-City Movement?" U.S. Bureau of the Census, Special Demographic Analyses, COS-801-1, March 1980.

inflation have relatively less capacity to raise revenues and meet the service needs of their residents. This can only increase the outward movement of their middle income residents and reduce the long-run economic prospects of the poor, unless offsetting and ameliorating steps are taken.

SUMMING UP: THE CHANGING NATURE OF URBAN POVERTY

The 1970s saw poverty increase in the largest central cities of the nation, particularly in those cities whose economies were troubled by loss of employment opportunities. The lack of economic opportunities in large cities characterized by high levels of resident need and declining total population appears to be a major factor underlying the increase in poverty in such cities. Within large cities the population groups most afflicted by poverty were blacks and female-headed households. Families headed by black women were most at risk of being poor. Black youth experienced very high levels of joblessness.

Growing poverty levels in the largest and

neediest central cities stood in sharp contrast to declining poverty levels in smaller cities, the suburbs and non-metropolitan areas. Yet, there is little evidence that poor residents of large needy central cities migrate to communities with expanding opportunities in significant numbers, in order to improve their earnings and quality of life. . . .

CLASSIFYING COMMUNITIES BY DEGREE OF COMMUNITY NEED

In recent years, the process of classifying major urban centers into a limited number of categories that measure degree of distress has been advanced as a means of improving our understanding of urban change and helping frame policy responses. Indices of central city need have been used by the Joint Economic Committee of the Congress, the Committee for Economic Development, the Congressional Budget Office, the Brookings Institution, and the Department of Housing and Urban Development.

Most of these approaches to ranking or measuring community needs rely on similar indicators of social, economic, and fiscal distress. These include:

income characteristics, including per capita income or the poverty rate.

economic characteristics, including the rate of change in the number of jobs and the extent of unemployment or underemployment.

fiscal characteristics including expenditures for different kinds of services, relative and absolute growth of tax base, relative and absolute tax burdens, and such proxies as age of housing.

population trends, measured as the absolute or relative population increase or decrease over a recent period.

There is no precise agreement on exactly which factors to include in an urban needs index or concerning what weights to assign to each. As a result, while most of the indices of urban need show agreement on a broad group of very needy and relatively less needy central cities, because of the different perspectives of their formulators, the indices differ on the relative ranking of some cities. . . .

The fact that different indices of distress result in somewhat different rank order listings does not mean that one method is right and the others wrong. Each provides useful insights into some of the complex characteristics of urban communities. Clearly, there is much to be learned about the limitations and utility of different indicators of distress and different ways to use indicators to define distress. Among the aspects that must be investigated further are: methods of defining change measures; the effects of combining several factors into a single needs measure; the interrelationships among different indicators of social, economic, and fiscal need; the ways in which the measures change over time; and the relative attention that should be given to measures that focus on a city's residents as compared to those that measure conditions within the geographic area of the city.

A typology or classification scheme has been developed for this Report. To the extent possible, it measures community need based on indices illustrating varied problems faced by community residents and indices reflecting community growth patterns. Both sets of indices are important. The first characterizes income levels and trends; the second, population change. Together they provide an approximation of a community's economic and social well being as well as its general fiscal capacity.

Resident Need

Four measures are used to define resident problems and the general ability of a community to respond to such problems. They are [listed in Table 3].

Each measure records or illustrates possible household problems. Collectively, they reflect trends in local conditions, particularly with respect to poverty and income. They also suggest the current burdens on a community with respect to neighborhood deterioration and community services. Finally, because income growth and pov-

erty are related to local fiscal strength, they indicate a community's ability to respond to local problems with its own resources.

Unfortunately, most measures of resident need suffer from shortcomings related to age and reliability of data. Clearly, the measures used to construct the resident need index, described above, are not without problems. For example, only the unemployment data are current. Even these data must be used with caution, given methodological difficulties associated with their collection.

But because the measures are used in a composite manner, they appear appropriate. Their pluses outweigh their minuses and use of all four together mitigates defects of individual measures. They, as indicated in later pages, help explain varied kinds of community distress better than most similar measures. They help establish linkages among economic, demographic, and social phenomena occurring in each community.

The poverty measure was allocated the heaviest weighting because it directly measures the concentration of low income households—those residents whose needs for public services tend to be greatest. It also provides a base (1969) upon which to estimate through more current measures the level of income and the rate of income change. Unemployment data provides a useful recent measure of the overall economic health of the community and its ability to provide residents with jobs. All of the measures used in the index indicate a community's fiscal health.

Developing the Needs Categories

Based on the measures described above and the weights assigned each measure, a

TABLE 3

Four Measures of Resident Need

Indicator	Weight
(1) Percent of population below the poverty level in 1969: Measures relative level of poverty population, and generally indicates the population in need of assistance.	40%
(2) Net growth of per capita income for 1969-1975: Records absolute growth of income in a community and average income level.	20%
(3) Percentage growth of per capita income from 1969-1975: Indicates relative growth of income.	20%
(4) Unemployment in 1978: Reflects job availability and provides an indicator of general economic health.	20%

resident needs index was calculated for each of the nation's 377 central cities. Cities were individually ranked in order of need and the list was divided approximately as follows:

The 30% of cities with the greatest need were categorized as having "Relatively High" need.

The 30% of cities with the lowest need, were classified as having "Relatively Low" need.

The remaining cities were characterized as having "Moderate" need.

KEY CONCEPTS

city-suburban income gap

community need index

people-versus-place poverty

poverty standard

31 Pollution, Prices, and Public Policy

Many urban areas face problems of environmental pollution. To solve these problems public authorities typically have relied upon government regulations and direct controls—the brute-force method. W. Lee Hoskins of Pittsburgh National Bank discusses economic facts of pollution and expresses the view, shared by most economists, that the brute-force method is normally uneconomical and that any given environmental objective can be achieved at lower cost by explicitly using the price mechanism. The author discusses two frequently advocated pricing schemes: pollution taxes and markets for pollution rights.

When Adam cast aside that first apple core in the Garden of Eden, he could hardly have known that the tendency of future generations to emulate this act would ultimately lead to a serious problem for his twentieth-century offspring. Yet millions of apple cores and megatons of other assorted refuse later, man finds himself straining the capacity of his skies, waterways, and lands as he forces them to assimilate the by-products of material progress and population growth.

Man cannot entirely wipe out pollution. Nor should he try. A little pollution is a "good thing" from society's point of view, since the cost of returning the environment to its pristine purity may well require stone-age living conditions. Man, however, can choose the quality of environment or level of pollution he desires if he is willing to pay for it. Air is free; clean air is not. Although the economics of the problem will not be the sole consideration affecting

From W. Lee Hoskins, "An Economic Solution to Pollution," *Business Review* of the Federal Reserve Bank of Philadelphia (September 1970), pp. 3-12. Adapted by W. Lee Hoskins.

man's choice of environmental quality, it certainly is a necessary ingredient in evaluating alternative measures for achieving various levels of pollution.

POLLUTION AND SCARCITY

An indomitable fact of life marking man's trek through time is scarcity. There are, and always have been, an unlimited number of competing uses to which man can devote his limited resources. Hence, even the wealthiest nation in the world cannot have all it wants of everything. Choices must be made. The pollution problem is eye-watering testimony to this pervasive and inescapable fact. A higher-quality natural environment can be had only at the cost of something else, perhaps a different mix of goods and services.

Man takes the resources of the earth and converts them into products that yield services. Although he may change the form of the resources, he cannot destroy them. Resources simply do not depart from earth and its atmosphere during the processes of production and consumption. Some are stored in the form of products—houses, factories, cars—that yield services. (The U.S. economy, for example, accumulates 10 to 15 percent of its annual material input in this fashion.)[1] A very small amount is recycled back into products. The greatest portion is returned to the environment, in its altered form, where it is stored while nature begins the task of breaking it down.

With the increases both in population and quantity of production, we are putting these "altered resources" or pollutants back into our skies, waterways, and lands at a rate so fast that they cannot be assimilated without creating increasingly harmful effects. The assimilative capacity of our natural environment is itself a scarce resource.

GETTING THE MOST FOR SOCIETY

The U.S. economy relies primarily on private incentives and consumer wants expressed through a competitive market process to settle problems posed by scarcity. The underlying notion behind this form of economic organization is simply that individuals in their role as consumers and producers attempt to achieve a more preferred position for themselves by putting their privately owned resources to uses most highly valued by society as a whole; that is, resources are put to socially desirable uses in the appropriate amounts. This notion works surprisingly well in a market-oriented economy when most of the costs and benefits associated with resource use are concentrated upon the person doing the producing or consuming. All the information needed to make the system work is provided by the often-maligned "market price."

Market Price: Provider of Information

The process works this way. Competitive prices are signals that direct the flow of resources to uses most highly valued by society as a whole. And consumers play the dominant role in determining which uses are most highly valued by bidding up the prices of goods they prefer more of relative to those they prefer less of. As a result, relative market prices reflect the tastes and desires, or values, consumers attach to having additional units of each good.[2] This information about society's tastes and desires is essential, for it tells producers where to direct resources.

Profit-seeking producers are important cogs in the workings of the system. Noticing a change in relative market prices (or anticipating one), a sharp-eyed producer bids resources away from the lower valued uses and directs them to the production of goods for which consumers have expressed a desire. His incentive to do this is an increase in wealth. But, as production expands, a point will be reached where the additional resources are going to cost the entrepreneur more than they can add to his return. He will stop producing goods that use these resources before that point is reached, if he is interested in achieving the largest return possible. Hence, market prices provide producers with both the necessary information and incentive to

---

[1] Robert I. Ayres, and Allen V. Kneese, "Production, Consumption, and Externalities," *American Economic Review* (June 1969), p. 285.

[2] More specifically, a consumer, taking account of his own tastes and wealth, tries to get the most for his money. How does he do this? He does this by spending his money so that the last dollar spent on an additional unit of a particular good represents the same personal value to him as that of the last dollar spent on any other good. All consumers doing likewise bid up the price of some goods that they prefer more relative to others that they prefer less. These relative market prices reflect the value society attaches to additional units. For example, if the price per pound of steak is twice that of hamburger, then the last pound of steak that an individual buys must be desired by him twice as much as the last pound of hamburger purchased.

insure that resources flow to uses most highly valued by society. And, as a consequence, any rearrangement of society's output would leave it worse off.[3]

Pollution:
The Uncounted Cost

Unfortunately, market prices do not always accurately refect the total costs of production and consumption to society. Why? One reason is that many important costs of using resources are not brought to bear on the individual making the consumption or production decision. As a result, the private cost associated with his use of resources differs from the social cost. It is this difference that gives rise to the pollution problem. For example, if the owner of a car had to pay the full cost of driving his car, including reparation for the damage he imposes on others in society by disposing of the gaseous wastes into the air, he would likely drive less. Resources would then tend to flow into other modes of transportation, such as mass transit, as they rose in value relative to the automobile. But auto drivers dump exhaust fumes, without charge, into the air. Since this residual affects other people, including the unborn, unfavorably, the social costs end up being greater than the private payments incurred by automobile owners.[4] People now drive cars more than they would if they had to pay the full cost of operating them. Hence, undesirably high levels of air pollution occur.

A key to lower levels of pollution is the removal of the wedge between private and social costs. One method of knocking this

wedge loose is to cause individuals to bear most of the consequences associated with their use of resources. This can be done by expanding our market system to include environmental products. Another method, which characterizes present attempts at pollution control, is to prohibit or regulate certain uses of resources that lead to the divergence between social and private costs. The method chosen will determine how much we must ultimately pay for a cleaner environment and the degree to which we are successful.

PRESENT CONTROLS:
AN INFORMATION GAP

Currently, lawmakers rely primarily on government regulations. They have passed zoning restrictions that prohibit some uses of property in certain geographical areas and have set air and water pollution-control standards in other locales. The tremendous problems associated with employing these direct controls make it clear why such laws have more often than not appeared to be unenforceable, uneconomical, and doomed to failure.

Direct pollution controls face two main problems. First, the level of pollution must be decided upon; second, techniques and incentives for achieving the goal must be implemented.

What Level of Pollution?

Complete elimination of most types of pollution is impossible. The hobgoblin, scarcity, means that cleaner air or water can be had only by giving up something else. Outdoor recreation, fresh air, and longer lives are things people enjoy, but so are powerful cars, electricity for heating and lighting, and cigarettes. The problem is to find the socially desired mix of these goods. But, since clean air, for example, has no market

---

[3] This statement takes as given the current distribution of wealth, that markets are competitive, and that individuals using resources bear all the consequences of their use.

[4] There would be no divergence between social and private costs if each producer and consumer compensated someone for all costs associated with their production or consumption.

price to provide information about its value to society, pollution fighters have no guide as to the level of pollution to seek. It might be possible to ask people how much they are willing to give up or pay for cleaner air or water. But everyone is for a much cleaner environment when only talk and not his wallet is involved. A truthful response may also be a scarce good.

The all-too-common chanting of facts, such as the amount of raw sewage dumped into rivers, is like crying in the wind. We need to know the gains to be had from reducing the discharge and what they cost. But gleaning this information is, in fact, a major problem of pollution control. On some of these costs, we can put dollar values. For example, if acid in our waterways reduces the operating life of boats and barges by 20 percent, one portion of the cost of polluted rivers is 20 percent of boat and barge expenditures. Closer to home are the additional expenditures on cleaning, laundering, and air conditioning that people incur as a consequence of polluted air. However, many other costs are more difficult to measure in dollar-and-cents terms—impairment of human health, wildlife and recreation loss, and everyday discomforts, such as smarting eyes. And these intangibles may be quite large relative to the measurable costs.

Of course, if the costs and gains—including those in the future—are known, a pollution-control agency would not have to select an arbitrary level of reduction.[5] The appropriate level of pollution would be where the additional cost of lowering the level of pollution begins to surpass the additional gains from the lower level. While the rule itself is simple, it often seems to be left on the shelf when debate waxes hot on serious social issues. Nevertheless, control agencies must make decisions with this rule in mind.

A Problem of Information and Incentives

Once the decision is made as to what is an appropriate level of pollution, the control agency must find a way to implement and enforce the decision.[6] Regulation through direct controls is one solution, but it may be an expensive one. If an agency wants to reduce air pollution in a metropolitan area by 5 percent, for example, it could simply require all sources to reduce pollution by 5 percent. Such a rule would be, among other things, grossly inefficient, for the total cost of reducing each source by 5 percent would be greater than the total cost of reducing the overall level by 5 percent. For example, it may be cheaper to reduce emissions of certain factories by 80 percent than to cut back auto emissions by 1 percent. The economist's decision rule is that the last dollar spent on controlling each pollution source should yield the same gain. To administer such a rule successfully, the control agency would have to have an enormous amount of facts about costs associated with controlling each source. Since obtaining this information is itself an expensive business, especially because it is always changing because of improved technology, the control agency would make its decisions with only rough estimates, giving up some portion of efficiency in the process.

Direct controls pose additional problems. For example, specific antipollution devices

---

[5] Such costs and gains can only be estimated. In addition, there is the problem of selecting the "right" discount rate to apply to future costs and gains.

[6] For a more detailed explanation of the problems associated with direct controls and cost estimation, see Larry E. Ruff, "The Economic Common Sense of Pollution," *Public Interest* (Spring 1970), pp. 73-78.

may be required or standards may be set allowing polluters to decide for themselves the cheapest method of meeting the standard. Neither method provides incentives to reduce pollution other than the threat of prosecution. In addition, both require constant inspections. Also the question of fairness arises. Why should automobile owners in North Dakota be forced to purchase manufacturer-installed control devices because the smog in Los Angeles is bad?

Another route might be to let the government (you and me) pay for keeping pollution down by building major treatment plants and subsidizing the cost. But this method would provide no incentive to reduce pollution; indeed, it would actually encourage it, since firms would pay nothing to dispose of unwanted by-products.

Finally, a pollution tax may be levied on polluters in order to achieve the desired level of pollution. The idea is that if an individual is charged for the cost of disposing of his junk, he tends to produce less of it. Now this alternative has possibilities, since it can induce a desire to curb pollution.[7] But administrators of such a program also suffer from a lack of appropriate information; namely, who should be taxed and how much in order to achieve the chosen level of pollution.

Public decision makers faced with pollution-control decisions can never be expected to duplicate the quality of resource-valuation information contained in a market price. Consequently, they must make decisions about pollution control with low-quality information that provides them with only rough ideas about pollution costs and benefits. In addition, they face the problem of giving polluters incentive to cut back—a necessary ingredient if long-run success is to be achieved. However, the quality of information received, the incentive system, and the consequent decision about controlling pollution can be greatly improved depending on how government alters the rights to resource use or chooses to control pollution.

BACK TO THE PRICE MECHANISM

An alternative to the present policies and techniques of controlling pollution, which often appear to be less effective than desired, is the extension of the market system to include environmental products, such as clean air and water. Expansion of the market system to deal with pollution requires the definition of rights to use environmental resources and the provision of a method for exchanging such rights.

"Everyone's Property is No One's Property"

Pollution most frequently occurs or is conveyed through air, rivers, lakes, oceans, and commonly owned lands, such as public parks and streets. In most cases, rights to use these resources are held by all of us in common or are simply unspecified by law. When rights to resources are vague or held in common, the rule is "first come, first served." A person has less incentive to maintain the purity of a lake or stream when he does not have the right to capture the value from doing so. Water in a private lake tends to be put to its highest-valued uses (including those in the future) when the owner stands to gain. If the owner can capture that value by selling the

---

[7] A gasoline tax may result in less gasoline being purchased and, hence, may reduce air pollution. But no incentives are provided to gasoline manufacturers to reduce the pollutants in their products (although a tax on lead in gasoline may provide such incentives). Nor do car owners have incentive to install control devices. Furthermore, the same level of air pollution may be achieved at less cost by muzzling another source.

lake, he has an incentive to protect the quality of the water. Unfortunately, no such incentive exists for our commonly owned air, water, and land. As a result, these resources are not being put to uses most highly valued by society—they are "overconsumed" (polluted), while other goods are "overproduced." One means of coping with this problem is to specify salable property rights in our commonly owned resources.

Selling rights to resource use provides a built-in mechanism for bringing any side effects associated with resource use home to the user's roost. For example, a homeowner's property is salable, so he stands to gain in the form of increased property value from favorably impressing other people by planting pansies or painting the house. In fact, he is induced to impress them. These side effects are *internalized* or brought to bear on his decision on how to care for the property. Conversely, beer cans and old tires scattered about an owner's property are also "internalized," and they are reflected in a lower property value. The fact that the rights to goods or property can be sold or rented forces owners to take account of the harmful or beneficial effects on others associated with using the goods or at least be aware of the gain forgone by not doing so. An important function of property rights or the rights to use resources is that of giving people incentive to internalize these side effects.

Substituting individual rights to resource use for common ownership has been a common practice. For example, the overstocking of grazing land was greatly reduced by replacing common land ownership with assigned rights to use the land. Today, common rights to land use consist primarily of parks and roads that incidentally suffer from a form of pollution—congestion.

Common ownership of air and water have remained intact because the cost of specifying rights to their use and then buying and selling them may have been greater than the expected gain. Now because of the increasing damage of pollution, the situation seems to be reversed.[8]

This does not mean that government, with pollution-control standards, has no role to play. Indeed, only government can create and enforce rights. Moreover, some types of pollution currently may be too costly to be solved by delineating property rights, so control standards may be the best alternative. But, by reducing the amount of common property rights so that the price system can resolve conflicts in resource use, the area in which control standards must be applied can be greatly reduced.

For Sale:
Rights to Pollute
There are a number of ways to employ a price-based control mechanism to reduce pollution. In most cases, they involve the sale of a right to use resources (see Box 1).

[8] If property rights could be costlessly exchanged and enforced, there would be no divergence between social and private costs, and undesirably high levels of pollution would not exist. An important circumstance that keeps pollution from being "internalized," and hence reduced, is that the cost of enforcing and exchanging rights to use property is greater than the gain from doing so. Just think of the cost involved in safeguarding your home from noise pollution, for example. Each passing airplane and loud car damages the physical attributes of your property and may cause it to decrease in value. (Notice the loss in market value of homes when an airport or auto race track is put into operation nearby.) Yet it would be a costly business to detect, catch, and bargain with every plane and car owner who bombarded your home with noise. Because of this, noise-makers are not induced to take account of the cost imposed on others when producing noise even if they could cheaply muffle it. The moral of the story is that the more expensive it is to enforce the laws pertaining to property rights, the more such rights will be violated. When enforcement and exchange costs are high, the end result is that the private cost of operating noisy airplanes or cars does not reflect accurately the cost to society. If homeowners could cheaply enforce the exchange rights, less noise would be produced by passing cars and airplanes, and prices of homes would more accurately reflect their value to society.

BOX 1

A POLLUTION MARKET

Let's put a price on pollution. As a starting point, the pollution-control agency for a particular region would calculate the tons of wastes dumped into the atmosphere and water during the previous year. Since some wastes cause more damage than others, an "equivalent ton table" must be drawn up. The control agency would then print up "Rights to Pollute" based on the number of equivalent tons emitted in previous years and require that polluters who wish to use the atmosphere or waterways to dispose of wastes purchase the appropriate number of rights. Population growth and increases in the number of plants operating in the region would drive the price of the rights up over time. The higher price would provide added incentive to cut down on pollution. For example, if a car owner (driving a particular model that, on the average, emits one equivalent ton of pollution per year) is faced with higher priced pollution rights, he may choose to change to a model with a lower emission rating, stop driving, or modify his car with a device that will provide a lower emission rating.

Besides providing strong incentives to reduce pollution by imposing its *full cost* on the polluter and the reduction in the quantity of information necessitated by direct controls, this system would offer a means of choosing the desirable level of pollution for the region. If people desire a lower level of pollution and are willing to pay for it with higher-priced pollution rights, they can make their feeling known by voting. The control agency could be required to allow the public to vote on the equivalent tons of pollutants to be released into the environment that year. A smaller number of tons would mean higher prices for pollution rights. One advantage of this method over stronger direct controls is that the costs are explicit, and the higher-priced rights can be directly related to the vote for a lower level of pollution.

This market system also offers conservation groups, anti-pollution associations, and individuals the chance to fight pollution by purchasing rights and holding them off the market. This would have a twofold effect: (1) the amount of wastes dumped into the region would be less by the amount of rights purchased; and (2) the price for the remaining rights would be higher, thus providing additional incentives to reduce pollution (which may result in the closing of plants that are heavy polluters).

A price-based system of controls attacks a major problem of pollution abatement: lack of power by the regional agency. Getting municipalities to join and agree to a regional pollution-control plan is often difficult, if not impossible. The fact that the pricing system of control can generate a sizable pool of loot to be divided among the participants can be a persuasive inducement for getting together. The workings of such an alternative for controlling water pollution are presented in detail by J.H. Dales, "Pollution, Property and Price" (Toronto: University of Toronto Press, 1968), pp. 77-97.

One way would be to allow the control agency to set prices on pollution, such as 10 cents per pound for industrial wastes discharged into a waterway or 20 cents per unit of sulfur dioxide emitted into the air. Of course, the price in principle should reflect the costs to society of the extra units discharged. However, any positive price would tend to reduce pollution. The more dangerous to society (more costly) the additional pollutants are, the higher the prices charged. Each polluter would be free to discharge any amount of waste so long as he paid the price. Polluters, acting in their own self-interest, would then seek to reduce their discharge up to the point where additional pollution abatement costs more than the pollution fee.

This form of pollution control has a number of advantages over direct requirements or standards. Incentives to cut down on pollution and to develop new methods for doing so are built in, and the operation of the plants or factories is not disrupted by inspectors checking to see if a certain device is installed and operating. The control agency needs no information about individual plants other than the amount of pollutants emitted. However, the control agency would have to juggle the price or fee charged until the desired level of pollution is achieved. The problem of the appropriate level of pollution would, unfortunately, remain.

The beginning of such a market for rights was started under the Carter Administration and continued with the Reagan Administration. Currently a company that reduces air pollution in a particular area (by closing a plant or cleaning up emissions) can receive emission credits from the Environmental Protection Agency. These credits can be sold to another firm in the area that needs an offset because of expansion. The idea is to keep the level of air pollution constant while allowing firms to save an estimated 40 to 90 percent of pollution-control costs.[9]

A Little Here,
A Little There

It seems unlikely that a full-fledged pricing system is going to spring forth one morning from the quagmire of 90 separate federal environment programs and untold number of state and local pollution regulations. More likely is a step-by-step adoption of the pricing technique by already existing agencies and departments. The

pricing method has long been used by local governments to reduce common property rights to city streets by selling rights to space via parking meters. A number of other possible applications come to mind.

The automobile may be a good starting place, since cars are associated with several pollution problems, such as air contamination and junk disposal. Most states have motor-vehicle departments that could tack a pollution price or fee onto the yearly registration charge. The fee could vary depending on the model, horsepower, or location of owner's residence and control devices installed. The accumulation of junked autos could be reduced by requiring all car owners to put up a deposit fee to be held by the states and paid to junk dealers upon recycling of the scrapped car.

Packaging also has caused some concern. The amount of packaging might be reduced by simply charging the full price of disposing of this refuse. The type of packaging can be influenced by charging more for items that are hard to dispose of, such as aluminum cans and plastic containers. However, it may be more efficient to tax manufacturers rather than charge consumers. Higher disposal charges might lead to increased use of the returnable bottle.

Potentially harmful insecticides and chemical fertilizers that fly off with birds or run off with water might be dealt with by some form of excise tax on the chemicals. The tax would make the user bear some the external cost of pollution, and, therefore, he may use less of these products.

CONCLUSION

The basic question we face today is not so much whether the price system can control many types of pollution, but, rather, are we

[9] "Market Booms For Rights To Pollute," *Wall Street Journal*, 16 June 1981.

willing to pay for a cleaner environment? If we are, the means employed to achieve lower pollution levels will have considerable impact on how far we will go and how much we will ultimately pay. The pricing system has in the past proved to be a useful and efficient method of dealing with the vast majority of scarcity problems in our society. And there is little doubt that it can become increasingly important in resolving the pollution issue, which is basically a problem of scarcity, if given the chance. That chance will not be forthcoming as long as lawmakers and others continue to focus the main portion of their attention on the noneconomic aspects of the problem, such as who to blame and the extent of the problem. The alarm has been sounded. It is time to implement measures that stand a good chance of success over the long haul. Price-based control mechanisms are certainly leading candidates.

KEY CONCEPTS

common property resources

efficiency

pollution rights

pollution tax

private costs

social costs

STEPHEN L. MEHAY

32   The Economics of Urban Crime Control

In this selection, general methods for improving urban government services are developed and applied to police services. If cities supply the types and quantities of police services desired by consumers and do so at minimun costs, then production is efficient. This selection identifies some major impediments to police efficiency and discusses two strategies—the administrative approach and the market approach—for helping police administrators make basic allocative decisions.

Between 1965 and 1979, municipal police spending, measured in either total or per capita terms, rose by more than 300 percent. Even after corrections are made for general inflation, real police spending approximately doubled. By the close of the 1970s, each taxpayer was paying about $125 yearly for the police protection services provided by state and local governments.[1] Seemingly impervious to this considerable rise in real resources devoted to local law enforcement, the major offense rate (per 100,000 population) rose by more than 85 percent during roughly the same period.

In the past, local officials could count on taxpayer support for bigger city budgets for police or other services. But the taxpayer revolt has reacquainted local officials with the realities of scarce resources. Faced with growing voter resistance to greater tax burdens, local administrators have been forced to explore ways of producing better police services on a fixed or declining budget. Traditional expenditure allocations among various inputs and programs have come under closer scrutiny.

[1] U.S. Bureau of the Census, *Statistical Abstract of the United States*, 1980.

EFFICIENCY IN GOVERNMENT

A common misconception is that greater efficiency in government simply means reducing operating costs. Economic efficiency means much more than that; it means supplying the correct type as well as quantity of services desired by consumers, while drawing upon a minimum of society's scarce resources. These conditions are fulfilled fairly well when goods and services are produced and sold in competitive markets. Consumer demands reveal which goods are desired and how much of them is desired, and competition among producers insures that only the most efficient firms survive to supply the market.

When government agencies supply services, profit incentives and external pressure from competitors usually are absent. The preferences of consumer-taxpayers for police or other local services are revealed mainly through the ballot box. But rational voter ignorance, infrequency of elections, and the fact that many issues are often decided by voting for a single candidate, all combine to make it unlikely that residents' preferences will be revealed clearly by voting. Consequently, the conditions for efficiency in local police departments may be weak or absent altogether.

Two complementary strategies are available to improve police efficiency. The first is the *administrative approach,* which involves the use of economic analytical techniques, such as cost-benefit and cost-effectiveness analysis, in internal decision making. The second is the *market approach,* which involves altering the structure of incentives by introducing *external* market forces. Which of these two strategies will work depends on the strength of the demand signals for each individual police service.

Many police services benefit particular individuals or firms and can potentially be priced and sold. For example, if the police provide special crowd control at a local concert or sporting event, the promoters of the event are directly benefited. If the police do not provide this service, the promoters will be obliged to provide it themselves. For these types of service, demand signals are strong, and a direct market approach to the allocation problem is warranted.

Crime prevention services, on the other hand—especially patrol, investigation, and apprehension—yield benefits to recipients who are difficult or costly to identify. Although these services deter crime, it is difficult to predict in advance which individuals will directly benefit. Because everyone enjoys a lessened probability of becoming a victim, crime prevention is characterized as a *public good.* Public goods cannot be left to the private market because the difficulty of financing them through voluntary payments will lead to an inefficiently low level of production. Because the market cannot be depended upon to reveal consumer demands for public goods, an internal administrative approach can be used instead to stimulate the market.

COST-BENEFIT ANALYSIS FOR POLICE SERVICES

Cost-benefit analysis begins by identifying the effects of a given police program. It then attempts to estimate the value of these outcomes to the community. In essence, this approach attempts to estimate the value, or benefits, consumers would obtain from a given level of this service, together with the amount they would be willing to pay for it. When the benefits are converted to monetary values, the dollar costs and benefits can be compared to determine whether the program should be expanded, contracted, or ended. In principle, cost-benefit analysis can be applied separately to each police activity so that maximum net social benefits can be obtained from a given police budget.

Often it is very difficult to assign a monetary value to the effects of a police program, such as a program that has the goal of deterring assaults. In this case, cost-effectiveness analysis can be used rather than cost-benefit analysis. To illustrate, suppose that two police programs, A and B, each cost $100,000 but A deters 100 assaults while B deters only 50. For an equal outlay, program A is clearly the preferred choice. Cost-effectiveness analysis can be used to compare the results of two programs that have equal costs, or to compare the cost of two programs that have identical outcomes.

Determining the Optimum Crime Level

One of the major decisions faced every day by the police is which type of crime to attack. The constraint imposed by a fixed budget means that choosing to allocate resources to one crime will leave less for attacking others. Cracking down, for example, on prostitution shifts resources away from other activities. The community may pay for less prostitution with more robberies and burglaries. Note, too, that by choosing how many resources to devote to each crime, the police implicitly choose the amount of each crime the community must tolerate.

How can the police gauge when a shift of resources from one crime to another yields positive benefits to the community? Police priorities should reflect the seriousness of different crimes as determined by the preferences of local residents. While several techniques are available to assess crime seriousness as perceived by voters,[2] one method is to estimate the dollar equivalent of the expected losses associated with each type of crime. To illustrate, suppose that the average loss associated with robbery is $1,000, consisting perhaps of cash,[3] medical expenses, and wages lost due to injuries. In addition, suppose that the average auto theft involves, say, $500 of losses, consisting of damages to the automobile plus the value of the forgone services of the lost vehicle. Each robbery prevention should then be weighed twice as heavily as each auto-theft prevention. In principle, other costs of crime, not simply those felt by victims, should also be included. The rest of society bears such costs as supporting the criminal justice sys-

tem, making expenditures on insurance or self-protection devices (locks, alarms, guard dogs) and altering one's behavior to avoid high-crime areas. Many social costs are difficult to quantify with any precision but they are nevertheless real (see Box 1).

Society is better off if police seek to minimize the cost of crime, rather than to minimize certain crime rates, because weighting crimes according to an index of seriousness helps to approximate the collective value that taxpayers place on prevented crimes. The social cost of a crime indicates the harmful impact of that crime on the community. Consequently, it also indicates the maximum amount the community would pay to avoid that crime.

Allocating Resources Among Programs

Optimal resource use involves allocating the fixed amount of budgeted resources among alternative programs so that the cost of crime to the city is minimized. Determining whether too few or too many resources are presently allocated to a particular crime-prevention program requires the use of *marginal analysis*. That is, the marginal benefits and costs associated with increasing or decreasing the size of a given program must be estimated and compared. Suppose, for example, that we wished to evaluate the desirability of adding another patrol unit to a specific patrol beat. The analysis would proceed as follows.

First, the expected number of crime preventions attributable to the additional patrol unit must be estimated. One approach would be to compare the crime rate on the experimental beat with a *base crime rate*.[4] The difference between the

---

[2] See Robert Anderson, "Towards a Cost-Benefit Analysis of Police Activity," *Public Finance* 29 (1974): 1-18.

[3] Technically, monetary transfers from one individual to another impose no real cost on society because there is no overall reduction in wealth or income. However, the thief who performs the transfer invests his capital and labor in illegal rather than legal pursuits, and this investment is wasted from society's viewpoint. If it is assumed that the amount transferred in each crime merely compensates the criminal for his investment, then that full amount can be chalked up as a social cost.

[4] The *base crime rate* can be computed either from the historical trend on the experimental beat, or the crime rate observed on a different beat but one with similar physical and demographic characteristics.

BOX 1

SOCIAL COSTS OF CRIME

Crime imposes costs on society far beyond those felt by victims. In principle, crime wastes scarce resources that have productive uses elsewhere. As a result, the total real output of goods and services is lower than it could be. The full social cost of crime includes those resources used by criminals to carry out crime and those used by society to prevent it as well as those resources used to deal with crimes once they have been committed. From society's viewpoint, criminals could be employed in productive legal jobs, and resources used by the police and the rest of the criminal justice system (prosecutors, courts, jails, rehabilitation agencies) could be funneled into other private or public endeavors. In addition, expenditures by private individuals and firms on protective services and devices have other desirable uses.

In 1974, crimes against persons resulted in estimated economic losses of $3 billion in the form of lost earnings and medical expenses. Crimes against property involved transfers and losses of $21.3 billion. Other crimes (such as drunken driving) involved losses and damages of $6.5 billion. In addition, illegal goods and services (such as drugs and gambling) involved losses of $37.2 billion. Public expenditures

on the criminal justice system were estimated to be $14.6 billion, and private protection expenditures totaled $6 billion. The sum of these admittedly rough, but very conservative, estimates of the cost of crime in the United States was $88.6 billion in 1974, about 8 percent of the gross national product. Assuming an inflation rate of 50 percent for the period 1974 to 1981, crime costs today would total $132 billion.

In practice, measuring the additional real costs above and beyond the monetary value of property damages or losses is no easy task. It is difficult to attach money values to the physical pain and mental suffering of victims of violent crimes. And even when a price tag is affixed to lost productive services of individuals killed or injured, the real losses to family and friends are impossible to estimate. It is also difficult to measure the losses when individuals alter their behavior to avoid living, shopping, and traveling in dangerous areas of the city. Thus, measurement of social costs frequently omits some of the more important aspects of the cost of crime.

Source: Daryl A. Hellman, *The Economics of Crime* (New York: St. Martin's Press, 1980), p. 23.

---

actual and base crime rate is the estimate of crimes prevented by the additional patrol unit. Suppose the extra patrol unit prevents 10 robberies and 10 burglaries per year. If the average loss is $1,500 from robbery and $1,000 from burglary, then the annual marginal benefit of the extra patrol unit on that beat is $25,000. If the annual cost of the unit is $20,000, then the net marginal benefit of the extra unit is $5,000, and the community would benefit by putting the additional patrol unit into service.

While the example involves the decision of where to deploy a patrol unit, in princi-

ple all police programs compete for funds. The $20,000 worth of resources represented by the patrol unit could be allocated to numerous programs in the department—for example, to detectives, to traffic control, or to community relations. The police are confronted by numerous resource trade-offs that would be aided by economic analysis. In principle, an additional dollar of funding should be added to (or subtracted from) each police program until the marginal benefit produced is equal in all programs. This rule will ensure that the maximum total social benefit will be obtained from a given police budget.

Obstacles to the Administrative Approach

While it is easy to describe the rule that should guide the allocation of resources, putting the rule into practice is much more difficult. Because of measurement problems, police effectiveness often is difficult to evaluate. Measurement problems are encountered in every step of the analysis and include problems of: (1) measuring the true crime rate; (2) measuring the amount of crime deterred by police actions; and (3) measuring the monetary value of each deterred crime. Because most crimes are underreported, it is difficult to estimate the true crime rate and the crime reduction attributable to police actions. Another obstacle is that crime is influenced by numerous environmental and economic factors outside the control of the police. Finally, measuring the full social cost of crime is also difficult. Many of the real costs of crime (such as pain and suffering) cannot be measured at all. Even if the costs are fairly easy to measure, the data are often unavailable.

However, even if measurement problems did not exist to complicate the analyst's life, it should be realized that simply instituting cost-benefit analysis or other economic techniques will not guarantee that efficient decisions will be made. These techniques can assist police officials by providing improved information about the likely economic effects of their decisions. But in practice inefficiency often remains the rule in government because of a failure of incentives. Government bureaus are neither guided by profit-and-loss statements nor confronted by competitive suppliers. The incentive structure seldom rewards managers for pursuing efficient strategies or penalizes them for pursuing inefficient ones. The basic incentive structure is not altered by the introduction of cost-benefit analysis. At best, such devices merely simulate the forces of supply and demand. A more effective alternative would be to directly introduce market-type incentives.

MARKET ARRANGEMENTS FOR POLICE SERVICES

Market forces can be introduced in one of two ways. First, some police services can be sold to beneficiaries rather than provided free of charge. A second approach is for services to be produced either by a private firm or by another governmental agency (such as the county) and provided on a contract basis to the city.

Introducing Competition

Private firms cannot always produce services cheaper than the government. Some private firms are as inefficient as government bureaus often are alleged to be. However, inefficient private firms, unlike inefficient government bureaus, will tend to earn losses and, eventually, to go out of business. When goods are produced in a reasonably competitive environment, a firm's very survival depends upon efficient operation.

Similar market incentives can be introduced by contracting out some police services through open competitive bidding. Local government would still decide how much service it desired and would continue to finance the service, but private profit-seeking firms would supply it. Fortunately, private suppliers already exist for many police services. For example, the services of chemical laboratories maintained by many large city police departments could be purchased from private research facilities or colleges. The training of police officers could be undertaken by private schools with tuition paid either by the trainees or subsidized by the city. Most research and planning, maintenance services, as well as follow-up investigation of property losses could also be farmed out to private suppliers.

There is some evidence to suggest that even basic crime-prevention services—for example, patrol—could be provided privately. It is not uncommon for residents of a neighborhood to collectively hire private firms to provide basic patrol services to supplement existing municipal police services. Some cities also hire private security firms to perform specialized tasks, such as patrolling high-crime housing projects and parks and providing security checks at airports.[5]

The Lakewood Plan

Under the *Lakewood Plan*, one level of government—usually the county—offers services on a contract basis to another level—usually a city. This service arrangement is relied on heavily in Los Angeles County where the County Sheriff's Department offers basic law enforcement services to 30 of the county's 77 incorporated cities. Services sold on contract include basic preventive patrol, traffic patrol, and accident investigation. Smaller cities are also offered specialized services, such as crime labs and forensic personnel.

The usual arrangement is for the contracting city to purchase the amount of service it desires, above some specified minimum. For example, the basic unit of patrol service is a patrol car that operates on 24-hour duty, seven days a week. The county usually sets an annual fee per car,

which is intended to cover the marginal cost of the service. The city may then purchase any multiple or fraction of this basic unit.

Although the Lakewood Plan involves contracting between governmental entities, it offers important lessons for advocates of the market approach. First, the plan demonstrates that market-type arrangements can be established even for basic crime-prevention services such as patrol. Second, although the county is not a profit-seeking firm, it faces some competition and, unlike the typical government monopoly bureau, it has some incentive to keep costs low. Competition comes from the purchasing city itself, which always has the option of providing its own police services if it becomes dissatisfied with the county.

Finally, if scale economies exist for some police services, contracting from a large-scale supplier, such as the county, allows small cities to reap cost savings without sacrificing local control over service levels. Research studies indicate that the expenditures by Lakewood Plan cities may be as low as one-half of those of neighboring Los Angeles-area cities, which maintain their own police departments.[6] Although this expenditure differential could simply reflect lower demands for police protection by contract-city residents, the fact that the size of the differential is so large suggests that at least part of it results either from scale economies of from incentives that induce the county to be efficient.

Pricing Police Services

Even if contracting out police services is

---

[5] The number of private security police in the United States equals or exceeds the number of state and local police officers. See Robert Poole, Jr., *Cutting Back City Hall* (New York: Universe Books, 1980).

[6] See Stephen L. Mehay, "Intergovernmental Contracting for Municipal Police Services: An Empirical Analysis," *Land Economics* 55 (February 1979); and Robert T. Deacon, "The Expenditure Effects of Alternative Public Supply Institutions," *Public Choice* 34 (1979).

infeasible, other market arrangements are possible. For example, some services can be sold to their recipients instead of being distributed free. User charges for any service improve efficiency by yielding information on the strength of consumer demand for it. If buyers are unwilling to pay an amount sufficient to cover the extra cost of the service, then the service is being over-produced and should be cut back. User charges not only provide useful demand information, they also ration available output and signal whether additional, long-run capital investment is warranted. Last but not least, user charges can yield revenue for municipal coffers strained by the tax revolt. This latter point should appeal to revenue-starved bureaus, even if the finer points about the efficiency of the approach are missed.

User charges are feasible only if police services have easily identifiable recipients and if those who are unwilling to pay can be excluded from receiving the service. These conditions pose an obvious problem for patrol, detection, apprehension, and other protective services. Yet, other routine services can be priced. Indeed, many cities already charge for copies of crime reports, traffic-accident reports, and fingerprint reports, for crowd-control services at sporting and entertainment events, for towing automobiles, for funeral escorts, and for serving civil papers. Services that are not currently priced, but that could be offered for a fee that covers operating costs, are accident-investigation services, extra patrols for businesses and homes, and searches for stolen automobiles.

A COMBINED APPROACH

If police efficiency is improved, the scarce resources available to city governments can be stretched to provide more and better public services. Because police services are provided by government bureaus, useful signals about consumer demand are unavailable. Consequently, the incentives to channel resources into the most efficient uses are at best weak. The administrative and market approaches are alternative ways of supplying the missing incentives. If police services can be priced and then sold or contracted out to private or large-scale governmental suppliers, the incentive structure will be realigned toward greater efficiency. At the very least, demand signals will be stronger regarding which services taxpayers most desire and in what quantities.

If services cannot be sold in the market or if contracting is impractical, cost-benefit analysis and other devices must be relied upon to provide information on the value the community places on police services. These latter approaches attempt to provide the same information that would be forthcoming automatically from a market structure. In principle, the enhanced information will permit better decision making. A rational combination of the two approaches may squeeze more crime prevention from strained police budgets and help stem the rising tide of urban crime.

KEY CONCEPTS

cost-benefit analysis

cost-effectiveness analysis

efficiency

Lakewood Plan

public goods

scale economies

KENNETH A. SMALL

33 Energy Scarcity and Urban Development Patterns

Kenneth A. Small, of Princeton University, analyzes the usual argument that higher gasoline and fuel prices will result in the increased centralization of our metropolitan areas. The author calculates the likely effects of very large increases in gasoline prices on relative commuting costs from the suburbs, and the effects of very large increases in fuel prices on relative residential heating and cooling costs in the suburbs. The author finds that these price increases are much more likely to result in energy-saving adjustments (for example, the purchase of more fuel-efficient cars and the insulation of buildings) than in migration of suburbanites back to the central city.

INTRODUCTION

Recent events have revived the question of whether limitations on the availability of energy sources will force a major reversal of post-war trends toward decentralized urban development patterns. If fuel is costly or difficult to obtain, the argument goes, central locations and high residential densities will become more attractive as people seek to shorten trips, take advantage of mass transit, and reduce home heating costs. Indeed, anecdotal evidence has appeared in the real estate news suggesting greater concern with such factors among homebuyers. Mayors claim that "the energy crisis has guaranteed the future of the American city" (Newark's Mayor Gibson, as quoted in Allman 1978, p. 56), and some planners foresee a metropolis shaped "almost entirely by energy availability: val-

ues and preferences may become submerged to necessity as our resource options disappear" (Van Til 1979, p. 321).

Two rather different arguments should be distinguished. Many writers in the popular press, noting the established connection between residential density and energy consumption, expect the energy crisis to result in greatly revived central cities, a view perhaps inadvertently fostered by professional use of such terms as "imploding metropolis" (Franklin 1974). Romanos (1978) and Anas and Moses (1978), on the other hand, reason from behavioral considerations that energy scarcity is most likely to foster a multinuclear pattern with strong suburban subcenters. Van Til (1979) arrives at the same conclusion working backward from assumed aggregate energy availability by sector and the assumption that a highly concentrated "super-city" is too costly. Keyes (1980) takes a more negative view altogether, showing that a variety of attractive energy-saving options are available to households and firms, and arguing that

Condensed from *International Regional Science Review* 5, 2 (1980): 97–117. Copyright 1980 International Regional Science Review. Reprinted with permission of the Regional Science Association and the author.

these "would make changes in residential locations ... and commercial or industrial siting less than optimal or even unnecessary" (p. 309). Yet none of these authors provides evidence on the crucial quantitative link between stimulus (energy prices or government-imposed constraints) and location response by private decision makers. Without such evidence, the impact energy scarcity might have on urban development patterns cannot be assessed.

This article focuses primarily on the central city relative to suburbs as a whole, although the calculations also shed light on the question of development of suburban nuclei. Data on energy consumption patterns by location, combined with empirical evidence on the effects of city-suburban cost differentials on migration are used to place an upper bound on the impact of energy scarcity on central cities. This impact is found to be very modest. The evidence that energy shortages foster a multinuclear pattern, though far from conclusive, is much stronger than that for a revival of central cities.

In the high energy cost scenario considered in Section III, growing world scarcity leads to ... a stable supply at much higher prices than those prevailing in the late 1970s. Another possible scenario is one of unstable supply, with intermittent disruptions recurring over an extended period. The uncertainty associated with such a course of events could conceivably influence location decisions more than price, since central locations provide more options for coping with short-term disruptions. ...

In any case, the ultimate locational response to severe shortages, like that to a price rise, will depend greatly on the extent to which various other adjustment mechanisms are used. This article begins

with an examination of those mechanisms and then proceeds to a much more detailed examination of intraurban location change in response to high energy prices.

ADJUSTMENT MECHANISMS

The primary incentives for readjustment of location patterns within urban areas appear to be related to automobile transportation and residential heating and cooling. These two items account for 13.1 and 11.9 percent, respectively, of all U.S. energy consumption in 1973 (Schurr et al. 1979, p. 75). Furthermore, they comprise most of the typical urban household's "energy budget," since all other residential uses combined amounted to only 8.6 percent of energy consumption in 1973. Industry and commerce account for more than half of all U.S. energy consumption; the dominant end uses (32.3 percent of all consumption) are process steam, process heat, and electric motive power, which are susceptible to reduction by technological but not locational changes. ...

In order to assess the extent to which urban location shifts might occur, the strength of the primary incentive (price or supply shortage) must be understood, as well as the relative amounts by which various other energy-saving mechanisms, from simple adjustments in day-to-day utilization patterns to alterations in long-lived capital stock, are utilized. If gasoline or heating fuel consumption at low density locations can be fairly easily reduced, less incentive exists to relocate in order to save fuel.

The adjustment mechanisms available for saving gasoline include changes in driving habits (e.g., speed or acceleration), discretionary trips, multi-purpose trips, carpooling, transit use, and the purchase of fuel-efficient cars. For reduction of space heating and cooling fuel requirements, households and businesses may alter domestic habits (e.g., thermostat settings or use of curtains), retrofit existing buildings (e.g., modified furnaces or insulation), or purchase new buildings with energy efficient design.

A good deal is known about the potential for achieving energy savings through these means. A substantial increase occurred in the use of multi-purpose trips in order to economize on travel during the 1973-74 gasoline shortage (Peskin et al. 1975). In 1974 a survey revealed that 89 percent of respondents claimed to "frequently" drive more slowly in order to save gasoline, and 31 percent reduced shopping and recreational trips (U.S. Congress 1975). During the mid-1970s, use of home heating fuel was reduced by an estimated 9 to 13 percent by adjustments in thermostat settings and other living habits, plus the modest amount of retrofitting of homes which occurred during the short time (Schurr et al. 1979, pp. 141–2).

Several authors have concluded that by far the most potent tool for achieving reductions in energy consumption in surface transportation is improvement in fuel economy of motor vehicles.[1] Legal regulation, rising gasoline prices, and intermittent shortages have already raised the fuel economy of newly purchased domestic cars in the United States by more than 40 percent between 1974 and 1978 through a combination of design modification and "downsizing." The new car standards of 27.5 miles per gallon, now mandated for 1985 model cars, would amount to an additional 50 percent improvement. Market

incentives may push the actual achievements even higher: General Motors has announced its intention to achieve a fleet average of 31 miles per gallon by 1985 (*Wall Street Journal*, July 10, 1980). . . .

Statistical evidence further strengthens the view that gasoline savings would come predominantly from changes in automobile fuel efficiency. Econometric estimates suggest that the overall price-elasticity of demand for gasoline ranges from .22 in a one-year short run to .78 in the long run, the latter being a combination of price-elasticities for fleet efficiency of .72, and for vehicle-miles of only .06 (Kain 1979, pp. 21–22). From a 1976 sample of individual households purchasing new cars, Lave and Train (1979) estimate a model of auto-type choice which implies a gasoline price-elasticity of 0.43 just from shifts among different size classes.

The technological possibilities for fuel savings in space heating and cooling are also striking (A.D. Little Inc. 1974; Hittman Associates 1977). A Resources for the Future study (Schurr et al. 1979, pp. 125-43) concludes that savings from simple alterations in furnaces can reduce consumption of heating fuel by at least 20 percent, whereas modifications which would be economical under modest tax incentives and a total price of $5.40 per million Btu (about 75 cents per gallon of fuel oil) would reduce consumption by 64 percent in existing structures and 77 percent in new ones! Clearly improvements over present practice are not only feasible, but are likely given the price increases already in force.

The thrust of this evidence is that a variety of avenues are available to reduce, with a minimum of expense and inconvenience, the consumption of energy in those sectors most strongly affected by potential scarcity.

---

[1] See particularly Altshuler et al. (1979), chapter 5; Schurr et al. (1979); pp. 143–159; and Kain (1979).

The use of such mechanisms would greatly reduce the impact of scarcity upon other aspects of life, including intra- and interurban location. Given the strength of the forces underlying recent migration patterns, these patterns may be relatively unaffected by energy scarcity. This possibility is considered in subsequent sections which analyze in greater detail the strength and pattern of the location incentives.

HIGH COST SCENARIO

Despite widespread pessimism, rising real energy costs over the next one or two decades are by no means a certainty. At present, the cost of energy is heavily influenced by the actions of the oil exporting nations through their international cartel. Various projections of the price of crude oil, under either free market or monopoly conditions, show it to be quite sensitive to the timing and eventual cost of such alternative sources as synthetic fuels, nuclear breeder reactors, solar, nuclear fusion, and low-grade sources of conventional fuels.[2] Favorable developments in any of these areas carry the potential for turning restrictive policies on the part of the oil producing nations against their long-term advantage. In addition, any further major oil discoveries can only increase the present cartel's potential for instability.

Nevertheless, should favorable developments not occur, recent price increases would continue. The relevant consideration for urban form is not the kind of temporary disequilibria reflected in the erratic spot market prices reported throughout 1979; it is instead the medium- to long-term price dictated by energy reserves and technolo-

gies. An upper limit appears to depend on the ability, within two or three decades, to develop substantial quantities of synthetic fuels including shale oil. Although the costs of these technologies are uncertain, most estimates reviewed by Schurr et al. (1979) place them below 40 dollars per barrel in 1977 prices, roughly four times the 1977 average domestic oil price in the United States. With around 38 gallons of refined products produced per barrel of crude, their real costs could therefore be expected to rise by no more than 75 cents per gallon. . . .

An increase in 1977 prices of $1.00 per gallon for gasoline and of $0.75 per gallon for fuel oil is considered here to be a reasonable upper limit for the rise in long-term price of liquid fuels. Natural gas is assumed to rise in price by the same amount . . . as fuel oil; electricity is assumed generated from fuel oil, with price rise dictated by a straight pass-through of fuel costs. Since all calculations shown below are proportioned to these assumed increases, any reader believing they are overly optimistic or pessimistic can easily adjust the results.

As discussed in the previous section, many responses to such price increases are likely besides locational changes, most of which reduce the incentive to relocate. For example, multipurpose auto trips could be expected to reduce automobile travel more or less proportionally from all residential locations. . . . Although certain adjustments (e.g., public transit) are more feasible in the city, others such as carpooling would probably bring about a larger proportional reduction in fuel use in the suburbs. To determine the net incentive for relocations, each of these behavioral changes must be quantified as a function of location. Doing so is beyond the scope of the present arti-

---

[2] See, for example, Nordhaus (1979), Symposium on the Economics of Exhaustible Resources (1974), Bernari (1976), and Houthakker and Kennedy (1978).

cle. However, if these other adjustments reduce energy costs proportionally at all locations, then the relocation incentive in the absence of any such adjustments is an upper bound on the actual relocation incentive. Therefore, in the remainder of this section the cost increases incurred at alternative locations are computed on the assumption that technological and behavioral patterns determining energy use are those prevailing in the 1970s, with two exceptions: automotive fuel economy is set at 20 miles per gallon, and home heating/cooling fuel efficiency is increased by 20 percent over 1977 levels. This is done for three crucial types of energy use: work travel, nonwork travel, and residential space heating/cooling.

Work Trips

The usual argument that higher gasoline prices will result in centralization of urban development patterns rests on two implicit assumptions. The first is that travel destinations are generally more centralized than residences, so that people can reduce automobile use by moving closer to the center. With respect to work trips, this assumption is not nearly as true as is commonly believed. Data for 1975 (U.S. Bureau of the Census 1979b) indicate that 47.4 percent of all jobs in metropolitan areas are located outside of central cities, compared to 58.9 percent of household residences. Only 18.6 percent of metropolitan jobs are filled by suburban residents commuting to the central city, and nearly half that number commute in the opposite direction.

The second implicit assumption is that residences, rather than jobs, will be relocated. Yet there is considerable evidence that employers try to locate near concentrations of labor. If workers become more resistant to long commutes, suburban locations should gain in attractiveness to firms, with a decentralizing effect. Thus, even the direction of the net effect on central cities is unclear. . . .

Table 1 shows the percentage distribution of all U.S. workers living and working within the same SMSA [Standard Metropolitan Statistical Area], according to a four-way breakdown by residence and employment site. It also reports the corresponding percentages of trips made by driving an auto, and the average trip lengths for auto

TABLE 1

High Energy Cost Scenario: Work Travel, 1975 National Sample, and Cost Increases

	Residence in City Employed in:		Residence in Suburb Employed in:	
	City	Suburb	City	Suburb
Percentage of workers in SMSA	34.8	8.1	19.5	37.7
Percentage of commuters who drive to work[a]	64.0	80.5	75.8	79.8
One way trip length in miles for driver[a]	5.6	10.1	11.5	7.4
Average annual cost increase per worker[b]	86	195	209	142

[a] The average car pool is assumed to contain 2.5 persons.
[b] The added cost per worker results from an added cost per auto driver of 5 cents per mile for 240 round trips per year.

Source: U.S. Bureau of the Census (1979b), Tables F, H, and 1.

drivers. The resulting average annual cost increase per worker, due to a $1.00 per gallon rise in gasoline price, is also shown for each of the four categories.

The absolute increases are small in comparison to total incomes or housing costs, and the differences among the four categories of workers are even smaller. The largest difference is for those who work in the city. They can reduce work-trip auto use by over 50 percent (from 11.5 to 5.6 miles per trip) by shifting from a suburban to a city residence. Nevertheless, such a move would reduce the incremental cost caused by the gasoline price rise by only $123 per year (from $209 to $86). In contrast, the average commuter to a suburban job uses *more* vehicle-miles from a city than from a suburban residence, and would face an additional $53 per year incentive to locate in the suburbs.

Note that the first row of Table 1 implies that the average household (with 1.18 workers) contains 0.64 workers employed in the central city and 0.54 in the suburbs. The bottom row shows the annual cost increase to such a family to be $160 or $210, depending on whether it resides in the city or suburbs. The *differential* increase, which provides a measure of the net incentive to centralize, is therefore only $50.

Another possible influence of gasoline prices on firms is through the increased cost of trucking. Although cheap truck transportation was a major factor in employment suburbanization (Moses and Williamson 1967), several reasons exist to think that increased fuel prices would not reverse this trend. First, the fuel component of the urban portion of freight shipments represents a very small cost for typical firms. Although a shift to rail for intercity freight shipments may well occur,

it would more likely be accommodated through an increase in truck-on-flatcar ("piggyback") than through relocations of firms. Trucks have an inherent service advantage for local pickup and delivery, and costly investment in new railroad sidings would be required to eliminate that advantage.

Nonwork Travel

Suburban residents drive more than city residents for nonwork purposes, and recent evidence described below indicates that the differential cannot be explained entirely by socioeconomic differences. Presumably inherent differences in living patterns, which would make suburban locations relatively less attractive in the event of rising gasoline prices, are at least partially responsible. An upper bound on the size of this relocation incentive can be estimated by determining the average number of additional vehicle-miles per household associated with suburban residence, holding constant those variables (such as income, age, marital status, and number of children) not likely to be altered as part of the location choice, but allowing variables closely related to location (such as housing type and tenure) to vary.

The necessary estimates of how nonwork automobile travel depends on these variables are provided by Sharp (1978), who used early 1970s household survey data to estimate statistical models of automobile ownership and use. Controlling for the first set of characteristics mentioned above, he identified the influence of housing type, housing tenure, and residence location on auto ownership and use. . . . Using his method, a suburban residence is associated with an additional 2260 vehicle-miles per year for the average household. At 20 miles per gallon fuel economy, the suburban-city differential in annual cost of nonwork travel by automobile would rise by $113 due to the hypothetical gasoline price increase.

Residential Heating and Cooling

Among the amenities which attract metropolitan residents to suburban locations is a greater predominance of single-family homes. In times of costly energy, this attraction is less compelling because such homes use more fuel for heating and air conditioning than comparably sized apartment units. According to Schurr et al. (1979, p. 128), energy consumption for space heating, per square foot of living area, is about 40 percent lower in multifamily than in single-family units.

An analysis based on engineering studies of prototype housing units in different regions of the country is shown in Tables 2 through 4. Table 2 lists the mix of structure types found in central cities and suburbs in the four major regions of the United States.

Table 3 shows energy consumption per 1000 square feet of floor space for prototype units representative of those structure types. The weighted average fuel consumption for various locations is shown in Table 4 for a 1280-square-foot unit, the average of the sizes shown in Table 3 weighted by their relative frequencies in all metropolitan areas in 1976. Although floor space may be somewhat dependent on location choice, it is held constant in these comparisons on the assumption that it is determined primarily by income and family size.

The city-suburb differentials shown in Table 4 are of about the same size as the regional differences, the latter being narrowed considerably by the inclusion of air conditioning. On balance, the city-suburban differentials of $63 to $136 per year resulting from a 75 cent per gallon price increase in fuel oil (or its equivalent in natural gas or electric utility rates) appear rather small inducements for city living. Once again, the differences (between sin-

TABLE 2

Percentage Distribution of Housing Structure Types by Region, 1976

Location of Residence	Mobile Home	Single-Family Detached	Single-Family Attached	Multifamily
Northeast:				
City	0.1	16.2	11.8	72.0
Suburb	1.6	64.5	5.9	28.0
North Central:				
City	1.0	48.8	3.4	46.8
Suburb	2.9	74.8	2.8	19.6
South:				
City	1.2	56.0	5.1	37.8
Suburb	6.3	68.4	3.3	22.0
West:				
City	1.8	55.0	3.3	39.9
Suburb	7.7	63.9	4.4	24.0

Source: U.S. Bureau of the Census (1978a), Tables B1, C1, D1, E1.

TABLE 3

Energy Consumption for Space Heating and Cooling:
By Structure Type and Region[a]

| Location of Residence | Structure Type and Floor Space (sq. ft.)[b] | | | |
	Mobile Home (720)	Single-Family Detached (1560)	Single-Family Attached (1100)	Multifamily (900)
Northeast:				
Heating	154	103	91	64
Cooling	11	6	5	4
Total	165	109	96	68
North Central:				
Heating	175	117	114	73
Cooling	20	10	9	6
Total	195	126	124	79
South:				
Heating	83	56	53	33
Cooling	65	44	42	25
Total	148	100	94	58
West:				
Heating	100	75	72	44
Cooling	63	45	43	27
Total	163	120	115	71

[a] Primary energy consumption at power plant assuming 33 percent conversion efficiency, in millions of British Thermal Units per year per 1000 square feet of floor space, for electrically heated homes with central air conditioning. Figures have been reduced by 20 percent to account for modest conservation measures beyond those embodied in the typical early-1970s building practices assumed. Differences between various heating fuels, between one- and two-story homes, and between low- and high-rise apartment buildings are too small to warrant showing them separately. Thus, the figures for 1- and 2-story single family structures are averaged; attached single family structures are duplexes sharing one wall; and multifamily units are three-story garden apartments.
[b] One square foot equals 0.0929 square meters.

Source: Arthur D. Little, Inc. (1974), p. 77 and Tables 3.5-3.9.

gle family and multifamily dwellings) within cities and within suburbs are more significant, and could conceivably result in a noticeable shift in demand for higher-density living.

A Perspective on Magnitudes

In portraying the impact of a high-energy-cost scenario, an attempt has been made to quantify the change in average city-suburban cost differentials as perceived by households making location decisions. Even the upper bound appears rather modest in terms of its likely impact on location

decisions. This upper bound—$256 annually for households consisting of $50 for work-trips, $113 for nonwork travel, and $93 for residential heating and cooling—is directly proportional to the assumed increase of 300 percent in crude oil prices, and thus can be easily modified for different assumptions. Due to other adjustments, the actual location incentives probably would be considerably smaller.

To assess better the possible impact of such incentives, evidence is useful regarding the effect of other cost differentials on intrametropolitan migration rates. The

TABLE 4

Energy Consumption for Space Heating and Cooling per Housing Unit:
Composite of Residential Structure Types by Location

Location of Residence	Primary Fuel Consumption[a] (gallons fuel oil per year)		Cost Increase[b] (dollars per year)		
	City	Suburb	City	Suburb	Difference
Northeast	721	903	541	677	136
North central	971	1105	729	829	100
South	783	867	587	650	63
West	937	1032	703	774	71
U.S. average[c]	848	972	636	729	93

[a] Same as Table 3 for a 1280-square-foot unit and assumes 5.8 million BTU's per 42-gallon barrel.
[b] Cost increase resulting from price increase of primary fuel of 75 cents per gallon of fuel oil.
[c] Weighted by number of year-round housing units in metropolitan areas by region, 1976.

Source: Computed from Tables 2 and 3.

responsiveness of household migration to tax disparities has been estimated by Frey (1979), who disaggregates the population flows to and within metropolitan areas and examines the determinants of destination locations. In a multiple-regression equation estimated on a sample of 39 large SMSAs, he finds that a high ratio of city to suburban taxes increases the likelihood that city movers will choose to relocate in the suburbs. His coefficient estimate implies that an increase of 0.1 in the ratio of suburban to city per capita taxes causes a decrease of 1.2 in the percentage of city movers who choose a suburban destination. Such a change would represent a reduction of 0.24 percentage points in the annual rate of outmigration (since 20 percent of central-city households move within their SMSA each year) and could be brought about by a change of approximately $110 in the average city-suburb tax differential in Frey's sample. Thus, if households react to the upper bound cost increases of $256 in the same way as they would to comparable tax increases, net outmigration from cities might decrease on average by 0.56 percent-

age points per year. This figure compares to 1970-78 net outmigration rates of 2.5 percent per year for St. Louis, 1.8 for Baltimore and Washington, D.C., 1.5 for New York, 1.4 for Philadelphia, and 1.2 for San Francisco.[3]

DISCUSSION

Energy scarcity, like other forces, can exert its full influence on urban structure only over a period of time long enough to permit adjustment of the capital stock. Only to a limited extent can changes in vacancy rates and postponement of building abandonment quickly absorb an increase in demand for city locations. In the short run much of the demand shift would instead be capitalized into higher prices for city properties. Nevertheless, the processes of migration, building abandonment, and suburban construction are ongoing ones. The rates at which they occur can change almost instantaneously, thus providing a

[3] Computed from U.S. Bureau of the Census (1980). Migration figure for cities not coinciding with a county equivalent are unavailable.

strong signal as to the likely course of future patterns of urban centralization. Furthermore, the price effects themselves would have an immediate positive effect on the city's fiscal health through lower tax delinquency and . . . a larger property tax base. Thus, although any restructuring of the urban landscape due to energy scarcity would take place only gradually, immediate and important effects should be apparent at once. Since a temporary shortage and a sharp price rise have in fact occurred recently, empirical tests of the primary result of this analysis possibly can be designed.

The incentives for location changes may perhaps be offset by capitalization of the new energy cost differentials into property values and rents, but only after densities have adjusted to their new equilibrium levels; until that time, capitalization serves as the mechanism through which increased demand for energy-efficient locations calls forth an increased density of dwelling units there, thus permitting the induced net migrations to occur. . . .

The evidence assembled here provides little support for the view that overall urban decentralization will be substantially altered in the next one or two decades by energy shortages. Existing opportunities and preferences both favor use of technological means of reducing energy consumption in the automotive and residential sectors. Even without such adaptations, the differences in energy consumption between central cities and suburbs are not large enough to induce any substantial "back-to-the-city" movement. Even under highly uncertain supply conditions, other means of adjustment would provide more flexibility with less disruption to life styles than large scale reversal of postwar decentralization trends.

Any discernible response in development patterns is more likely to be in the form of greater *nucleation* of both suburban and city development. The relative energy-cost differences between low- and high-density developments, between transit-accessible and highway-oriented developments, or between close-in and outlying suburbs, are considerably greater than the average differences between central city and suburbs. Furthermore, a substantial shortening of average work trips could occur simply through interchanges of the residential locations of suburban workers, without any net change in the overall degree of concentration of population. The extent to which these changes would occur deserves greater attention and might have important implications for travel patterns. However, they do not alter the basic conclusion that substantial revitalization of central cities will not occur as a result of energy scarcity and price changes.

REFERENCES

Allman, T. C. 1978. The urban crisis leaves town. *Harper's,* December, pp. 41–56.

Altshuler, A., with Womack, J. P., and Pucher, J. R. 1979. *The urban transportation system: politics and policy innovation.* Cambridge, Mass.: The MIT Press.

Benari, Y. R. 1976. *Depletable resource pricing and output strategies in light of a possible future substitute.* Ph.D. Dissertation, Princeton University.

Franklin, H. M. 1974. Will the new consciousness of energy and the environment create an imploding metropolis? *American Institute of Architects Journal,* 62, 2: 28–36.

Frey, W. 1979. White flight and central-city loss: application of an analytic migration framework. *Environment and Planning A,* 11: 129–147.

Hittman Associates, Inc. 1977. *Residential energy consumption: detailed geographic analysis,* Report No. HIT-650-11 prepared for U.S. Department of Housing and Urban Development.

Houthakker, H., and Kennedy, M. 1978. Long-range energy prospects. *Journal of Energy Development,* Autumn.

Kain, J. F. 1979. *The future of urban transportation: an economist's perspective.* Cambridge, Mass.: Department of City and Regional Planning, Harvard University, Discussion Paper D79-12.

Lave, C. and Train, K. 1979. A disaggregate model of auto-type choice. *Transportation Research* 13A: 1–9.

Little, Arthur D., Inc. 1974. *Residential and commercial energy use patterns, 1970-1990,* Vol. 1 of U.S. Federal Energy Administration, *Project Independence Blueprint,* prepared for U.S. Department of Housing and Urban Development.

Moses, L. N., and Williamson, H. F., Jr. 1967. The location of economic activity in cities. *American Economic Review* 57, 2: 212–222.

Nordhaus, W. D. 1979. *The efficient use of energy resources.* New Haven: Yale University Press.

Peskin, R. L., Schafer, J. L., and Stopher, P. R. 1975. *The immediate impact of gasoline shortages on urban travel behavior,* U.S. Federal Highway Administration, April.

Romanos, M. C. 1978. Energy-price effects on metropolitan spatial structure and form. *Environment and Planning A* 10: 93–104.

Schurr, S. H., Darmstadter, J., Perry, H., Ramsey, W., and Russell, M. 1979. *Energy in America's future: the choices before us.* A study by the staff of the Resources for the Future National Energy Strategies Project. Baltimore: The Johns Hopkins University Press.

Sharp, D. P. 1978. Projections of automobile ownership and use based on household life-style factors. Ph.D. Dissertation, University of Pittsburgh.

Symposium on the Economics of Exhaustible Resources. 1974. *Review of Economic Studies,* special issue.

U.S. Advisory Commission on Intergovernmental Relations. 1973. *City financial emergencies,* Report No. A-42.

U.S. Bureau of the Census. 1978a. *Current Housing Reports,* Series H-150-76, Part A. General Housing Characteristics for the United States and Regions.

U.S. Bureau of the Census. 1978b. *Current Housing Reports,* Series H-170-76, No. 45. Housing Characteristics for Selected Metropolitan Areas: Cleveland, Ohio SMSA.

U.S. Bureau of the Census. 1979a. *Construction Reports,* Series C25–78, No. 13.

U.S. Bureau of the Census. 1979b. *Current Population Reports,* Series P-23, No. 99. The Journey to Work in the United States: 1975.

U.S. Bureau of the Census. 1979c. *Statistical Abstract of the United States: 1979.*

U.S. Bureau of the Census. 1980. *Current Population Reports,* Series P-25, No. 873. Estimate of the population of counties and metropolitan areas: July 1, 1977 and 1978.

U.S. Congress. 1975. *Energy, the economy, and mass transit.* Washington, D.C.: Office of Technology Assessment.

Van Til, J. 1979. Spatial form and structure in a possible future: some implications of energy shortfall for urban planning. *Journal of the American Planning Association* 45, 3: 318–329.

KEY CONCEPTS

Multinuclear development patterns

Price-elasticity of demand

INDEX